Keeping Score:
Music, Disciplinarity, Culture

KNOWLEDGE:
Disciplinarity and Beyond

SERIES EDITORS

Ellen Messer-Davidow · David R. Shumway · David J. Sylvan

Keeping Score:
Music, Disciplinarity,
Culture

EDITED BY

DAVID SCHWARZ

ANAHID KASSABIAN

LAWRENCE SIEGEL

Robert Dulgarian,
Special Assistant

UNIVERSITY PRESS OF VIRGINIA

Charlottesville and London

THE UNIVERSITY PRESS OF VIRGINIA
© 1997 by the Rector and Visitors of the University of Virginia

First published 1997

♾ The paper used in this publication meets the minimum requirements of the American National Standard for Information Sciences—Permanence of Paper for Printed Library Materials, ANSI Z39.48-1984.

Library of Congress Cataloging-in-Publication Data

Keeping score : music, disciplinarity, culture / edited by David
    Schwarz, Anahid Kassabian, and Lawrence Siegel.
       p. cm.—(Knowledge, disciplinarity and beyond)
    Includes bibliographical references and index.
    ISBN 0-8139-1699-2 (cloth : alk. paper).—ISBN 0-8139-1700-x
(paper : alk. paper)
    1. Music—Instruction and study. 2. Interdisciplinary approach to
knowledge. 3. Music—Theory. 4. Musical criticism. 5. Musicology.
6. Music and society. 7. Music—History and criticism.
I. Schwarz, David, 1952– . II. Kassabian, Anahid. III. Siegel,
Lawrence. IV. Series.
MT1.K32 1997
780—DC21

                                    96-45044
                                        CIP

Printed in the United States of America

FOR JAKOB, MARAL, ELI, AND CLAIR

CONTENTS

PART 2:

DISCIPLINED AND DISCIPLINING MUSIC

ACKNOWLEDGMENTS

The editors thank David Shumway, Ellen Messer-Davidow, and David Sylvan for their long-term help, support, and guidance from the outset of this project. We thank, as well, all of our contributors who put much hard work into the book. We thank Timothy Buell of the University of Calgary for organizing the Resonant Intervals conference at which the idea for this book first came into being. We thank Mark T. Abbott of the School of Music at the University of Illinois, Urbana, for expert and careful work preparing and editing musical examples using Finale 3. 5. 1. David Schwarz thanks David Shrader, Dean of the College of Music at the University of North Texas for generous institutional support; he thanks, as well, Lisa A. Raskin, Dean of the Faculty at Amherst College, as well as the faculty of the Music Department at Amherst College for their generous support of this project. Special thanks to Marlies and Jakob. Anahid Kassabian gives special thanks to Leo and Maral for their patience. Lawrence Siegel thanks his mentors, guides, and comrades in the exploration of culture and society: Richard Leppert, Janet Levy, Susan McClary, Leonard Meyer, and the University Press of Virginia for its commitment to this work.

Keeping Score:
Music, Disciplinarity, Culture

ANAHID KASSABIAN

Introduction: Music, Disciplinarity, and Interdisciplinarity

T he study of music is ancient, but the disciplined study of music dates back only some two centuries. Such study began by basing its discourse on the assumptions and methods of science and on the values of the arts. In the *Musikwissenschaft* of late nineteenth-century Germany, historical musicology began to diverge as modern concepts of history gained ascendancy in scholarly writing. In the course of the twentieth century, musicology, ethnomusicology, theory, and composition have become separate disciplines, each to be mastered, taught, and perpetuated by their own professional societies. Thus music has followed the broad pattern of Western culture to divide its experience of the world into branches of thought, from the classical division of philosophy into logic, ethics, and physics, through the medieval trivium (grammar, rhetoric, dialectic) and quadrivium (arithmetic, geometry, astronomy, music) to the modern proliferation of arts and sciences. But throughout these changes in music studies the epistemological ground has remained much the same. The self-critical historical scholarship that came to dominate many disciplines in the 1970s and 1980s is only slowly emerging in music. It was not until 1985 that Joseph Kerman, in *Contemplating Music*, traced the histories and interests of music and the extent to which they are formalist and positivist: his call for a new (and implicitly interdisciplinary) music criticism has guided much of the work in this volume.

Keeping Score is a book of essays about the discipline of music that interrogates the "natural" status of organizing the academy into disciplines, that is, according to object of study. It is informed by a series of works on, and ongoing debates about, disciplinarity: Thomas Kuhn's model of paradigm/postparadigm cycles, Michel Foucault's connection of disciplines and bodies,

Stuart Hall's sense of interdisciplinarity as critique. Many of music's splintered disciplines (or subdisciplines) conform to a Kuhnian postparadigm phase, and *Keeping Score* explores the various emerging and receding paradigms. With Foucault (and with Katherine Bergeron and Philip V. Bohlman in *Disciplining Music*) we see music as a discipline in the sense of a mode of representing and deploying power. Within and through the discipline of music, the docile bodies of performers are molded, and the minds of theorists, musicologists, ethnomusicologists, and composers are shaped by received methodologies and ideals. Hall's discussion of sociology and literature in "The Emergence of Cultural Studies" also describes one connection between music and critical theory in this volume; *Keeping Score* consciously articulates how the new paradigms emerging in music studies themselves exceed and examine disciplinarity.

The structure of the volume as a whole reflects these understandings of disciplinarity. We begin with a look at the construction of disciplines in music in part 1: in a variety of ways, these authors write about what David Shumway and Ellen Messer-Davidow have called "boundary-work." We call this section of the book "The Construction of Musical Disciplines" to suggest the ideological status of scholarly writing in the drawing or erasing of disciplinary boundaries, from McCreless's critique of post–World War II music theory, to Covach's claim that music analysis can benefit popular music studies, to Cohen's argument that the text/context binary obscures music's relation to place, to Hooker's demonstration that cultural anxiety lies at the "origin" of American musical culture.

While the essays in part 1 interrogate the epistemological and ontological status of music as an object of disciplined study and music as a disciplining structure, the essays in part 2 examine the status of music as disciplined and disciplining consumption—of structures of normative listening practices (Stockfelt), of listeners' aesthetic judgments (Walser) and desires (Winkler), of sexual identity (Rycenga) and gender representation (Kallick), of implicit and explicit representations of national identification and assimilation (Kassabian), and of structures in early development that (re)present and are (re)presented by subjective positions in music (Schwarz). In short, the authors of part 2 show how disciplines and discourses inform music and its reception, and how music, most importantly, is an expression of a wide variety of forces: historical, political, social, ideological, and psychoanalytic.

From multiple, often contradictory schools of cultural theory, *Keeping Score* as a volume critiques the ideological underpinnings of the disciplines and subdisciplines of music. As some essays explicitly argue, music studies depend on Enlightenment ideologies to define their fields of practice and methods of inquiry. The subdiscipline of historical musicology, like the discipline of history, depends on the presumption of a transparent access to the past. Ethnomusicology, like anthropology, assumes the ability of an outside observer to collect data and report back on the musical-cultural practices of other cultures. Music theory, like structural linguistics, assumes that musical texts are specific enactments of a generalized musical language, the basic material of which lies far beneath the surface of a text. Academic music composition, like other fine arts such as painting, has embraced the notion of artistic inspiration, natural talent, and autonomy at the expense of reception. Traditional musicology, music theory, and composition all depend on Kantian concepts of the beautiful as ahistorical and universal, but replace the Kantian ethical underpinning with romantic notions of genius and authorship. We—and the contributors to *Keeping Score*—proceed from analyses of the crises of Beauty and Truth in postmodernity by considering what might supplement them. With Derrida, we see the supplement qualitatively shifting the nature of both theory and the textual object of study; we see, however, a revision of music studies necessarily linking music to social, economic, political, and subjective issues. This interdependence defines the relationship between theories of culture and of music in *Keeping Score*.

As *Music and Society* firmly established, once it is no longer a given that we know what constitutes the best of music, we no longer have a guarantee that we know what music is best to study. And once we can no longer state with any certainty that what is beautiful now will always (or eventually) be beautiful to all peoples in all times, we can no longer depend on the structures internal to music to be the sole or even the primary sources or explanations of its powers. While similar a priori underpinnings of such disciplines as literature and the natural sciences have been called into question, this epistemological project is just beginning to take hold in music studies. Because all of the essays in the collection are grounded in related interrogations of the same assumptions, what binds them, above and beyond the topic of music, is a fundamental philosophical concern with the production of meaning by "producers" and "consumers" among musical and cultural texts. By both examining and crossing disciplinary boundaries, *Keeping Score* both exposes the complicity of the disciplines of music studies with Enlightenment ideologies and proposes alternative analytical strategies.

In "Rethinking Contemporary Music Theory," Patrick McCreless examines the discipline of music theory, exploring its historical depth and unpacking its relations to musicology, ethnomusicology, and composition. McCreless applies a nuanced reading of Michel Foucault (*The Order of Things, The Archaeology of Knowledge, Discipline and Punish*) both to the history of the discipline of music theory and to the role of music theory in contemporary American academia. McCreless focuses on four crucial moments in the history of the discipline (the late nineteenth century in Germany, the mid 1950s and the late 1970s in the United States, and the current text/context debate), in each case interrogating the often polemical binary between music theory and musicology by exposing tensions within music theory's own practice (for example, theory's "poor fit" of research and pedagogy) and by unpacking the political and methodological forces at work within the new musicology's recent critique of music theory. McCreless's boundary-work is retrospective and prospective: he examines the political and methodological forces that have contributed to the drawing of disciplinary boundaries around music theory and suggests how music theory can function in the future.

In "Terminal Prestige" Susan McClary critiques the prestige that surrounds post–World War II music theory in American academic institutions. She argues that theory in general and musical analysis in particular are produced as commodities to be accumulated and protected at the expense of social context. McClary's article is a classic statement in the text/context debate, and her assumptions and charges against certain musical-theoretical practices spark reactions in John Covach's essay.

Although popular music is increasingly disciplined by academic institutions in courses of instruction, scholarly journals, articles, and books, much tension surrounds the issue of musical analysis and popular music. Some argue that popular music is a function of social context, historical and geographic specificity, gender, and economic conditions. Others argue that popular music is a collection of texts like any other and can be studied, analyzed, and disciplined in ways that relate detail to totality and basic structure to surface manifestation. Social context scholars can accuse analysts of making a social representation into an aesthetic object; analysts can accuse social contextualists of reducing music to a frozen signifier of social relations without contours, specific features of syntactic structure. In "We Won't Get Fooled Again," John Covach builds a bridge between these two positions. He argues that the technologies of musical analysts can enrich and be enriched by the study of rock music without bracketing social context. While remaining sensitive to the vast difficulties of applying theory to music outside the Western art tradition, Covach suggests that a music theory of rock would force theory to develop new procedures that in turn could be applied to the analysis of art music as well. Covach argues for a reciprocal relationship between analysis and social context in popular and classical music studies.

Sara Cohen argues against the text/context binary itself, showing the reciprocal relations between the two in British popular music. In "Liverpool and the Beatles," Cohen shows how the place of Liverpool, the tourism industry, and the reception of the Beatles' music in Liverpool were crucial elements in the construction of the Beatles as a cultural phenomenon. Cohen shows through ethnographic research how text and context can shift positions in a song and in geographical location. Penny Lane is a Liverpool street that serves as a setting for the Beatles' famous song of the same title; the song, on the other hand, is a context for the street's significance to the Liverpool tourist industry. Cohen argues that the text/context binary obscures the complex relations among music, fans, the social conditions of communities, and received and produced histories.

As Cohen blurs the text/context binary in popular music studies, Richard Hooker shows how the production of American musical culture arose from a complex web of social, theological, and aesthetic contexts. "The Invention of American Musical Culture" focuses on a particular historical and cultural moment, a period of literary anxiety preceding the establishment of a fine-arts culture in the antebellum United States. American fine-art musical culture at its inception is almost solely a literary phenomenon and serves as a sort of library for what Hooker calls "technologies" of musical acculturation. In identifying the literary rules predetermining musical meaning in early American musical culture, the article fundamentally challenges the practices of musical historiography. Musical history as we have been writing it since the eighteenth century installs the hierarchy "music and performance/writings on music"; this dyad operates in even the most radical challenges to the ideological neutrality or formal absoluteness of musical texts. However, the history of music in cultural terms—and this includes all discussions of affect and meaning, contemporaneous or otherwise—is always implicated in a set of nonmusical and specifically literary pre-texts. Hooker's work addresses a writing that at once produces an anxiety (the absence of a real, authentically American musical culture) and a musical and scholarly tradition in the American academy that continues up to the present. Hooker calls for a new disciplinary paradigm synthesizing historiography, literary criticism, and music studies.

We open part 2 with "Adequate Modes of Listening" by Ola Stockfelt. The essay begins with listening. Stockfelt recounts how, while waiting for his transatlantic flight to depart, he was suddenly appalled to hear a rendition of Mozart's Symphony No. 40 in G minor, bowdlerized for "easy listening," piped over the aircraft's sound system. Stockfelt defamiliarizes his own reaction by examining the history of the symphony's reception since its inclusion as one of our first "masterpieces" at the formation of the classical canon. He considers the ideological structure of "masterworks" to have inaugurated the formation of the bourgeois listener: locked passively into position in the concert hall as challenging musical meaning imprints itself upon his receptive subjectivity. The uses of the symphony, he argues, have progressively shifted in Western cultural history to the point of its commercialization as "easy listening" fodder. The article invites us to listen actively to music in all of its many positions in the public and private spaces of Western culture, and hence to recognize the bourgeois listening paradigm, despite its ideological privilege, as only one among these positions. Stockfelt's approach is anti-disciplinary: he shows how disciplinary boundaries structure listening practices, and he listens around such boundaries to hear their contingent status.

The necessity of hearing contingently is also the concern of Rob Walser in "Out of Notes: Signification, Interpretation, and the Problem of Miles Davis." Walser reveals the dependence of musical aesthetic evaluation on several levels of racial, class, and aesthetic ideology. Walser begins by considering three traditional responses to Davis's mistakes: (1) ignoring them; (2) apologizing for them; and (3) explaining them away. Walser proposes that all three responses are inadequate to the task of explaining the apparent discrepancy between the presence of obvious mistakes in Davis's performances on the one hand, and Davis's equally obvious status as a great musician on the other. Walser theorizes Davis's mistakes using a model from Henry Louis Gates Jr. to show an intimate *connection* between Davis's "greatness" and his "mistakes." As opposed to "signifying" (characterized by logic, denotation, and fixed meaning), Walser argues that Davis's music and mistakes are "signifyin'" (characterized by reference, gesture, and dialogue). Providing technical, aesthetic, and ideological evidence to support his claim, Walser's essay points out the politics of aesthetic judgment.

Stockfelt and Walser are, in effect, "listening awry," to borrow a term from Slavoj Žižek. In "Writing Ghost Notes," Peter Winkler listens to the music of Aretha Franklin while focusing on transcription, the technology of studying musical sounds through the medium of written notation—a technology on which all the subdisciplines of music depend. Using a phenomenological account of his attempt to notate a recording by Franklin, Winkler argues that although a transcription may seem to be an accurate representation of what is "really there" in the recording, the appearance of objectivity is illusory. Winkler maintains that transcription is an intensely subjective practice, an inevitable insertion of the speaker's own desire, fantasy, and cultural bias into the musical text. He concludes that the true value of transcription lies in the intense and infinite involvement it creates between music and transcriber: it is less an analytical than a pedagogical tool. Winkler warns musicians in the academy to beware the damage we may do to music if we deify the notion of objectivity in transcribing and inscribing music into the discipline. In carrying out this quite specific exploration of ways that ideology and analysis function within popular music studies, Winkler begins with a hermeneutic approach aimed at "getting it down on paper" and ends with a self-reflexive swerve into his own desire.

While Winkler theorizes a failure to close the hermeneutic gap between critical act and performed instance of an Aretha Franklin song, Jennifer Rycenga charts a complex web of relations connecting her listening subjectivity and music in "Sisterhood: A Loving Lesbian Ear Listens to Progressive Heterosexual Women's Rock Music." Rycenga theorizes lesbian listening subjectivity in radical ways that synthesize body, mind, listener, performer, producer, music as artifact, and music as object. She avoids a notion of synthesis that would subordinate some factors to others or that would finalize one meaning at the expense of another; instead, she listens in and around all aspects of this music—those that evade description no less than those she can name with ease. And her discussion of theological structures embedded within recent heterosexual women's rock music opens an important cross-disciplinary conversation between music studies and religious studies.

In "Janáček's *Jenůfa* and the Tyranny of the Domestic," Jenny Kallick moves back and forth across thresholds of the drama upon which the opera is based, the libretto, the score, and the processes of creating meaning through listening. Her notion of the "tyranny of the domestic" is informed by feminist theory of recent decades, contemporary feminist musicology, and a nuanced analysis of how music both reproduces and produces gendered structures. Kallick's interdisciplinarity not only synthesizes but transforms approaches of feminist literary criticism and historical musicology.

My own "At the Twilight's Last Scoring" continues Kallick's trans-formational synthesis. I consider how music in contemporary Hollywood action-adventure films constructs complex representations of U.S. nationality. Through particular processes of identification based on musical semiotics and on the relationships among musical, visual, and narrative elements, I argue that the paths of identification are produced and registered in a variety of ways, some transparent, some troubled, and some blocked. I contribute to a psychoanalysis based not on the phallus and its (re)deployments but on liminal encroachments of subjective positions enunciated in representations that are produced and registered in public space.

A different approach to psychoanalysis and music is offered in David Schwarz's "Listening Subjects: Semiotics, Psychoanalysis, and the Music of John Adams and Steve Reich." Schwarz's theory of listening implicitly treats the ear as producer as well as encoder of musical meaning. He suggests that, contrary to the formalist models of listening implicit in mainstream music studies, listening subjects are produced when an element of musical experience creates a fantasy that refers back to an early stage of the subject's development—the "sonorous envelope" or the "acoustic mirror"—a stage charged with sound. Crucially, Schwarz shows both that music is a subjective process and that musical processes are not contained by the music itself. Schwarz analyzes music theory and psychoanalysis as disciplines belonging to different logical classes: music theory postulates fixed meanings that are produced as surface and depth produce one another in syntagmatic structures; psychoanalysis charts the relationship between necessary structures (the sonorous envelope, the acoustic mirror, the triangulation of desire) and contingent subjective positions. Listening to music awry, Schwarz uses each discipline to let music sound against the other, producing an unstable representation of sounds at music-theoretical and psychoanalytic thresholds.

It was within the context of interdisciplinarity broadly conceived that this volume first came into being. In May 1991 the editors met at a five-day conference organized by Timothy Buell at the University of Calgary entitled

"Resonant Intervals: Interdisciplinary Perspectives of Music." The conference included works by physicists, literary critics, experimental psychologists, musicologists, filmmakers, and many others. The underlying aim of the conference was to celebrate the plural and heterogeneous approaches to music within the academy. While we were thrilled by the energy and freshness in the theoretical air at Calgary, we used the "Resonant Intervals" celebration of pluralism as a springboard to a different approach. We understand *Keeping Score* to be organized around interdisciplinarity more as Stuart Hall, in "The Emergence of Cultural Studies," describes it: not "a question of which disciplines would contribute . . . but of how one could decenter or destabilize a series of interdisciplinary fields" (16). Rather than celebrating the pluralism of the academy, we think of disciplines as a web of critiques; we learn, in other words, as much about music from what sociology, literary theory, and philosophy teach us as we do from music theory, and mutatis mutandis about and from other disciplines. Thus while the trajectory of our thinking begins within the established academic disciplines of composition, musicology, ethnomusicology, and music theory, *Keeping Score* does not require, like other works on disciplinarity and music, the revamping or correction of those disciplines. As a whole, *Keeping Score* articulates instead a range of reasons for giving up the project of defining disciplines wholly according to object of study.

In this sense, *Keeping Score* is part of a growing body of other studies concerned with the integrity and impermeability of disciplinary boundaries. In literature (Graff, Shumway, Messer-Davidow, Herrnstein-Smith), in anthropology (Clifford, Marcus), in sociology (Game, Clough), and in many other disciplines, the practices, assumptions, and methodologies of those disciplines are being called into serious question. In music, Lawrence Kramer's 1990 *Music as Cultural Practice* uses an essentially traditional comparative technique to illuminate one trope underlying two disparate texts, one musical and one literary; such a cross-disciplinary comparative technique qualitatively alters the relationship between text and theory previously separated by disciplinary standards of legitimacy and expertise. We seek adjacency as well with the recent volume *Disciplining Music* (1992, edited by Katherine Bergeron and Philip V. Bohlman) that theorizes, criticizes, and extends the limits of the various canons within music studies. Despite a theoretically rigorous introduction, however, *Disciplining Music* pulls back from calling the organization of the academy or the intellectual role of canons and canonicity into question, choosing instead to focus on the gentler project of revising those institutions.

Feminism and queer theory have played especially important roles in questioning disciplinarity, and *Keeping Score* owes a substantial debt to three books that theorize music, gender, and sexuality: Susan McClary's *Feminine Endings*; *Musicology and Difference*, edited by Ruth A. Solie; and *Queering the Pitch*, edited by Philip Brett, Elizabeth Wood, and Gary C. Thomas. In

Feminine Endings, McClary theorizes how a wide variety of musics from Monteverdi to Diamanda Galás produce, represent, perpetuate, and problematize gender. *Musicology and Difference* explores with extraordinary subtlety how music, gender, and difference are structured in musical texts. Its authors build on McClary's methodology and assumptions to bring nuances stemming from an awareness of gender issues to more traditional forms of research and analysis. All three of these books have opened theoretical and musical spaces that subtend the work of *Keeping Score*. With Brett, Wood, and Thomas, one "emphasis is on throwing into question old labels and their meanings so as to reassociate music with lived experience and the broader patterns of discourse and culture that music both mirrors and actively produces" (viii–ix). And *Queering the Pitch* reorients the connections among bodies, sexualities, and musical pleasures in ways that provoke a wholesale rethinking of music disciplines.

It is important to realize that there is no unified object such as music studies in the United States. There is no single disciplinary organization, no annual meeting that brings (for example) our authors together for a single conference. For those of us familiar with the meetings of organizations such as the Modern Language Association, "music studies" is an extraordinarily heterogeneous construct, unreflected by institutions, organizations, or publications. Nevertheless, each of our authors interrogates an aspect of the disciplinary/interdisciplinary status of their relationship to the study of music. Thus *Keeping Score* both accounts for the status of the disciplines of music in the mid-1990s and points ahead to how music studies can function in the coming decades. The essays examine the topography, history, technologies, and ideologies of the disciplines of music and consider approaches that their self-definitions proscribe. They address two primary audiences: (1) music scholars, who will find in them a range of contemporary research that extends the materials and methodologies of the traditional subdisciplines of music studies; and (2) cultural studies theorists, who will find familiar ideas refigured within the immanent (and previously largely unfamiliar) materials of music analysis. Both the content of each article and the organization of the volume as a whole speak to specialists in both audiences. Theorists will find an entire realm of everyday cultural life—music not only on tapes and CDs, but on television—opened up to analysis. Musical scholars will find critiques of their disciplines that suggest theoretical and analytical possibilities in a postparadigm era. In short, *Keeping Score* speaks to music studies from within its own languages and enters into the conversations already taking place across disciplinary boundaries throughout the academy.

We have chosen to represent the discipline of music studies as a heterogeneous intersection of traditional musical disciplines (theory, musicology, and ethnomusicology) and cultural studies (ethnic studies, postcolonial studies, Marxism, and feminist anthropology). As such, *Keeping Score* is an anthology in the traditional sense of bringing together different texts, voices, and contexts. The heterogeneity of the book is not a call to an uncritical celebration of tension; it is a reflection of and a reflection *on* the flux with which we who are at once within and without disciplinary positions work. The heterogeneity of approaches in the book as a whole is often, but not always, reflected in conflicting methodologies at work within some of the individual articles themselves. In short, *Keeping Score* is a snapshot of the profession of music studies: there are main objects readily recognizable (the big disciplines of musicology and music theory, for example), and there are more marginal objects as well. We hope that, like a snapshot, *Keeping Score* has a fresh "thereness," a sense of being, and, above all, an expression of subjectivities in time and space and place. We hope as well that, as in a snapshot, we have caught at the margins of the frame ideas, approaches, catachreses, and ideologies that in the future we will recognize as having been there all along within our personal and collective ears.

Part 1
The Construction of
Musical Disciplines

PATRICK McCRELESS

Rethinking Contemporary Music Theory

> There is no power relation without the correlative constitution of a field of knowledge, nor any knowledge that does not presuppose and constitute at the same time power relations.
>
> **Michel Foucault**

A well-known cartoon from the *New Yorker* shows two overweight and presumably retired executives sipping martinis and relaxing in bathing suits on the deck of a not insubstantial yacht. "I used to think I was intelligent, ambitious, and hard-working," remarks one to the other. "By the time I discovered I was merely obsessive-compulsive, I'd already made my pile."

This retired executive might well stand for contemporary American music theory in the mid-1990s, thirty-five to forty years after its advent in our universities and conservatories—time enough for a full career, from underling to executive, from assistant professor to professor emeritus. Unlike the character in the cartoon, music theory is presumably not resigning itself to the depressing prospect of watching its own sunset. Yet the time is ripe for a reevaluation of music theory as a discipline. Theory is now firmly established in academic music in the United States and is remarkably successful as an export to Canada, the British Isles, Germany, France, and Australia. At home, however, it is under attack as never before: it is held to be guilty of analytical formalism, of detaching musical works from their historical and social context and pretending that they are transparent to "purely musical" interpretations, and of thus purveying an outmoded and unexamined "aesthetic ideology." Its analysis-based research program is seen as self-reflexive and self-serving, spurning insights from and addresses to other fields.

Why is the academic discipline of music theory under siege? What historical perspective could explain the intellectual position that music theory now occupies? What is the best course of action for those of us who are committed to the discipline? To answer such questions, we must first situate music theory as an academic discipline in the 1990s.

Since the Greek *theoria*, the etymological root of the word *theory*, is the

1 3

noun form of a verb meaning to inspect, observe, or consider, one might suggest that *all* rational contemplation of music—whether practical, historical, or analytical—could in a broad sense be regarded as theory.[1] But the modern distribution of the intellectual disciplines of music classifies theory as only one member of a trio that also includes musicology and ethnomusicology. Of the three, musicology focuses on the music of the Western tradition, from antiquity to the present, from a historical, documentary, and critical point of view. Ethnomusicology has been variously defined as the study of non-Western, folk, traditional, and popular musics; or as the study of music in its social role; or simply as the study of the music of the Other. Music theory, more than musicology and ethnomusicology, is both a research program and a pedagogy.

As a research program, it includes the development and analytical application of theories, often empirically based, of the structure of tonal and atonal music (and occasionally pretonal music); the history of music theory; the pedagogy of musical skills, from fundamental to advanced; and music perception and cognition.

Distinctive of music theory among the three academic musical disciplines, at least as practiced in English-speaking North America, is the centrality of pedagogy, which has a role in music-theoretical life that far exceeds its rather modest role as an object of music-theoretical research. It is the formidable task of music theory to teach fundamental and traditional musical skills such as harmony, sightsinging and ear training, and counterpoint. This pedagogical obligation of music theory distinguishes it sharply from its sister disciplines, musicology and ethnomusicology in that, although these disciplines are similarly committed to both research and teaching (musicologists teach music history and literature, and ethnomusicologists teach courses in folk and non-Western musics), they are by no means responsible for carrying out, on a massive scale, the perpetuation of a nonacademic, skills-oriented pedagogical discipline that is more the professional discipline of an art than the intellectual one of the sciences or humanities. Today's music theorists thus occupy a position precariously situated between those of scholar and of skilled artisan. As members of the academy they must define and pursue areas of research just as their colleagues in the sciences and humanities do. At the same time they must possess sufficient musical competence, training, and pedagogical skill to teach the fundamentals of music theory, usually in a manner that has more in common with musical pedagogy of the eighteenth and nineteenth centuries than it does with late twentieth-century scholarly research.

The configuration of the three academic musical disciplines in modern American musical education must be unpacked if we are to understand the current intellectual position of music theory. In one sense, music theory is by far the oldest of the three, inasmuch as it can trace an uninterrupted lineage back to Aristoxenos in the second century B.C.E. Musicology and ethnomu sicology are much younger. Even if there were sporadic attempts to narrate a history of music in the sixteenth through the eighteenth centuries—Calvisius in the sixteenth century, Printz in the seventeenth, and de La Borde, Burney, Hawkins, and Forkel in the eighteenth—the historiography of music and the notion of musical history as an academic discipline are unquestionably products of the nineteenth century. *Musikwissenschaft,* the "science of music"— an all-inclusive discipline of Western music including historical, stylistic, critical, and theoretical studies—was the creation of German scholars in the latter half of the nineteenth century and was the first of our three fields to be established as a modern intellectual discipline. American musicology descended directly from German *Musikwissenschaft,* inheriting its positivist historiography and its concern with stylistic evolution, while downplaying its concern with criticism and theory, to the extent that the American version of the discipline was, until quite recently, almost exclusively a historical discipline, not a critical or theoretical one.[2] Ethnomusicology, or *vergleichende Musikwissenschaft* ("comparative musicology"), also German in origin, was a late nineteenth- and early twentieth-century offshoot of *Musikwissenschaft.* But paradoxically, music theory, the oldest of the disciplines historically, is easily the youngest of the three as a modern academic discipline. Furthermore, it is of American, not German, provenance. Even though *Musiktheorie* was (and still is) included in the German *Musikwissenschaft,* the modern, academic incarnation of music theory is peculiarly American and may be dated to about 1960, when the "professional music theorist" came onto the scene—that is, when "music theory" in American universities began to define itself as a discipline distinct from musicology, on the one hand, and composition, on the other, and when a few music schools began to employ "music theorists" rather than composers, musicologists, or performers who also taught theory, to administer their music theory curricula. The birth of the new academic discipline was also marked by the establishment of the *Journal of Music Theory*, the first journal devoted to the new field, at Yale in 1957, and of *Perspectives of New Music* at Princeton in 1962; and, within the next decade, numerous graduate programs at both university music departments and conservatories.

The present essay attempts to rethink this contemporary music theory— to address the questions of where it is, how it got there, and where it is going—by viewing it through the lens of the interpretations of the history of knowledge, of power, and of disciplinarity developed by the French historian and philosopher Michel Foucault between the late 1950s and his death in 1984 (a historical period, we might note in passing, that is coterminous with the establishment and growth of modern music theory). Despite the complexity of his analyses, the fundamental import of what Foucault has to say is clear enough, and his critique of "human sciences" such as psychiatry, medicine, and criminology has been enormously influential in the humanities and social sciences for the past two decades. What I shall attempt here is by no means a wholesale mapping of Foucault's ideas onto music theory—a task of dubious value for which I am in any case unqualified—but rather a reading of its history and current situation in the light of his work, which can, I think, illuminate the discipline in a fresh and original way.

Foucault, among others, has encouraged us to see the history of thought not as a continuous, transparent unfolding of truth that ineluctably evolves toward the present but as a succession of discourses that generally do not proceed gradually or linearly but are marked by disjunctions, gaps, and sudden reconfigurations. In the 1960s Foucault's historico-philosophical project focused on discourse itself. Although he categorically denied being a structuralist, he nevertheless, in harmony with the structuralist rage that had engulfed intellectual life in France and elsewhere at that time, attempted to map out for the human sciences the principles by which discourses in different disciplines constituted and regulated themselves.[3] Such principles were, according to Foucault, not only not consciously known by the practitioners of the disciplines but were also structurally independent of the actual social practice of these disciplines, so that the language of discourse would control the practice of the discipline, rather than the discipline controlling the discursive language or the two interacting to condition each other. Realizing the implausibility of such a claim, Foucault in the 1970s turned his attention to the social practice of the disciplines and began to concern himself with the interaction of such practices and disciplinary knowledge. In this later work, which he referred to as the "genealogy" of, rather than the earlier quasi-structuralist "archaeology" of knowledge, his intent is to show that knowledge is not pure but is conditioned by and found to be in collusion with "power," so that what is known should be seen less as abstract truth and more as a product of a discourse that shapes itself so as to manufacture types of knowledge that empower particular individuals or groups. Central to his work on knowledge and power are what he calls the "disciplines of man," which for him are social institutions that all trace their origins, at least in France, to the period just after the French Revolution and that epitomize the repressive use of the knowledge/power axis: the psychiatric asylum, the hospital, the prison, the military barracks, and the primary school. Each institution claims its power over the individual on the basis of a newly found empirical knowledge, and each uses that knowledge to rank, classify, distribute, and regulate the "docile bodies" that the discipline controls. Throughout his work, both archaeological and genealogical, he tends to focus on discourse as an abstract site of knowledge, and to remove from this arena the motivation and action of the individual subject. Although it goes without saying that this strategy prohibits him from writing history modeled on biography and human action, it enables him to articulate in a novel and original way how disciplines operate and how their discourses function.[4]

The central features of Foucault's thought upon which the present essay depends are (1) the collusion of knowledge and power; (2) the tendency in the evolution of thought and of individual disciplines to proceed in starts and stops, in periods of stability followed by severe disjunction; (3) the focus on discourse rather than human subjects; and (4) the interdependency of disciplinary history and the knowledge/power configuration. I shall begin by examining music theory as a conventional body of knowledge and a set of shared practices—first as it exists now, in its modern form, in the 1990s, then as it began to assume this form, in the late 1950s, and then more broadly as a historical discipline many centuries old. Only historical understanding of continuities and discontinuities in the evolution of the discipline can offer a nuanced reading of why music theory has taken the form that it has in the past thirty-five years. This reading will open into the second large part of the essay, which will be concerned with a Foucauldian interpretation of music theory as knowledge and power: first, in the positive sense of how theory has used its distinctive knowledge and practice to establish for itself and its practitioners a secure position in the academic world, in the form of jobs, publications, places in undergraduate and graduate curricula, and so forth; and second, in the negative sense of how theory has rendered itself a "docile body" by submitting willingly to a larger and more powerful disciplinary institution than itself—the university. Finally, in the light of this interpretation, I shall pursue in greater detail the criticisms to which music theory has recently been subjected by postmodernist musicology, examine its stresses and fractures, both self-induced and imposed from the outside, and offer some suggestions for its continued vitality and intellectual and artistic health.

MUSIC THEORY AS KNOWLEDGE

The most reliable indicator of what knowledge the discipline of music theory now claims as its own is what it has produced: in conference papers, articles, books, and courses in undergraduate and graduate curricula. Naturally, the topics and questions that have generated activity in the discipline have varied and currently seem to be expanding in a number of directions. But a number of broad trends in research have been obvious enough, trends that clearly define music theory as an academic discipline. Whatever objections can be lodged against it, music theory cannot be accused of not knowing what it is about. It turns on five distinct areas that may be viewed both as bodies of knowledge and as programs of research: (1) theoretical systems, (2) musical analysis, (3) the history of music theory, (4) the pedagogy of music theory, and (5) music perception and cognition.

The first two categories are difficult to separate in practice because most music-theoretical systems are constructed to be used as analytical tools. Whatever the balance of theory proper and its analytical application, the central thrust of the discipline is in fact powerfully directed toward analytical theory and its use. For what music theorists do, at least in terms of original intellectual work, is, first and foremost, the analysis of music in the Western tradition, using both existing theories such as those of Heinrich Schenker, the early twentieth-century Viennese theorist of tonal music, and newer theories. Until very recently, music theory graduate programs have centered almost wholly on theory-based analysis and still provide extensive training in Schenkerian analysis of tonal music and in some version of pitch-class set theory and twelve-tone theory for atonal and twelve-tone music, respectively.

The third area of music theory as a contemporary knowledge is that of its own history as a discipline. The impulse to develop a historical narrative of music theory and theoretical systems, like the impulse to establish an academic discipline around the history of music itself, dates to the mid- to late nineteenth century. The two most prolific music historians of the nineteenth century, François-Joseph Fétis and Hugo Riemann, both founders of the discipline of musicology, wrote histories of harmonic theory, classic nineteenth-century progressivist histories in that their authors treated the history of harmonic theory as an evolution through stages of imperfection to a triumphant arrival at their own harmonic systems.[5] In the twentieth century, although no scholar has undertaken a work on the scale of Riemann's monumental *Geschichte der Musiktheorie*, the quantity and quality of research has been impressive. The British theorist Matthew Shirlaw published a history of harmonic theory, the first in English, in 1917, and in the first half of the twentieth century numerous musicologists researched various aspects of the history of theory, often not so much to trace the history of the discipline itself as to use theory to elucidate the practice of music in a particular historical period. Since the founding of American music theory around 1960, American (as well as, for example, German) scholars have, in the space of just over thirty years, filled in enormous lacunae and exploded many misconceptions of earlier scholarship, while at the same time expanding our understanding of the history of the discipline in new and unexpected ways.

Fourth, music theorists are charged with teaching a substantial body of knowledge and practical skills regarding the art—the rudiments of music (intervals, scales, keys, chords, rhythm, sightsinging, ear training), harmony, rhythm, counterpoint, and so forth. These practical areas of theoretical activity tend mostly to entail the passing on of traditional musical skills. For example, musicians in the Western tradition, which is heavily dependent upon musical notation, need to be able to represent in their minds the sound of music that they see in score—to hear how it will sound while composing it, or while preparing to sing, play, or conduct it. Traditional music theory pedagogy develops this skill through posing graduated tasks such as dictation exercises—having students write down melodies or harmonic progressions that they hear—and singing melodies at sight. Anyone who has taught such skills knows that the ability to acquire them differs radically among individuals: musically gifted students (those with a "good ear") can often easily perform such tasks on the first try; others require patient guidance, and their progress is painstakingly slow. Since musical skills of this sort clearly involve raw perception and intellectual concepts, both highly gifted and less gifted students develop them insofar as theory moderates their direct perceptions by giving a set of names to musical elements, so that they develop a theory-based working knowledge and set of expectations about how music behaves. It is here that theory, whether as a historically based received knowledge or a contemporary research program, intersects with pedagogy. A musically sensitive and intellectually coherent theory can vastly improve the efficiency of the learning of both fundamental and sophisticated musical skills. Research in the area of music theory pedagogy—that is, music-theoretical knowledge that involves not just the passing on of a tradition but the ongoing development of new knowledge—focuses on both perception and theory, as well as the interaction of the two.

The final and most recent enterprise adopted by music theory is that of music perception and cognition. Like music theory itself, research into the perception and cognition of music has both an ancient and a modern history. The former dates back to the seventeenth century, when musicians of an empirical turn of mind (for example, Vincenzo Galilei, father of Galileo), as well as leading intellectual and scientific figures of the time (Descartes, Mersenne, Kepler, Galileo, Huygens), theorized and conducted experiments regarding sound and human sound perception. Certain aspects of the work of Helmholtz, the founder of the modern science of acoustics in the later nineteenth century, and a substantial body of empirical work in the generations that succeeded him—that of Carl Stumpf, William Wundt, James Mursell, and Carl Seashore, for example—legitimately addresses aspects of music perception. The contemporary discipline focusing on music perception and cognition had its origins only in the 1960s and 1970s in cognitive psychology and in fields such as music education or music theory pedagogy, where researchers investigated aspects of musical learning. Whatever the modalities of their interactions, it is clear that a growing number of music theorists are showing an interest, and even doing research in, these areas, and cognitive psychologists with an interest in music are reaching out to music theory as a discipline that can be used to direct and validate their work. The field of music perception and cognition has arguably separated itself from both psychology and music and established itself as an independent discipline. There are now a number of journals in the area (e.g., *Music Perception*, which began publication in 1984), as well as major conferences every year. At the same time, music perception and cognition are critical to both the theoretical/analytical and the pedagogical side of music theory, which now accepts these areas as a viable subdiscipline.

In 1987 the Society for Music Theory devoted the plenary session of its tenth annual conference to papers addressing the accomplishments of what we are here calling modern music theory—which, in 1987, was for all practical purposes the work done by members of the society and their predecessors since about 1957. The papers at the session were each devoted to a major research area of modern theory and were published in 1990 in the society's journal, *Music Theory Spectrum*.[6] Both the topics of the papers and their relative weighting substantiate my account of how music theory constitutes itself as an academic discipline. Three papers address analytical theory and analysis—one Schenkerian analysis, one the analysis of nineteenth-century music, and one atonal and twelve-tone music. Two papers are devoted to the history of music theory—one to sixteenth- and seventeenth-century, the other to eighteenth- and nineteenth-century theory.[7] One paper each involves pedagogy and music perception. A final paper, "New Research Paradigms," is less a tabulation of accomplishments than a transdisciplinary speculation on possible new directions in which the field might move.

That such a paper should be presented at this conference of the society was strangely appropriate. By 1987 music theory had come under increasing fire, both within the discipline and from without, for what seemed increasing intellectual rigidity. Although, as we have noted, the term *theory* suggests no necessary limitation to the way music could be considered rationally, in practice music theory had come to mean—at least so far as research was concerned and despite the discipline's duties to teach basic musical literacy—a "normal science" of Schenkerian theory and pitch-class set theory, plus a modest amount of research in the history of theory, pedagogy, and music perception and cognition.

Since the 1987 meeting, the discipline has become more self-reflective and self-critical, connecting tentatively with disciplines such as literary and critical theory and the history and philosophy of science and becoming more seriously involved in research in music perception and cognition. But even as early as 1980, the preeminent musicologist Joseph Kerman had already blasted the music-theoretical enterprise in the journal *Critical Inquiry* for limiting itself to the theory-based analysis of musical works—usually works in the mainstream Germanic tradition since the eighteenth century or else modern works that in many ways perpetuate that tradition—to the virtual exclusion of any consideration of the historical context, social function, or expressive resonance of that music.[8] Kerman's title, "How We Got into Analysis, and How to Get Out," hints at the tenor of his polemic: music theory's concentration on analysis constitutes a hyperrationalistic formalism that views works of art as "black boxes," the meaning of which is internal to the works themselves, in their "purely musical" relationships, denying their richer meaning to composers, performers, and listeners. What is needed, in Kerman's view, is not *analysis* but *criticism,* a broadly based interpretive strategy that, while not eschewing analysis altogether, appropriates it only in association with a historically and culturally "thick" description of the work in question—a description that does take into account the life and possible intent of the composer, the intended audience, the cultural and aesthetic norms and semiotic traditions for the communication of meaning at a given time and place. Since Kerman's initial salvo, and his further critique in the widely read *Contemplating Music* of 1985, the attacks on music theory have grown progressively more strident, particularly from the various proponents of a "new musicology" dedicated not to the stylistic and documentary researches of the past but to a culturally, intellectually, and critically aware interpretation of works in their social, historical, and semiotic contexts. Musicologists of a wide variety of critical persuasions have seconded Kerman's objections to formalist theory and added their own: Leo Treitler, Susan McClary, Lawrence Kramer, Ruth Solie, Rose Rosengard Subotnik, Carolyn Abbate, and Richard Taruskin.[9]

What has made the discipline of music theory vulnerable? To answer this question, we must go back to 1957 and examine its origins more closely. There is no better point of entry to the early history of modern music theory than a reminiscence by Milton Babbitt—twelve-tone composer, theorist, and by any account one of principal founders of the discipline: "We have produced now at least two generations of professional theorists. I really think of our professional theorists beginning with the generation of Allen Forte [that is, in the 1950s]. The notion of professional theory is almost totally new. There were virtually no professional theorists in this country. . . .There was no such thing as a professional theorist at any university that I can think of when I began becoming involved with universities."[10]

Babbitt attributes the rise of the professional theorist in the United States to two factors. First was the immigration of a number of Schenker's students—notably Hans Weisse, Felix Salzer, Oswald Jonas, and Ernst Oster—to this country in the 1930s and 1940s. Either as private teachers or from positions at conservatories or universities (Weisse, for example, taught at the Mannes School of Music in New York, Jonas at Roosevelt University in Chicago), these students of Schenker began to introduce the notion that the masterpieces of the tonal repertoire should not be merely *described* but should be *explained*. To explain works of art by uncovering a deep structure, as Schenker's system made possible, was to move beyond theory in its pedagogical sense, which is what most teachers of theory were employed to teach at the time, into theory in the sense of an intellectually coherent, empirically validated system. The creation of a music theory that was not only new but also rigorous—*real theory*—goes hand in hand with what Babbitt invokes as the second impetus to the development of a new discipline: the simple fact that teachers of music theory taught in universities. For Schenkerian theory, and indeed any rigorous theory, was precisely what such teachers needed to attain intellectual respectability, which in turn was what they needed in order to survive in the university environment. Out of the theory teacher was thus born the music theorist.

The term *music theorist* was a neologism, coined, as far as I can determine, around 1957, the year of the first issue of the *Journal of Music Theory*. (German has long had a compound word for music theory, *Musiktheorie,* as in Riemann's *Geschichte der Musiktheorie*; but German scholars do not tend to refer to those who practice the discipline of music theory as *Musiktheoretiker*. Indeed, the term *Theoretiker*, or theorist, often carries the pejorative connotation of a dry, stuffy, pedant, as does the English *theorist*, or especially *theoretician*, a locution whose additional syllables seem to capture for performers and critics the distance they perceive between the theoretical thinker and their own musical worlds.) Even *music theory,* certainly not a new term in 1957, was somehow reified by the new journal and the research program on which the new discipline embarked. We shall see later that what in fact made this reification possible was precisely the reconstitution and expansion of a received knowledge and the hitching of this knowledge for the first time to the trappings of academic power—an ambitious and intellectually respectable research agenda, a journal, expanding curricula, and new graduate programs.

Again, Babbitt's reminiscence articulates in a personal way how music theory was new in the 1950s and how it has grown since that time: "The idea of serious theoretical thinking about music, analytical thinking worthy of the name of theory (as theory would be worthy of its name in almost every other field except our benighted one), is something new and for which I am grateful. There are probably six magazines now devoted almost entirely to serious theoretical-analytical issues; there were none whatsoever when I began this racket."[11] The novelty and desirability, even the necessity of theory, in the intellectually ambitious sense conveyed by Babbitt, shines forth on virtually every page of the early issues of the *Journal of Music Theory*, flush with the energy and excitement of the founding of a new discipline. The foreword to the first issue casts a longing glance at ancient days of music-theoretical glory and calls for a return of the discipline to real theoretical discourse, rather than unexamined, mindless pedagogy:

> In centuries past the formulation of laws regarding the practice of music was regarded as the highest aim for a musician; and, in many instances, musical laws were the inspiration or the source for more general laws regarding material or spiritual experience. Music was the image of the universe, hence, a source of truth; and it was the music theorist [*sic*: this modern term is projected upon the past here] who sought, discovered, and expressed both natural and divine law. But in our own time it is the rare musician who knows how his art offers a key to universal understanding. Music theory has become a discipline in stylistic definition or, still less, a

system of nomenclature and classification that offers no valid laws even regarding music. It is to the restoration of music theory as more than a didactic convenience, more than a necessary discipline, as, in fact, a mode of creative thought that this journal is dedicated.[12]

These words, and many more like them in succeeding issues, were written by the first editor of the journal, David Kraehenbuehl, a Yale theorist whose scholarship has not remained influential but whose ability to galvanize the energies of the new discipline and to articulate its goals clearly was indispensable in establishing it on secure footing and making a place for it in the university and the conservatory. The central theme in Kraehenbuehl's polemics is the notion that music theory is a venerable discipline "that has fallen into a state of almost universal academic disgrace" and that its mandate in the late 1950s was to restore it as a vital intellectual discipline.[13]

The intellectual program that Kraehenbuehl outlines in the foreword is almost precisely the program that has been carried out by music theory since 1957: namely, to focus both on analytical technique and "pure" theory, as well as on pedagogy and the history of music theory. Only the discipline's later venture into music perception and cognition was not foreseen. What was seen as important in the late 1950s was to theorize about and to analyze music, to research the history of the discipline, and to develop a theoretically based (rather than an unthinking and traditional) pedagogy. What was emphatically, almost violently, rejected was the notion of music theory as *just* pedagogy. All the early volumes of the journal, while devoting enormous space to reviews of pedagogical books and to the occasional pedagogical article, betray a uniform scorn for the "theory pedagogue." Kraehenbuehl identifies the real theorist rather donnishly as a "rare bird" who is often not "distinguished from his domesticated and more common distant relative, the theory pedagogue, who . . . seldom possesses the identifying features of a true professional theorist."[14] For Kraehenbuehl, the true professional theorist is (1) a first-rate practicing musician, as a composer or performer, (2) a skilled and logical thinker, (3) a professional who spends most of his time learning, thinking, and theorizing about music, and (4) a musician and thinker interested in and knowledgeable about earlier music-theoretical systems.

Kraehenbuehl's polemical essays in the early issues of the *Journal* pinpoint with remarkable accuracy what modern music theory is, what it does, to what intellectual standard it holds itself, and the kind of multi-talented person that the theorist must be. Both these essays and the comments of Babbitt also juxtapose *theory* and *pedagogy*, making it clear that it is the task of the new discipline, at least as a mode of knowledge, to found itself on the former, not the latter.

How does such a discipline compare with the centuries-old tradition of music theory that the new theory inherited in 1957? Certainly it betrays a continuation of the tension that has existed between speculative and practical theory throughout the history of the Western musical tradition. It was Aristotle who divided human mental activity into three spheres: the theoretical, the practical, and the poetic, or creative. Through the Renaissance, the first two categories—the speculative, or theoretical, and the practical—ordered music theory. Conceptually, Renaissance theory strictly divided *musica theorica* from *musica practica*. *Musica theorica* was a scholarly activity, inherited directly from the Middle Ages and ultimately from the Greeks, involving a traditional body of knowledge concerning tuning systems and their mathematical bases. As such, *musica theorica* was a part of the medieval quadrivium (with the other mathematical arts of arithmetic, geometry, and astronomy), and was far removed from actual musical practice. *Musica practica*, on the other hand, was not for the scholar but for practical musicians—usually singers in chapel choirs—who did not need to know the pure numerical ratios of musical intervals or how such ratios reflect the harmony of the spheres and the mind of God but did need to know how to sing chant melodies at sight and to realize correctly the mensural notation in their choirbooks.

Despite its conceptual separation of *musica theorica* and *musica practica*, the Renaissance also gradually evolved an ideal whereby the best musician would be one who had mastered *both* theoretical and practical musical knowledge. The Renaissance theorist Gaffurius, in his *Theorica musice* of 1492, after describing the theoretical and the practical musician separately, designates the "true musician" as one "lacking neither theory nor practice." [15] And Zarlino's *Le istitutioni harmoniche* (1558), the music-theoretical *summa* of Renaissance polyphonic practice, achieved the status that it did in part because it consciously and masterfully combined the theoretical (books 1 and 2) and the practical (books 3 and 4).

At the turn of the seventeenth century, the great tradition of *musica theorica* gradually died out in most European countries, leaving theory for the time being to deal primarily with the practical questions of figured bass realization, ornamentation, and counterpoint. In German theory, however, the tradition of *musica theorica*—the notion of music as Zarlino's *numerus sonorus*, or "sounding number," with all the associated trappings of a neo-Pythagorean, theological cosmogony—survived for another century. Echoing Gaffurius and Zarlino, the German theorists preached an ideal of combining the theoretical and the practical. Thus the late seventeenth-century Lutheran organist, composer, and theorist Andreas Werckmeister wrote in 1686 that "it is nevertheless ever so much better if one can be a theoretical and practical musician at the same time; but not everyone can do everything."[16]

It is precisely this ideal, espoused by both Zarlino and Werckmeister, that drives modern music theory and that has in important respects also driven the historical discipline of theory since the Renaissance. But the simple division of music-theoretical activity into *musica theorica* and *musica practica* is no longer supportable—indeed, it was supportable through the Renaissance only because *musica theorica* represented a closed body of received knowledge that had its basis in a wider intellectual tradition. From the time of Zarlino until the present, it still makes sense to divide the discipline into the theoretical and the practical, but the situation is more complex. Traditional *musica theorica* carried the connotation of being generally divorced from musical practice. But in modern theory, and in fact in theory since the time of Zarlino, the activity of theory-making is not only *not* divorced from the actual practice of music, but it is also not divorced from the pedagogy of music. The best theorists—Zarlino, Rameau, and Schenker, for example—are able to articulate original formulations of the principles that govern certain aspects of existing practice. If those principles are conceptually right and useful, they are ultimately incorporated into pedagogical theory as well.

Since the Renaissance, systematic theory-making in music does not necessarily entail recourse to ideas outside music. Many of the lasting original contributions to music theory have been "speculative," not in the sense that they are connected to a system of ideas external to music, but in the sense that they uncover principles hitherto undiscovered or used haphazardly with no awareness of their real significance: Lippius's articulation of the notions of the triad, inversion, and octave equivalence; Rameau's fundamental bass and his use of the concepts tonic, dominant, and subdominant; Kirnberger's essential and unessential dissonance; Schenker's *Ursatz* and structural levels. To be sure, often those theorists who in their theories develop the concepts and models most useful in purely musical terms—Zarlino, Lippius, Rameau, and Schenker, for example—also explicitly base their theories on concepts external to musical practice (the relation of harmonic consonance to a Christian, neo-Pythagorean cosmogony in the cases of Zarlino and Lippius, or the relation of the triad to "Nature" and to the overtone series in the cases of Rameau and Schenker). But our understanding of the theories need not necessarily take their extramusical components into account; we can, and theorists generally do, simply incorporate these useful new musical conceptualizations into our musical practice, discourse, and pedagogy, leaving the broader intellectual ramifications of the theories to historians or ignoring them altogether. (Postmodernist critics would argue, of course, that this continual untying of the "purely musical" aspects of music theories from their sociocultural moorings betrays a deep cultural bias in modern Western thought toward seeing music as a self-enclosed referential system rather than a contingent cultural product and that all music theory since the Renaissance, even the most nonspeculative, practical theory, masks sexist or authoritarian ideologies.[17] Foucault himself might well adopt such a position, and it is one that we will consider in detail when we bring music theory into contact with postmodern musicology.)

It should thus be clear how theoretical musical thinking is gradually transformed into practical musical activity and teaching. Lippius's identification of the triad and octave equivalence, and Rameau's fundamental bass, for example, constituted by any account theoretical advances in the history of Western music. Yet their notions were soon incorporated into musical pedagogy, simply because the conceptual leaps of the theorists clearly articulated something already functioning in musical practice and intuitively understood by musicians, and they thus established cognitive categories—*teachable* categories, in the sense of the *musica practica* of music theory—for phenomena that had previously had no name and participated in no describable relational function. The fact that the notions of triad, octave equivalence, and harmonic function now seem to be entirely the province of practical, rather than speculative theory, only demonstrates how successful they have been as theoretical constructs.

To suggest that speculative theory generates pedagogical theory is, of course, not to deny the existence of theory that is primarily pedagogical. Guido's system of solmization, Fux's of contrapuntal pedagogy (derived and codified, to be sure, out of the work of generations of Italian contrapuntal theorists), countless figured bass manuals in the eighteenth century, and countless harmony texts in the nineteenth and twentieth centuries, to cite just a few examples—all were developed for pedagogical purposes, not speculative ones. It has been the goal of contemporary music theory to teach musical skills in a way that preserves the best of these pedagogical methods (those of Guido and Fux, for example), while at the same time attempting to incorporate concepts from the best recent speculative theory in teaching as well.

So in the activity of music theory for the past few centuries, Aristotle's categories of the theoretical and practical turn out to describe the discipline, although perhaps not purely: the theoretical may or may not invoke concepts outside music, and it may merge with the practical or even serve as a model for it. But what about his third category, that of the creative, or poetic? Medieval and Renaissance theorists for the most part ignored this category and concerned themselves only with *musica theorica* and *musica practica*. In association, however, with Luther's program of humanistic education and his emphasis on music, German theorists of the sixteenth and seventeenth centuries introduced *musica poetica* into music theory. What was significant about *musica poetica* was not only that it explicitly claimed to teach the creation of music, or musical composition, but that it adopted the classical art of rhetoric as its conceptual and pedagogical model. In so doing it introduced a way of thinking about music and musical composition that, although it did not bear the fruit of a wholesale conceptual shift in music theory until the beginning of the nineteenth century, added a new and significant component to musical thinking.

To understand what was new about *musica poetica*, we must understand the compositional pedagogy of the time. In the seventeenth and eighteenth centuries most music theory—even theory with a strong speculative component, like that of the seventeenth-century German theorists who preserved *musica theorica*, or Rameau—was directed toward practical musical ends: how to compose a sacred choral piece, how to realize a figured bass, how to ornament a melodic line, how to use figured bass as the basis of composition, how to compose in the conservative church style according to the teaching of Fux and his predecessors, how to make harmonies follow one another coherently—in sum, those traditional compositional skills that Carl Dahlhaus has called *Satzlehre*.[18] *Musica poetica* added to these conventional skills the notion that music *says* something, in the same manner that a rhetorical oration does. The original impetus behind the idea concerned vocal music. The locus classicus of this sort of thinking is Joachim Burmeister's famous analysis, in his *Musica poetica* of 1606, of a motet by Orlando di Lasso—an analysis that shows, albeit in a primitive way, how rhetorically derived musical figures can intensify the musical setting of a text and how a musical setting as a whole can be organized like an oration.[19] Although the history of the *musica poetica* tradition is far too complex to detail here, what ultimately evolved out of it was that eighteenth-century writers, beginning especially with Johann Mattheson in the 1720s and 1730s, not only continued the tradition of musical figures with respect to vocal music but, more importantly, began to conceive of *instrumental* composition in terms of rhetoric, so that a completely new branch of theory arose that dealt with what eighteenth-century writers called the theory of melody (as in Mattheson's *Kern melodischer Wissenschaft* of 1737), but that we would call musical *form*. After Mattheson, writers of composition treatises, at least those dealing with melody, phrase structure, and "form" (the term is an anachronism: it was rarely used in the eighteenth century) frequently distinguished musical "grammar," the traditional skills of harmony, figured bass, and counterpoint (*Satzlehre*), from musical "rhetoric," which involved the rhetorically based organization of the melody of an entire piece.[20] Central to this tradition of compositional theory and pedagogy (a tradition that was simultaneously speculative and practical) are: (1) the first explicit development of the notions of motive and theme in the context of instrumental music (the eighteenth-century terms are widely variable and include *motivo*, *Thema*, *Idee*, and many others); (2) a growing sense of how to deal conceptually with an entire piece, rather than with the details of counterpoint and harmony that comprise the object of *Satzlehre*; and (3) an evolving aesthetic that valued instrumental music as much as or more than vocal music and that fostered the development of theoretical means to validate, in musical or music-theoretical terms, this aesthetic ideal.[21]

The conceptual shift that *musica poetica*, as introduced in the sixteenth and seventeenth centuries, and reconstituted for the sake of instrumental music in the eighteenth, ultimately made possible in music theory—a shift that took place in the first decade or two of the nineteenth century—was the turn from compositional pedagogy to *analysis*. The *musica poetica* treatises of the seventeenth century and the *Melodielehre* treatises in the tradition of Mattheson, Riepel, Koch, and Galeazzi in the eighteenth century were directed at the composer. The nineteenth century, of course, also produced numerous composition treatises. But near the beginning of the century there began to coalesce, from a daunting complex of influences—the shift from a mimetic to an expressive aesthetic,[22] the associated growth of the concept of the creative genius, the further development of the eighteenth-century notion of the detached contemplation of art, the idea of the autonomous work of art, and the development of what we now call romantic subjectivity, to name a few— a new point of view, one directed not to prospective composers but to an educated musical audience that could learn to appreciate musical masterworks without necessarily being able to produce them. This shift is clearly articulated by the change in music-theoretical writing about melody and "form" from a guiding metaphor of rhetoric to describe musical works to a metaphor of *structure*. Carl Dahlhaus has noted that E. T. A. Hoffmann, in his famous reviews of Beethoven's Fifth Symphony and other works, was the first critic emphatically to use the word *structure* with respect to music.[23] And a survey of the music-theoretical literature in the late eighteenth and early nineteenth centuries shows that over the course of this period the elements of musical composition that in the eighteenth century were described in terms of rhetoric (phrase structure, melodic succession, theme and thematic development, disposition and repetition of materials, tonal plan) gradually begin to be described in terms of the metaphor of the organism, and in terms of structure and form.[24]

The roots of modern music theory—*our* music theory—lie in this aesthetic ideology that developed around the turn of the nineteenth century. Our concern for the structural autonomy of the masterpiece, for structure and form, for teleological motivic development, for musical logic: all have their roots in the conceptual shift that took place at that time. We can begin to understand our current situation in music theory by observing the tensions this shift produced in nineteenth-century composition and theory. For musical composition the new ideology introduced a tension between a traditional, eighteenth-century compositional aesthetic, which turned on the conventional *Satzlehre* of harmony and counterpoint and the rhetorically based *Melodielehre*, and the more recent aesthetic of genius and originality, which encouraged composers to transcend these traditional practices and to learn their craft by studying the works of the greatest masters, against whose standard their own originality would be measured.[25] In music theory the new ideology reconfigured the entire discipline. We have seen that most seventeenth- and eighteenth-century theory was ultimately directed toward practicing musicians—composers and performers—who would learn from theory the practice of a relatively stable musical style. But in an era that valued originality, and thus change over stability, the question necessarily arose as to whether theory should take as its task the *preservation* of the traditional stability (by teaching the traditional music-theoretical virtues), the *explanation* of that stability (the development of theories to explain how musical practice works), the *pedagogy* of originality (the teaching of original composition, to the extent that such a thing is possible), or the *explanation* of that originality once it is brought into existence (analysis).

What nineteenth-century theory did, of course, was all of the above. Much of nineteenth-century theory simply recycles or adds new pedagogical twists to eighteenth-century methods or else takes some aspect of more recent theory as the basis for a hardened pedagogical system: the conservative Viennese figured-bass manuals of the first half of the century, the pedagogy of harmony and counterpoint in the Paris Conservatory, the *Grundsätze* of Simon Sechter, the practical treatises of North German theorists such as Richter and Jadassohn, and the standard *Formenlehre* treatises of the second half of the century all exemplify this tendency. Some nineteenth-century theory is more speculative and attempts to formulate new principles to explain standard musical practice: the harmonic theories of Vogler (developed in the eighteenth century but more influential in the nineteenth), Fétis, and the North German harmonic theorists of the second half of the century— Hauptmann, Oettingen, and Riemann. Nineteenth-century compositional theory generally attempts to resolve the tension between received musical skills (such as harmony and counterpoint) and originality by means of the comprehensive composition treatise, which rolls into a single theoretical work the musical grammar (harmony and counterpoint, or *Satzlehre*) and rhetoric (or melodic and formal theory) that the eighteenth century tended to separate, *plus*, in some cases, the use of actual masterworks as models for composition: the composition treatises of Momigny, Reicha, Czerny (including his compilation of Reicha's works in a simultaneous French and German edition), and the *Kompositionslehren* of Marx, Lobe, and Riemann. In most of these treatises there exists a fine line between invoking actual musical compositions as *models* for composition and as *objects* for analysis. The passages in such composition treatises that deal with real musical works, as well as essays by such writers as Hoffmann, Berlioz, and Schumann, and the more explicitly analytical-explanatory endeavors of Marx, Westphal, Riemann, and numerous others in the later nineteenth century most clearly exemplify the conceptual shift from compositional pedagogy to analysis and the ideological impulse to classify certain works as masterworks, worthy and even demanding of analytical scrutiny and explanation.

It would be pointless to continue this survey of how the tensions inherent in nineteenth-century theory were played out in early twentieth-century theory. For it was really only in German theory that they were played out. German-language theory tends to address head on such stresses between speculative and pedagogical theory, between compositional and analytical theory, or between competing harmonic systems and analytical approaches in the rich and vital theoretical discourse typical of the early years of the twentieth century—discourse that included the continuing work of Riemann, the radically new and intellectually powerful voices of Schenker and Schoenberg, the original analytical approaches of Ernst Kurth and Alfred Lorenz, and many others. French theory, the only national tradition even remotely competitive in the nineteenth century with German theory for speculative activity and in originality, was, after the turn of the century, essentially confined to the ossified pedagogical practice of the Paris Conservatory. British theory offered the brilliantly original Donald Francis Tovey, whose impressive analytical output, however insightful, lacked explicit theoretical content.

As for the United States, in the late nineteenth century, and even in the first half of the twentieth, there was in effect no original speculative American theory. As we have seen in the polemical statements of Babbitt and Kraehenbuehl, American theory was for all practical purposes coterminous with pedagogy: in the terms of our survey above, it was a combination of eighteenth-century *Satzlehre*, pedagogically oriented nineteenth-century harmony, often presented in garbled textbooks that combined conflicting harmonic traditions in a single undigested mix, and conventional nineteenth-century *Formenlehre*, as interpreted for English-speaking music students by the British pedagogue Ebenezer Prout and the German-trained Americans George Wedge and Percy Goetschius.

With this enriched historical context we can now return to Babbitt's reading of the state of American theory (or "theory") in the 1950s and understand more clearly what he means when he claims that the modern theory arose from the confluence of the immigration of Schenkerian theorists and the location of theory teaching at the site of the university. What the ideas of Schenker brought, in a way that the ideas of no other theorist could do, to a theory in a "state of universal academic disgrace" was not only the rigor that Babbitt cherishes but an engagement with all the vital tensions and issues of nineteenth- and early twentieth-century theory: the tension between speculative and practical theory—indeed, the very notions that there exists a speculative theory of value, and that it is intimately bound up with pedagogy; the tension between *Satzlehre* and original composition, expressed by Schenker as the tension between strict composition and free composition; the aesthetic ideology of genius and of organic and autonomous musical structure; and the notion of analysis as the explanation of the masterwork. It was precisely these tensions and issues that formed the horizons of Schenker's own work, so that the importation and dissemination of his ideas by his immigrant students in the 1940s and 1950s not only brought a weak and derivative American music theory into contact with a formidable theoretical mind but also brought it into contact for the first time with an intellectually and musically vital theoretical tradition. From this point of view—that is, from a point of view that sees Schenker not only as an original theoretical thinker but also as the bearer and upholder of a richer tradition—Schenker seems almost predestined for life in the American university. William Rothstein has shown in insightful and entertaining detail the thorough, if improbable, Americanization of his system and his ideas.[26] And William Benjamin, in a well-known review of the English translation of Schenker's summa, *Free Composition*, has argued that the value of Schenkerian theory in modern musical life is that it makes possible a kind of active engagement with the tonal repertoire that is impossible with any other analytical system.[27] To this I would add that Schenker makes such engagement possible not only with the repertoire but with both the speculative and practical sides of the Western European tradition. For in coming to grips with Schenker we not only learn a creative and relatively rigorous system for dealing with tonal music; we also are forced to test Schenker's ideas—and our own—on *Satzlehre*, *Formenlehre*, motivic relations, and many other aspects of theory that were never examined in this country before the advent of Schenkerian theory in the 1950s.

Schenkerian thought is central in the establishment of modern music theory's research program of theory-based analysis of tonal masterworks—a program that brings to its task not only Schenker's intellectual and artistic force but also, unwittingly, his aesthetic ideology as well (no matter how much theorists have tried to repress that ideology). His thought has also clearly served as a stimulus to contemporary theory's interest in the history of music theory—not only of the texts that Schenker himself so valued, such as those of Fux and C. P. E. Bach, but also of those that prefigured his work in important ways (Bernhard and Heinichen, for example), and even those against whom he so strongly reacted (Marx, Riemann, Kurth).

Schenkerian thought is even central, in a paradoxical way, to the other side of modern theory's theoretical-analytical program: that of atonal and twelve-tone music—a music that was summarily rejected as a nonmusic by Schenker himself. If the inspiration for such theory was Schoenberg, especially Schoenberg as interpreted and formalized by Babbitt, still it was Schenker who established a model of a systematic explanatory theory for a music. Babbitt's admiration of Schenker is apparent throughout his theoretical work, and a dogma that is found frequently in the writings of Princeton composers and theorists, especially in the 1960s, is the notion that there are two musics for which there are adequate explanatory theories: tonal music, as modeled by Schenker; and twelve-tone music, as formalized by Babbitt and his students. Similarly, Allen Forte, at Yale, structured the graduate program in music theory around the two central poles of Schenkerian analysis, for tonal music, and his own pitch-class set theory, for atonal music. In a 1981 article, Benjamin describes this "marriage of convenience"—the hitching together of Schenkerian theory and twelve-tone and set theory as the driving intellectual forces of the discipline.[28] If this marriage of convenience is both improbable and ostensibly illogical, it does, when viewed from a greater distance than Benjamin was able to achieve, make a certain amount of sense. Schenkerian theory and the current theories of atonal and twelve-tone music, however mutually exclusive in terms of the repertoires that constitute their objects, both share a value system that explicitly privileges rigor, system, and theory-based analysis and implicitly share an aesthetic ideology whereby analysis validates masterworks that exhibit an unquestioned structural autonomy.

The twelve-tone theories of Babbitt, to which should be added the pitch-class-set theoretical work of Allen Forte, John Rahn, John Clough, David Lewin, Robert Morris, and many others, do revitalize an aspect of the Western theoretical tradition that had been more or less moribund since the neo-Pythagoreans of the seventeenth century: the relation of music and mathematics. The connection between the two systems, of course, no longer concerns the arithmetic ratios of tuning systems but rather those branches of mathematics, such as set theory and group theory, that are particularly capable of describing various kinds of relations within the twelve-pitch-class system. Mathematically based theory and analysis of this sort is utterly foreign to historical musicology and constitutes one of the most distinct and original contributions of contemporary American theory.

We have seen how modern music theory exists as an academic field of study, as a body of knowledge and a research program now in the 1990s, how it constituted itself as an independent discipline in the late 1950s, and how it relates to the broader historical tradition out of which it came. The next section of the paper will show how modern music theory, with its newfound disciplinary knowledge, has negotiated a place for itself in the economy of power of the modern university and conservatory and how it has also unwittingly left its intellectual program vulnerable to attack.

MUSIC THEORY AS POWER

Can we not read the birth of modern music theory in the 1950s in terms of the Foucauldian dyad of knowledge and power? Foucault has shown that knowledge is in collusion with power and that new forms of knowledge create power where it had not been before. Similarly, he has shown that, although the disciplines, as bodies and practices of knowledge that make possible the exercise of power, can be repressive in that knowledge can be used to control individuals and groups, still a function of the disciplines is *production*—not only the production of discourses and practices that constitute knowledge and make it possible but even the production of *individuals* ("Out of the music theory teacher was thus born the 'music theorist'"): "the individual is no doubt the fictitious atom of an 'ideological' representation of society; but he is also a reality fabricated by this specific technology of power that I have called 'discipline'. We must cease once and for all to describe the effects of power in negative terms: it 'excludes' it 'represses' it 'censors', it 'abstracts', it 'masks', it 'conceals'. In fact, power produces; it produces reality; it produces domains of objects and rituals of truth."[29] That is, internalized structures of disciplinary power serve as a force to motivate individuals to define themselves within the discipline by "producing," so that by thus strengthening their connection to the discipline, they strengthen the discipline itself both by expanding its knowledge and by validating its hold upon them.

To read modern music theory into this configuration merely requires that we examine the space in which music theory constituted itself, that we identify its knowledge, and that we show how it appropriated power in a way that made its existence possible. We have already seen in detail how music theory staked out, or indeed created, a knowledge that it could call its own—a knowledge with some boundaries to be shared with its sister discipline of musicology, but a distinct and relatively self-contained knowledge nonetheless. That it has wielded this knowledge effectively in the academic economy of power is a simple matter of history. Since the 1950s music theory has changed itself from a pedagogical service with no intellectual respectability to a full-fledged discipline of the academy—one that retains its pedagogical mandate but one that has also made of itself a viable field of research. Whereas Babbitt could look back and see no serious music theory journals in the early 1950s but at least six in the 1980s, we can now, in the 1990s, see at least ten. Whereas virtually no university or conservatory in the 1950s employed anyone who called him- or herself a music theorist, now most schools have at least one or two, and some as many as eight or ten. Whereas in 1950 no American university offered a Ph.D. in music theory, now at least fifteen do. American music theory occupies a central place in undergraduate and graduate music curricula, provides jobs for its practitioners, supports a vital academic society, produces countless volumes of research and pedagogical materials, exports its ideas, and serves as a model for fledgling disciplines of music theory in Europe and elsewhere. Surely modern music theory, if it is anything, is an *industry*—one that defines and controls individuals, provides employment, manufactures products.[30]

How did modern music theory become a growth industry? It did so by creating its own knowledge and asserting its power in terms of the disciplinary configuration it saw as already existing and against which it would create itself and establish its boundaries. We have already seen that in the late 1950s music theory defined itself against a rejected form of itself: that is, the new music theory was *not* a pedagogy, didactic convenience, a discipline in a state of "academic disgrace." It would be instead a site of "serious theoretical thinking about music," a "creative mode of thought"—possibly even a new *musica theorica*. Twenty years later, when the discipline experienced another beginning—this time the beginning of a new academic society, the Society for Music Theory in 1978—it defined itself against, not only its old self, but its sister disciplines of musicology and composition, since many of the new society's members came from either the American Musicological Society or the American Society for University Composers.[31] In contradistinction to musicology, music theory would deal with the music itself, and deal with it systematically and with rigor, rather than as categories of style and historical evolution or as positivistic historical facts allegedly irrelevant to true musical understanding. In contradistinction to composition, it would be a scholarly field rather than a purely artistic one. By thus defining itself—against the unsophisticated pedagogical theory of its own American past and against musicology—it pulled itself up by the bootstraps to constitute itself as a disciplinary knowledge with a clear focus and boundaries. In so doing it also made its play for entering the academic economy of power in that it claimed now not just to provide a pedagogical service but to be a bona fide intellectual discipline. Musicology had long been recognized as a scholarly field in good standing in the humanities. Music theory was not, and it saw its mission as laying out a field of knowledge and practice whereby it could insert itself into the academic arena by filling a gap that it perceived in musical studies.

That it has done so, and done it well, is a matter of record. But music theory's very success masks strains that have made it difficult to reconcile the disciplinary knowledge that theory claims and the power structure of the modern university. We shall examine three such strains, two here and one in the final section of this essay: (1) the tension between a power structure that tends to enforce a separation between the sciences, the humanities, and the arts, and a disciplinary knowledge that shares aspects of all three; (2) the tension between the disciplinary expectations of the research university, for which modern theory groomed itself, and those of the university music schools, conservatories, or liberal arts colleges where most music theorists are employed; and (3) the tension between modern theory and musicology.

Foucault's concept of the disciplines can clarify our understanding of these tensions. His work employs the notion of "discipline" in two different ways—ways that he does not in fact distinguish himself but are crucial to our rethinking of contemporary music theory. In his quasi-structuralist works, *The Order of Things* and *The Archaeology of Knowledge, discipline* generally refers to the various sciences, social sciences, or humanities: to discrete bodies of knowledge and practices with well-defined objects of study and intellectual traditions. These works assume a distant and detached point of view in order to focus exclusively on disciplinary discourse as language detached from social context. But in later works, especially *Discipline and Punish*, discipline takes on both a broader and a narrower meaning: broader, in the sense that discourse and social practice interact, precisely as the interaction of knowledge and power; and narrower, in the sense that disciplines are now institutions (in particular, the hospital, the factory, the prison, the military barracks, and the primary school) that take on an altogether more ominous and repressive aura, because they are not disciplines of the mind but disciplines of the body developed in close association with the rise of capitalism.

If we view contemporary music theory in the light of these two senses of "discipline," an intriguing play of knowledge and power emerges between music theory as an intellectual discipline and the university as the controlling institution to which it is subject. Music theory is in fact, like all academic disciplines, a "docile body"—an object of control—with respect to the university, just as, in another sense, most music theorists, as individuals and employees of universities, are "docile bodies."[32] We have seen what music theory gained by voluntarily becoming a docile body: its submission to the institutional discipline of the university made possible its very existence; it created the "music theorist" as an individual and stimulated his or her *production*.

But music theory also paid a price in this interaction. Although it unquestionably profited enormously from the requirements of focus and productivity that it imposed upon itself in testing its wings as an academic discipline, it also took on the difficult problem of defining itself within the university in terms of the sciences, humanities, or arts. The very terms of music theory's entrance into the university place it in the difficult (if not impossible) position as a discipline that is in its essence simultaneously science, humanistic discipline, and art, of having to fill all three roles in the institutional setting. I can think of no other discipline that shares this problem. In the field of music as a whole, musicology and ethnomusicology are humanistic disciplines, while composition and performance are arts. In academic art departments there is a clear demarcation between the art historians, who are humanistic scholars, and the practicing painters and sculptors, who are artists.[33]

But music theorists share traits of all three. Under the powerful influence of Babbitt in the 1950s and 1960s, music theory in its formative years adopted, explicitly (in the case of Babbitt and his students) or implicitly (in the case of many other theorists), the philosophical foundation of logical positivism for music theory. Babbitt's program, as expressed in his famous dictum "There is but one kind of language, one kind of method for the verbal formulation of 'concepts' and the verbal analysis of such formulations: 'scientific' language and 'scientific' method,"[34] and his own theoretical work encouraged modern music theorists from the very beginning to model their work on the formal methods of mathematics and the hard sciences. Although, to be sure, not all theorists followed along this path, many did, and the discipline has produced a substantial body of mathematically based work that exemplifies the methods and practices of the sciences much more than those of the humanities and arts. More recently, Matthew Brown and Douglas Dempster have attempted to revive the notion of a formal music theory modeled on the empirical sciences,[35] and this strain of thought will undoubtedly continue to occupy a central position within the discipline. In addition, the growing field of music perception and cognition adopts an empirical stance, although this work, like psychology and the social sciences, stands in an uneasy relation to the hard sciences and has generally not been accepted by theorists of the Babbitt-positivist tradition.

Much of the work of the discipline has also been humanistic in its mode of thought. Certainly all work in the history of music theory is humanistic in its method. But what about theory proper and theory-based analysis? Some of this work—that of twelve-tone theory, for example—follows the model of the sciences. And the vast Schenkerian literature? For all that recent theorists (especially Princeton theorists) have done to formalize Schenker and impart to Schenkerian analysis the aura of rigorous science,[36] and for all the harsh criticisms of his work by Joseph Kerman and Leo Treitler as being "formalist" in the sense that structuralist literary criticism or anthropology is formalist, Schenker considered his work an aspect of musical art pure and simple and would surely find it bizarre to see his work invoked in either the name of science or that of humanism. Still, to the extent that Schenkerian theory, or any other analytical theory, for that matter, attempts to explain artistic products of human culture, the theory-based analytical enterprise of contemporary theory is inevitably humanistic. (Not all theorists will subscribe to this interpretation, of course: some, such as positivists who see no difference between the sciences and humanities, will find the whole notion of the humanities irrelevant, and others will consider their discipline to be art pure and simple.)

The pedagogy of traditional musical skills as inherited in many respects from the eighteenth and nineteenth centuries embodies the craft of an art rather than the methodology of a scientific or humanistic discipline. Even if we insist on rigorous use of language in pedagogy, as Babbitt does, what pedagogy seeks to accomplish is the transmission of a skill, not training in the formulation of empirical theories or critical study of human culture. Furthermore, the practice of music theory depends more fundamentally on its practitioners' possessing adequate musical skills than mathematical, logical, or interpretive ones. It is these latter skills, as exercised by many theorists, that have gained them and their discipline successful entry into the academy. But in a discipline in which the object of study is music and in which virtually everyone uses musical skills on a daily basis in pedagogy and analysis, musical ability is essential. As William Benjamin has rightly and authoritatively pointed out, even Schenkerian analysis, with all its sophistication, by no means requires that those who practice it have the minds of scientists or humanistic scholars: "[Schenker's method of analysis] does not demand an unusual capacity for logical thought, a prodigious grasp of abstraction, or a way with words, and it certainly does not call for interdisciplinary competence."[37]

The work of Howard Gardner illuminates this problem. Gardner suggests that intelligence is not a single, monolithic, unassailable category empirically demonstrable only by means of IQ tests but a descriptor of a variety of independent human mental capacities (musical ability, logical reasoning, mathematical reasoning, for example) that can take a variety of forms and styles in behavior and that can be measured in different ways.[38] Many music theorists do possess extraordinary musical skills (fine pitch discrimination, powerful memory, improvisatory facility, sensitivity to tonal and motivic relations, and the like), without possessing comparable skills in logical or mathematical reasoning. But others, some with exceptional musical ability and some not, also possess an extraordinary capacity for mathematics or for critical and interpretive thinking. And it goes without saying that those who possess a wide range of capacities, musical and intellectual (whether cognitively separate as claimed by Gardner or not) and who bring these skills together in what they produce as theorists, either as teachers or scholars, stand the best chance of success in the discipline.

That the tasks and modes of thought of music theory are thus distributed across the methodologies of the sciences, humanities, and arts and that the cognitive capacities of individual theorists are similarly distributed across a range of abilities appropriate to those methodologies is surely an advantage to music theory, which thereby demonstrates its intellectual and artistic breadth and vitality. Yet this situation is also disadvantageous, both for the discipline itself and for the relation of the individual music theorist to the institutionalized practice of the discipline in the university.

Herein lies the second troublesome tension within music theory. The task of the institutional discipline, the university, is to enclose, partition, distribute, and rank those individuals who subscribe to a particular intellectual discipline.[39] But the university is hardly the monolithic institution that my discussion thus far would suggest. The practice of modern music theory in the United States takes place not in the abstract "university" as a Platonic idea but in real-world institutions: liberal arts colleges with small music departments, state universities with prestigious music schools, state universities with less prestigious music schools or departments, major private research universities with music departments, and conservatories. These different types of institutions have different demands on music theory and different ways of valuing it. Conservatories and state university music schools require extensive conventional pedagogy for their thousands of students who are training to be performers and music educators; often they require the teaching of modern music theory, in its academic, *musica theorica* sense as well, for graduate students in composition, musicology, and music theory. Liberal arts colleges usually have not music schools but music departments—a crucial and often overlooked distinction. They too require pedagogy, but on a smaller scale, with perhaps some scholarly music theory in addition. Large private research universities, like liberal arts colleges, generally have music departments, not schools; they do not train practicing musicians, and they deal with music primarily as a scholarly rather than as a practical discipline.

When music theory made its move in the late 1950s and 1960s to enter the academy, it did so by reconstituting itself as a scholarly discipline modeled on either the sciences or the humanities rather than as an artistic or purely pedagogical one. In so doing it willingly submitted itself to evaluation *as a scholarly discipline* by the institutional discipline of which it sought to be a part. And as a disciplinary knowledge, modern music theory was born, not at the conservatory or the small liberal arts college, but at Princeton and Yale; the academy to which it originally sought admission was not the schools of music at Indiana University and the University of Michigan but the Ivy League research university.

Music theory's ambition to make a place for itself in such institutions touched off a disciplinary reaction, the dust from which has not entirely settled. In its new form, music theory claimed a sophisticated scholarly knowledge, turning itself into a new *musica theorica* and repressing its *musica practica* traditions to gain entrance to the academy. Did it gain the power that it sought? Yes, if by academy we mean university conservatories and music schools, and liberal arts colleges. No—or at least, not convincingly—if by academy we mean the research universities to which theory sought entrance. With the exception of Yale, which created the first prestigious doctoral program in music theory, and Princeton, where there has never been a graduate program in theory but where there has been a lively practice of theory under the auspices of composition, music theory has only with great difficulty made inroads into the music departments of private research universities. For decades the faculties of such departments included only composers and musicologists, both of which have tended to view the discipline of music theory with suspicion. Most do not offer graduate programs in music theory, and some (Cornell and Harvard, for example) did not hire a "professional music theorist" in the modern sense of the discipline until the late 1970s or even the 1980s. Many musicologists, as humanistic scholars working in divisions or colleges of humanities, have seen the program of modern music theory, on the one hand, as too narrow and formalistic—that is, too positivistic on the model of the sciences and too unconcerned with, even ignorant of, broader historical and social concerns—and on the other, too tainted by pedagogy, which they have seen as offering no possibilities for original research. And composers in these departments have sometimes tended to oppose the encroachment of theory as well, for their own reasons, often simply the resistance of one type of creative artist to theory of any sort, or else protection of disciplinary turf. Music theory has gained entrance to such institutions, but its success has been hard won, and it still tends to play a secondary role to musicology and composition.

But in other types of institutions music theory has established a more secure place for itself. Where music theory was quickest to thrive, and where it has consistently done well, is in university music schools, or in conservatories with close ties to universities—and here I include not only the schools of music at institutions like the University of Michigan or Indiana University but also institutions such as the Peabody Conservatory, which functions as a unit within a private university (unlike, say, the Juilliard School of Music and the Curtis School of Music, which have no such connections), and the Eastman School of Music, which, while also functioning as a unit within a private university, has tried to transcend the gap between the conservatory and the research university to offer aspects of both. The reasons for music theory's success in such institutions are not difficult to determine: these institutions need and value music theory's traditional *musica practica* while they provide a scholarly environment that encourages and rewards research. And although modern music theory has not made its way into the most traditional and prestigious conservatories, such as the Juilliard School of Music and the Curtis Institute, which still rely entirely on traditional pedagogy and reject the academic side of the discipline, it has found a secure place in the liberal arts college, where the music theorist is often valued as a versatile artist-scholar who can perform and teach practical theory as well as teaching and practicing the scholarly side of the discipline.

There thus exists a striking tension between the goals that modern music theory set for itself and its actual practice in the world. Theory envisioned itself thirty-five years ago as a new scholarly discipline capable of acceptance into the academy at the highest and most prestigious level. To the extent that it sought a base of power in music departments at private research universities, which are driven by scholarship and research and which neither valued nor imagined themselves to need conventional music-theoretical pedagogy, it had to base its knowledge on an explicit research program that would be legitimated by the academy at this level and to repress its conventional ties to pedagogy. Without question, that research program has been productive and influential. But at the same time, the knowledge that most distinctively defines the program, theory-based analysis (our modern *musica theorica*), was designed for the power structure and disciplinary requirements of precisely the kind of institution where it has had the most difficulty gaining a foothold. Conversely, the knowledge that academic music theory has tended to disclaim, the practical musical knowledge of a contemporary *musica practica*, is what the power structure and disciplinary requirements of the kind of institutions that in fact provide activity and employment for most music theorists have demanded of them.

This poor fit of disciplinary knowledge and power also has important ramifications for the individual theorist. For music theory, the usual and much-
publicized tension between scholarship and teaching is exacerbated by the
fact that the theorists with the best musical and pedagogical skills (whom the
music schools and colleges need in order to teach heavily enrolled classes in
music theory) sometimes have neither the interest nor the capacity for the
kind of original scholarship by which their own discipline chose to define
itself and which virtually all institutions—university music schools as well as
music departments in research universities—now require for promotion and
tenure. Likewise, theorists with the greatest capacity for research sometimes
lack the pedagogical skills that the music schools or colleges, in a practical
sense, require. Indeed, in university music schools the individual music theorist is often caught between a performance faculty (usually the majority of the
faculty in such schools) that operates on the model of the conservatory and
is thus concerned only with his or her being a skilled and dedicated teacher
for budding practical musicians, and an academic faculty that operates on
the model of the research university and is concerned primarily with scholarship and research. This schizophrenic position of the theorist contrasts
markedly with that of the musicologist and ethnomusicologist, who in all
types of institutions are viewed as humanistic scholars who will teach and
produce research in their own fields, or that of composers, who are viewed
as artists who teach composition and write music. Pedagogy is thus both a
blessing and a curse for modern music theory: a blessing because it provides
employment and enables the discipline to offer a valuable service to thousands of musicians, a curse because it has, and will forever, compromise music theory's position as a purely academic discipline.

Historically, the first institutionalization of music theory as a modern discipline (in Foucault's sense of the new kinds of disciplines that arose around
the time of the French Revolution) produced precisely the opposite result:
with the establishment of the Paris Conservatory in 1795, under the aegis of
the Directoire government,[40] French music theory opted for the conservatory, not the university. The complex of political and intellectual forces and
institutions may have given music theory no real opportunity to enter the
university; but the institutionalization of music theory in the conservatory is
nonetheless instructive because, then as now, there were both speculative
(generally Rameau-influenced) theorists and practical ones, and the distribution of theorists on the table of professional positions had in effect the
opposite result from what has happened in contemporary American theory:
namely, the most powerful positions went to the practical rather than to the
speculative theorists. And the regulatory function of the social institution
(the government-sponsored conservatory, the modern university) controlled
or controls the production of the intellectual discipline in both cases: Paris
Conservatory theory has pursued a doggedly practical, antispeculative pro-

gram for two centuries, with no sign of change, while modern American theory, though it has produced both speculative and practical theory, has tended to value the former above the latter.

Nevertheless, practical theorists in American colleges, universities, and conservatories have done very well in positions, publications, financial rewards, and all the trappings of academic life, despite the nascent discipline's self-defining opposition to practical theory. What the competent practical theorist has to offer—essential training in musical skills—is likely to remain essential to the broader discipline of music as an art. And if the role of the *practical* theorist, the teacher of *Satzlehre*, lacks the intellectual force and prestige of that of the research scientist or humanist scholar, the role of *speculative* theorist offers no such prestige either, at least in the eyes of the general public, to whom the term *music theorist* is no more prestigious, and certainly less comprehensible, than *music theory teacher*.

MUSIC THEORY AND MUSICOLOGY

If the first two tensions that characterize modern music theory concern its relation to the university at large, the third involves its relation to its sister discipline of musicology. Musicology has served as a subtheme throughout this essay, and in this final section we must bring music theory face to face with it. We have seen that music theory is far older than musicology as an intellectual discipline, yet much younger as a contemporary academic discipline. We have also seen that, at the time of the formation of the Society for Music Theory in 1978, the new discipline defined itself and its practice—theory-based analysis and pedagogy rather than positivistic historical studies—*against* musicology.

What spurred theorists to break from the musicological society at that time were the limitations of musicology's research program. Joseph Kerman finds postwar American musicology remarkably similar to the German positivist history of the late nineteenth century: the unrelenting search for new data in the discovery and publication of new documentary sources, the compilation of vast riches of resource material, the detailed examination of evidence—all done in the positivist spirit of collecting knowledge, with little concern for criticism or interpretation.[41] It was in fact musicology's single-minded adherence to this limited program, to the virtual exclusion of theory, analysis, or criticism, that created the intellectual gap in academic musical studies that theory was only too happy to fill. The success of music theory since the 1950s has thus been predicated not only on its own real strengths but also on musicology's weaknesses.

Given musicology's lack of interest in theory and analysis and its obsession with manuscripts and historical documents as opposed to theory's project of theory-based analysis and its more direct participation in music-making with its ongoing pedagogical responsibilities, it was easy enough for music theorists to crow that it was they, and only they, who really engaged music *as music*. Such a climate motivated music theorists to embrace a thoroughgoing formalism. Babbitt had already set forth an influential empirical-scientific program from Princeton; Allen Forte implicitly adopted the same philosophical basis for his teaching at Yale; and both Babbitt and Forte, as well as Schenkerians of various stripes, glibly linked the new music theory to the "formalism" of Schenker—a formalism that laid no claim to positivist empiricism but one that staunchly proclaimed, like Hanslick, the purely musical structural autonomy of the individual musical work. Music-theoretical normal science became the project of analyzing works and extending theory, often in creative and musically sensitive ways (for example, the work of Leonard Meyer, Wallace Berry, and David Epstein; new theories of tonal rhythm, some based in the work of Schenker, some not; extensions of Schenker's theory of hidden motivic parallelisms) in the very best traditions of historical speculative music theory, but generally with no consideration of the troublesome aspects of social context and meaning.

Since all was ostensibly well, most music theorists did not anticipate the historico-critico-musicological broadside that would score a direct hit on their discipline in the 1980s. Yet once musicology inevitably began to realize the limitations of endless studies of archives and documents and productions of historical editions, and to value critical interpretation, as it did beginning in the early 1980s, trouble between musicology and music theory was inevitable. One way in which we might read this recent trouble is to suggest that, by the mid-1980s, both theory and musicology had claimed the explication of the "work" as disciplinary turf: theory because of the very nature of its modern research program, the very existence of which depended on claiming for itself the space of "explaining" the individual work; musicology because of the dissatisfaction of at least some of its practitioners with positivistic historical musicology and the sense of a need for the interpretation of music in culture and in a social context. By the time the enterprise of positivist musicology began to lose steam, theory had so highly committed itself to formalist ideologies of analysis that it had unwittingly allowed a new disciplinary space to open, that of interpretation and criticism as opposed to analysis—a space that many musicologists began to explore and occupy. The "new musicology" has thus done to theory precisely what "modern music theory" had done to musicology decades earlier: it has created a new disciplinary identity by claiming a space that was ignored or repressed by a competing discipline.

We could also read the tension between theory and the new musicology in terms of modernism and postmodernism. Modern theory, as a product of the 1950s and 1960s, predictably bears a distinctive stamp of structuralism and formalism; it has been grounded philosophically in the same positivism that for so long guided historical musicology, except that theory has leaned toward the model of the sciences, developing and extending explicit and testable theories for analysis, while musicology followed a more humanistically based program and concerned itself less with theory proper than with a positivist view of what constitutes historical data and how that data may be organized into historical "facts." The new musicology, on the other hand, as a child of the 1980s, exhibits the traits of postmodernist thought: rejection of the structural autonomy and immanent meaning of the work of art, questioning of the received canon of works, concern with surfaces rather than deep structures, and viewing the work less as a self-contained coherent whole than as a complex product of the signifying practices and social norms of a particular culture. In their approach to the work, then, modern theory and the new musicology are respectively modernist and postmodernist. The difference between the two is that between *explaining* and *interpreting*: "The postmodern concern with surfaces rather than with deep explanations implies that instead of explaining, postmoderns are interpreting. I mean by this that instead of taking themselves to be discovering an independently given reality governed by law-like regularities, they see themselves as doing something more like interpreting texts. Moreover, instead of assuming that every text has a single unifying structure, they think that texts are almost infinitely complex. The postmodern paradigm is not profundity but complexity."[42]

This is not to assert that all theorists are modernists and all musicologists are postmodernists. As we have seen, theory began to expand its disciplinary horizons in various directions in the late 1980s. And on the musicological side of the ledger, many musicologists subscribe to the old paradigm of what that discipline is about and remain hostile to the postmodernist influence. Such musicologists find it easier to align themselves with modernist theory than with the new musicology, since theory and positivist musicology share a common philosophical basis and aesthetic ideology. Since both theory and musicology claim a spectrum of practitioners ranging from the most traditional (positivistic musicology) to modernist (modern theory) to postmodern (the new musicology), we might fancy an emerging configuration that distinguishes disciplinary practice not according to theory or musicology but according to traditionalist and modernist versus postmodernist paradigms. In such a world we might imagine a number of possible scenarios: the current one, in which both theory and musicology experience the tension between modernism and postmodernism; one in which modernists would gradually gravitate to one discipline (theory, for example) and postmodernists to the other; or the improbable one (which would have the same effect) of redividing the disciplines according to new paradigms—the Society for the Modernist Study of Music and the Society for the Postmodernist Study of Music.

More likely, and probably more healthy, would be a situation where both theorists and musicologists found value in, if not actually themselves being comfortable or competent in, both the modernist and postmodernist paradigms. David Couzens Hoy, in an essay examining the issue of whether Foucault was modern or postmodern (not surprisingly, he finds both tendencies in Foucault's work), articulates this problem in a way that could be illuminating for our disciplines of theory and musicology:

> Historical breaks do not occur everywhere for everyone at the same time. The same person, discipline, or institution can be traditional in some respects, modern in others, and postmodern in yet others. Furthermore, since there is no necessary progress, no forward movement in history, and perhaps no such thing as history (in the absence of a convincing metanarrative), the postmodern cannot imply that there is any normative advantage that comes from being either later in time or a sign of the future. Postmodernism cannot and should not claim to be better, more advanced, or more clever than whatever preceded it. That modernism does assume this superiority is what distinguishes it from postmodernism, and what postmodern pastiche disruptively reveals. So a postmodern cannot argue that those who are traditional or modern must eventually follow the path to postmodernism.[43]

Hoy's perspective suggests for music theory and musicology that they learn to see modern and postmodern points of view—or, as they are now reified in music studies, analysis and criticism—as complementary rather than necessarily hostile and mutually exclusive. An obstacle to such a rapprochement has been the polemical language of the recent debate between analysis and criticism. Lawrence Kramer, in an article ostensibly intended to bridge the gap between analysis and criticism, nevertheless has harsh words to say about analysis: "This hermeneutic trend [that is, the postmodernist tendency to interpret musical works as complex cultural products rather than as "transhistorical" structural wholes] has not yet had much impact on either the theory or practice of musical analysis. It has been hard enough for a discipline grounded in the ideal of positive knowledge to come to terms even with older modes of criticism that share its assumptions about musical autonomy and unity, let alone with postmodernist critical modes that challenge those assumptions. Even at its most concessive, analysis has tended to fall back on privileging its own province of knowledge and its own version of what Michel Foucault calls the will to truth."[44]

Such critical views of theory-based analysis constitute in part a delayed reaction to the philosophy expounded by theorists such as Babbitt, who airily dismissed any discourse about music that he perceived as lacking rigor. For example, with respect to catchwords such as "back to Bach" and "neoclassicism," ubiquitous in standard historical and critical writing on Stravinsky, Babbitt asserted that they should only "be talked about by those who could not and should not talk about the music."[45] Whether one agrees with Babbitt's positivist platform, his apparently objective, rigorous language in fact bristles with exclusionary hostility, especially in the context of what discourse about music in the late 1960s and early 1970s was like. Richard Taruskin's postmodernist reading of Babbitt's language is predictably pointed: "As always with Babbitt, for 'talk' read 'talk shop'; the reason for dismissing the language of public converse is simply and wholly its lack of 'pertinence to professional activity or professional discourse.'" To equate music, for purposes of discussion, with the techniques of manufacturing music, to regard the manufacturing of music as the only legitimate professional concern of musicians, and to sanction only such locutions as may describe or analogically represent that manufacture, is of course merely to practice another politics of exclusion."[46]

Taruskin's analysis of Babbitt brings together a number of strands of this essay. Babbitt's words from twenty years ago simply articulate (however baldly) the research space that contemporary music theory claimed for itself in the 1950s: a rigorous research program of theory-based analysis—a program whose very existence in the university depended on its excluding other sorts of discourse about music (e.g., historical discourse and unrigorous critical discourse). And this research program in turn entailed that modern music theory would in fact be an exclusionary discipline. If nothing else, the unusual combination of cognitive capacities required to practice it, as it was envisioned in the 1950s and established in the years since, requires that it be so. Modern music theory is thus, for better or worse, and by its own making, the province of what Richard Littlefield and David Neumeyer have called "professional interpreters,"[47] or what Margaret Murata, in a different context, has called an "expert subculture."[48] The language of the expert subculture is by definition not the language of the general public, nor is it the language of the postmodernist critic.

But this is not to say that it is a language without value. Scott Burnham has responded to Lawrence Kramer's attempt to bridge the gap between analysis and criticism—an attempt that, it must be admitted, has criticism, not analysis, calling the shots—with a passionate defense of theory-based analysis against the "shrill marauders" of postmodernism.[49] Burnham defends analysis by showing, contra the postmodernists who have gleefully shown what it *cannot* do, what it *can* do: that is, identify ways in which music signifies, self-referentially, in the "space between a tacit, internalized sense of general style [a sense that it is the task of theory to describe, articulate, and formalize] . . . and the claims of the individual work."[50] For Burnham, as for most contemporary theorists, there is palpable and describable meaning in this purely musical space—a meaning that, on the one hand, neither denies nor devalues the extramusical, socially based meaning that so fascinates postmodern critics, and on the other, is vastly more rich and complex than the straw man of "pure formalism" that such critics so easily dismiss. The value of theory, as he points out, is that it provides a stable and consistent music-centered standpoint in terms of which to read musical works. Without such a music-based technology, even if it rests in the hands of an expert subculture, it would be difficult to control a subjectivism that, in some postmodernist and deconstructionist projects, often threatens to overstep the boundary between criticism and free association.

Taruskin's critiques also point up the dangers of postmodernism's own exclusionary tendencies: if Babbitt's language is exclusionary, so is Taruskin's. Indeed, postmodernist attacks—whether on theory-based analysis, positivistic musicology, or anything else—that attempt to bury the adversary as a useless relic of the past (or the present) begin to take on the same aura of claiming transhistorical truth that they denounce in structuralism and formalism. Taruskin seems to relegate Babbitt, his language, and the program of theory and analysis that he represents to a modernist trash heap—a sizable dump that also apparently includes positivist musicology and much of the historical performance movement as well. Taruskin's virtuosic unmasking of modernist ideology, whether of "authentic performance" or of modern theory and analysis, is one of the most impressive performances of the new musicology. But he has his own peculiar blind spot. In his attacks on the historical performance movement—attacks that rightly uncover and explode that movement's characteristic modernist assumption of superiority—he virtually always defends traditionalist performers of the standard repertoire (Toscanini, for example) while he pounds away at the authentic instrument devotees. Taruskin argues, at least in part, that to reject traditionalist performers is to reject real musicians who creatively engaged music in their own time and established musical significance for themselves in their own way.[51] But Taruskin refuses to concede the same to adherents of either the early music movement or modern theory and analysis, most of whom are weighed in the balance of a postmodern version of truth and found wanting. Yet surely these musicians are also embodiments of the musical thought, discourse, and activity of their time, for whom music is just as much a social and cultural practice as it was fifty or a hundred years before: if they are guided by an unconscious ideology, is it more false, or more malignant, than that of the 1890s or the 1930s?

Similarly, another postmodernist, Rose Rosengard Subotnik, in an essay entitled "Toward a Deconstruction of Structural Listening: A Critique of Schoenberg, Adorno, and Stravinsky," attempts to discredit the kind of listening that modern theory and analysis have encouraged and taught: listening for structural formal, tonal, and motivic relationships, and locating musical meaning, in real-time hearing, in the play between musical syntax and the individual work, between expectations conditioned by style and realizations in the actual music.[52] Theorists of all stripes, even those in bitter opposition on theoretical and analytical issues, from proponents of strict Schenkerian theory to those of the implication-realization theories of Leonard Meyer and Eugene Narmour, have all been in general agreement on this program of how to listen. Subotnik levels against structural listening the predictable postmodernist charges: it ignores the musical surface, it is blind to extramusical meaning, it shirks the obligation of the musical interpreter "to seek carefully reasoned ways of investigating and assessing the social and moral significance of the values discerned in music."[53] She is right: structural listening does none of these things, for it is founded on the ideology of structural autonomy that has always driven modern theory. But she goes further:

> Of all methods, structural listening, even in its "replete" version, seems the least useful for entering the semiotic domain of sound and style. For carried to its logical conclusion, this method in all its versions, as an exclusive or even as the primary paradigm for listening, is not in a position to define much of a positive role for society, style, or ultimately even sound in the reception of music. Discounting metaphorical and affective responses based on cultural association, personal experience, and imaginative play as at best secondary not only in musical perception but also in the theoretical accounts we make of such perception, this method allows virtually no recognition to non-structural varieties of meaning or emotion in the act of listening. Since these are of course precisely the varieties favored by the overwhelming majority of people, structural listening by itself turns out to be socially divisive, not only in what it demands but also in what it excludes or suppresses.[54]

Music theory must concede Subotnik's eloquently argued main point: structural listening, at least in its more limited forms, is self-reflexive and hermetically sealed from social issues. But it is hardly more socially divisive than learned treatises on Adorno or virtuoso performances of deconstructive criticism that require a lifelong education in the loftiest realms of Western art, culture, and criticism to even begin to comprehend.

And for flesh-and-blood talented musicians with quick ears and long memories, it is not socially divisive at all; it is simply the way life and listening happen to be. Such musicians are perfectly capable of listening for, thinking about, writing about, and proselytizing about the social meaning of music. Subotnik rightly charges that our educational system has for years insisted on structural listening at the expense of socially aware listening, and that if our system of values prizes the former excessively over the latter, young musicians will remain insensitive to extramusical meaning, or, alas, like many music theorists, simply ignore it. But structural listening does not logically or perceptually exclude other types of listening. Those with a gift for structural listening and theoretical abstraction should use such gifts. Joseph Kerman himself has noted that musicologists "look to theory and analysis for tools to help them with their own work."[55] Kerman has also written of "the very real attractions" that Schenker's theory can offer to a certain kind of mind,"[56] and, in his *New Grove* essay on Beethoven, of "Beethoven's fascination for musicians of a certain turn of mind."[57] That "certain kind of mind" is embodied in the modern music theorist, whose insights into music constitute a unique contribution to musical culture in the past few decades.

To return to the image of the cartoon with which I began this essay: music theory, like the retired executive on the yacht, has, whether one likes it or not, established itself in an enviable position of power: it has already "made its pile." It has learned that its claim to power, and indeed its central research agenda, at least in the view of some, was compromised from the outset by a questionable ideology. The power that it now enjoys may even have been gained in part through the dark workings of an unconscious obsession, rather than the virtuous hard work and search for truth that it always imagined to be its driving force. But what should it do? Should it flatly deny that it has been compromised and proceed with business as usual? Should it abrogate its power and begin again, trying better to match its vision and its practice the second time around? Or should it, like the executive in the cartoon, wisely accept the reality that no knowledge or power is ever pure, and revel in its accomplishments anyway?

To no one's surprise, I, as a practicing music theorist, would opt for the third course: for a music theory that comes to grips with postmodernism while continuing to build on and value its own achievements of the past. A truly postmodern music theory would not practice the exclusionary politics of some postmodernists or some of its own practitioners but would form itself along the lines suggested above by David Hoy. It would recognize and accept the facts that modern music theory was from the beginning based on the ideological assumption of the structural autonomy of the musical work and that its disciplinary boundaries as well as its disciplinary production proceeded from this ideology. That the ideology has been uncovered and brought into the open not only by musicologists but from within the theory community itself can only be a sign of the vitality and health of the discipline.[58] But instead of either denying the problems inherent in the ideology (and thus the discipline) and forging full speed ahead or rejecting its own history wholesale once it has discovered that history to be compromised by a problematic ideology, music theory would attempt to integrate its own history, combining traditional, modern, and postmodern practices where desirable, but also letting them exist side by side as well. It would recognize that its power in the world of the university and conservatory is inevitably founded upon a knowledge that shares aspects of art, science, and humanistic disciplines and of traditional, modern, and now postmodern thought. Modern music theory would see itself neither as regressing from a period of triumph to a period of hunkering down for a siege nor as progressing from a period of benighted modernist darkness to postmodernist enlightenment but rather as participating in an ongoing play of knowledge and power in which disciplinary spaces open up, are appropriated to amass power, produce new knowledge, and create practicing disciplinary individuals, only to open up still other disciplinary spaces that establish yet newer configurations of knowledge and power.

NOTES

I am grateful to Roger Graybill, Douglass Green, Lawrence Kramer, Richard Leppert, and David Schwarz for their insightful readings of earlier versions of this paper. The epigraph is taken from Michel Foucault, *Discipline and Punish: The Birth of the Prison* (New York: Vintage/Random House, 1977), 27.

1. See Claude Palisca's article "Theory," in Stanley Sadie, ed., *The New Grove Dictionary of Music and Musicians* (London: Macmillan, 1980), 18:741–42.

2. For an insightful and far more detailed retrospective on the history and traditions of American musicology, see Joseph Kerman, *Contemplating Music: Challenges to Musicology* (Cambridge: Harvard Univ. Press, 1985), especially 11–59.

3. Michel Foucault, *The Order of Things: An Archaeology of the Human Sciences* (New York: Vintage/Random House, 1973), xiv.

4. My account here is indebted to the critical reading of Foucault's oeuvre in Hubert L. Dreyfus and Paul Rabinow, *Michel Foucault: Beyond Structuralism and Hermeneutics*, 2d ed. (Chicago: Univ. of Chicago Press, 1983). For those unfamiliar with Foucault's work, his first important books were *Madness and Civilization: A History of Insanity in the Age of Reason* (New York: Vintage/Random House, 1973) and *The Birth of the Clinic: An Archaeology of Medical Perception* (New York: Vintage/Random House, 1975), both published originally in French, in 1961 and 1963, respectively. His next two major works represent his quasi-structuralist project on discourse: *The Order of Things* and *The Archaeology of Knowledge* (New York: Harper Colophon, 1972), published in French in 1966 and 1969, respectively. His last works, which connect discourse to social practice and examine the relation between knowledge and power, are *Discipline and Punish*, published in French in 1975, and *The History of Sexuality, Volume I: An Introduction; Volume II: The Uses of Pleasure;* and *Volume III: The Care of the Self* (New York: Vintage/Random House, 1978, 1985, and 1986, respectively).

5. François-Joseph Fétis, *Esquisse de l'histoire de l'harmonie considerée comme art et comme science systématique* (Paris: Bourgogne & Martinet, 1840); Hugo Riemann, *Geschichte der Musiktheorie im IX.-XIX. Jahrhundert* (Leipzig: Max Hesse, 1898). For bibliographic references to English translations, see David Damschroder and David Russell Williams, *Music Theory from Zarlino to Schenker: A Bibliography and Guide*, Harmonologia Series, no. 4 (Stuyvesant, N.Y.: Pendragon Press, 1990), 86–87 and 272.

6. "The State of Research in Music Theory: Papers of the Plenary Session, Rochester, 1987," in *Music Theory Spectrum* 11, no. 1 (Spring 1989).

7. The absence of a paper on the history of music theory before the sixteenth century is indicative of the fact that the research on theory before 1500 has generally remained the province of musicologists rather than theorists.

8. Joseph Kerman, "How We Got into Analysis, and How We Can Get Out," *Critical Inquiry* 7 (1980): 311–31.

9. See, for example, Leo Treitler, *Music and the Historical Imagination* (Cambridge: Harvard Univ. Press, 1989); Susan McClary and Richard Leppert, eds., *Music and Society: The Politics of Composition, Performance, and Reception* (Cambridge: Cambridge Univ. Press, 1987); Susan McClary, *Feminine Endings: Music, Gender, and Sexuality* (Minneapolis: Univ. of Minnesota Press, 1991); Lawrence Kramer, *Music as Cultural Practice 1800–1900* (Berkeley and Los Angeles: Univ. of California Press, 1990); Ruth A. Solie, ed., *Musicology and Difference: Gender and Sexuality and Music Scholarship* (Berkeley and Los Angeles: Univ. of California Press, 1993); Rose Rosengard Subotnik, *Developing Variations: Style and Ideology in Western Music* (Minneapolis: Univ. of Minnesota Press, 1991); Carolyn Abbate, *Unsung Voices: Opera and Musical Narrative in the Nineteenth Century* (Princeton: Princeton Univ. Press, 1991); and Richard Taruskin, "She Do the Ring in Different Voices," review of Abbate's *Unsung Voices, Cambridge Opera Journal* 4 (1992): 187–97.

10. Milton Babbitt, *Words about Music*, ed. Stephen Dembski and Joseph Straus (Madison: Univ. of Wisconsin Press, 1987), 121.

11. Ibid.

12. David Kraehenbuehl, Foreword, *Journal of Music Theory* 1, no. 1 (1957): 1.

13. David Kraehenbuehl, Introduction, "The Nature and Value of Theoretical Training: A Forum," *Journal of Music Theory* 3, no. 1 (1959): 31.

14. David Kraehenbuehl, untitled paper in "The Professional Music Theorist— His Habits and Training: A Forum," *Journal of Music Theory* 4, no. 1 (1960): 62.

15. Franchino Gaffurio, *The Theory of Music*, trans. Walter Kurt Kreysig (New Haven and London: Yale Univ. Press, 1993), 42.

16. "Jedoch ist es umb so viel besser wenn jemand ein Theoreticus und Practicus zugleich seyn kan; Sed non omnia possumus omnes." *Musicae mathematicae Hodegus curiosus* (Frankfurt am Main and Leipzig: Theodor Philipp Calvisius, 1686), 10.

17. See, for example, McClary, *Feminine Endings*.

18. Carl Dahlhaus, *Die Musiktheorie im. 18. und 19. Jahrhundert, Erster Teil: Grundzüge einer Systematik*, in *Geschichte der Musiktheorie*, bd. 10 (Darmstadt: Wissenschaftliche Buchgesellschaft, 1984).

19. Joachim Burmeister, *Musica poetica* (Rostock, 1606). For an English translation and extensive commentary on the treatise, see Burmeister, *Musical Poetics*, trans. and with Introduction and Notes by Benito V. Rivera (New Haven and London: Yale Univ. Press, 1993). See also the classic commentary on Burmeister's analysis of the Lasso motet in Claude Palisca, "*Ut oratoria musica*: The Rhetorical Basis of Musical Mannerism," in *The Meaning of Mannerism*, ed. Franklin Westcott Robinson and Stephen G. Nichols Jr. (Hanover: Univ. Press of New England, 1972), 37–65.

20. For an extensive discussion of the eighteenth-century distinction between musical grammar and musical rhetoric, see Mark Evan Bonds, *Wordless Rhetoric: Musical Form and the Metaphor of the Oration* (Cambridge: Harvard Univ. Press, 1991), 68–80. A valuable historical survey of eighteenth-century music theory is Joel Lester, *Compositional Theory in the Eighteenth Century* (Cambridge: Harvard Univ. Press, 1992).

21. John Neubauer traces in detail the development of the philosophical and aes-

thetic arguments legitimating instrumental music in *The Emancipation of Music from Language: Departure from Mimesis in Eighteenth-Century Aesthetics* (New Haven and London: Yale Univ. Press, 1986).

22. The classic account of this shift is M. H. Abrams, *The Mirror and the Lamp: Romantic Theory and the Critical Tradition* (Oxford: Oxford Univ. Press, 1953).

23. Carl Dahlhaus, *The Idea of Absolute Music*, trans. Roger Lustig (Chicago: Univ. of Chicago Press, 1989), 7. See also Klaus Kropfinger, "Der musikalische Struktur-begriff bei E. T. A. Hoffmann," in *Bericht über den internationalen musikwissenschaft-lichen Kongress Bonn 1970* (Kassel: Bärenreiter, 1973), 480.

24. Bonds, *Wordless Rhetoric*, 140–48. A valuable anthology of nineteenth-century analytical writing is available in Ian Bent, *Music Analysis in the Nineteenth Century*, 2 vols. (Cambridge: Cambridge Univ. Press, 1994). For essential critical background in the ideology under discussion here, see Terry Eagleton, *The Ideology of the Aesthetic* (Cambridge: Harvard Univ. Press, 1990) and Lydia Goehr, *The Imaginary Museum of Musical Works: An Essay in the Philosophy of Music* (Oxford: Oxford Univ. Press, 1992).

25. Dahlhaus discusses the tension in nineteenth-century composition between *Satzlehre* and the aesthetic of originality in *Die Musiktheorie im 18. und 19. Jahrhundert*, 29.

26. William Rothstein, "The Americanization of Heinrich Schenker," in *Schenker Studies*, ed. Hedi Siegel (Cambridge: Cambridge Univ. Press, 1990), 193–203.

27. William E. Benjamin, "Schenker's Theory and the Future of Music," *Journal of Music Theory* 25, no. 1 (1981): 159–61.

28. Ibid., 171.

29. Foucault, *Discipline and Punish*, 194.

30. For the notion of modern music scholarship as industry I am indebted to Carolyn Abbate and Roger Parker, Introduction "On Analyzing Opera," *Analyzing Opera* (Berkeley and Los Angeles: Univ. of California Press, 1989), 17.

31. For an informative retrospective on the formation of the society, see Richmond Browne, "The Inception of the Society for Music Theory," *Music Theory Spectrum* 1, no. 1 (1979): 2–5.

32. Foucault, *Discipline and Punish*, 136.

33. For a related discussion of similar issues, see Edward T. Cone's early essay "Music Theory as a Humanistic Discipline" (originally published, appropriately enough, in 1957), in *Music: A View from Delft*, ed. Robert P. Morgan (Chicago: Univ. of Chicago Press, 1992), 29–38.

34. Milton Babbitt, "Past and Present Concepts of the Nature and Limits of Music," in *Perspectives on Contemporary Music Theory*, ed. Benjamin Boretz and Edward T. Cone (New York: Norton, 1972), 3. Since, for Babbitt, any meaningful discourse requires rigor and since only the language of "scientific" discourse apparently meets his standards of rigor, the conventional distinctions separating the arts, sciences, and humanities evaporate: "Without even engaging oneself in disposing of that easily disposable, if persistent, dichotomy of 'arts' and 'sciences' (or, relatedly, 'humanities' and 'sciences')—that historical remnant of a colloquial distinction—it only need be insisted here that our concern is not whether music has been, is, can be, will be, or should be, a 'science,' whatever that may be assumed to mean, but simply

that statements about music must conform to those verbal and methodological requirements which attend the possibility of meaningful discourse in any domain" (Babbitt, "Past and Present Concepts," 3).

Foucault, it should be pointed out, makes a clear distinction between the "natural" sciences and the "human sciences." See Dreyfus and Rabinow, 115–17.

35. Matthew Brown and Douglas J. Dempster, "The Scientific Image of Music Theory," *Journal of Music Theory* 33, no. 1 (1989): 65–106. See also the critiques of this essay by Benjamin Boretz, Nicholas Cook, John Rahn, and Richard Taruskin, in the same volume, as well as Brown and Dempster's response, "Evaluating Musical Analyses and Theories: Five Perspectives," *Journal of Music Theory* 34, no. 2 (1990): 247–80.

36. For example, Michael Kassler, "A Trinity of Essays" (Ph. D. diss, Princeton University, 1967). A growing body of work concerns itself with the language of modern American theory, especially with respect to the ways in which it replaces the organicist metaphors of Schenker with seemingly objective, neutral language. See Rothstein, "The Americanization of Heinrich Schenker" (n. 26 above); Marion A. Guck, "Analytical Fictions," *Music Theory Spectrum* 16, no. 2 (1994): 217–30, and "Rehabilitating the Incorrigible," in *Theory, Analysis, and Meaning in Music,* ed. Anthony Pople (Cambridge: Cambridge Univ. Press, 1994), 57–76; Robert Snarrenberg, "Competing Myths: The American Abandonment of Schenker's Organicism," in *Theory, Analysis, and Meaning in Music,* 29–56.

37. Benjamin, "Schenker's Theory and the Future of Music," 161.

38. Howard Gardner, (New York: Basic Books, 1983). American, pragmatic, empirical, democratic, Gardner ostensibly exemplifies the intellectual polar opposite of Foucault. Yet a thematic thread connects the two, a thread to which we will appeal more than once in attempting to sort out the intellectual and political positions of contemporary music theory. Both seek to deconstruct the sort of unexamined truths that we tend to accept unquestioningly. Both resist what Foucault calls "master discourses" or "totalizing histories" that obscure the detailed complexity of history as it is experienced and lived. Foucault repeatedly invokes his virtuosic knowledge of miniscule details of, say, medical history or social practice, to reject Freudian or Marxist accounts that he sees as projecting unyielding interpretations—unjustified by historical detail, in his view—onto events or individuals. Likewise, Gardner disallows the labeling of individual persons as intelligent or not intelligent on the basis of IQ tests. Indeed, the IQ test might be seen as a classic case of the loss of individual freedom occasioned by the establishment of a "human discipline" of knowledge, with its inevitable collusion with power: the experts, empowered by a knowledge and an institutionalized apparatus for its operation, rank, classify, distribute, and thus regulate the individuals that are subjected to their technology.

39. See Foucault, *Discipline and Punish,* 141–56.

40. See Cynthia Gessele, "The Institutionalization of Music Theory in France, 1764–1802," Ph. D. diss., Princeton University, 1989, and Renate Groth, *Die französische Kompositionslehre des 19. Jahrhunderts,* Beihefte zum Archiv für Musikwissenschaft, no. 22 (Wiesbaden: Steiner, 1983).

41. Kerman, *Contemplating Music,* 31–32.

42. David Couzens Hoy, "Foucault: Modern or Postmodern?" in *After Foucault:*

Humanistic Knowledge, Postmodern Challenges, ed. Jonathan Arac (New Brunswick: Rutgers Univ. Press, 1988), 28.

43. Hoy, "Foucault," 38.

44. Lawrence Kramer, "Haydn's Chaos, Schenker's Order; or, Hermeneutics and Musical Analysis: Can They Mix?" *Nineteenth-Century Music* 16, no. 1 (1992): 4.

45. Milton Babbitt, untitled memoir in *Perspectives of New Music* 9, no. 2–10, no. 1 (1971): 106.

46. Richard Taruskin, "Back to Whom? Neoclassicism as Ideology," *Nineteenth-Century Music* 16, no. 3 (1993): 288.

47. Richard Littlefield and David Neumeyer, "Rewriting Schenker: Narrative—History—Ideology," *Music Theory Spectrum* 14, no. 1 (1992): 52.

48. Margaret Murata, "Scylla and Charybdis, or Steering between Form and Social Context in the Seventeenth Century," in *Explorations in Music, the Arts, and Ideas: Essays in Honor of Leonard B. Meyer*, ed. Eugene Narmour and Ruth A. Solie (Stuyvesant, N.Y.: Pendragon Press, 1988), 84. Murata's "expert subculture" is one of practicing musicians, not one of theorists.

49. Scott Burnham, "The Criticism of Analysis and the Analysis of Criticism," *Nineteenth-Century Music* 16, no. 1 (1992): 70–76.

50. Ibid., 72.

51. Richard Taruskin, review of various recordings of Beethoven symphonies recorded by ensembles from the early music movement, in *Opus* 3, no. 6 (1987), 31. Taruskin is not opposed to the historical performance movement in principle, but only to its excessive "modernist" claims of authenticity, which often, in his opinion, simply serve as a cover for perfunctory and unimaginative performances.

52. In *Explorations in Music, the Arts, and Ideas*, 87–122.

53. Subotnik, 117.

54. Ibid., 115–16.

55. Kerman, 64.

56. Ibid., 82.

57. Joseph Kerman and Alan Tyson, *The New Grove Beethoven* (New York: Norton, 1983), 108.

58. See Littlefield and Neumeyer, above, or Kevin Korsyn, "Brahms Research and Aesthetic Ideology," *Music Analysis* 12, no. 1 (1993): 89–102.

SUSAN McCLARY

Terminal Prestige: The Case of Avant-Garde Music Composition

Good evening. Welcome to Difficult Listening Hour.
The spot on your dial for that relentless and
impenetrable sound of Difficult Music [Music . . . Music . . . Music . . .]
So sit bolt upright in that straight-backed chair,
button that top button,
and get set for some difficult music:
Ooola.

Laurie Anderson, "Difficult Listening Hour"

When composer/performance artist Laurie Anderson performs "Difficult Listening Hour" as part of her extended work *United States*, she satirizes several aspects of the present-day music scene. Perhaps the first thing that strikes one is the sound of her voice. As she speaks into a vocoder, the pitch of her voice is thrown down into a much lower range so that she no longer sounds like a woman at all. Rather she evokes the insinuating delivery typical of announcers on classical music stations—the low, velvety, patriarchal voice that soothes and seduces while congratulating the listener on his or her status as a connoisseur of élite music. Ordinarily such "cultured" voices serve to render affirmative and nonthreatening their presentations of high art: kick off your shoes, sit back, and relax to (say) *Death and Transfiguration*. By contrast, Anderson instructs us (with that familiar congenial/sinister voice) to deny ourselves all the usual trappings of physical comfort as she braces us for that most alienating of musical experiences: the encounter with the avant-garde, with Difficult Music.

Lest we miss the lethal accuracy of Anderson's satire of the avant-garde, I would like to turn first to a strikingly parallel formulation from Roger Sessions's essay from 1950 "How a 'Difficult' Composer Gets That Way": "I have sometimes been told that my music is 'difficult' for the listener. There are those who consider this as praise, those who consider it a reproach. For my part I cannot regard it as, in itself, either the one or the other. But so far as it is so, it is the way the music comes, the way it has to come."[1] Sessions (presumably the agent who composes these pieces) is strangely absent from this explanation: it is *the music itself* that can't help it, that demands the kind of complexity that listeners by and large find incomprehensible. And while Sessions professes not to care whether the assessment of "difficult" is intended as praise or reproach, the title and tone of the essay make it quite clear that he wears "difficult" as a badge of honor.

Better still, this is Arnold Schoenberg's "How One Becomes Lonely" from 1937:

> But as soon as the war was over, there came another wave which procured for me a popularity unsurpassed since. My works were played everywhere and acclaimed in such a manner that I started to doubt the value of my music. This may seem like a joke, but, of course, there is some truth in it. If previously my music had been difficult to understand on account of the peculiarities of my ideas and the way in which I expressed them, how could it happen that now, all of a sudden, everybody could follow my ideas and like them? Either the music or the audience was worthless. . . . One of the accusations directed at me maintained that I composed only for my private satisfaction. And this was to become true, but in a different manner from that which was meant. While composing for me had been a pleasure, now it became a duty. I knew I had to fulfil a task: I had to express what was necessary to be expressed and I knew I had the duty of developing my ideas for the sake of progress in music, whether I liked it or not; but I also had to realize that the great majority of the public did not like it.[2]

Here again we find that a piece is worthless if it is not so "difficult" as to be incomprehensible and that acceptance on the part of the audience indicates failure. Note, too, that what is described in the first of these paragraphs as Schoenberg's own oppositional idiosyncracies ("the peculiarities of my ideas") becomes in the second "the duty of developing my ideas for the sake of progress in music, whether I liked it or not." Once again, it is the music itself that demands such sacrifices by community and artist alike.

Finally, here is Milton Babbitt in "The Composer as Specialist," infamously—though probably appropriately—retitled by the editors of *High Fidelity Magazine* as "Who Cares If You Listen?" from 1958: "I dare suggest that the composer would do himself and his music an immediate and eventual service by total, resolute, and voluntary withdrawal from this public world to one of private performance and electronic media, with its very real possibility of complete elimination of the public and social aspects of musical composition. By so doing, the separation between the domains would be defined beyond any possibility of confusion of categories, and the composer would be free to pursue a private life of professional achievement, as opposed to a public life of unprofessional compromise and exhibitionism."[3]

Music functions and is valued variously in different human societies: it may participate in ritual, facilitate the physical motions of dance or labor, serve as entertainment, provide pleasure, stand as a manifestation of ideal beauty or order, and so on. Within many societies, there exists a hierarchy among musical discourses that attributes greater prestige to some of these functions than to others.

Perhaps only with the twentieth-century avant-garde, however, has there been a music that has sought to secure prestige precisely by claiming to renounce all possible social functions and values, just as Wagner's Alberich renounced human love in exchange for the Rheingold. Schoenberg was relieved and gratified when audiences again turned against him: it had not been his fault that they had thought temporarily that they liked him—they really had not understood him in the first place.[4] The prestige value of this music, in other words, is inversely correlated with public response and comprehension.

This strange posture was not invented in the twentieth century, of course. It is but the reductio ad absurdum of the nineteenth-century notion that music ought to be an autonomous activity, insulated from the contamination of the outside social world.[5] The motivation for this position can be traced in part to the breakdown of the aristocratic patronage system and to the problems the composer faced as a freelance artist, reluctantly dependent on the bourgeois audience. Within the context of industrial capitalism, two mutually exclusive economies of music developed: that which is measured by popular or commercial success and that which aims for the prestige conferred by official arbiters of taste. Pierre Boulez, for instance, in defending the integrity of avant-garde music against the option of pluralism, states: "The economy is there to remind us, in case we get lost in this bland utopia: there are musics which bring in money and exist for commercial profit; there are musics that cost something whose very concept has nothing to do with profit. No liberalism will erase this distinction."[6]

The terms for this double economy are already recognizable in Robert Schumann's criticism in the *Neue Zeitschrift für Musik*, with his castigations of what he perceived as the vulgar virtuosity of Philistine Goliaths such as Liszt and his championing (through his imaginary group of aesthetic underdogs, the "League of David") of the cerebral, organic constructs of composers such as Brahms.[7] If Schumann helped set the groundwork for the Great German Canon that is still the mainstay of the bourgeois concert audience, he also articulated a position that would ultimately lead to the self-alienation of the composer from that same audience.

Schumann's writing is to some extent motivated by the social idealism that marks much of European culture in the first half of the nineteenth century— by a desire to wean the indiscriminate middle-class audience from empty, manipulative display and to instill in them what he regarded as the liberatory, dialectical habits of thought articulated in the complex music of serious composers. Adorno's interpretation of Schoenberg argues compellingly that his private-language games likewise are motivated by the impulse of social critique, even if Schoenberg's solutions end up reinscribing the very contradictions he sought to transcend.[8]

But idealism thwarted easily turns into contempt. In this century (especially following World War II), the "serious" composer has felt beleaguered both by the reified, infinitely repeated classical music repertory and also by the mass media that have provided the previously disenfranchised with modes of "writing" and distribution: namely, recording, radio, and television. Thus even though Schoenberg, Boulez, and Babbitt differ enormously from each other in terms of socio-historical context and music style, they at least share the siege mentality that has given rise to the extreme position we have been tracing: they all regard the audience as an irrelevant annoyance whose approval signals artistic failure.

But no musical repertory can truly be autonomous from social values and networks. If it can be demonstrated that these composers disdain commercial and popular success or even political effect (for instance, contributing to the utopian enlightenment of the masses), this does not mean that they are entirely indifferent to socially conferred reward nor that they can truly exist as artists independent of any social framework.

Quite the contrary: the avant-garde composer requires a discursive community for support every bit as much as does any musician. But the constitution of this community and its values are those of the ivory tower. Babbitt, for instance, writes: "But how, it may be asked, will [the withdrawal from the audience] secure the means of survival for the composer and his music? One answer is that after all such a private life is what the university provides the scholar and the scientist. It is only proper that the university, which—significantly—has provided so many contemporary composers with their professional training and general education, should provide a home for the " complex," "difficult," and "problematical" in music." [9] And further on, Babbitt adds: "Granting to music the position accorded other arts and sciences promises the sole substantial means of survival for the music I have been describing. Admittedly, if this music is not supported, the whistling repertory of the man in the street will be little affected, the concert-going activity of the conspicuous consumer of musical culture will be little disturbed. But music will cease to evolve, and, in that important sense, will cease to live." [10]

By aligning his music with the intellectual élite—with what he identifies as the autonomous "private life" of scholarship and science (this at the height of the Cold War!)—Babbitt appeals to a separate economy that confers prestige but that also (it must also be added) confers financial support in the form of foundation grants and university professorships.[11]

The rhetoric of survival—the survival not merely of serial or electronic music but of music *tout court*—runs through virtually all of these documents.

We are back to the Fall of Rome with the barbarians at the gates; we are encouraged to perceive the serious composer as an endangered species and to provide public subsidies underwriting music that most proudly announces itself to be incomprehensible. Babbitt's rhetoric has achieved its goal: most university music departments support resident composers (though many, I must emphasize, find the "Who Cares If You Listen" attitude objectionable); and the small amount of money earmarked by foundations for music commissions is reserved for the kind of "serious" music that Babbitt and his colleagues advocate.

In many ways, however, the academic prestige market is even less stable than the commercial market. Within the commercial market, it is at least clear that (for whatever reasons) a certain number of concert tickets or recordings have been sold. A popular artist may go from adulation to obscurity overnight, but some measure of that short-term fame will have been evident. By contrast, the claim that one's music is valuable precisely because of its autonomy from social function is itself precariously dependent on particular social definitions of prestige.

And those definitions have been shifting for about the last twenty years. Perhaps Philip Glass signaled best the beginning of the end of that era when he described his contact with the Boulez scene in Paris as "a wasteland, dominated by these maniacs, these creeps, who were trying to make everyone write this crazy creepy music."[12] For a while, avant-garde music's glory lay in the illusion that it had transcended social context altogether—that it was too difficult for the uninitiated to comprehend. But proud declarations of uselessness can be—and are now beginning to be—seen as admissions of uselessness. The obvious question becomes: "Who cares if you compose?"

Babbitt's claim that music will cease to exist if academic music is not publicly subsidized rests on an extraordinary assumption: that there really is no other music. Boulez's argument acknowledges the existence of other artifacts parading as music, though he summarily dismisses them as commercial. But just who are the barbarians in this picture? What is the whistling repertory of Babbitt's man in the street?

It would undoubtedly come as surprise to that whistling barbarian that music is an endangered species, the last remnants of which are being carefully protected in university laboratories. Because to anyone who has not been trained in terms of the modernist party line, it is quite obvious that the twentieth century has witnessed an unparallel explosion in musical creativity. But whereas the music of the canon is the repository of aristocratic and, later, hegemonic middle-class values, this unruly explosion in the twentieth century is the coming to voice of American blacks and latinos, of the rural and working classes, of women, and (in the case of those we might call postmodern) of those whose training in those "creepy" institutions did not quite take.

For all the rhetoric of survival and attempts at eliminating other forms of musical productivity by simply refusing to acknowledge them, these arguments have had little influence on the musical world or ultimately, I would predict, on music history. The music produced under those hothouse conditions has been heard by few and has had next to no social impact. It is the last hurrah of a historical bloc that lost its hegemonic grip on culture at the turn of the century.

As the end has become increasingly evident, supporters have occasionally called upon the avant-garde to recast its rhetoric of difficulty-for-the-sake-of-difficulty. In a sympathetic open letter in *The Village Voice* in 1984, Gregory Sandow invited Babbitt to explain what his music is about *in human terms*.[13] A couple of years before, Sandow had criticized Paul Griffiths's *Modern Music* for continuing the tradition of writing about Babbitt's music exclusively in terms of the quasi-mathematical models Babbitt himself had formulated.[14] Sandow even sketched out why he liked Babbitt's music *as music*: as works of art that resonate with the human condition in the mid-twentieth century, that could (if explained and presented differently) even come to influence the listener's perception of the world and the self.

But in his recent article "The Unlikely Survival of Serious Music," Babbitt argues quite adamantly that he prefers still to hold the hard line.[15] He continues to exalt difficulty, to denigrate the alternatives as "public circuses of music, the citadels of show biz," to characterize his own position at Princeton as "our little humble house," and to define thus the kind of understanding he expects the listener to have of his music:

> Not that kind of understanding which reduces the rich manifestations, the rich ramifications, of musical relationships to some mundane banalities, not some sort of many-one mapping of all those wonderfully rich ramifications of musical relations to some sort of representation of the world out there but understanding of music and understanding of a great many other things by a fairly obvious process.
>
> I am not going to try to summarize, and I have certainly not offered you anything more than what is a description of one aspect of this crisis in music, with no solution being offered because I know of no solutions. I think therefore you can understand why those of us who dare to presume to attempt to make music as much as it can be rather than as little as one can get away with—music's being under the current egalitarian dispensation—and who have entered the university as our last hope, our only hope, and ergo our best hope, hope only that we're not about to be abandoned.[16]

It seems necessary at this point to confront the inevitable charge of anti-intellectualism, for the avant-garde has consistently protected its endeavors by hurling this invective at its would-be critics. To deal with the human (i.e., expressive, social, political) dimension of this music need not qualify as retreating into anti-intellectualism, as Babbitt repeatedly suggests. On the contrary: the orthodox, self-contained analyses that appear in most music theory journals require little more than a specialist's grasp of combinatorial techniques; by contrast, explication of this music as historical human artifact would involve not only knowledge of serial principles but also grounding in critical theory and extensive knowledge of twentieth-century political and cultural history.

We would gain from such discussions of avant-garde music a greater sense of human connectedness—the repertory can be heard as articulating poignantly some of the contradictions human subjects are experiencing at this moment in social and musical history. But at the same time, we would lose the mystique of difficulty, which might well be replaced by the acknowledgment of human vulnerability. What if underneath all that thorny puzzle-playing and those displays of total control there lurked the fear and confusion (clearly recognizable in all the defensive quotations already cited) that mark most other forms of contemporary culture? In other words, one could, as Sandow does, explain on many levels how this music is meaningful in other than quasi-mathematical terms. But the point is that such an agenda would violate the criteria of prestige the avant-garde has defined for itself. Better to go down with the ship than to admit to meaning. We have here, in other words, a case of terminal prestige.

By retreating from the public ear, avant-garde music has in some important sense silenced itself. Only to the tiny, dwindling community that shares modernist definitions of the economy of prestige does the phenomenon make the slightest bit of sense: thus the urgency with which Babbitt throws himself on the mercy of "the mightiest of fortresses against the overwhelming, outnumbering forces, both within and without the university, of anti-intellectualism, cultural populism, and passing fashion."[17] For if the patronage of the university fails, "to consign us to the great world out there, however seriously or however viciously, is to consign us to oblivion. Out there in that world outside the university, our music and our words are bound to fall on unheeding or, at least, uncomprehending ears. Don't forget, out there we're an academic, and there is no more sturdy vestige of anti-intellectualism than the fact that the very term academic is conceived to be an immediate, automatic, and ultimate term of derogation."[18] In the face of this pathetic scenario, only a Simon Legree would press for eviction. Why not extend refuge? What does it matter, after all, if a few people in universities continue to write music intended only for themselves and a few colleagues?

The presence of this group of artists in universities has had several perhaps unexpected but nevertheless serious consequences besides the presumably benign survival of the avant-garde. First, because the prestige of these composers (and, not coincidentally, their livelihood) is dependent on the transmission of their antisocial assumptions to subsequent generations of musicians, academic music study has gradually and subtly become restricted to the reproduction of this ideology. Most studies of twentieth-century music manage to ignore completely the existence of jazz or rock.[19] In the last decade, the popular success of certain postmodern musicians (Philip Glass, Laurie Anderson, Steve Reich, Meredith Monk) has precipitated a vigorous response on the part of academic composers who are attempting to reassert their greater prestige. Ironically, the avant-garde no longer identifies with the new: institutionalized as it is in the universities, it has become the conservative stronghold of the current music scene, as it holds stringently to difficulty and inaccessibility as the principal signs of its integrity and moral superiority.

The power of the avant-garde lobby within higher education is such that both popular and postmodern musics are marked as the enemy, and there is still considerable effort exerted to keep them out of the regular curriculum. American popular music, when taught at all in music departments, is usually presented as part of ethnomusicology—the culture of the "primitive," the ethnic Other—a clear indication of the economy of prestige at work. More often it is left for American Studies or sociology departments to deal with on the grounds that it really isn't music at all.

The treatment of newer forms of experimental music by the academy is perhaps even more puzzling at first glance. Neotonal composers such as David Del Tredici or George Rochberg have had to be extremely defensive about moving into terrain that most people in cultural circles would readily recognize as postmodern: the composition of music that draws upon images and gestures of past repertories.[20] When I gave a talk about Glass at the Walker Art Center in Minneapolis after a local performance of his *The Photographer* a few years ago, I was chastised by colleagues for having broken rank. The fact that Glass has attracted a considerable following is regarded by some as prima facie evidence of his lack of seriousness: in Boulez's terms, one can attain money or prestige, but not both. (One wonders a bit here about Boulez's professional fees and his base of institutional support in contrast to those of your basic black, working-class musician dreaming of producing a Top 40 hit.) As is the case with popular music, postmodern composers are discussed (if at all) in programs devoted to cultural studies or in sociology.

Self-proclaimed "serious" musicians often make a great deal of the artificial demand that must be created for popular music by means of advertisement and image manipulation. But an interesting irony here is that much of the university curriculum is devoted to a usually futile attempt at instilling a very artificial demand for academic music in young musicians. We shame students for their incorrigible tastes in popular music and browbeat them with abstract analytical devices in hopes that they will be influenced by, say, stochasticism and will maintain the illusion that this kind of abstract experimentation informs the future of music. For everything rests on some community continuing to think that this audienceless music is prestigious: otherwise, prestige simply evaporates. It begins to feel a bit like the make-believe worlds of *The Glass Menagerie* or *The Wizard of Oz*, in which enormous amounts of energy are poured into keeping a fantasy of denial alive.

Since students (despite all our efforts) have access to the outside world, most of them are aware of these other musics on some level—even if they have bought into the academic prestige racket. But the influence of the avant-garde on universities has been more extensive than simply its attempted blackout of the competition. Because avant-garde music's prestige relies on its having transcended social use or signification, its advocates have naturalized this position and have projected it back onto the whole of the European canon. It has become heretical to address the signifying practices of, say, Bach or Beethoven for at least two interrelated reasons: first, their present-day prestige in the modernist academy hinges on the abstract patterns of order in their music rather than on signification;[21] second, the argument that their music likewise is nothing but abstract constructs in turn helps legitimize the avant-garde. The more obviously socially grounded sources of meaning in the music are bracketed and declared irrelevant—if not causes for embarrassment.

In his introduction to *Beyond Orpheus* (which boasts a foreword by Milton Babbitt), David Epstein writes: "The fact that Schoenberg's approach to music had at its roots concepts from studies of tonal music from Bach through Brahms is of more than purely historical interest. It suggests that serial concepts themselves—as explicit viewpoints and procedures—may yield insights into similar viewpoints and concepts of earlier, tonal music."[22] He goes on to set the limits of his project, first to the classic-romantic tradition from Haydn through Brahms and then to the German-Viennese tradition—"the most seminal [sic] body of music that emerged during this broad period."[23] Finally, he says that his studies "are confined to absolute music": "Our understanding of structure is still sufficiently unclear that it seems advisable to avoid the further complications of words and/or dramatic action—implicit or explicit—and their relations to structure, or their effects upon it. A final limitation: the matter of 'expression' in music is beyond the confines of these studies. The limitation here is a practical one alone; the question of what music 'says' is vast and complex and demands separate study. [Music's] materials are the means as well as the medium of its communication. Indeed, in attacking this problem it is first of all essential clearly to perceive, to recognize, and to comprehend what it is we hear, free of external or misconstrued meanings."[24]

He then proceeds to explicate Beethoven's *Eroica* as the efficient genetic unfolding of two pitch cells: a triad and a chromatic cluster. Epstein claims to leave open the possibility of dealing with "expression" for other studies. However, if one has really accepted his structuralist account as, in fact, what we are able "to perceive, to recognize and to comprehend, free of external or misconstrued meanings," then one would be rather hard pressed to come up with anything in the realm of meaning other than the implicit one that meaning inheres in this efficient genetic unfolding of two pitch cells.

Now this tends to be the way many music theorists—the individuals responsible for teaching students how music operates—are currently being trained, especially in the most prestigious departments on the East Coast, which also house the most prestigious composers. Any music that is worth bothering with (i.e., that is sufficiently prestigious to warrant attention) *was always already difficult music.* Only the ignorant—Babbitt's whistling man on the street—could have responded to music as though it had anything to do with desire, with experience of the body, with social meaning. I recently spoke with a prominent music theorist who thought I was very bizarre to suggest that Debussy's *Prélude à l'aprés-midi d'un faune* might be erotic.

These strange priorities also infect anyone who tries to play the prestige game with other musics. Recently jazz has been introduced into élite musicological and music theory circles; but it is permitted a place in the limelight only if its social context is scraped off and if its artifacts can be demonstrated to be every bit as complex and difficult to hear as serial music.[25] In his bid to be granted prestige by serious-music circles, Anthony Braxton, for instance, has written program notes as abstruse as those of any electronic composer; and, as Ronald Radano has demonstrated recently, Braxton has paid the price of being held to be somewhat suspect by both the avant-garde and jazz communities.[26] As long as Philip Glass was straddling the fence between the academy and the audience, he wrote program notes that explained in excruciating abstract detail how his compositional constructs operated.[27] However, now that he has attracted an audience and has become comfortable about composing for people, his writing is extremely accessible and deals precisely with those matters Epstein fastidiously bracketed: the relationships among music, words, movement, and drama.[28]

Thus far I have presented my argument as though the only "enemies" against which the avant-garde has pitted itself were popular culture, postmodernism, and—in general—socially grounded signification. But a position has begun to emerge recently among cultural critics and historians that recognizes High Modernism as also having been motivated stongly as a repudiation of femininity. In "Mass Culture as Woman: Modernism's Other," Andreas Huyssen traces the retreat of "serious artists" from the contaminating qualities regarded as "feminine" (e.g., expression, pleasure, community) to that refuge of masculine prestige which is modernism.[29]

This repudiation can, of course, be understood as targeting not actual women, but rather what is feared to be the "feminine" dimension of the male artist—or even the practice of art itself, which is often classified as an "effeminate" activity: it is perhaps more obviously a product of homophobia and anxiety over masculine identity than of misogyny per se. However, Eve Kosofsky Sedgwick's *Between Men: English Literature and Male Homosocial Desire* reveals ways in which masculine anxiety, homophobia, and misogyny form a tight system of pathological interdependencies in Western culture, and her *Epistemology of the Closet* deals specifically with the impact of these anxieties in the emergence of modernism.[30]

And thus, not surprisingly, the retreat to the boys' club of modernism was not simply a matter of sloughing off soft, sentimental, "feminine" qualities for the sake of more difficult, "hard-core" criteria. Littering the path of this retreat are countless mutilated representations of women—the self-conscious defacements of what had previously been upheld in art and society as "the beautiful"—which have been protected from critical scrutiny by modernist appeals to autonomy, objectivity, abstraction, artistic liberation from bourgeois constraints, stylistic innovation, and progress. The debate that broke out a few years ago over Picasso—the visual artist of modernism's early avant-garde—finally forced the issue of the misogyny that marks the content of much of his art:[31] the content which has often made me flinch from his paintings as though they were images of criminal atrocities, but which I (as a "cultured" individual) could protest only at the risk of exposing my Philistine ignorance or "feminine self-interest." Susan Gubar and Sandra Gilbert are now analyzing these issues with respect to modernist literature,[32] and Klaus Theweleit's *Male Fantasies* documents (perhaps far more thoroughly and enthusiastically than one would wish) the links between German modernist culture and its backlash against the masses, Jews, and female contamination—all of which turn out to blur into a single threatening "red tide."[33]

Feminism has been very late in making an appearance in music criticism, and this is largely owing to the success composers, musicologists, and theorists have had in maintaining the illusion that music is an entirely autonomous realm. But the gender politics that assign prestige to "masculinity" mark the emergence of modernism in music as much as in the other arts. Witness, for instance, Charles Ives's pathetic insistence on his own exaggerated masculinity and his homophobic renunciations of predecessors and contemporaries (including friends and colleagues);[34] Adorno's hysteria over the "castrating" effect of mass culture;[35] the ongoing resistance to admitting women into the field of composition; formalist attitudes of revulsion in the face of expression (i.e., effeminate romantic excess); and, of course, the celebration of the unyielding, "hard-core" procedures of academic music apparent in virtually all the quotations above.[36]

It is symptomatic of the modernist attitude that the most widely used undergraduate textbook on twentieth-century music, Joseph Machlis's *Introduction to Contemporary Music*, is heavily illustrated with famous modernist paintings of female nudes (giving the book a deceptively interdisciplinary and "liberal" appearance) with captions that exclusively address formal considerations. The reader is offered these images for delectation but at the same time is bullied into regarding them not as the bodies of women, but rather as innovative ways of construing line, color, and form.[37]

Much of the avant-garde musical repertory similarly both flaunts and conceals its misogynist content. On the one hand, modern music claims autonomy—demands that one focus on the combinatoriality that gave rise to the technical choices in the compositional process. But, on the other hand, the violations of musical continuity and of traditional bourgeois expectations that characterize modern music are coupled (far more often than can be purely coincidental) with texts that feature the slashing of women. In other words, the most prestigious games in town (both the battle for artistic license—which regards the violation of social taboos as evidence of the artist's liberation—and also the battle for stylistic innovation) tend to be played out over female bodies. In piece after piece, some of the most extraordinarily vicious subject matter is trotted out unproblematically in the interest of artistic freedom and progressive experimentation with sound: see, for instance, Hindemith's *Murderer, Hope of Women*, Berg's *Lulu*, or Morton Subotnick's "The Last Dream of the Beast" from *The Double Life of Amphibians* (in which a "beast" dies during his "final love moment" with a blind, armless woman). The masculine prestige of modernism both protects and encourages such content.

To be sure, one wants to avoid reducing the accomplishments and complexity of modernist culture to simple expressions of misogyny. And there are ways of interpreting the literary and musical content of many modernist pieces that would argue for the artists' sensitivity with respect to the female victims represented. To take what may be an especially sympathetic instance, Babbitt's *Philomel* (its Ovid-inspired text commissioned by the composer from poet John Hollander) can be read quite straightforwardly as an *anti-rape* statement, in which the victim is transformed into the nightingale to sing about both her suffering and her transcendence.[38] The violent distortions and ruptures of the singer's voice in the piece bear witness to Philomel's rape and to the fact that her tongue has been ripped out. The shattered fragmentation of her human voice (which is reassembled serially into "a million Philomels"), her change from material being into music ("I am becoming my own song," "As if a new self / Could be founded on sound"), and her forging of triumph from violence ("Suffering is redeemed in song") all serve to acknowledge the horror of the crime and yet the possibility of survival. They also resonate strongly with many of the modernist problematics (the anxiety over decentered identity; the reconstitution of subjectivity through complex recombinant procedures; the retreat from the material world into pure, autonomous sound) discussed throughout this essay. Anyone who has seen Bethany Beardslee perform this piece live—who has watched her as her own shredded, electronically transformed voice is thrown back at her from loud speakers—can attest to the great theatrical and emotional power of *Philomel*.

Yet Babbitt's writings discourage one from attempting to unpack his composition along these lines. Indeed, he warns us not to get hung up trying to map the events of pieces onto the "mundane banalities" of real life—for it is in this objective, unsentimental attitude that prestige resides. But if content is really not at issue, why such horrendous subject matter? Many of my female students have trouble listening passively to *Philomel* as yet another instance of serial and electronic manipulation: they have difficulty achieving the kind of objective intellectual attitude that would permit them to focus on considerations of sterile compositional technique. For to most women, rape and mutilation are not mundane banalities that can conveniently be bracketed for the sake of art: especially an art that attaches prestige to the celebration of such violations.

Now, I am not arguing that composers should cease to be housed in the university. But I am no longer willing to be party to the transmission of the "prestige" ideology—especially when that means abdicating responsibility for problematic content or silencing the kind of music criticism that aims to understand music in its social context. And I am especially concerned that we cease blocking the teaching of popular and postmodern music, for these are the musics (for better or for worse) most influential in shaping lives, subjectivities, values, and behaviors at the present moment.

The avant-garde must be studied as well, to be sure, though not exclusively in accordance with the autonomous terms it has tried to enforce. All music—even that of the most austere avant-garde composer—is inevitably tied to the social conditions within which it is produced, transmitted, preserved, or forgotten. Among the conditions that need to be explored by the historian striving to make sense of the midcentury avant-garde are the formation of the university-as-discursive-community as well as the economy of prestige upon which this music has depended for survival.

As we have seen, *survival* is a key word that appears over and over again in these documents—and even in compositions such as *Philomel*. Recent titles of essays concerning new music continue to announce this doomsday orientation: see, for instance, Rochberg's *The Aesthetics of Survival* or John Struble's article in a recent *Minnesota Composers Forum Newsletter*, "Survival Strategies for the End of the Millennium," a critique that resonates with Sandow's and my own.[39] As Babbitt (once again) puts it: "But I am not prepared to admit that anything less than, anything other than, sheer *survival* is at stake, and that such *survival* seems unlikely when the conditions necessary for that *survival* are so seriously threatened. These conditions are the corporal *survival* of the composer in his [sic] role as a composer, then the *survival* of his [sic] creations in some kind of a communicable, permanent, and readable form, and finally, perhaps above all, the *survival* of the university in a role which universities seem less and less able or willing to assume [my emphasis]."[40] Threatened with extinction, the serious composers who have confined their interests to their own careers, and to the perpetuation of a music they themselves refuse to justify, continue to hurl invectives at the "rubbish" of popular culture.

But the avant-garde holds no monopoly on survival rhetoric. In that popular rubbish, one can also find survival as a central theme—though not the survival of the avant-garde for the avant-garde's sake. As I was writing this paper in 1988, I found that whenever I typed the word *survival*, I began humming a tune that was then very popular: "System of Survival" by Earth, Wind & Fire.[41] Moreover, this strange, oblique intrusion from the dreaded popular realm was far from annoying: the fortuitous presence of this song in my own cultural memory had the effect of undercutting the gravity of all those doomsday arguments, since each appearance of the "S-word" triggered not the intended gloom but rather the infectious rhythms of Earth, Wind & Fire. Finally, it proved impossible to remain too morose over predictions that "music will cease to evolve, will cease to live" in the face of such an irrepressible counterexample. Thus while the connection between Babbitt's appeals and this *particular* popular song is admittedly rather tenuous, I wish to close by examining "System of Survival" and the ways in which it presents quite a different raison-d'être for music—a different economy of prestige—than that articulated by the avant-garde.

To begin, let us address forthrightly the issue of money. Yes, the recording is commercial: I bought it at a store, as did some hundred-thousands of others. And, yes, it aimed to be, and succeeded in being, a popular hit: for those traditionally excluded from the marketplace, the achievement of a commercial hit accrues extraordinary prestige (though valuing commercial success is not the same, as Boulez suggests, as producing music solely for profit—only someone in very comfortable conditions could thus disparage economic gain). Without question, the song is multiply mediated through musical discursive practices, electronic technology, marketing decisions, and the recording industry's distribution patterns: no more than any other piece of music is it the pure representation of authentic experience. However, its message— namely, that music can provide sustenance to those who somehow continue living in the face of institutional contempt and neglect, that the joyful engagement of one's body in dance can be the oppositional moment in lives almost overwhelmed by poverty and racism, that the survival of a people and its values can occur through the medium of music—is extremely eloquent up against the *musique, c'est moi* harangues of our last descendents of musical absolutism.

To be sure, its many levels of complex mediation are rendered as transparent as possible to facilitate communication—if one is familiar with the discursive norms of fusion, one can respond strongly to it on first hearing without a special seminar in advanced analytical methods. But this is not to say that "System of Survival" is simplistic or conventional in its construction, for musical excellence and imagination are demanded as much within this economy of prestige as within the modernist academy.

"System" begins with a montage of snippets from then-recent news broadcasts, which provides the political backdrop up against which the song articulates its exuberant opposition. The song itself is marked by the intricate communality of performer participation characteristic of African-based music, a communality that stands in stark contrast to the alienated composerly control of Schoenberg or Babbitt. The virtuosity of the singers—especially the highly controlled, apparently effortless falsetto of Phillip Bailey—might qualify as "extended vocal technique" if presented in the context of experimental music. Survival itself is enacted musically in this song through the pungent dissonances that refuse to resolve, the continual resistance to harmonic closure (which would spell rhythmic death), and the effusive sax solo that dramatizes the noise of defiance. Moreover, the bass line enters only after a considerable length of time—the group sings of survival, even in the absence of the secure harmonic foundation that ordinarily grounds such music; yet the rhythm track is constantly present to inform the dance and to guarantee continuity.

As is the case with most African-American music, the rhythm itself constitutes the most compelling yet most complex component of the song. I would argue that the skill required to construct a groove with the degree of vitality characteristic of "System of Survival" is far greater than what goes into the production of the self-denying, "difficult" rhythms derived by externally generated means. One need only observe professional classical performers attempting to capture anything approaching "swing" (forget about funk!) to appreciate how *truly* difficult this apparently immediate music is.

Of course, "System of Survival" also requires tremendous technological sophistication for its execution. A recent volume of *Roland Users Group* (a trade magazine for musicians who use electronic gear in music production) presents a daunting "difficult music" description of the electronic devices and computer hookups necessary for duplicating Earth, Wind & Fire's studio compositions in live performance. The following is actually one of the simpler passages in the article, but it is included here as an example because it pertains to the song under discussion: "For the song 'System of Survival,' McKnight [the keyboard technician and programmer] had to take the opening dialogue ('The biggest unanswered question is, Where is the money?'), a cash register sound, the vocoder encoded 'System of Survival' and the words 'Everybody Get Up' and sample them into the S-550 so that Phillip Bailey could play the various parts from different pads on his Roland Octapad (PAD-8). For their older material, McKnight had to recreate the analog sounds that were in vogue when the original albums came out. 'The JX-10 is perfect for those types of analog sounds,' Mike says. 'One of the things I do is take the ROM presets from the JX-10, copy them to one of the blank slots and just go nuts.' " [42]

The exhaustive discussions of the mechanical details of execution in this article strongly resemble many program notes for "serious music." For anyone who continues to demand complex, jargon-laden analyses for the appreciation of music, such an article might serve to confer [modernist]prestige on the group: if you want difficulty, you've got it. At the very least, one can no longer pretend that their music is "natural" or "primitive" given their sophisticated control of state-of-the-art electronics, which shames much of the home-made-sounding electronic music produced through university laboratories. However, no one in Earth, Wind & Fire or in popular music criticism would mistake such technical descriptions for the content of the pieces. The electronic nuts-and-bolts dimension of the music is highlighted in this trade journal partly for the sake of other professionals (who indeed are interested in how certain effects were achieved) and partly for the sake of advertising Roland equipment. But this mechanical display is not the intended reception of the song—this is not what it means, and this is not the principal way it strives to acquire prestige.

The kind of intelligence that shines through this song is of quite a different order: it is an intelligence that accepts the experiences of the body—dance, sexuality, feelings of depression and elation—as integral parts of human knowledge that accrue value precisely as they are shared and confirmed publicly. "System of Survival" is, in other words, a song that gives no credence whatsoever to the mind/body split or to the defensive autonomy that infects so much of Western music, especially that of the avant-garde which fetishizes intellectual work for its own sake. At the same time, it is an extremely *smart* piece: musically, socially, politically. And it draws upon and celebrates forms of sedimented cultural memory that have miraculously survived a history of extraordinary oppression and that threaten to persist indefinitely—even if not acknowledged within the academy.[43]

Adorno and others (including the composers cited above) have regarded modernism and mass culture as inseparable opponents in the same cultural world and have consequently bestowed prestige upon the avant-garde as a defense against the degradation of mass culture. But at this moment in the history of the dichotomy, the terms of the debate have shifted so much as to make earlier definitions and moral positions no longer credible. This is in part owing to the avant-garde's deliberate self-reification from within—most explicitly displayed by the "who cares if you listen" attitude. But it is probably the case that the avant-garde was always fighting a losing battle. If one reflects on the demographic shifts of this century, the emergence of energetic, previously disenfranchised voices to displace a moribund, élite status quo is not at all surprising. Nor, I think, is it cause for lamentation. Debates over culture now tend to concentrate on the various models articulated and distributed through the popular media. Some of these models are worthy of celebration, others seem highly problematic with respect to images of violence and misogyny—though none more so than much of what the avant-garde has consistently dished up. In any case, the avant-garde is scarcely even a factor in cultural discussions now, except in a few sealed rooms in the academy.

This is not to suggest that there are no longer standards or that anything goes. Rather there are now many alternate sites of prestige-formation—all with their own stringent criteria—that correspond to communities hitherto excluded from the musical élite's crumbling economy of prestige.[44] In describing "System of Survival" above, I discussed some of the qualities that have made Earth, Wind & Fire an extremely influential group during the last twenty years. The fact that this song reaches a wide audience, that it speaks in a comprehensible language of exuberant hope in the face of hardship, is regarded not as evidence of selling out but as a mark of success in an economy of prestige that rewards communication and political effectiveness. Earth, Wind & Fire cares if you listen.

> Everybody get up
> Do your dance
> Stay alive.
> **Earth, Wind & Fire, "System of Survival"**

NOTES

This article was first written for an interdisciplinary conference at the University of Minnesota, The Economy of Prestige, in 1988. It was published, along with other papers from that conference, in *Cultural Critique* 12 (Spring 1989), a special volume edited by Richard Leppert and Bruce Lincoln. In the years since its publication, "Terminal Prestige" has become quite controversial. See, for instance, Elaine Barkin, "Either/Or," *Perspectives of New Music* 30 (1992): 206–33, and Linda Dusman, "Unheard of: Music as Performance and the Reception of the New," *Perspectives of New Music* 32, no. 2 (1994). My responses follow each article. I have updated a few references for this republication. The epigraph is taken from Laurie Anderson, "Difficult Music," *United States*, part 2. Recorded live at the Brooklyn Academy of Music, February 7–10, 1983. Available from Warner Bros. Records Inc., 1984. The texts are also published in book form (New York: Harper & Row, 1984). For more on Anderson, see "This Is Not a Story My People Tell: Musical Time and Space according to Laurie Anderson," in my *Feminine Endings: Music, Gender, and Sexuality* (Minneapolis: Univ. of Minnesota Press, 1991), 132–47. Permission to reprint this article granted from Oxford University Press—eds.

1. Roger Sessions, "How a 'Difficult' Composer Gets That Way," in *Roger Sessions*

on Music: Collected Essays, ed. Edward T. Cone (Princeton: Princeton Univ. Press, 1979), 169.

2. Arnold Schoenberg, "How One Becomes Lonely," in *Style and Idea*, ed. Leonard Stein, trans. Leo Black (Berkeley and Los Angeles: Univ. of California Press, 1975), 51, 53.

3. Milton Babbitt, "Who Cares If You Listen?" *High Fidelity Magazine* 8 (Feb. 1958): 126.

4. Schoenberg, "How One Becomes Lonely," 51–53.

5. By thus criticizing the notion of "autonomy" as it now circulates in music studies, I do not mean to advocate social determinism, which stands as the opposite of "autonomy" in some critical traditions, but rather to insist that music always has social meanings that need to be acknowledged. See Janet Wolff, "The Ideology of Autonomous Art," foreword to *Music and Society: The Politics of Composition, Performance and Reception*, ed. Richard Leppert and Susan McClary (Cambridge: Cambridge Univ. Press, 1987), 1–12.

6. Michel Foucault and Pierre Boulez, "Contemporary Music and the Public," trans. John Rahn, *Perspectives of New Music* 23 (Fall/Winter 1985): 8.

7. Robert Schumann, *Gesammelte Schriften über Musik und Musiker*, 2 vols. (Leipzig: Breitkopf & Härtel, 1883). Several collections of these essays exist in English translation.

8. Theodor W. Adorno, "Schoenberg," *Prisms*, trans. Samuel Weber and Shierry Weber (Cambridge: MIT Press, 1981), 147–72.

9. Babbitt, "Who Cares," 126.

10. Babbitt, "Who Cares," 127.

11. See Serge Guilbaut, *How New York Stole the Idea of Modern Art: Abstract Expressionism, Freedom, and the Cold War*, trans. Arthur Goldhammer (Chicago: Univ. of Chicago Press, 1983).

12. Quoted in John Rockwell, "Philip Glass," *All American Musican Music: Composition in the Late Twentieth Century* (New York: Knopf, 1983), 111.

13. Gregory Sandow, "An Open Letter to Milton Babbitt," *The Village Voice* (5 June 1984): 81–82.

14. Sandow, "A Fine Madness," *The Village Voice* (16 March 1982): 73.

15. Milton Babbitt, "The Unlikely Survival of Serious Music," *Milton Babbitt: Words about Music*, ed. Stephen Dembski and Joseph N. Straus (Madison: Univ. of Wisconsin Press, 1987), 163–83.

16. Ibid., 182–83.

17. Ibid., 163.

18. Ibid., 180.

19. For two prominent recent examples, see Robert P. Morgan, *Twentieth-Century Music: A History of Musical Style in Modern Europe and America* (New York: Norton, 1991) and Glenn Watkins, *Soundings: Music in the Twentieth Century* (New York: Schirmer Books, 1988). A very few studies have tried to present pictures of twentieth-century music that do not honor the high art division between "serious" and "popular" musics and that deal with many kinds of musics on an equal footing. See, for instance, Rockwell, *All American Music*, and Billy Bergman and Richard Horn, *Recombinant Do. Re. Mi: Frontiers of the Rock Era* (New York: Quill, 1985).

20. See Rockwell, "David Del Tredici: The Return of Tonality, the Orchestra

Audience and the Danger of Success," *All American Music*, 71–83, and George Rochberg *The Aesthetics of Survival* (Ann Arbor: Univ. of Michigan Press, 1984). For fuller treatments of the phenomenon of postmodernism in music, see Georgina Born, "Modern Music Culture: On Shock, Pop and Synthesis," *New Formations* 2 (1987): 51–77 and Jann Pasler, "Postmodernism, Narrativity, and the Art of Memory," *Contemporary Music Review* 7 (1993): 2–32.

21. For a response to this position that argues in favor of autonomy, see Nicolas Temperley, "Tonality and the Bourgeoisie," *Musical Times* (Dec. 1987): 685–87.

22. David Epstein, *Beyond Orpheus: Studies in Musical Structure* (Cambridge: MIT Press, 1979), 5.

23. Ibid., 11.

24. Ibid.

25. See, for instance, Wynton Marsalis, "What Jazz Is—and Isn't," *New York Times* (31 July 1988), sect. 2, 21, 24. Marsalis advocates rule-bound, difficult-music accounts of jazz in an attempt at elevating it to the status of high art. To be sure, the old mystified stories Marsalis argues against, in which jazz artists spring full-blown as the unmediated products of their miserable social conditions, are detestable; and, indeed, jazz must be acknowledged as the most significant musical genre to emerge in the first half of this century. But such revisions in jazz reception cannot afford to erase the oppressive social conditions that shaped the discursive practices of jazz, within and in spite of which its extraordinary practioners worked to develop their complex art.

One of the better attempts at dealing structurally with jazz is Lewis Porter, "John Coltrane's *A Love Supreme*: Jazz Improvisation as Composition," *Journal of the American Musicological Society* 38 (1985): 593–621. Although Porter concentrates on formal matters in this article, he also states in his introduction: "Furthermore, Coltrane required more than abstract interest from his music. He used it to express profound spiritual moods. While retaining the goal of intellectual involvement, he sought to communicate nobility, dignity, peace, or even violent outrage" (593).

26. See Ronald Radano, "Braxton's Reputation," *Musical Quarterly* 72 (1986): 503–22.

27. See Glass's formal "Notes on *Einstein on the Beach*," included with the recording (CBS Records, 1976).

28. Philip Glass, *Music by Philip Glass* (New York: Harper & Row, 1987).

29. Andreas Huyssen, "Mass Culture as Woman: Modernism's Other," *After the Great Divide: Modernism, Mass Culture, Postmodernism* (Bloomington: Indiana Univ. Press, 1986), chap. 3.

30. Eve Kosofsky Sedgwick, *Between Men: English Literature and Male Homosocial Desire* (New York: Columbia Univ. Press, 1985) and *Epistemology of the Closet* (Berkeley and Los Angeles: Univ. of California Press, 1990).

31. This controversy became quite public with the publication of Arianna Stassinopoulos Huffington's sensationalist *Picasso: Creator and Destroyer* (New York: Simon & Schuster, 1988). Huffington concentrates too heavily on Picasso's personality in accounting for his imagery, thus making this dimension of his art seem exclusively a product of his own psychopathology. However, similar readings of modernist art—which emphasize discursive conventions rather than individual idiosyncracy—had already been available. See, for instance, Carol Duncan, "Virility and Domination in

Early Twentieth-Century Vanguard Painting," *Feminism and Art History: Questioning the Litany*, ed. Norma Broude and Mary D. Garrard (New York: Harper & Row, 1982), 293–314. See also Leo Steinberg, "The Philosophical Brothel" (1972), reprinted in *October* 44 (Spring 1988): 7–74, for a pioneering discussion of the sexual politics articulated in Picasso's paintings, especially *Les Demoiselles d'Avignon*, and of how formalist criticism serves to mask such issues.

32. Sandra M. Gilbert and Susan Gubar, "Tradition and the Female Talent," *The Poetics of Gender*, ed. Nancy K. Miller (New York: Columbia Univ. Press, 1986), 183–207. See also their *No Man's Land: The Place of the Woman Writer in the Twentieth Century*, 2 vols. (New Haven: Yale Univ. Press, 1988, 1989).

33. Klaus Theweleit, *Male Fantasies*, 2 vols., trans. Stephen Conway (Minneapolis: Univ. of Minnesota Press, 1987, 1989).

34. This obsession is manifest in almost every document Ives wrote. For instance: "Well, I'll say two things here: (1) That nice professor of music is a musical lily-pad [one of Ives's several derogatory terms for insufficiently masculine men]. He never took a chance at himself, or took one coming or going. (2) His opinion is based on something he'd probably never heard, seen, or experienced. He knows little of how these things sounded when they came 'blam' off a real man's chest. It was the way this music was sung that made them big or little—and I had the chance of hearing them big—a man's experience of men!" (*Charles Ives' Memos*, ed. John Kirkpatrick (New York: Norton, 1972), 131. For a psychoanalytic discussion of this and other aspects of Ives's character, see Maynard Solomon, "Charles Ives: Some Questions of Veracity," *Journal of the American Musicological Society* 40 (1987): 466–69. Solomon writes: "He [Ives] is both drawn to music and repelled by it. 'As a boy [I was] partially ashamed of' music, he recalled 'an entirely wrong attitude but it was strong—most boys in American country towns, I think felt the same. And there may be something in it. Hasn't music always been too much an emasculated art?' To ward off such feelings, Ives would eradicate the traces of the 'soft-bodied' and the 'decadent' in his own work, perhaps employing the techniques of modernism to conceal the atmospheric, lyrical, yielding strata which often underlie his first ideas" (467).

For a discussion of how early modernists reacted against women composers and also against what what they viewed as femininity, see Catherine Parsons Smith, "'A Distinguishing Virility': Feminism and Modernism in American Art Music," *Cecilia Reclaimed: Feminist Perspectives on Gender and Music*, ed. Susan C. Cook and Judy S. Tsou (Urbana: Univ. of Illinois Press, 1994), 90–106. See also my *Feminine Endings*, 104–9.

35. "The aim of jazz is the mechanical reproduction of a regressive moment, a castration symbolism. 'Give up your masculinity, let yourself be castrated,' the eunuchlike sound of the jazz band both mocks and proclaims, 'and you will be rewarded, accepted into a fraternity which shares the mystery of impotence with you, a mystery revealed at the moment of the initiation rite'" (Adorno, "Perennial Fashion—Jazz," *Prisms,* 129).

36. See Fred Maus, "Masculine Discourse in Music Theory," *Perspectives of New Music* 31, no. 2 (1993): 264–93.

37. For instance, for the caption for a reproduction of Modigliani's *Nude*, 1917 (painting of a sleeping woman in full frontal nudity), he writes: "The economy and purity of style which characterizes Webern's music may also be found in the elegant

simplicity of Modigliani's work. A supreme draftsman, his elongated figures are linear yet sculptural in the impression of roundness and volume which they convey" (Joseph Machlis, *Introduction to Contemporary Music*, 2d ed. [New York: Norton, 1979], 272). See also the captions for Manet's *Le Déjeuner sur l'herbe*, 84, and Gauguin's *The Spirit of the Dead Watching*, 17.

38. Babbitt, *Philomel* (1964), recorded by Bethany Beardslee on AR, in collaboration with Deutsche Grammophon.

39. Rochberg, *Aesthetics of Survival*, and John Warthen Struble, "Survival Strategies for the End of the Millennium," *Minnesota Composers Forum Newsletter* (Apr. 1988): 5–7.

40. Babbitt, "The Unlikely Survival," 163. For the most recent such statement, see the interview with Babbitt in the special 150th anniversary issue of *The Musical Times* 135 (June 1994).

41. Skylark, "System of Survival," on *Earth, Wind & Fire: Touch the World*, produced by Maurice White for Kalimba Productions (CBS, Inc., 1987).

42. Tony Thomas, "The Sound of Earth Wind & Fire," *Roland Users Group* 6, no. 2 (1988): 49. For more on the cultural and musical complexity of sampling and groove-construction in African-American music, see Tricia Rose, *Black Noise: Rap Music and Black Culture in Contemporary America* (Hanover, N. H.: Wesleyan Univ. Press, 1994) and Robert Walser, "Rhythm, Rhyme, and Rhetoric in the Music of Public Enemy," *Ethnomusicology* 39, no. 2 (1995): 193–217.

43. The concept of sedimented cultural memory in popular music is being most eloquently developed by George Lipsitz. See, for instance, his "Cruising around the Historical Bloc—Postmodernism and Popular Music in East Los Angeles," *Time Passages: Collective Memory and American Popular Culture* (Minneapolis: Univ. of Minnesota Press, 1990).

44. For an excellent discussion of popular culture as a site of class struggle, see Stuart Hall, "Notes on Deconstructing 'The Popular,'" *People's History and Socialist Theory*, ed. Raphael Samuel (London: Routledge & Kegan Paul, 1981), 227–39.

JOHN COVACH

We Won't Get Fooled Again:
Rock Music and Musical Analysis

"Meet the new boss
Same as the old boss"
Pete Townshend

In 1971 the British rock band The Who released their seventh album, entitled *Who's Next*.[1] The final track on the LP, the eight-and-a-half-minute "Won't Get Fooled Again," is for the most part a hard-driving rock number. The arrangement to this song is perhaps most noteworthy for its use of a repeated-note figure played by the organ, occurring especially in the introduction and in two instrumental interludes; and for Roger Daltry's two excruciating screams, the second of which, occurring immediately before the final verse, must surely be among the most famous screams in all of rock music. The lyrics of "Won't Get Fooled Again" represent Pete Townshend at his cynical best. Writing in the first person, Townshend portrays a feeling that political revolutions change very little for those not in political power: for the average person—or at least for the average restless youth—nothing seems to have changed significantly the day after the revolution. Following the second organ interlude, which terminates with a Keith Moon drum solo, Daltry lets out his famous scream. It is a scream of recognition and horror: our singer discovers that the "new boss" is no different from the "old boss."[2]

This essay will explore issues in the analysis of rock music. Within the academic community of musical scholarship, musical analysis is usually considered to fall within the domain of the discipline of music theory. Certainly musicologists and popular music scholars incorporate musical analysis into their work to some degree, but it is music theorists who have developed and routinely employ a number of sophisticated techniques and systems for analysis. This essay will focus in part on how music theorists might approach the analysis of rock music within their own disciplinary contexts. I will, however, also be concerned with the ways in which music theory and analysis can make a contribution within the disciplinary context of popular music studies generally. The question of how music theorists might approach the analysis of popular music—and even whether they should consider popular music at all—is one that affects both the disciplines of music theory and of popular music studies. These two disciplines, however, have tended to ignore each other: theorists have been occupied almost entirely with the analysis of music within the European art-music tradition, and popular music scholarship has tended to focus its attention more on cultural, social, and economic contexts and less on the musical texts themselves.

I will confine my remarks in this essay to rock music, since that is the area within popular music that my own research addresses. I will argue that Townshend's parable-like lyrics sound a warning that must be heeded as we consider, first, the role popular music might play in the ways in which theorists will think about music and music theory in the future, and second, the role that musical analysis should play in the study of popular music in a broad sense. In the first case, theorists might well ask themselves why they should be concerned with popular music at all. Having adapted Townshend's song title for my essay, I feel obliged to explain first how I believe theorists have been in some sense "fooled"; after all, if one has not been fooled initially, how could one avoid being fooled again?

Second, I will consider two positions that address the analysis of popular music and that have been forwarded outside of the discipline of music theory. The first position comes from the field of musicology and the second arises from popular music studies. Both positions are critical of the notion that traditional analysis can offer much to popular music studies, and even assert that such analytical perspectives can distort an interpretation of the music in fundamental ways. I will argue that both of these positions have problems. Finally, I will suggest a number of reasons why I feel some theorists may want to consider investigating rock music, why I feel the study of rock music can make a positive contribution within the music-theoretical discourse, and how the analysis of popular music can make a significant contribution to the field of popular music studies.

It is probably safe to say that music theory as a professional discourse is currently in a period of critical self-reassessment. At music theory conferences one often hears such Kuhnian terms as *paradigm shift* and *post paradigm period* bandied about by colleagues engaged in informal discussion.[3] Much of this discussion can be organized around two intimately related questions: first, how theorists should look at music; and second, what music they should look at? In terms of analysis, for example, techniques and methods influenced by literary theory have made significant inroads.[4] For musical works that theorists analyze and theorize about, criticism that the canon of "great works" is too narrow and must be expanded to include a wider range of styles and cultures has perhaps caused some theorists to explore the analysis of non-Western and popular musics.[5]

In order to examine the question of analytical paradigms in music theory,

I turn first to a brief consideration of the work of the Viennese music theorist Heinrich Schenker. I turn to Schenker's work in part because his theories form one of the dominant paradigms within the discipline of music theory, and if one can propose that theorists have been fooled to some extent by their own theories, then one should expect to find this situation in the work of Schenker and his various students and followers. I also choose Schenker because the relationship of his theory to the musical literature it addresses is quite clear-cut. This is important because I will focus below on whether or not Schenker's theories—and analytical theories generally—can be separated from a literature to which they have been intimately bound.

Schenker's written work, and especially his theoretical writings after 1904, is principally concerned with the music of a relatively limited group of composers, all of whom are German, Austrian, or strongly identified with the German musical tradition.[6] Schenker's notion of the superiority of the German musical genius is in fact central to his musical worldview.[7] Schenker's well-known position, in a nutshell, is that a certain group of German composers, living over a period of roughly two hundred years, raised music to the status of the masterwork. Music before Bach is viewed as evolving toward the masterwork; music after Brahms (and the music of Wagner and his followers) is degenerate.

Many critics of Schenker's view would probably label it "ethnocentric" and "elitist."[8] Conservative supporters of Schenker's position might maintain that Schenker was right: the music he discusses *is* superior to other music. Moderate supporters of Schenker's theories might claim that whether or not Schenker was right about the literature he explored, we must study his writing *as if* he were right, suspending judgment for the sake of a hermeneutic understanding. But I am not concerned here with engaging the question of Schenker's musical values in any absolute sense. I would merely suggest that the success of Schenker's theories—and by Schenker's theories I mean not only the *Ursatz*-dominated late writings, but also the early and middle-period works[9]—depends to a large part on the constraints Schenker placed on the body of musical works that he considered. Schenker's writings are as powerful as they are because he was able to draw out generalizing principles from a body of musical works that he knew were related to one another before he ever began. Schenker started with a repertoire of German masterworks, and with the famous exception of Wagner's works, studied these masterworks— or other works in the same tradition—throughout his entire career.[10] His theory is not intended to prove that these pieces truly are masterworks: after all, Schenker felt it was his responsibility not to test masterworks but to learn from them.[11] Instead, what his theory tells us, with only a few exceptions, is *how these masterworks are related to one another.*[12]

If Schenker's theories can really be seen as generated from a specific literature, then one might wonder how effective these theories can be when applied to literatures other than the one upon which Schenker focused.[13] While

Schenker certainly believed, as he states in *Free Composition*, that his "concepts present, for the first time, a *genuine theory of tonal language*,"[14] one is tempted to add "in pieces that are important to me." Of course, his a priori position is that there really are no great tonal pieces outside the tradition with which he is concerned; therefore the whole question is—for him at least—meaningless. One might, however, accuse Schenker of making too broad a claim for his theory: perhaps there are pieces that are tonal but operate according to principles that are in some significant way different from those principles he describes.

Two approaches have tended to dominate Schenkerian thought: either theorists stick with the analysis of pieces within the repertoire circumscribed by Schenker himself, or theorists attempt to modify Schenker's late theory in order to apply it to the analysis of music outside of that repertoire. Especially noteworthy with regard to modifying Schenker's late theory have been the pioneering work of Felix Salzer, Lori Burns's more recent work on modal middle grounds in Bach, and Matthew Brown's analyses of Wagner, Debussy, and Jimi Hendrix.[15] But if there is a real danger of the Schenkerian being fooled in some sense, it lies in the alluring analytical power of Schenker's theory when it is applied to the repertoire for which it was designed. Schenker's late theory provides the theorist with a powerful analytical apparatus for approaching the music of Mozart, Beethoven, and Brahms;[16] is it any wonder that some theorists are only too happy to remain within the world of the great German masterworks and rarely stray into other repertoires?

This discussion of Schenkerian theory has ultimately been in the service of making a very simple point: when a theorist has a strong paradigm from which to work—and this is not restricted to the Schenkerian paradigm—repertoire decisions can sometimes be made on the basis of the pieces that are likely to work best within that paradigm. The paradigm under consideration could just as easily be pitch-class set theory or twelve-tone theory: in any of these cases it is perfectly possible to choose repertoire in terms of the theoretical paradigm itself. And by pointing this out I do not also mean to object to such a practice. But a common image (or caricature) of music theorists held outside the discipline—and held especially, as I will argue below, by popular music scholars—is that the only music music theorists value is music that they can get to fit into their established analytical models. Ultimately, this opinion goes, theorists ignore any music that does not fit into one of their preestablished conceptual molds. While this characterization of the discipline is certainly exaggerated, it is not entirely without foundation. Theorists *may* at times determine *what* music they look at by *how* they plan to look at it.

If we return for a moment to Pete Townshend's lyrics (and work the metaphor of political revolution for paradigm shift a little harder), I would argue that the established theoretical paradigms could be thought of as a kind of "old boss"—an old boss that may have the effect of overdetermining the repertories to which a theorist is drawn. But as the theorist endeavors to expand her work to include the analysis of new repertories—in this case popular music—the question that might follow naturally is: What threatens to assume the role of the "new boss," and how can music theorists avoid being fooled again? As the traditionally trained theorist turns his analytical attention to popular music, are there traps lying in wait that need to be avoided? In order to pursue these questions, I turn to two arguments that have been made outside the field of music theory with regard to the relationship between analysis and popular music.

In her 1989 article "Terminal Prestige: The Case of Avant-Garde Music Composition," musicologist Susan McClary offers what is essentially a response to Milton Babbitt's 1958 essay "The Composer as Specialist" (an essay frequently referred to by the title given it by the editors of *High Fidelity Magazine*, "Who Cares If You Listen?").[17] McClary argues that avant-garde composers—she quotes Arnold Schoenberg, Roger Sessions, Pierre Boulez, and Babbitt—essentially relish the difficulty of their music. The average concertgoer finds this music impossible to understand, and this, McClary contends, validates the difficulty of this cerebral music in the eyes of its avant-garde composers. The problem, as McClary sees it, is that these composers insist that their music be understood strictly in terms of its structure; any attempt to understand this music in more "human terms" (whatever that is supposed to mean) is discouraged by the very composers themselves, despite the fact that such a perspective might actually provide a kind of aesthetic entré for at least part of their alienated audience. The prestige of this music depends on its difficulty, and since relatively few are listening, avant-garde composers suffer from a condition McClary diagnoses as "terminal prestige."

I will not consider here the many problems in McClary's portrayal of Schoenberg, Sessions, Boulez, and Babbitt. Instead, I want to focus on the way McClary employs popular music rhetorically in the course of her argument. There is much the advocate of popular music can agree with in her article. She points out that music scholars in the academy, or at least those in music theory, have tended to ignore almost all forms of popular music; while avant-garde composers are predicting the end of music, vital music is breaking out all around them. McClary claims that various popular musics have played a crucial role in musical life in the twentieth century and calls for the serious and careful study of popular music. So far, then, we know *what* music we need to look at, but the big question is, *How* should we look at it? And it is this second question that I find troubling in McClary's argument.

McClary examines an Earth, Wind, & Fire song, "System of Survival."[18] She is mostly concerned that the tune addresses social and political issues and that it was conceived, in contrast to the music of Babbitt, by musicians who do care whether you listen. McClary is careful to stress the fact that "System of Survival" is not a simple song; it is carefully produced and recorded. But she adds: "The kind of intelligence that shines through this song is of quite a different order: it is an intelligence that accepts the experiences of the body—dance, sexuality, feelings of depression and elation—as integral parts of human knowledge that accrue value as they are shared and confirmed publicly." [19] McClary is referring mostly to the lyrics of the song, and to some very brief remarks she makes about the rhythm tracks, the singing, the harmonic structure, and various other aspects of the music.

What is troubling about McClary's reading of Earth, Wind, & Fire is that she seems to have accepted uncritically the notion that popular music is uncomplicated in the traditional sense, or that even if it is complicated structurally, or engages our attention along structural lines, that is nonetheless not how the song was meant to be heard anyway. In fact, McClary seems to be saying to those difficulty-mongering avant-garde critics of popular music: "OK, you're right, this stuff isn't very interesting structurally, so here are some ways in which it *is* interesting." Based on her description, one might think that most of the Earth, Wind, & Fire album on which "System of Survival" appears is given over to the type of hip political statements she praises so warmly in her article. But in fact there are really only two or three other numbers that contain lyrics addressing social issues.[20] For the most part, the rest of the album is, like much art music, music about itself or music about other music. There are a number of extremely interesting structural moments, some clever references to other tunes and styles, and a lot of masterful playing, singing, production work, and songwriting. As McClary states, this music is popular, and that popularity is certainly the result of a number of factors, including such things as the marketing of the product, radio and MTV airplay, and the like. But surely one factor that accounts for the effect of this music is the structure of the music itself.[21]

Along with McClary, I believe we need to devote more scholarly attention to popular music, and I agree with most of the historical reasons she gives for doing so.[22] But in McClary's argument a "new boss" emerges that threatens to replace the old one. For her, the most valuable interpretation of a piece is one that is most informed by its social and cultural context. Like the Schenkerian paradigm discussed a moment ago, a strong sociological paradigm can also attract the scholar to a certain repertoire; McClary is drawn to consider *this particular* Earth, Wind, & Fire song because it can be shown to do some of the things that she presumably wants to see music do. But if there was a chance of being fooled before, it is equally possible in the present instance; and McClary's choice of a musical example in this case is just as motivated by ideology as are the choices of any theorist she might care to cite, although I am not sure that she would disagree on this point.[23] By carefully considering her examination of "System of Survival," the reader unquestionably comes to a greater understanding of McClary's intellectual position; but I am not sure one learns very much about the music of Earth, Wind, & Fire, or about popular music in general.

McClary clearly directs the reader's attention to popular music because it raises issues that are routinely ignored in the professional discourse of academic musicology and music theory. In McClary's argument, popular music constitutes a kind of disciplinary disruption to the standard picture that scholars routinely paint of music in the twentieth century. But while the example she chooses is effective in such a role, it is certainly not the case that all popular music—or even all Earth, Wind, & Fire music—has this disruptive effect. Casting popular music in the role of the significant disruption, and in so doing emphasizing the ways in which it is different from art music (a difference that is asserted rather than argued), proves ultimately to be just as distorting as any attempt to emphasize the similarities between the two broad styles.

While McClary devotes only a few sentences to an examination of the music-technical aspects of "System of Survival," she does use technical terms that are usually employed in the analysis of European art music. She writes, for example, of "pungent dissonances that refuse to resolve," of the "continual resistance to harmonic closure," and of the "absence of the secure harmonic foundation that usually grounds such music."[24] These technical descriptions are, of course, used in the service of supporting her sociologically informed reading of the song. But there are a number of scholars in the discipline of popular music studies who might advise McClary to be cautious in her use of such traditional analytical terms. For popular music scholars such as Richard Middleton, John Shepherd, or Peter Wicke, descriptive terms derived from the study of Western art music are ideologically loaded: by even employing such technical terms and the conceptual prejudices that they are thought to imply, one risks interpreting the music according to analytical criteria that are foreign to the music itself. In other words, since most of our music-analytical paradigms have been developed to examine music in the European tradition, they are inherently unsuited for the analysis of popular music.

Here, surprisingly, our conservative Schenkerian and radical cultural theorist take a similar position with regard to the what and how of analysis. Both maintain that an analytical system and the musical repertoire it describes should be perfectly matched. The Schenkerian may avoid analyzing rock music because the music may not produce satisfying results according to the paradigm; the sociologically oriented popular music scholar will probably be glad to see the conservative analyst avoid popular music altogether. In proposing that rock music must not be analyzed according to what he terms "the Beethoven tradition," for example, Peter Wicke writes: "Thus, in order to take rock seriously as music, we need to investigate the conception of music which underlies it rather than apply aesthetic criteria and musical models that are completely alien to its cultural origins."[25] Along similar lines, John Shepherd writes: "While it is true that historical musicology has developed a formidable range of analytic techniques and terms for coming to grips with the internal parameters of 'music,' such techniques and terms have a very limited application. It is not possible, for example, to agree with Wilfrid Mellers that there are such things as objective 'musical facts,' necessarily susceptible to explanation through a terminology 'which has been evolved by professional musicians over some centuries.'"[26] Richard Middleton, in a careful and instructive assessment of the applicability of traditional modes of analysis to popular music, writes: "On the other hand, terms are commonly ideologically loaded. 'Dissonance' and 'resolution' immediately suggest certain *harmonic* procedures, and a string of associated technical and emotional associations. 'Motive' immediately suggests Beethovenian symphonic development technique."[27]

I will return below to Middleton's position with regard to the use of traditional analytical techniques for popular music. For now, I would like to focus on the problem that these popular music scholars have posed for music theorists interested in the analysis of rock music. According to Middleton, Shepherd, and Wicke, the application of analytical paradigms developed in the study of art music to popular music (and rock) is likely to produce distorted interpretations.

A common target for this kind of criticism is the work of Wilfrid Mellers. Mellers's books on the music of the Beatles and Bob Dylan are often accused of presenting the music of these artists *as if it were* art music. Middleton, for example, takes Mellers to task for privileging "the areas of tonality, melodic contour and, especially, harmony"; he is especially concerned with Mellers's Beatles analyses, where "almost any analysis can be taken as an example of the way harmonic progressions are automatically seen as the most interesting, the most interpretively important, aspects of the music."[28] Rock critic and sociologist Simon Frith finds Mellers's lack of attention to the social dimension of this music troubling. Frith states that "Wilfrid Mellers's scholarly books on the Beatles and Bob Dylan, for example, describe in technical terms their subjects' transcendent qualities; but they read like fan mail and, in their lack of self-conscious hipness, point to the contradiction at the heart of this aesthetic approach."[29]

I find at least two serious problems with this critique of traditional analytical approaches. First, none of these authors demonstrates a close familiarity with music theory and analysis as it has been practiced in the discipline recently; one often wonders who they are talking about, and even whether they are reacting to the discourse of music theory at all. (It sometimes seems as though these writers are reacting principally against the way theory and analysis were taught when they were students, rather than against any identifiable contemporary position.) Middleton does devote a considerable amount of discussion to possible applications of Schenkerian analytical techniques to popular music; nonetheless, he writes not as a professional theorist but rather as someone who has explored theoretical approaches to popular music.[30] Writers in popular music scholarship sometimes set up the theorist or musicologist as a straw man, as a caricature that serves as a foil to their own ideas. It is as if these writers were against the idea of theorists examining popular music *as a matter of principle*.

The second problem I find with this approach has to do with the theme I have been following throughout this essay: that is, these scholars, by insisting that we *cannot* view popular music through our current set of analytical lenses, risk allowing a set of a priori assumptions to dictate methodology. It seems clear that the time to judge the fruitfulness of an approach is *after* a significant amount of sophisticated work has been done, not before it has been done. And if such work is to be done, it seems obvious that music theorists and analysts possess the technical skills to do it.

To summarize my argument up to this point: it is a mistake to ignore the analysis of rock music because it does not fit current music-theoretical and analytical paradigms in obvious ways. I have argued that it would also be unwise to take up the study of rock music simply because it works nicely according to a more sociologically oriented paradigm, and to insist in so doing that rock music cannot work in more traditional ways too. Finally, I contend that rejecting the applicability of current analytical methods to rock music is premature, and unnecessarily limiting.

To consider why theorists might be interested in the analysis of popular music in general, and rock music in particular, I wish to return to the questions *what* music should we look at, and *how* should we look at it? Is it, for example, possible to adapt current analytical approaches to the task of analyzing rock? Recent analytical work has suggested that it is. Walter Everett, Peter Kaminsky, and Matthew Brown have used modified Schenkerian approaches in recent work examining the music of the Beatles, Paul Simon, and Jimi Hendrix.[31] Far from demonstrating that this music is somehow "just like" art music, these analyses suggest that while rock music can at times hold certain structural characteristics in common with Schenker's "masterwork literature," it also has musical characteristics that are all its own. Rock music raises issues in tonal theory that simply do not come up in the consideration of the masterworks. That this music is different in these often tacit ways is partly what we mean when we say that rock constitutes a different style of music. To the extent that theorists are interested in developing their theories of tonal music in ways that cross repertory boundaries, the analysis of rock music can make a significant contribution.

As mentioned above, Schenker's theory is one that arises from a particular repertoire. There are other theoretical approaches, however, that do not arise from some specific body of works. Style theory, for example, especially as articulated by Leonard Meyer, considers how styles can evolve in general ways.[32] Meyer's notion of style change, for example, generalizes across a number of historical and geographically situated styles. Rock music provides a ready testing ground for many of Meyer's notions of how styles change; because rock music is disseminated almost immediately after it is produced, the time frame within which style change can and does occur is drastically speeded up. Consider, for example, the amazing development of rock music from the British invasion of the 1964–66 period to the psychedelia of 1967–69, to the explosion of widely divergent rock styles in the early 1970s. One only needs to compare an early Beatles album with, say, King Crimson's *In the Court of the Crimson King* of some five years later to underscore the speed and magnitude of this stylistic transformation. This rapid style change is sometimes thought to be due to a superficial demand on the part of the rock consumer for constant variety. But one might also posit that styles changed so quickly because innovation could be absorbed and adopted almost instantaneously by the musicians who produced it. In any case, I am convinced that the general music-technical mechanisms of style change in the rock music of the 1960s and 70s are ultimately not much different from those operative in other historical periods.

As mentioned at the beginning of this essay, music theory has begun to incorporate techniques and methods drawn from other disciplines. Rock music can serve as a focal repertory for testing the effectiveness of some of these ideas for musical analysis, especially because approaches borrowed from other disciplines are not as repertoire-dependent as those developed inside of the discipline. Thus, as I have attempted to show in recent articles, notions of stylistic competency and intertextuality can be very useful in unpacking the effect of certain kinds of rock music.[33] These notions are especially applicable, for instance, to the new-wave groups of the latter third of the 1970s—groups whose music depends upon the listener's ability to identify references to earlier styles in rock music.

In addition to enriching our perspective on current analytical paradigms, the study of rock music also suggests that there are particular analytical issues that arise in the analysis of rock that may not arise as obviously in other, more traditionally studied repertoires. Consider tone color and instrumentation, for example. A large part of the aesthetic effect of much rock music depends upon certain precise timbres: What would the Moody Blues be without their Mellotron, Jimi Hendrix without his Stratocaster, or the Byrds without Roger McGuinn's Rickenbacker electric twelve-string guitar? These sounds can become referential in precise ways, and this referentiality in the work of later groups can take on a tremendous significance. Developing an analytical apparatus that tracks these and other kinds of timbral relationships in rock music could in turn be applied to other repertoires, even those in the art music tradition. Thus, I think that while rock music benefits from the application of established analytical approaches, it also, at least potentially, has something to give in return: it can perhaps address our attention to aspects of familiar repertoires that have been less carefully examined within the discipline. And it is the intradisciplinary benefits of this possible reciprocal relationship that I wish to stress.

In short, my position is not that theorists and analysts should consider rock music simply "because it is there," even though that may be a good enough reason for musicologists to consider it.[34] Theorists should pay more attention to rock music *because it is interesting*; and it is interesting because as a repertory it challenges some of our assumptions about what music is, how it can work, and how we experience it. I do not think one should use rock or popular music as a kind of club with which to beat the avant-garde and the structuralism or formalism that their music may be seen to represent. I also do not think that we must *necessarily* adopt a sociological orientation in our study of rock music.[35] Certainly the socially determined elements in rock music must be considered, and this will enrich analysis, but whether or not the analytical argument principally addresses sociological concerns is ultimately a question of interpretive emphasis, and, ultimately, an issue of intellectual freedom.

While I have argued that music theory would benefit greatly through a closer engagement with popular music, popular music studies would also be tremendously enriched by the kind of careful and close musical analysis that theorists could bring to the field. As John Shepherd has pointed out, popular music scholars often treat the music itself as a kind of "inscrutable black box."[36] In fact, most popular music scholars would not object to the suggestion that some kind of analysis of the actual musical text needs to be done; the real question is what kind of analysis this should be.

It seems clear that attempting to force popular music into models created for the analysis of Western European art music is bound to produce distortions. At the same time, however, asserting that an entirely new approach to musical analysis needs to be devised especially for popular music seems extreme. One problem with developing entirely new modes of analysis specifically for popular music is that it presumes that popular and art music are entirely different from one another, but this certainly need not be the case. In considering the question of using analytical approaches developed in the study of European art music to study popular music, the matter comes down, in large part, to disciplinary assumptions and prejudices. Popular music scholars are quick to note what they take to be the silent assumptions of theorists and analysts, and clearly the analyst must admit that there are significant differences between the music of Elvis Presley and Richard Wagner. Residing outside the discipline of music theory, these scholars are able to detect interpretive biases that may go undetected within it.

But the crucial point in sounding out silent prejudices is to avoid replacing one set of assumptions with another, equally insidious set. Thus one must be wary of rejecting too quickly an entire approach to musical analysis, with all the sophisticated techniques that theorists have developed for accounting for the musical text, on the assumption that because such techniques were developed to study art music they could never produce anything but a distorted reading of popular music. Indeed, if we as theorists or as popular music scholars do not want to be "fooled again," we must resist the temptations that disciplinary paradigms can create, or at least be keenly aware of the ways in which these pressures can operate.[37] As musical scholarship pays increasing attention to popular music, we need to be sure that we avoid creating a "new boss, just like the old boss."

NOTES

An earlier version of this essay was presented at the annual meeting of Music Theory Midwest in Madison, Wisconsin, 16 May 1993. I would like to thank Susan Cook, Marianne Kielian-Gilbert, Allen Forte, and Walter Everett for reading the earlier version and offering many helpful comments. This essay is also published in *In Theory Only* 13 (1996). Used with permission. The epigraph is taken from "Won't Get Fooled Again," words and music by Pete Townshend, from the LP *Who's Next*, Decca DL 79182, 1971.

1. While this was The Who's seventh U.K. release, it was only the fourth to be released in the United States.

2. It should be pointed out that, according to this interpretation, Daltry should have employed the word *no!* for this scream. Instead, he employs the word *yeah!* The latter is, however, the standard word/syllable employed in rock screams; yeah! should thus not be understood literally in this case—and this is obvious from the context—as suggesting that illusory political change is somehow positive.

3. Thomas Kuhn, *The Structure of Scientific Revolutions*, 2d rev. ed. (Chicago: Univ. of Chicago Press, 1970).

4. To observe the influence that literary criticism has had on music theory—and many articles could be cited—one need only consider such recent articles appearing in the journal of the Society for Music Theory such as Richard Littlefield and David Neumeyer, "Rewriting Schenker: Narrative—History—Ideology," *Music Theory Spectrum* 14, no. 1 (1992): 38–65; and Patrick McCreless, "Syntagmatics and Paratagmatics: Some Implications for the Analysis of Chromaticism in Tonal Music," *Music Theory Spectrum* 13, no. 2 (1991): 147–78. See also the 1992 Society for Music Theory Keynote Address by Ian Bent, "History of Music Theory: Margin or Center," *Theoria* 6 (1992): 1–21.

5. Lewis Rowell's work on the music of India, for example, culminates in his recent *Music and Musical Thought in Early India* (Chicago: Univ. of Chicago Press, 1992).

6. Joseph Kerman's harsh criticism of Schenker on this point is well known. He writes that "in his tacit acceptance of received opinion as to the canon of music's masterpieces, Schenker exemplifies more clearly than any of its other practitioners one

aspect of the discipline of analysis" ("How We Got into Analysis, and How to Get Out," *Critical Inquiry* 7 [1980]: 317.) In Schenker's defense, it might be added that while he may have focused his attention on the music of a restricted number of composers, within that particular body of musical literature Schenker knew and studied a great number and tremendous variety of works.

7. For a careful consideration of the role of the genius in Schenker's thought, see Nicholas Cook, "Schenker's Theory of Music as Ethics," *Journal of Musicology* 7, no. 4 (1989): 415–39.

8. See, for example, Nicholas Cook's discussion of Schenker's "elitist" attitudes in his *A Guide to Musical Analysis* (New York: George Braziller, 1987), 57–59.

9. In the United States, theorists tend to view Schenker's theoretical work as culminating in *Free Composition* and the *Meisterwerk* essays. Thus, earlier writings tend to be viewed as teleologically oriented toward the later writings, and Oswald Jonas's annotations in the English translation of Schenker's *Harmony* are just the most obvious instance of this teleological approach. When one therefore speaks of "Schenker's theory," one almost always means Schenker's *late* theory, and so the Schenkerian paradigm with which American theorists work is essentially one founded on Schenker's late work. For a discussion of the issues surrounding the reception of Schenker's work in the United States, see William Rothstein, "The Americanization of Heinrich Schenker," *In Theory Only* 9, no. 1 (1986): 5–17. For a critique of what he calls the "teleological straightjacket" in Schenkerian writing, see Allan Keiler, "The Origins of Schenker's Thought: How Man Is Musical," *Journal of Music Theory* 33, no. 2 (1989): 273–98. See also Patrick McCreless, "Rethinking Contemporary Music Theory," in this volume.

10. In the 1906 *Harmonielehre*, Schenker describes a passage from Wagner's *Tristan und Isolde* as a "masterpiece of poetry and articulation" (*Harmony*, ed. Oswald Jonas, trans. Elisabeth Mann Borgese [Chicago: Univ. of Chicago Press, 1954; repr. Cambridge: MIT Press, 1973], 112). Nicholas Cook discusses Schenker's later more negative assessment of Wagner in his "Schenker's Theory of Music as Ethics," 418.

11. Throughout his writings Schenker maintains a high level of respect for the music he considers to be of masterwork caliber. Schenker assumes that it is he who must rise to the greatness of the masterwork, not that the masterwork must be vindicated by analytical scrutiny.

12. I do not mean by making this claim to also assert that Schenker himself would necessarily have seen his theory in this way. Instead, I see a Schenkerian graph as "situating" a particular musical work within the much larger group of works that constitute Schenker's masterwork literature. Graphing a piece, then, tells us less about the piece in isolation from other works (i.e., in an "absolute" sense) than it does about how that piece is similar or differs from other works within the specified literature. According to this interpretation of Schenker's theory, meaning in a graph is *relational and contextual*.

13. That Schenker's theory arises from the pieces themselves, and not from preconceived theoretical notions that are subsequently applied to pieces, suggests a parallel with the mode of inquiry Goethe proposed as a sort of corrective to Newtonian scientific methodology. See Dennis L. Sepper, *Goethe contra Newton: Polemics and the Project for a New Science of Color* (Cambridge: Cambridge Univ. Press, 1988).

14. Heinrich Schenker, *Free Composition*, trans. and ed. by Ernst Oster (New York: Longman, 1979), 9.

15. See Felix Salzer, *Structural Hearing: Tonal Coherence in Music*, 2 vols., 2d ed. (New York: Dover, 1962); Lori Burns, "J. S. Bach's Chorale Harmonizations of Modal Cantus Firmi," 2 vols., Ph.D. diss., Harvard University, 1991; Matthew Brown, "Isolde's Narrative: From *Hauptmotiv* to Tonal Model," in *Analyzing Opera: Verdi and Wagner*, ed. Carolyn Abbate and Roger Parker (Berkeley: Univ. of California Press, 1989), 180–201; "Tonality and Form in Debussy's *Prélude à "L'aprés-midi d'un Faune,"* *Music Theory Spectrum* 15, no. 2 (1993): 127–43; and *"Axis Bold as Love*: Jimi Hendrix and Psychedelic Blues," paper presented to the Society for Music Theory, Oakland, California, November 1990.

16. It seems to me that Schenker's early and middle-period work stands up quite well on its own and that in terms of refining theoretical models, there are still a number of roads not yet taken within Schenkerian theory. See, for example, Joseph Lubben's "Schenker the Progressive: Analytic Practice in *Der Tonwille*," *Music Theory Spectrum* 15, no. 1 (1993): 59–75.

17. See Susan McClary, "Terminal Prestige: The Case of Avant-Garde Music Composition," *Cultural Critique* 12 (1989): 57–81, reprinted in this volume; and Milton Babbitt, "Who Cares If You Listen?" *High Fidelity Magazine* 8, (Feb. 1958), reprinted under its original title in *Esthetics Contemporary*, ed. Richard Kostelanetz (Buffalo, N.Y.: Prometheus Books, 1978), 280–87.

18. Skylark, "System of Survival," on Earth, Wind, & Fire, *Touch the World*, produced by Maurice White for Kalimba Productions, Columbia CK 40596, 1987.

19. McClary, "Terminal Prestige," 80.

20. The lyrics to "Evil Roy," "Money Tight," and "Touch the World" suggest that the individual needs to rise above material circumstances. In the case of "Touch the World," the lyrics by Rev. Oliver Wells suggest turning to Jesus. These songs are not nearly as cynical as "System of Survival" and cannot be thought of as political in the sense of suggesting the need for change in one's *external* circumstances.

21. Consider, for example, the instrumental cut "New Horizons," composed, produced, and arranged by Bill Meyers.

22. See also Susan McClary and Robert Walser, "Start Making Sense! Musicology Wrestles with Rock," in *On Record: Rock, Pop, and the Written Word*, ed. Simon Frith and Andrew Goodwin (New York: Pantheon Books, 1990), 276–92.

23. For McClary's critique of the field of music theory, see her Afterword, "The Politics of Science and Sound," in Jacques Attali, *Noise: The Political Economy of Music*, trans. Brian Massumi, *Theory and History of Literature* (Minneapolis: Univ. of Minnesota Press, 1985), 16, 149–58.

24. McClary, "Terminal Prestige," 78.

25. Peter Wicke, *Rock Music: Culture, Aesthetics, and Sociology*, trans. Rachel Fogg (Cambridge: Cambridge Univ. Press, 1990), 2. It seems to me that the categorial assertion that the European tradition is completely alien to the origins of rock music is wrong-headed and that this link is worthy of far more careful consideration than it has been given in popular music studies.

26. John Shepherd, "A Theoretical Model for Sociomusicological Analysis of Popular Musics," *Popular Music* 2 (1982): 146. Shepherd is quoting Wilfrid Mellers, *Twilight of the Gods: The Music of the Beatles* (New York: Viking Press, 1973), 15, 16.

27. Richard Middleton, *Studying Popular Music* (Milton Keynes: Open Univ. Press, 1990), 104.

28. Ibid., 113.

29. Simon Frith, "Towards an Aesthetics of Popular Music," in Richard Leppart and Susan McClary, eds., *Music and Society: The Politics of Composition, Performance, and Reception* (Cambridge: Cambridge Univ. Press, 1987), 136.

30. Middleton's chapter on analysis is, along with the work of Philip Tagg, undoubtedly the best music-analytical work to come out of the field of popular music studies. See *Studying*, chap. 6. Philip Tagg outlines his analytical approach in "Analysing Popular Music: Theory, Method, and Practice," *Popular Music* 2 (1982): 37–67.

31. Brown, *"Axis Bold as Love"*; Walter Everett, "Swallowed by a Song: Paul Simon's Crisis of Chromaticism," in John Covach and Graeme Boone, eds., *Analyzing Rock Music* (New York: Oxford Univ. Press, forthcoming); and Peter Kaminsky, "The Pop Album as Song Cycle: Paul Simon's *Still Crazy after All These Years*," paper presented to the Society for Music Theory, Kansas City, October 1992. See also Everett's forthcoming book (Oxford Univ. Press) on the Beatles.

32. See especially Leonard Meyer, *Style and Music* (Philadelphia: Univ. of Pennsylvania Press, 1989).

33. John Covach, "The Rutles and the Use of Specific Models in Musical Satire," *Indiana Theory Review* 11 (1990): 119–44; "Stylistic Competencies, Musical Satire, and 'This is Spinal Tap,'" in Elizabeth West Marvin and Richard Hermann, eds., *Concert Music, Rock, and Jazz since 1945: Essays and Analytical Studies* (Rochester, N. Y.: Univ. of Rochester Press, 1995); and "Yes, 'Close to the Edge,' and the Boundaries of Rock," in Covach and Boone, *Understanding Rock Music*.

34. I take up the relationship between rock music and musicology, as well as the relationship between musicology and popular music studies, in "Popular Music, Unpopular Musicology," in *Rethinking Music: Musicology in Context*, ed. Nicholas Cook and Mark Everist (Oxford: Oxford Univ. Press, forthcoming).

35. In making this point I do not mean to suggest that I am opposed to approaching popular music in a way that is essentially sociologically oriented. McClary's discussion of Madonna's music, for example, employs analytical techniques usually associated with the analysis of art music in the service of a sociologically oriented approach. I am merely arguing that an investigation of popular music need not be motivated exclusively by sociological concerns. See Susan McClary, "Living to Tell: Madonna's Resurrection of the Fleshly," in *Feminine Endings: Music, Gender, and Sexuality* (Minneapolis: University of Minnesota Press, 1991), 148–66.

36. John Shepherd, *Music as Social Text* (Cambridge: Polity Press, 1991), 206.

37. Though I have been considering these assumptions as disciplinary ones—which in itself is a kind of distancing technique of which one must constantly be aware—one should remember that the assumptions to which I refer are also likely to have some basis in each scholar's own experience and background. Thus for a popular music scholar the assumption may not simply be that the discipline of music theory has nothing interesting to say about rock music, but also that *music theorists like the ones I've known* couldn't possibly have anything interesting to say. This, of course, applies equally to the biases of music theorists and analysts. The argument then is not just about bringing disciplines together—something that seems comfortably abstract—but also about bringing people together.

SARA COHEN

Liverpool and the Beatles: Exploring Relations between Music and Place, Text and Context

In the extensive literature on the Beatles, their connection with the city of Liverpool has often been portrayed as one of text and context, whereby their songs have been treated as texts and contextualized in relation to the place and time in which they were born and brought up with Liverpool of the 1950s and 1960s embodying a juxtaposition and conjunction of particular social, cultural, and economic factors. "Why did the Beatles happen?" and "Why Liverpool?" are questions commonly posed. In books, articles, photographs, and films featuring the Beatles, Liverpool is typically depicted as adjacent context, as backdrop, as the beginning or starting point of the Beatles phenomenon.

This essay problematizes such a notion of text and context, viewing the relationship between music and place from an alternative perspective. It does so through an account of some of the ways in which the relationship between Liverpool and the Beatles is currently being used and discussed by different resident groups within Liverpool, focusing in particular upon those involved with music and tourism industries. The first part of the essay reverses the text/context, music/place model referred to above, considering how music and music-making not only reflect but also produce a city. The second part of the essay emphasizes the contested nature of this process by highlighting a few rather different and conflicting perspectives on the Beatles, Liverpool, and the relationship between them. In the third and final part of the essay, the complex and dynamic interaction between music and place is discussed in terms of the text/context metaphor.

PRODUCING BEATLE CITY: GLOBAL SUCCESS, LOCAL ORIGINS

The Beatles were the first British band to make it in the American market, and they have also been described as the first rock/pop band to make their local origins (embodied in their accents, humor, and style) a part of their global success. An article in *Music Week* began: "Think Liverpool and you immediately think The Beatles." The article went on to suggest that "the Merseyside Tourism Board, taking its lead from US cities with similar musical heritage such as Memphis, Nashville and New Orleans, exploits links with the Fab Four to the hilt."[1] But have these links been capitalized upon in Liverpool and, if so, then how and with what effects?

The four members of the Beatles were born in Liverpool and were based in the city until the band's spectacular success in the early 1960s led them to move to London. Their last live performance in Liverpool was in 1963 at the famous Cavern Club. During the 1970s several individuals who had been involved with the Beatles organized a few informal social gatherings for Beatles fans. A Beatles shop opened and a small Beatles convention was organized.

In the decade or so since then the potential contribution of tourism to regenerating depressed urban areas has been increasingly emphasized. Many British and American cities have made tourism a component of their economic policy. It is viewed as one means of improving their image, enabling them to compete with other cities to attract not just tourists but potential investors, transnational corporations, national and international funding bodies. Culture and the arts have increasingly been seen to have an important role in this race between places to create distinct place identities, leading to an emphasis upon "cultural tourism," involving the commodification of local culture and heritage and to interconnections between tourism, art, education, and shopping.[2]

The seriousness of Liverpool's current economic decline was marked in 1994 when Merseyside received Objective One status, which is the European Community's highest funding category. This is the latest in a long line of British and European funding schemes targeted at the region. Yet compared with other large industrial cities in Britain and the United States, Liverpool has been relatively late in turning to tourism or the arts and cultural industries as a means of regeneration. During the early 1980s its Militant City Council was understandably concerned to concentrate instead upon an urgent local need for housing and regarded tourism as a poor substitute for secure employment. The council allocated no funds specifically for tourism, and in 1981 it handed all responsibility for tourism over to Merseyside County Council. At that time the linking of Merseyside with tourism was still a rather alien, and to many quite an amusing, concept in view of the region's notorious social, economic, and image problems.

DEATH AND COMMEMORATION

The promotion of local tourism by Merseyside County Council largely depended upon one particular employee who also happened to be a Beatles fan. He pushed the connection between the Beatles and tourism, although his efforts did not meet with much enthusiasm from colleagues or other public institutions. (In fact, Beatles tourism has been dominated by the private sector which, until 1993, lobbied unsuccessfully for public funds.) In 1980 the death of John Lennon triggered an urgent desire in many Beatles fans to travel to Liverpool; in 1981 Liverpool City Council agreed that four new streets could be named after the individual members of the Beatles; and by 1982 the County Council employee had begun promoting Liverpool as the birthplace of the Beatles. He organized a regular Beatles Walk, the training of Beatles tour guides, and the production of a guidebook. He also helped establish the Beatles convention as an annual event, and he introduced Beatle coach tours and package weekends.

In 1983 Cavern City Tours was established, a private company that became the main promoter of Beatles tourism when Merseyside County Council was abolished in 1986.[3] It was set up by three official Beatle guides, and it remains the only Liverpool-based tour operator, producing Beatles-related postcards and maps, organizing a daily Beatles bus tour, Beatles weekend breaks and the annual Beatles convention, and running the new Cavern Club, which was built on the site of the original club. Besides Cavern City Tours, the only other major players in the local Beatles industry are the Beatles shop selling souvenirs, memorabilia and other Beatles-related merchandise, and a Beatles Museum entitled "Beatles Story."[4]

During the second half of the 1980s, the small Beatles industry struggled to survive. Most Beatles visitors are day-trippers with limited impact on the city's economy. Those connected with Beatles tourism describe it as a case of always "missing the boat," "a story of missed opportunities," and the city "shooting itself in the foot," while overseas visitors, particularly Americans, have commented on how badly managed it is.[5] The demolition of the original Cavern Club in 1973 on the orders of Liverpool City Council is seen as the prime example of such incompetence.

In 1993, however, Cavern City Tours successfully organized a street festival in conjunction with the annual Beatles Convention. The festival had a Merseybeat focus but also involved other musical styles. It was seen by its organizers as a means of attracting Liverpool people as well as visitors, and a means of getting convention participants and their spending out of the hotel that hosts the convention and into the city. That same year Liverpool City Council employed its first ever tourist officer. Part of that officer's brief was to investigate Beatles tourism and review the possibilities regarding a role for the council. The council recently allocated some funding and support for the local Beatles sector.

SELLING, MARKETING, AND PRODUCING THE CITY

Alongside local developent agencies, Liverpool's present City Council now emphasizes Liverpool as a place that can be professionally developed, packaged, and sold. The rhetoric of such organizations involves a language of visitor services, "key assets," "core products," "destination marketing," "product quality," and "style." Those working in Beatles tourism use similar language in their struggle to get Beatles tourism recognized by the public sector, and they adopt a rather pragmatic view, pointing out that the Beatles are perceived worldwide as "synonymous with Liverpool" and that the city must capitalize upon its "direct links with the most important and successful entertainment phenomenon the modern world has ever witnessed." The Beatles are advocated as a useful "tool in improving the city's image" and developing the local economy, "packaging the city on the backs of the Beatles," as one tourism official put it. Such views have been increasingly reflected in articles on Beatles tourism featured in the local press.

This brief chronology of Beatles tourism indicates a complex interaction between music and place—in this instance the city of Liverpool. The Beatles were born and brought up in Liverpool, and sometimes they deliberately represented the city in their music, although their music and music-making could be seen to reflect social, cultural, and economic factors peculiar to the city in more diverse and less overt ways.[6] But the music and music-making of the Beatles have also played a role in "producing" Liverpool, and the city is more than just an inert context, backdrop, or beginning. A city is a material setting comprising the physical and built environment; it is a setting for social practice and interaction; and it is a concept or symbol that is represented and interpreted. To describe a city as being "produced" is to emphasize the processes that shape the city's material, social and symbolic forms. Music is part of such processes. Music reflects aspects of the city in which it is created, hence "different cities make different noises,"[7] but music also produces the city, influencing social relations and activities in the city, people's concepts and experiences of the city, and the city's economic and material development. In other words, the Beatles and their music contribute to Liverpool's economy and visitor industry, although in other cities the impact of music may be more significant if often hidden. Music plays a role, for example, within an evening economy of bars, clubs, pubs, and it generates income through festivals and street performances.

When the Beatles became famous, so too did Liverpool. Although Liverpool's development agencies aim to promote the city as a place of excellence, fine architecture, and leading universities, with a strategy based around the theme of Maritime City, debates about whether or how Liverpool should capitalize upon its connection with the Beatles, using music to sell and develop place, became increasingly pertinent as the city's image and economic situation worsened and as interest in the Beatles and in Beatles and pop memorabilia burgeoned following the death of John Lennon.

Through sounds, images, events, and artifacts the Beatles have thus been used to represent or symbolize Liverpool, influencing the ways in which people think about or imagine the city, distinguishing it from other places and associating it with particular meanings, values, and sentiments. This influences the way people act in relation to the city. The music of the Beatles, for example, has attracted visitors to Liverpool, and Beatles tourist officials point such visitors towards bars, pubs, exhibitions and other places, rituals and events that have Beatles connections or where Beatles music is played. The music often marks such spaces as tourist spaces, and it constitutes a focus or frame for social practice, establishing, maintaining and transforming social relations and playing a role in the social production of place.

In this manner music can also influence people's experiences of place. The textual metaphor tends to depict music and culture in general as representational practice that can then be interpreted to reveal meanings, but music is not just represented and interpreted. The songs of the Beatles, for example, are not always theorized about, textualized, or read; they are also heard and felt, and music has a peculiar ability to affect or articulate mood, atmosphere, emotion, and consequently to trigger the imagination. This occurs in a multitude of different ways and contexts. Liverpool's Beatles industry, for example, uses the music of the Beatles to enable visitors to enter another time and world. The promotional literature of the Beatles Story museum proclaims "see it, hear it, feel it," advertising the exhibition as an "experience" that will bring 1960s Liverpool back to life.

Music's social, sensual, symbolic, and economic role partly helps to explain why it is so highly valued by people in Liverpool, as it is in many other places. Travel writers and journalists often single music out as representing the essence, soul, or spirit of a place, perhaps because music appears to be "more natural" than visual imagery since its social semiotics is less familiar, but also because music produces place in a very particular way that differs in some respects from the role of other art or symbolic forms.[8] For many people music acts as a publicly acceptable means of expressing ideas and emotions that are not so easily expressed through other means; this makes music a valuable resource in the production of place and local subjectivity. As popular culture, the music of the Beatles is also of course a particularly powerful and accessible resource.

MUSIC AND CITY AS CONTESTED: SACRED JOURNEYS

A city can thus be produced socially, symbolically, and materially through music, emerging as both text and context. Interaction between music and the city is revealed further in the following account of some of the ways in which the relationship between the Beatles and Liverpool is discussed and debated by young Liverpool rock musicians and those involved with Beatles tourism.

For many Liverpool fans and followers, the Beatles are something to be proud of, and their connection with the city something to be commemorated and celebrated. In Liverpool a tourist is often stereotyped as a Japanese Beatles fan wandering around Penny Lane with a camera round their neck and a lost, bemused expression on their face.[9] Meanwhile, those working within the Beatles industry classify Beatles visitors in terms of nationality, length of stay, the amount of money they spend, and frequency of visit. Besides those with a general interest in the Beatles, they identify "pilgrims" who make a once-in-a-lifetime trip to Liverpool, and "fanatics" who make repeated visits.

The Beatles fanzines emphasize the religious, pilgrimage aspect to Beatles fandom, featuring articles with titles such as "A Born Again Beatle Fan." Brocken refers to the "completist" nature of Beatles fans (as with many other fans), their desire to read every book, buy every record, know every fact and figure: "The Beatles have been transformed," he states, "from musicians into a collector's hobby, like bus or train numbers." He also suggests that there is a desire to view the Beatles in terms of a comfortable linear historical narrative with a beginning, middle and end, hence the disappointment that often greets any attempt by a former Beatle to continue his recording career, and the current unease over the musical collaboration among the three remaining Beatles.[10] The death of John Lennon heightened a sense of closure and finality experienced after the breakup of the band. Thus for Beatles fans Liverpool may be a collector's item, another link in a chain of Beatles connections to be traced, or experiences to be had, or some sort of Mecca to be visited in order to get closer to the Beatles or expand knowledge about them.

INDIGENOUS INTERPRETATIONS

Overriding the categories of Beatles visitor outlined above, those working within the Beatles industry distinguish between "the fans" and "the people of this city," viewing them as two separate markets that cannot be mixed, partly because they are seen to reflect different attitudes toward the Beatles and partly because of their different spending power. The local market is described as "extremely difficult to reach."

There are, of course, local Beatles fans, and a Liverpool Beatles fan club was reestablished in November 1993. According to its fanzine: "For many years the one thing that has dismayed Beatles fans more than anything else has been the way that the Beatles heritage . . . has been neglected . . . . There has certainly been a reluctance by the city authorities to maintain the legacy we have." Thus for many local fans the Beatles are a source of pride, and a credit to the city. Their fanzine, *Across the Universe*, along with Beatles tourist literature and souvenirs, emphasizes Liverpool as the creative origin of the Beatles, the source or author. Liverpool is described as the place "where it all began," the place that gave "birth" to and "shaped" the Beatles; hence the frequent reference to The Beatles as Liverpool's "sons." That same desire to posit "a beginning" is revealed by fanzine articles in which people recount the moment they first became Beatles fans, or "The Day I First Saw The Beatles."[11]

The local Beatles fanzine and Beatles industry also construct a connection or opposition between Liverpool and "the world." The Beatles are described as "four lads from Liverpool who shook the world," and the phrase "From Liverpool to the world" is emblazoned across tourist literature. A printed Cavern City Tours Beatles guide refers to the media focus on Liverpool at the time of Lennon's death and to press reports implying that people in Liverpool did not care. It continues: "But Liverpool did show the world how it cared in a very splendid way." A Liverpool fan said of the Beatles: "They were ours, they were Liverpool's, they belonged to us . . . they were there one minute and gone the next . . . [it was given] out that they were going to London, expecting everybody to be pleased, but . . . for the ordinary fans, we felt a bit deserted . . . . Why did they have to go and leave us? . . . We lost them to the world . . . After they'd gone, after they'd made it, I didn't go to *any* of their concerts, I didn't buy *any* of their records."[12]

DESERTING, BETRAYING

The description of the Beatles as "deserters" is quite common in Liverpool. A tourist official suggests that it is a major reason for a general lack of local interest in Beatles tourism (personal communication). Some resent the idea that the city's fortunes should depend upon four pop musicians, and its image summed up by them, emphasizing that the city is "more than" the Beatles. Others, Liverpool Development agencies for example, promote instead an image of the city linked to "high" culture.[13]

In March 1994 one of the directors of Cavern City Tours, Dave Jones, spoke at a two-day seminar on the music business held at Liverpool University.[14] About sixty people attended, comprising a cross-section of those involved with music (particularly rock and pop music) on Merseyside, including musicians, promoters, managers, and educators.[15] Dave Jones began by telling his audience that Cavern City Tours was initially based upon the heritage of the Beatles, and although for many of them this "may be a big yawn . . . The Beatles will be here forever . . . . The Beatles are to Liverpool what the Pope is to Rome and Shakespeare to Stratford. If you can milk it then you should. But believe me, if there is one thing that sells this city worldwide then it's the Beatles, whether you like it or not." Dave's rather defensive tone is reflected in an unpublished 1994 report produced by the Beatles sector that refers to a question locals and journalists always ask: "What have the Beatles ever done for Liverpool?" Still, the Scousers (i.e., Liverpudlians) say: "So what? They left Liverpool in 1964. The Beatles themselves have never done anything positive to help this area."

LEFT BEHIND

In response to what it calls "this betrayal theory" the report argues that the Beatles have never forgotten their roots; they have paid homage to those roots in their music; they have donated to local charities, and Paul McCartney is currently establishing an Institute of Performing Arts in the city. The report refers to debates over who should be awarded the title of "the fifth Beatle," [16] and states that "the fifth Beatle was and always will be the city of Liverpool itself." It concludes, "The Beatles may have left Liverpool, but Liverpool will never leave them." The first article in the first newsletter of the new Beatles fan club is entitled "Did The Beatles Turn Their Backs on Liverpool? The article says: "Genuine fans know that The Beatles were too big for any one city, or any one country. They were true megastars and belonged to the world." This is followed by an article on the Institute of Performing Arts, suggesting that it represents "perhaps the best indication of Paul's true feelings for Liverpool."[17]

In his talk at the music business seminar Dave Jones described the activities and finances of Cavern City Tours, emphasizing that he and his colleagues earned little from the business but pointing out the contribution of the convention and festival to the local economy. The owner of a local recording studio asked him about financial support for the festival from the Beatles themselves, pointing out that bands such as U2 had invested in their home towns, and suggesting that supporting the festival was "one way in which The Beatles could put something back into the city." Dave agreed but added, "You can also turn around and say 'we can do it without you.'"

So although many fans and followers of the Beatles commemorate, celebrate, and take pleasure in the band's connection with Liverpool, in Liverpool itself the connection tends to be viewed skeptically. As successful, high-
earning stars, the Beatles are often perceived as being in a position of power
compared to Liverpool. For some, the Beatles' music represents the band's
love for, and commitment to, Liverpool, but for others it embodies the way
in which the Beatles have exploited the city, drawing inspiration from it, making money through it, and giving little in return. Some resent the idea that
the city's fortunes should depend upon four working-class pop musicians and
its image summed up by them. Alternatively, the Beatles might embody the
feeling that the city has been socially and economically deserted, left behind,
and ignored.

THE CURSE OF THE BEATLES

The image of Liverpool as a city "left behind" has been reinforced by the
British media, which have often portrayed Liverpool as chained to the past,
"a city relying on former glories,"[18] and British and overseas media typically
relate Liverpool's contemporary music scene to the Beatles, typically describing it as lying "in the shadow of the Beatles." Not surprisingly, this is a view
resisted by young local rock musicians. These musicians are overwhelmingly
white, working class, often unemployed men in their twenties or thirties.
They join and form bands for social, economic, and cultural reasons.[19] A
band offers, for example, a particular way of life, structuring time and space
through various rituals, routes, and routines (band meetings, and rehearsals,
for example), and it provides its members with goals and ambitions. Many
have an overwhelming desire to "make it" with their band, signing a deal with
a record company that will bring their band's music to a wider public and
provide them with an income. This intensifies their commitment to, and statements of belief in, their band, and their investment of emotion, money, and
time in their music-making. Such music-making provides young men with a
means of communicating ideas, sentiments, and messages that they cannot
convey through other means. Musical performance can be a frustrating, agonizing experience, but one that can also give intense pleasure and a sense of
achievement.

Many of these rock musicians have been influenced by the Beatles and by
other bands but at the same time strive to make music that is original and
different. To succeed with that music, they must try to attract the attention
of record company representatives in London, where the record industry is
based: many musicians feel obliged to visit London in an attempt to attract
those record companies' notice. There are, moreover, a large number of
bands in Liverpool, only a tiny minority of which get signed; competition
between bands for resources and attention is thus intense.

When local musicians achieve some degree of success (such as signing contracts with London-based record companies) they often leave Liverpool, taking their earnings with them. Nor is it only musicians who have left the city. Over the past thirty years, Liverpool's population has decreased from 800,000 in 1961 to 500,000 in 1991; many have left the city for economic reasons. The music industry is monopolized by five multinational companies and concentrated in capital cities such as London, New York, and Tokyo, making it hard for cities like Liverpool to retain the income of their successful musicians. Despite the successes of the Beatles and other local bands, Liverpool has a dilapidated music industry from which hardly anyone in the city profits. The small businesses that comprise it face a constant struggle for survival.[20]

Many young Liverpool rock musicians acknowledge their debt to the Beatles and to local history and heritage, but the Beatles are also felt to be a constraining factor on their music, image, and career. Resentful comments such as "every other band wants to get away from the legacy of the Beatles" are common. Hence a recent article on Liverpool's rock music scene in an Israeli national newspaper was entitled "The Curse of The Beatles."[21] In 1990 a large concert was held to mark the tenth anniversary of Lennon's death. Members of the local rock scene, resenting the funding and attention lavished upon this event, organized their own concurrent festival entitled "Liverpool now." A local journalist wrote that "while the city wallows in nostalgia, on the other side of town 1990 fights back."[22]

The economic situation in Liverpool has heightened sensitivities surrounding the connection between local musicians and the city. At the seminar on the music business held at Liverpool University much debate concerned the departure of local musicians for London, particularly the successful ones like the Beatles, who take their earnings with them. As one band manager put it: "Liverpool is good at producing good artists and products which we then send to London." He criticized the belief that musicians have little choice but to leave the city, and advocated "keep[ing] success local": "We've got to stop the haemorrhage," added a local musician. The rhetoric of rock in Liverpool is thus pervaded by a sense of loss. Musicians are seen to leave Liverpool because they are greedy and misguided, because they "sell out"; because to use music as a way out is part of rock ideology; because there is nothing for them in Liverpool and they are thus forced to leave; and because if they do become successful their activities and lifestyle necessitate living elsewhere.[23]

A 1991 report on Merseyside's music industries, entitled "Music City," stated that "Liverpool, unlike its neighbour Manchester, seems to have established a trend for its successful bands *not* investing in major projects in their city." The report suggests that Paul McCartney's plan to set up an Institute of Performing Arts in his old school building "set[s] a valuable precedent."[24] A well-known Manchester music entrepreneur repeatedly contrasts Liverpool musicians and their commitment to their city with Manchester musicians. During a lecture at Liverpool University in 1990 he suggested that "if the Beatles had done to Manchester what they did to Liverpool," the people there would have been furious: "Well-known bands from Manchester . . . it's nice because they are seen around . . . . No-one has put anything back into [Liverpool, which has] . . . a history of leaving and not reinvesting." Paul McCartney's recent initiative was, he suggested, "too late."[25]

RELATIONS OF POWER AND PLACE

The connection between Liverpool and the Beatles can be described as a social relationship involving interaction between people and relations of kinship, friendship, and fandom that bind them to places physically, conceptually, emotionally. The relationship between the Beatles and Liverpool is even presented as a kinship relation, with Liverpool as mother-creator and the Beatles as her favourite sons, which carries the implication that the Beatles' obligation to the city parallels that of children to a parent. Liverpool is commonly described as a large extended "family," particularly by Liverpool city councillors, journalists, and other spokespersons concerned to promote an image of a united city in the face of social and economic pressures, and hostility toward the city expressed in the national media and by central government. Other images or metaphors implying integration or bondedness are also used to link the city with a sense of security and belonging. Death has a profound effect on social relations in these and other situations. The sudden and shocking nature of John Lennon's death intensified feelings of loss, leading to expressions of collective grief and to an emphasis upon his relationship with the city, the family, or home to which he belonged but from which he had strayed so far.

Social relations, including those of kinship, involve notions of exchange, reciprocity, investment, and indebtedness. People are seen to "put something into" such relations and to "take something out." The notion of debts to places (for example, what the Beatles owe Liverpool) is a reified notion of debts between people. Such notions may be stronger in places like Liverpool, which many people have left for economic reasons.

All social relations are also power relations. The case material highlights issues of dependency, accountability, responsibility, and access surrounding the relationship between the Beatles and Liverpool. Liverpool exploits the Beatles, just as some might see the Beatles as having exploited Liverpool. But the relationship between Liverpool and the Beatles is an unequal one, with one side perceived as contributing more than the other or as more needy, deserving, or exploitative than the other (hence the above comment "we can do it without them"). In the media, Liverpool's contemporary music-makers are commonly described as being constrained by the Beatles, remaining in their shadow or under their curse.

The discourses of loss at the music business seminar surrounding the departure of the Beatles and other musicians from Liverpool represent those of powerlessness revolving around notions of dependency and opposition between Liverpool's musicians, music scene and industry, and Liverpool's policymakers or London. London was described during the seminar as "the glittering bright lights at the end of the motorway." The London music industry constantly beckons and dominates; the London music press defines and controls. Local musicians are described as being "sucked out" of Liverpool to London, and Liverpool is described as a music colony whose subservience to London is maintained through various means. This is reflected in expressions of hostility toward London. Musicians declare loyalty to their city, censuring other musicians for leaving it, yet the city can also seem a "prison," as one musician described it, with popular music offering one of the only ways out. If musicians achieve success, their relationship with the city becomes intensely scrutinized and lines of debt and accountability more tightly drawn. Those who remain may be perceived as relatively immobile and dependent, and as tied to the city.

The Beatles are thus implicated in a spatial politics involving local relations and inequalities. The Beatles, for example, are linked to suburban South Liverpool, which is commonly opposed to Liverpool's working-class and less affluent North End; local/regional relations (hence the common references to the Beatles and other musicians in order to emphasize an opposition between Liverpool and nearby Manchester); local/national relations (hence through bands like the Beatles Liverpool is opposed to London, and the British North to its South); and local/global relations (hence through the Beatles Liverpool was opposed above to America or to the world).

Such relations are bound up with class and other issues. The precise class position of the Beatles is much debated in Liverpool, although Beatles literature often emphasizes the band's working-class status and represents the band in a manner that constructs an opposition between them and their middle-class (and homosexual) manager, Brian Epstein. An issue of the London-based Beatles fanzine describes Brian ordering smoked salmon and "fine wine" from a posh London restaurant while "the boys" preferred "cheese sarnies" (sandwiches) and "cups of tea."[26] The article typically emphasizes the quirky humor of the boys in contrast to the seriousness and moodiness of Epstein. Meanwhile a printed Cavern City Tours guide to "Beatles Liverpool" states that Epstein's home "is quite a contrast to any of The Beatles homes you have already seen. It was Brian's well-educated, businesslike manner that appealed to The Beatles, and it was also a significant factor in their meteoric rise to stardom." In Beatles literature it is "the boys" rather than Epstein who are taken to embody Liverpool, and through them representations of Liverpool as northern, working class, cheeky, disrespectful, and masculine Other are reinforced. Such representations are particularly strong in Beatles films such as *A Hard Day's Night*, where the band are also linked to kinship, Irishness, and roots.

TEXTS IN ACTION

The relationship between Liverpool and the Beatles is thus created through social practice and interaction, bound up with issues of success and failure, fame and fortune, death and debt, power and dependency. The relationship is used, interpreted, and represented by different social groups (musicians, tourists, tourist officials, and policymakers) in various, often conflicting ways. It is used, for example, to construct boundaries between us and them, insiders and outsiders, then and now, here and there. For many Liverpudlians, it is an important part of their sense of local identity and history; but while some celebrate and take pride in the relationship, others downplay, ignore, disown, or feel constrained by it. For some the city is more than the Beatles; for others the Beatles are synonymous with Liverpool. The music and the place are thus contested symbols, and both can be described as cultural maps of meaning, a principal means by which identities are constructed, sustained, and transformed, and powerful sources of belongingness and division.

All this emphasizes the importance of studying music and place, text and context, through socially and historically specific situations, events, and processes. "Penny Lane," for example, is the title of a well-known Beatles song and refers to a particular street in Liverpool. Through its lyrics, through the semiotic coding of its sounds and structures, and through the many ways in which it has been presented visually and in writing, the song has been linked with particular images and meanings (for example, with notions of Englishness or Liverpoolness). This does not mean that there is any essential correspondence between the musical symbols and meaning: on the contrary, the song has come to mean different things to different individuals who might associate it with personal events and relationships, and to different social groups who might interpret it collectively. Elsewhere I have explored ways in which a musical category such as "the Liverpool Sound" is described by particular social groups.[27] It is not a fixed, unchanging sound that directly reflects characteristics of the city; rather, it is interpreted in different ways, and it is used to construct different images and concepts of place and the local, although people may be guided by various social groups and institutions (the media, for example) toward certain preferred meanings.

Today Penny Lane is a rather run-down, suburban-looking street, but it is featured on the postcards, keyrings, pens, and other souvenirs sold to visitors to the city, and it is the highlight of the Cavern City Tours "Magical Mystery" bus tour. The bus takes a journey through the city, constructing a Beatles geography consisting of places and buildings in which the band lived and performed or places referred to in their songs. As the bus passes through Penny Lane, the song is played and the tour guide points out aspects of the street featured in the song. The bus stops at the end of the street to allow visitors to photograph the street sign. Penny Lane thus appears as song and narrative, object and image, street and journey.

Some city councillors have advocated the renovation of Penny Lane and the installment of plaques, signposts, and a monument to commemorate the Beatles.[28] The councillors claim that its current state is an embarrassment to the city and gives visitors a bad impression of it. Cavern City Tours respond to this by pointing out that they have been dealing with Beatles tourism long before the City Council finally awakened to the idea, and that in their experience tourists appreciate the fact that Penny Lane *is* run-down and remains "just as it was," just as they pictured it through the song. They also stress the dangers of overdoing things in "tacky," "mickey mouse" style, pointing out that "if Penny Lane was in the US it would be a theme park by now."

Hence while the song represents the street, the street now represents the song. Liverpool played a part in the selling of the Beatles, and now the Beatles are sold specifically to sell Liverpool. The relationship between the Beatles and Liverpool, and that between music and place more generally, is thus dialectical and shifting. Rather than freeze a text like Penny Lane at a particular time and place, texts could be put in action, interpreted in ways that attempt to create a sense of depth and movement, illustrating social processes such as those through which The Beatles, Penny Lane, and Liverpool itself are continually textualized. At one moment and situation Penny Lane could be treated as text (in the form of transcript, narrative, object, or image), while at another it may become context (song as street, journey, environment), highlighting the importance of looking not just at relations between text and context but at intertextual and intercontextual relations. Penny Lane can thus be seen as both music and place, text and context. It is produced through social and economic practice, social relations and processes; it is a contested symbol, and it is also aesthetic and sensual experience.

CONCLUSION

This essay began by referring to literature on the Beatles in which their connection with the city of Liverpool has often been portrayed as one of text and context, whereby Beatles songs are treated as texts and Liverpool as adjacent context. Most of the academic literature on the Beatles is confined to musicology, with musical contexts often not considered at all, and if they are, then a homology between text and context is often uncritically and rather simplistically constructed, so that text simply reflects context. Such approaches reflect a notion of music as a text that can be read and interpreted, translated or transcribed, with the textual metaphor used in a way that privileges the reading of the textual expert, ignoring alternative readings. A separation between text and context, text and reader, is also implied; hence the textual metaphor tends to flatten culture, detracting, for example, from the dynamic quality and depth of musical sounds. In addition, it is a metaphor derived from literary studies, and as a visual metaphor it is in some ways inappropriate for the study of sound. M. Jackson points to the visual bias in Western societies, and thus to the ethnocentrism inherent in the text/context metaphor and the way in which it reproduces Western academic practice as an approach to the study of culture.[29]

This essay has attempted to view the relationship between music and place from an alternative perspective. It has focused on the ways in which the Beatles are used and discussed in contemporary Liverpool. There is of course no neat homological fit or essential correspondence between music and place.[30] This essay has considered how the music and music-making of the Beatles not only reflect but also produce the city, and it has indicated the complex and contested nature of this process, exposing underlying concepts and values, preoccupations and tensions. In doing so it has highlighted the dynamic and complex interaction between music and place, and it has problematized the familiar text/context metaphor applied to music, indicating that it can be used in a way that misrepresents music's role in the social, sensual, symbolic, and material production of place.

Popular music studies have tended to draw upon disciplines such as communication studies, literary criticism, and musicology for inspiration. In anthropology and in some other social science disciplines, issues of text and context are currently being discussed in interesting ways. Strathern, Appadurai, Harvey, and other anthropologists have problematized the notion of context.[31] Strathern, for instance, rejects the notion because it "implies the bringing to bear of previous, a priori features which are added to what is manifest in order to understand/know what it is."[32] She uses instead the figure/ground metaphor[33] to draw "attention to effects, which facilitates attention to what emerge as figure and what as ground in social interactions."[34] Rather than present place or music, text or context, as relatively fixed, inert, or bounded entities with continuity over time and space, the discussion in this paper has presented them as the location, intersection, and juxtaposition of social relations, interactions, and geographical routes.[35] The relationship between the Beatles and Liverpool is represented and promoted through social practice and interaction between people, sounds, images, artifacts, and the material environment. This is a contested process, the study of which requires a situational approach, highlighting the specific dynamics of power involved.

NOTES

I would like to thank the Leverhulme Trust for funding the research project upon which this paper has drawn.

1. *Music Week* Jan. 22, 1994. Merseyside is the region surrounding Liverpool.

2. Common examples of cultural tourism include the construction and restoration of historical buildings and waterfronts; the organization of festivals, conventions, and other special events; the development of museums, galleries and heritage centers; participation in competitions such as European "City of Culture"; and geographical theming and sloganeering ("Robin Hood country"; "Glasgow's miles better"; "Manchester: the life and soul of Britain"). See also Kevin Robins, "Tradition and Translation: National Culture in Its Global Context," in *Enterprise and Heritage: Crosscurrents of National Culture* (London: Routledge, 1991).

3. The Merseyside Tourism Board, which took over responsibility for local tourism from Merseyside County Council, placed little emphasis on the Beatles.

4. The first Beatles museum, entitled "Beatle City," went bankrupt in 1985.

5. Brocken, "Some Theories about Signification: Postmodernism and The Beatles' Cover Versions," M.A. thesis, University of Liverpool, 1993.

6. See, for example, Richard Meegan, "Local Worlds," in *The Shape of the World* (Oxford: Oxford Univ. Press, 1995), on musical influences apparent in the Beatles' music.

7. See John Street , "(Dis)located? Rhetoric, Politics, Meaning and the Locality," in *Popular Music: Style and Identity*. ed. Will Straw et al. Proceedings of the 7th Conference of the International Society for the Study of Popular Music, 1993.

8. See Sara Cohen, "Sounding Out the City: Music and the Sensuous Production of Place," *Transactions* (Winter 1995).

9. This is an image that probably reflects a common view of both fans and tourists as unimaginative, undiscerning, and undiscriminating.

10. Brocken, "Some Theories about Signification: Postmodernism and The Beatles' Cover Versions."

11. Quoted from *Across the Universe* (Autumn 1993).

12. "Celebration," program on the Cavern, Granada Television (August 1993).

13. For example: "I also agree, as quite a number of the committee have said, that once they left Liverpool that was it. They haven't put a penny back into this city that they've taken their living out of" (Liverpool City Councillor quoted on Radio 4 29.19.82—"Dancing in the Rubble"). And: "In my long life of public work I come across people who I think statues should be erected to far more than the Beatles—people who have really contributed to the city" (another Liverpool Councillor, ibid.).

14. The seminar was organized by Liverpool Music House—a music production company, in association with Liverpool University's Institute of Popular Music.

15. Most participants were from Merseyside, and most were working class, male, and in their twenties and thirties.

16. For example, Stuart Sutcliffe, the band's original drummer, or George Martin, who produced the band's music.

17. *Across the Universe* (Autumn 1993).

18. *Music Week* (22 Jan. 1994).

19. See Sara Cohen, *Rock Culture in Liverpool* (Oxford: Oxford Univ. Press, 1991).

20. See Sara Cohen, "Popular Music and Urban Regeneration: The Music Industries on Merseyside," *Cultural Studies* 5, no. 3 (1991): 332–46.

21. *Ha'aretz Weekly Supplement* (2 Sept. 1994).

22. *Melody Maker* (26 May 1990). Meanwhile it is the older musicians who used to be members of 1960s Merseybeat bands who participate in the Beatles convention (along with various friends and relatives of the Beatles), and who lobby for certain buildings associated with the Beatles to be preserved. Local black musicians, on the other hand, note the overwhelming emphasis on the Beatles and other White Merseybeat bands, and point to the black bands that performed and recorded in the city at the same time, and to the influence of black musicians, particularly African-American musicians, on the Beatles, an influence that is generally not locally recognized.

23. See Cohen, *Rock Culture in Liverpool.*

24. Ibid.

25. Ibid. One should remember the long-standing rivalry between Liverpool and Manchester.

26. See Tony Barrow, "Brian Epstein's Secret Hideaway," *The Beatles Book* (London: Beat Publications: Oct. 1993).

27. Sara Cohen, "Mapping the Sound: Identity, Place, and the Liverpool Sound," in *Ethnicity, Identity: The Musical Construction of Place*, ed. M. Stokes (Oxford: Berg, 1994).

28. *Liverpool Echo* (25 Oct. 1993).

29. See Michael Jackson, *Paths toward a Clearing* (Bloomington: Indiana Univ. Press, 1989), 11, as well as Paul Stoller, *The Taste of Ethnographic Things: The Sense in Anthropology* (Philadelphia: Univ. of Pennsylvania Press, 1989).

30. See, for example, Philip Tebbs, *Blues as Ethnomusicology,* Ph.D. diss: Oxford University, 1995.

31. See Maryln Strathern, "Between a Melanesianist and a Feminist," in *Reproducing the Future: Essays on Anthropology, Kinship and the New Reproductive Technologies* (Manchester: Manchester Univ. Press, 1992), 64–89; Arjun Appadurai, "The Production of Locality" (unpublished paper, 1993); and Penelope Harvey, "Auto-Anthropology at the Expo '92: Can We Do Anthropology When Culture and Context Become Self-Evident?" (unpublished paper, 1994).

32. Ibid.

33. This is also, of course, inappropriate for the study of music. [Some would dispute this point, perhaps productively.—Eds.]

34. Ibid.

35. See, for example, Doreen Massey, "Power Geometry and a Progressive Sense of Place," in *Mapping the Futures*, ed. Jon Bird et al. (London: Routledge, 1993), on places as moments and nodal points in networks of social relations.

RICHARD HOOKER

The Invention of American Musical Culture: Meaning, Criticism, and Musical Acculturation in Antebellum America

In 1820, in an era of ambitious but short-lived journals, John Rowe
Parker began publication of an ambitious but short-lived journal *The
Euterpeiad or Musical Intelligencer*, a journal dedicated solely to disseminating knowledge and appreciation of fine-art music.[1] Despite low readership
and a chronic lack of funds, the weekly journal managed to hold on for three
years, which was to be the average life of the dozen or so musical journals
that appeared over the next several decades—all overestimating, it seems, the
American interest in cultured music. Although the first journal dedicated
solely to musical criticism and theory, *The Euterpeiad* was by no means the
first American musical journal: a journal called *The Musical Visitor* appeared
at the beginning of the nineteenth century but served mainly as a weekly
publication of art songs. Nor was it the first institutionalized appearance of
European art music on this side of the Atlantic: institutionalized concerts of
fine-art music in the United States go as far back as 1788, to the first concert
of the Independent Musical Society in Boston. The Handel and Haydn Society of Boston gave its first concert in 1815, and the Musical Fund Society
of Philadelphia, formed in 1820, put together its first concert in 1821. The
originality of Parker's journal instead lies in its systematic articulation of an
ambition and program that was to occupy American musical criticism and
theory over the next four decades: the invention of an American fine-art musical culture. At the start of the nineteenth century, the United States had, to
be sure, a distinct and vigorous musical tradition represented by a body of
native music, patriotic and religious choral tunes, and a musical performance
theory, all easily understood and mastered, simple, sentimental, and an integral part of the American community.[2] However, within the larger project of
fashioning an American culture equal to but distinct from that of Europe, the

task at hand, as the American writers on music saw it, was to redefine, if not abandon outright, indigenous but "debased" American musical attitudes, tastes, and practices. Beyond a simple feeling of shame-faced inferiority, antebellum musical critics regarded music as an acculturating force, an elevated but ultimately pragmatic tool to remedy the defects of society: music could represent, even forge the basic (if only potential) character of American culture, what constituted America as a cultural idea.

The Euterpeiad inaugurated a cultural moment in American musical history in which the establishment of a fine-art musical culture took on great social urgency. This musical culture faltered somewhat in the concert halls and the churches but flourished in theory and criticism. Nevertheless, the historical assessment of American music-making and musical thought of the early (and even the later) nineteenth century has tended in recent decades to privilege what H. Wiley Hitchcock refers to as the "vernacular" musical traditions, finding in the minstrel shows, the tunebooks, and the ballad operas the distinctly "American" music of the time.[3] The "cultured" musical tradition, on the other hand, lacks interest because of its highly derivative nature, being little more than a geographical extension, and an often mediocre one at that, of European musical taste, performance, and composition.

Yet the musicians, journalists, lecturers, amateur musicians, and concert audiences of the early nineteenth-century United States would not necessarily have shared this view. Indeed, there is no evidence that the audiences, performers, and composers of the musics of the marketplace thought of their music as "originally" American. The aspirations towards a cultured musical tradition, as derivative, unoriginal, and deficient as this often turned out to be in actuality, reflect what is peculiarly American as much as, and probably more so than, the diverse musics of the marketplace. The "idea" or character of music may lie not in the intrinsic aspects of the music itself or of anonymous musical styles and genres but rather in the construction, or preconstruction, of musical meaning in nonmusical discourse.

The early attempts to found an American musical culture open up a wider area of inquiry than that normally encompassed by music historiography: the reflection in music and musical taste of broader cultural concerns and the relation of ideologies of musical taste to concepts of social structure. In both Europe and America in the early nineteenth century, this relation between musical culture and social forms went beyond superficial correspondences: as a cultural project, musical activity came to be regarded as a means of constructing social actuality. It is, of course, partly along this tangent that the distinctly modern concern with musical meaning originally developed—a concern that still informs at a deep level our historico-critical obsession with identifying uniquely "American" music.

As a social and cultural phenomenon, what distinctly sets the early American fine-art musical tradition apart from that of Europe is its overwhelming *literary* quality: the invention of American musical culture for the most part took place in the press, the lecture hall, and the bookstores, and to a considerably lesser extent in the concert hall. Despite the steady flow of European musicians to the United States, the dearth of concert culture was a constant source of embarrassment to the American lovers of fine-art music. Although the Handel and Haydn Society of Boston began annual concerts in 1815, they could not muster more than twenty or so musicians for their orchestra in the first few years. The Musical Fund Society, which began operation in Philadelphia in 1821, also presented no more than one concert a year for most of its existence. The Philharmonic Society of New York (the present-day New York Philharmonic) was not founded until 1841, and on such a shoe-string budget that the orchestra members doubled as ushers; the society presented only four to five concerts every year before the start of the Civil War. To all but their most dedicated supporters, these early concert performances were principally marked by their incompetence.[4] In contrast, the stream of weekly and monthly journals was almost continuous between the appearance of Parker's journal and 1860. No fewer than twenty-nine journals dedicated solely to musical theory, review, and criticism appeared in this period, with a real flowering of musical journalism occurring in the 1840s. The number of these journals does not even begin to reflect the journalistic activity devoted to musical criticism going on in other, specifically literary, journals. The era is, it seems, one of abundant talk and opinion: the flood of writing about music in America does not supplement, but *deliberately* constitutes the central activity in early American music-making.

This literary character of early American music culture hangs on an issue of anteriority. Writings on music abounded as plentifully in Europe as in America and served largely the same ostensible purpose of disseminating knowledge and arbitrating musical taste. In Europe, however, composition, performance theory, and concert life are rhetorically installed in musical criticism as distinctly anterior to the writing about music. In the United States of the 1820s to the 1850s, however, writing on music was generated specifically as a response to an absence of music, or rather an absence of quality performance and composition, as T. B. Hayward and H. Theodore Hach express it in the prospectus to *The Musical Magazine*: "the task will be arduous, if they [the editors] must rely for its [the magazine's] contents on the resources to be found in this country. There is comparatively no musical literature here."[5] The issue is not so much lack of musical literature, but rather the proliferation of inferior music; Parker legitimates musical criticism as a means of decrying "useless, unnecessary and pernicious productions."[6]

Musical art, as T. B. Hayward noted, was only "in its infancy" in America, and for that reason needed to be preceded by "dissemination of information."[7] The literary inventors of musical taste in America saw their mission as laying down the foundation for future musical composition and performance; in practice, however, they simply produced literary texts that arguably usurped the place of the absent music, installing linguistic and textual issues that are literary in origin and focus.

It is the overwhelmingly literary nature of early American musical culture that this essay will explore—in what way and for what purpose musical experience was rendered textual by the first writers on music in America and the critical problems they encountered in this endeavor. In antebellum America, the nature of writing on music made for an extreme perception of music as an exclusively literary text that, by being so characterized, acquired the acculturating or reformative purposes normally reserved for written or oral texts. The ability of music to define or refine the American character, the central justification for a fine-art musical culture in America, was tied indissolubly with the concept of music as a literary text and the possibility that this text could be, and must be, properly and precisely read.

MUSICAL EDUCATION AND
THE AMERICAN CHARACTER

The announced intention of early nineteenth-century American writing on music is a specifically educative one, arising originally out of the solely technical pedagogic mission of early American composers and consonant with the socially formative role postulated for music in the establishment of public school musical education.[8] John Rowe Parker heralds his journal from the start as a "General Extension of Musical Information," and in the prospectus to *The Musical Magazine* Hach and Hayward locate their journal within a broader educational project: "The present period is believed to be particularly auspicious for the establishment of a periodical devoted to Music. The public have become . . . awake to the importance of its [music's] cultivation . . . . Throughout the northern and middle States, Music, in its moral and social importance, is evidently fast rising in the public regard."[9]

At the forefront of musical reform, Lowell Mason, William Channing Woodbridge and Thomas Hastings all emphasized musical education as being of the utmost social significance. Americans, if left to themselves, would naturally favor music of low quality; America, they believed, as a civilization was woefully imbrued by degraded musical tastes.[10] This state of affairs did not just bode ill for the establishment of an American concert culture, it represented a moral and social desuetude of the highest order. The educational project, then, committed to the establishment of cultured musical taste and the rejection of all "uncultivated" musics, was first and foremost an act of moral and social responsibility; the development of a cultivated musical taste could bring about the general improvement of moral judgment on a national scale. For Hayward and Hach, musical acculturation would accomplish no less than the development of "self-sufficiency," the redemption of the young from "dissipated modes of life," and the spreading of "social happiness" throughout the young nation [11]

In European musical thought, the cultivation of musical taste had often a particular *individual* motive; among the amenities that admit individuals to higher social classes and circles is the appreciation of fine music. The only consequential exception was Pestalozzi's musical educational method, immensely popular in the United States, particularly among the pedagogues, which emphasized the moral importance of discipline and obedience developed in performance education.[12] In the United States, however, musical education—by this term I include not only the introduction of music into the public schools but also all American writing generated specifically to disseminate musical "intelligence" and "cultivate" taste—acquired an essentially social purpose. In a practical sense, musical performance was seen as developing certain social skills, such as discipline, as well as "habits of order, and obedience, and union" that could serve other aspects of life as well.[13] In this regard, American musical thought simply aped the Pestalozzian program of musical education; but the cultivation of musical taste in America assumed an even more fundamental social function beyond these purely practical concerns.

In the essay "Music and the Temperance Reform," Hayward explicitly defines the role musical education might serve in the reformation of society. He divides human faculties between the intellect and the feelings and posits the latter as the basis of all human happiness, religion, and morality. It becomes ethically and socially necessary, then, to cultivate those faculties over the intellectual faculties: "Should we not feel a strong degree of confidence, that if we could have the formation and cultivation of the sentiments and tastes of an individual in early life, we should thereby at least exert a strong influence in the determination of his future character? And yet this whole business, as a matter of public education, is entirely neglected by us. Young persons are possessed of all these faculties, that is, of passions, affections, feelings, tastes, though we may neglect them; and we may rest assured, that if we do not direct their development and provide proper and wholesome food for their enjoyment, the young persons will furnish it themselves, from whatever means, good or bad, that may fall in their way."[14]

As derivative as these ideas sound, the cultivation of sentiments and tastes, especially through music, and their determinate relation to the development of character reveal Hayward's inversion of the Cartesian relationship between affect and ethos, an inversion at the heart of Hayward's theory of the moral affect of music. Hayward in the passage quoted above openly draws on a psychology of art inaugurated by Descartes's *Les passions de l'ame* that came to constitute a dominant thread of European expressive theories of music well into the nineteenth century. In this work, Descartes specifically concerns himself with the physics and physiology of feeling, passion, and sentiment; external stimulation resonates with the particular physiological make-up, the ethos or character, of the individual. Affect—emotion resulting from an external stimulation—arises from the peculiar consonance or dissonance between the external stimulation and the internal character. A person's character, then, displays itself in each and every response to the outside world.[15] The relation between affect and ethos in Descartes's treatise, although immensely influential on European theories of art, played a purely explanatory and formal role in European musical aesthetics and theories of musical semiosis. However, in Hayward's plea for the cultivation of musical taste, as in numerous American writings on musical education, the inverted relation between affect and ethos serves as a foundation for the moral and social functions of music. Music in Hayward's essay influences "future character" to the extent that it refines the "feelings," that is, whereas in the Cartesian tradition affect is determined by the ethical (physiological) character of the individual, the process is formulated here as working in the other direction as well— training individuals to be affected correctly by music, in essence, develops the ethical (physiological) character of that individual. Learning to properly appreciate music becomes a physical exercise of the moral character.[16]

Since the feelings, passions, and sentiments are for Hayward the basis of all moral, religious, and social character, the direct physiological access to the ethical constitution of the individual through affects lends music a more determinate social and religious role largely unclaimed for music in European aesthetics.[17] But what exactly does musical exercise do for character? Hayward and Hach in their "Criticisms" relate musical cultivation particularly to "self-sufficiency."[18] Woodbridge, who also claims for music a principal role in the development of character and morals,[19] likewise justifies musical cultivation for its ability to develop self-sufficiency: "Bodily exercise is the sister of pure and simple music; and as exercise imparts health to the body, so music imparts the power of self-government to the soul."[20] Woodbridge here equates the development of musical taste with physical exercise, also drawing on the physiological basis of character and the relation of that character to affect. But he goes further: this particular physiology of character provides for the development of a moral "self-government" through the "exercise" of refined taste. To learn to respond properly to music is to learn to respond properly—morally, socially, and religiously—to all other aspects of life, in other words, to develop moral self-government: an internally and physiologically generated rule of behavior.

At the heart of this notion of character development through the refinement of affects lies a principle of correct and limited interpretation. For if the musical experience is able to form a child's character—or reform the base character of an adult—through affective "exercise," then the affects, which in the Cartesian aesthetic tradition are absolutely dependent on character, take on a relatively independent status of interpretation, rather than response, and so can be taught or developed. The affective response is no longer solely psychological but primarily literary and in this way related distantly to late eighteenth-century and Romantic expressive theories of musical semiosis in which the speech-act of music primarily consists of a vaguely determinate communication of emotion and sentiment[21]—the syntagmatic chain of a musical work produces both interpretation and emotional response.[22] In the moral and social educational program in which American writers stress musical cultivation, the notion of a proper interpretation of the sentiments or feelings communicated in a musical work is conflated with the notion that the emotional response generated by a musical text arises specifically out of the (physiological) character of the individual. This conflation lies at the theoretical heart of the musical education movement and primarily fuels the concern with the textual, specifically literary, basis of the musical text. The musical text cannot be allowed any kind of affective indeterminacy or be subject to the chaos of individual responses, which are implied in both the Cartesian psychology of affect and expressive theories of music. The establishment of a proper, single affective response to any musical text makes possible the affective refinement of character and posits for the musical text a communicative determinacy and univocality traditionally reserved only for the literary text. It would seem that developing moral self-government through music begins with the imposition from outside of a proper response to or interpretation of the musical text.[23]

THE LOCATION OF THE MUSICAL TEXT

It is this communicative determinacy that Thomas Hastings, in *A Dissertation on Musical Taste* (1822), requires for music if it is to develop the affections.[24] Hastings's project is to develop rules of criticism, a critical method, and language that could make possible the development of an American fine-art musical culture; the *Dissertation* is largely concerned with "talking" about music.

Music is a specifically "literary" subject, a "refined species of elocution." [25] This literariness, in part, justifies talking about music without the aid of musical notation.[26] The rules of criticism Hastings wishes to forge are principally directed at the reformation of church music, considered by Hastings and his contemporaries as potentially the highest and most refined of fine-art musical traditions. But these rules of criticism are distinct from rules of composition.[27] They are, in fact, directed almost entirely at the level of performance and the correct interpretation of a composer's intentions by a performer. At some functional level, the role of the performer as an interpreter of the musical text is identical to the role of the critic as an interpreter of the

musical text; musical criticism, then, takes a prior position to musical performance. Hastings is explicitly looking for rules of interpretation; musical
taste and musical refinement cannot be properly taught without determining
proper and limited interpretations of the musical text.

It is the production of a specific "sentimental feeling" that Hastings claims
music shares with lyric poetry. The less the lyric poet is able to elicit a precise
sentimental feeling, the less "excellent" his work becomes, and the same can
be applied to the composer. In Hastings's formulation, the representation of
feeling in the musical text, equated essentially with literary representation
(lyric poetry), is an act of communication between composer and listener: the
composer, as it were, communicates sentiment and feeling by producing it
in the listener. In this Hastings does not depart significantly from European expressive theories of music. However, in European aesthetics, musical
semiosis was considered highly indeterminate—essentially nonrepresenta-
tional—and allowed for a free play of emotional response in the listener; the
relative malleability of musical signs is, in Romantic aesthetics, the particular
virtue of music and what distinguishes music from literature. Hastings, however, goes on to assert for musical expression a univocal and determinate
communicative intentionality and meaning:

> A great composer does not usually set himself to work, without having in
> view a *distinct* object and design. Like the skilful [sic] writer or eloquent
> orator, he endeavors to adapt his performance, in some measure, to the
> science, taste and sensibility of those for whom it is chiefly intended: and
> unless his piece is to be a mere lesson or an exercise for the mechanical
> display of talent, it is his constant object to make an appeal to their feel-
> ings; and every thing that relates to his design is managed accordingly. The
> distinguished performer is chiefly solicitous on his part, to produce that ef-
> fect on the audience which was contemplated by the composer whose
> piece he attempts to execute . . . .
>
> It has been hence imagined by some, that the principles of musical taste
> are so uncertain and variable, that no definite rules of criticism can be es-
> tablished. But, were our attention confined to such compositions as have
> been pretty generally acknowledged to be chaste and interesting—compo-
> sitions that are somewhat adapted to our musical knowledge and taste, and
> that are calculated to excite feeling . . . and would our performers endeavor
> to produce the *precise* effects contemplated by composers . . . our taste
> would probably become less fickle and more refined; and we should then
> find less difficulty in establishing rules of criticism and applying them [em-
> phasis mine].[28]

Hastings here conflates music with the literary text in several ways: the
communicative intention of the composer to induce "precise emotional effects" is likened to the communicative intentions of the "writer or orator" as
regards not intellect but sentiment and feeling. The discovery (one might

even say standardization) of the precise affective meaning of the composer's music makes possible "definite rules of criticism," that is, an interpretive, specifically literary, basis on which music can be understood and evaluated. If the unlimited semiosis postulated for music in European musical aesthetics, which Hastings is attacking here, makes possible a free play of emotional response in the listener, the translation of musical experience into writing— the "definite rules of criticism" Hastings is looking for—becomes an impossible project. The resemblance of music to oration or writing is more than a passing remark: the musician shares with the orator and the writer (and later, the lyric poet) the specific intention of appealing to or communicating precise emotions. In addition, the presence of an essentially determinate meaning within the musical text makes it possible to misread the music, specifically at the level of performance, and this misreading has tremendous moral and social consequences: "Music is a language of feeling. When cultivated *merely* for the purpose of personal gratification, emulation, distinction or display, it is of course liable, in many instances, to awaken among its patrons and devotees some of the baser passions of the human heart."[29]

In his definition of the "distinguished performer," Hastings reveals one of the immediate obstacles faced in the literalization of the musical text: unlike oration or writing, the precise location, if you will, of the musical text is uncertain. It is obvious to Hastings that the composer does not directly communicate to the listener, but rather indirectly through the performer. Hence, the specifically interpretive activity of the performer in his reading of the music becomes a text itself that gains in virtue the more it resembles the composer's intentions; the performer is "distinguished" to the extent he produces "that effect on the audience which was contemplated by the composer whose piece he attempts to execute"[30] It follows that the inferior artist is one who above all else does not interpret or communicate correctly the expressive intentions of the composer, whose text is a miswriting of the composer's text: "The pedant or inferior artist pursues an opposite course. Imagining himself to excel in scientifick skill, genius, or execution, his object is similar to that of a narrow minded writer, or conceited orator, who is more anxious to display himself, than his subject . . . . Unfortunately, however, musical science and taste are yet in a state of infancy in this country, and hence not only pedants and inferior performers, but the most illiterate pretenders, too often pass for men of real talent."[31]

Earlier Hastings had likened the composer's activity to that of a writer or orator; the confusion concerning the location of the musical text is here emphasized in his application of the same metaphor to the performer ("a narrow minded writer, or conceited orator"). What was earlier a text written by the composer (and also referred to as a performance) here becomes the "subject" of the performer's written text, a text that can be miswritten to the extent that it does not resemble expressively the anterior text that constitutes its subject. What causes the performer to go astray are internally generated principles of musical interpretation, the desire to "display himself" rather than to read properly the composer's text. It is no accident that inferior performers are characterized as "illiterate"; their fundamental failure is a failure of reading.

Correct performance education, then, becomes as critical an element in the establishment of a musical culture as the general diffusion of musical appreciation, because it is vital to the precise communication of musical meaning that the text of the performance render as closely as possible the expressive meaning of the composer's text. This mediation of the musical text through the text of the performance, which can potentially misread and therefore miswrite the composer's text, threatens the communicative intention of music and hence the peculiar social and moral value of affective expression, particularly of church music.[32]

It is for this reason that Hastings, as well as the crowd of musical journalists, devoted much paper and ink to proposing and disseminating rules of correct performance. The chief object of criticism for the early reformers of music, such as Hastings and Mason, was not so much American music as it was American performance standards. Hastings's dissertation on "musical taste" is by and large an attempt to reform performance standards, particularly in the church, a reformation directed centrally at musical interpretation. This reformation drive in general was directed at what Hastings in the passage quoted above called "illiteracy" in music. This term does not distinguish "oral" from "written" musical traditions or the ability or inability to read notes on a page, for Hastings and others group virtuosic but expressively empty performances under the rubric of musical illiteracy. Rather, musical illiteracy, the inability to "read" music, primarily applies to the interpretive project of the performance. The instruction in the correct way to listen to music more importantly guarantees the correct technical and especially expressive means to perform music on which so much moral and social importance lay.

The focus on performance and interpretation opens up within Hastings's argument a fundamental aporia at the level of original textual production: how is it that musical texts are written in the first place? It would seem in Hastings's analysis of performance that there is an originary moment anterior to the interpretive act in which the musical text is conceived and composed; the character of this anterior moment is a proper or elevated affect willed into sensual, musical existence. What possible rules of criticism can guide this originary composition? That is, how can musical criticism distinguish between refined music and less refined music? Composition, it turns out, is equally dependent on interpretation; the composer is enjoined to study "specimens" of great music and learn from them the "ideas," which seem to be a conflation of technical methods and the sentiments they elicit. Originary composition, founded always on an interpretive specularity, recedes into infinite repetition: "Though our modern readers prefer, with much propriety, the *diction* and the *imagery* of later times, yet every first rate poet, of every age, has well known how to avail himself of the assistance that is to be derived from a study of the works of his ancient predecessors—and he has drawn largely from their materials. Many of his finest thoughts have been little else than literal translations into a more polished dialect, illustrated, perhaps by a modern style of imagery."[33]

The composer shares with the poet the sole duty of restatement, of repeating what has come before. The composer, in addition, proleptically indicates his own imitation, his own reinscription into this endless process of repetition. But still the aporia remains: where does original composition and invention arise? For Hastings, originality and invention arise only in the number and combination of sources the composer restates; the unoriginal composer restates only one source of musical "ideas": "unless we go through the same course of preparatory studies that he did, we shall be, at best, but second-hand artists in copying from him as a model. While his style has been formed by compilations from an immense number of different models, which compilations have been polished, refined and enriched, by his own cultivated taste and furtilized [sic] invention; ours will consist but of tasteful imitations of a single individual. His style will be, to every useful purpose, original: ours will abound in palpable plagiarisms."[34]

The composer differs little from the performer: the composer must properly rewrite a combination of musical texts whereas the performer must properly rewrite a single musical text. A composer falters when he does not fully understand a musical text; what criticism reveals to be a text imitating multiple sources, the deficient composer reads as a single, homogeneous text. The performer, for all practical purposes, is identical to the inferior composer in that he imitates or interprets a single musical text; the critic, on the other hand, like the excellent composer, has as his object the identification and proper interpretation of myriad musical texts. Again, criticism takes an anterior position to music, in this case, excellent composition. The location of the musical text is never fully resolved, however; all compositions, like all performances, are rewritings of rewritings. The composer's duty is to identify properly the rewritings embodied in individual compositions to avoid misunderstanding these compositions as original; this misunderstanding leads to a miswriting by the deficient composer that results in a loss of communicative force.[35]

WRITING IDEOLOGIES

For Hastings, music history is a history of expressivity, a progress of sentiment, although it is a history he narrates backwards in order to privilege the contemporary: "In turning over a volume of specimens, and proceeding gradually down from the compositions of our immediate predecessors, to the earliest fragments, we now perceive a constant decrease of melody, harmony, and rhythm. The little fragments of Greek and Roman musick are indeed rhythmical . . . but in this and almost every other respect they now appear uninteresting to us; nor can we easily conceive how they could ever have appeared otherwise."[36]

This musical chronology has a contemporary horizontal equivalent both social and cultural in nature: "If again we compare the refined specimens of modern composition, with those that still continue most in favour with the illiterate, and proceed from these to the rude songs of less refined and of barbarous nations, we shall also perceive a decreasing interest in the specimens, equally as striking as in the former case."[37]

The term *illiterate* is again no accident as this horizontal social axis mirrors the development of language.[38] The placing of the musically illiterate midway between the primitive and the refined along a scale mirroring linguistic capability begins to unveil an ideology of music that is the obverse side of the "moral self-governance" of the refined musical aesthete. Uncultured and unrefined musical taste reveals the noncommunicative and nonsocial character of the American masses; moral self-sufficiency is replaced by a depraved self-satisfaction.[39] This ideology is throughout the text marked in social terms by the "disgust" felt by the refined toward rude and rudely performed music and inscribed formally in the more neutral term "mechanical," "unexpressive," and so forth. There is a metaphorical dynamo running throughout the *Dissertation* that links unrefined musical taste to moral depravity to the prelinguistic or barely linguistic. Music is, first and foremost, a language of feeling, a language particularly suited to moral "feeling."[40] Inattention to musical art, then, is in its principal terms a species of "moral depravity" as well as illiteracy; the decline of sacred music metonymically points to an especially depraved age of the world.[41]

One other term in this metaphorical vortex may help unpack its operations: throughout the text, the term most often associated with unrefined music or musical taste is the rather cryptic *indifferent*, in part a polite pejorative, and in part a foregrounding of the nonlinguistic or barely linguistic properties of vulgar musical culture. The term constellates around the narcissistic tendencies of "illiterate" music in which music or performance fails to cross the boundaries of mere self-communication: "There is another class of individuals, who are willing to admit that their musick is indifferent . . . . *Their* voices do not need cultivation, for they can now sing in such a manner as to satisfy themselves."[42]

This peculiar brand of monomaniac, the self-satisfied, self-pleasing performer or composer, appears again and again throughout Hastings's polemic against American music and American performance standards. The semiotic narcissism, earlier expressed in the discussion of the inferior artist, so seriously undermines music in its linguistic, moral function, that its only social product is disgust.[43] Silence, from a social point of view, is infinitely preferable.[44] Unrefined music and musical performance first and foremost explode the linguistic status of music; music becomes subject to the chaos of internally generated principles—a nonlanguage of feeling—and threatens to elicit only base emotions in its auditors: disgust, unconcern, unsociability. This musical narcissism is not limited to popular music and deficient performers. The overrefined, if they are not careful to compose at the level of public understanding, fall into the same sort of self-satisfaction, for they fail in the intersubjective transaction that grounds the linguistic: "Hence the distinguished musician and his patrons are constantly refining beyond the taste of the vast multitude of listeners. They cultivate for themselves, a peculiar dialect, and when they make use of it in their transactions with the rest of the world, they marvel at not being understood."[45]

The ideology animating these metaphorical shifts is for Hastings essentially inscribed not within music itself but rather within the interpretive act, within the founding act of reading the musical text. The threat to American musical culture embodied in taste and practice, as Hastings saw it, was communicative and interpretive narcissism, a fundamental crisis of semiosis where the language of feeling fully present in a musical composition becomes a nonlanguage of feeling in the musical performance, a self-contained, self-representational, and self-generated act, or, on the compositional side, music that pleases only its composer. Hastings's prime example of such a musical solipsist is the composer of compound fugues and canons; and the immense popularity of fuguing tunes in American churches betokens their insufficiency as a musically refining force: "The exercise of ingenuity and the conquering of difficulties in constructing these complicated pieces, could render them sufficiently interesting to their fabricators we may suppose; but what connection had these circumstances with the public ear? Could any person be benefitted with listening, when twenty or thirty individuals were disputing on four or five different subjects at the same time? . . . as ignorance was in those days, esteemed '*the mother of devotion*,' we may easily conceive that no want of expression would be complained of as a defect in composition."[46] Mere contrapuntal contrivances give rise only to "senseless productions."[47] Worse than silence, this non-language of feeling introduces a chaos of affects—it is indifferent. In place of a community united by refined feeling erupts the basest and most antisocial mob of isolated affects. This rupture of the linguistic precision of music underlies Hastings's placing of vulgar music and rude performance midway between the refined and the barbarous, a dichotomy incorporated into the dichotomy between the linguistic and the prelinguistic. Rude musical taste and performance reveal a failure of reading and a failure of language that founds a failure of community and moral union.

Again, Hastings's text opens up a fundamental aporia not directly resolved in his argument: if popular music is unexpressive, whence arises any kind of self-satisfaction? Although the music is a nonlanguage of feeling, unexpressive and insignificant[48] whence arises whatever meaning or value it has for the self-satisfied composer or performer, or, more importantly, for the audience? Hastings continually relates the language of popular music with extrinsic associations, with signifying systems alien to the music itself; music of this sort gains meaning through "association:"[49] "A great portion of our fashionable ballads, duets, trios, etc. are either extracts from dramatic compositions, or imitations of such extracts; and this is probably the principal reason why so many of them are deficient in character and exceptionable in sentiment. Not in the least to excuse the immoral tendency of such productions, we may suppose that many of them had, in their original situation, some characteristic effect, that rendered them interesting to the frequenters of the theatre; but when they are thus detached, this effect is necessarily lost."[50]

Only the "unaffected language of feeling alone" can produce music of a genuine character.[51] The "associations" that lead people to admire deficient, expressionless music arise out of the heterogeneous and variable myriad of experience itself. Even "contemptible" music becomes a source of satisfaction if it is first heard under "favourable circumstances" or before cultivation has taken place.[52] These "associations," which are the basis of inferior music, preserve in part the linguistic status of refined music, which is still an unsullied language of feeling, and create the basis for the private, self-satisfying pleasure that seems to accrue to "senseless" music as well. The contingency of associations, which may or may not be shared, opens up for these musical texts limitless meaning, which, of course, forecloses the possibility of any precise communication of feeling, moral or otherwise, that is, any "refinement."

Music as cultural meaning, as ideology, becomes fully dependent on the literary text: the definite rules of criticism that inaugurate precise reading of the musical text. These definite rules of criticism can structure a community based on common feeling and affect, which, through the equation of musical feeling with moral enlightenment, leads to a community of common, homogeneous moral constitutions. Beyond this, however, Hastings reiterates what many of his contemporaries continually advocated as one of the principal justifications for fine-art music: its potential to unify the disunited, rebellious American community. The danger of the heterogeneous monomania, which, for Hastings, more than anything else characterized the debased musical taste in early America, implies nothing less than the hopeless moral fragmentation of American culture.

NEW HISTORIES OF MUSIC

I opened this essay, which remains fundamentally a historical and cultural study, with a thinly veiled but fundamental challenge to musical historiography, which has only in recent years begun to penetrate the cultural ideology of music. Musical history as we write it, and have written it since the eighteenth century, installs the hierarchy of "music and performance / writings on music" as the stuff of musical culture as it advances its way to the present. This hierarchy operates in even the most radical challenges to the ideological neutrality or formal absoluteness of the musical text. However, the history of music in cultural terms—and this includes any discussion of affect or meaning, contemporaneous or otherwise—is always implicated in a set of nonmusical, specifically literary, pretexts. In our histories of music, these literary texts are the privileged subalterns to the supposedly anterior musical text, the handmaidens that provide insight into the cultural or affective meaning of the music that is the subject of these texts. But music itself is always a nonobject of critical and historical musicological discourse even though it may be its principal subject; music in its cultural, social, and psychological dimensions—music that has meaning—is only a secondary object of historical discourse (or any other kind of discourse). Rather, the central object of all writing on music is always literary texts, anterior writings acknowledged and unacknowledged, which are reiterated, reworked, and shuffled around from one musical text to another.

The challenge is to rethink this dyad and the primacy of the musical text over the literary text in the cultural and ideological histories of music. The shift in the modern world to a criticism of music, a literary discourse of music, has fundamentally reconstituted the experience of music, an epistemic shift radically evident in the early invention of American fine-art musical culture. Through discourse, music has come to be inscribed in ideologies of affect, particularly ideologies of uniform, standardized interpretation; these ideologies predetermine the way we listen to music.

Music historiography has largely passed over the music critics in early America. This period, at least from the perspective of fine-art music, has as a result been of little interest to musical, or literary, historiography. Contemporary historians, unintentionally reiterating Hastings's nomenclature of vernacular music, find only the "uninteresting" and "unexpressive" in antebellum American fine-art music, which, as a result, necessarily fails as a bearer of cultural meaning—again, an unintentional reiteration of Hastings's argument. The invention of an American fine-art musical culture was primarily geared to the reformation of the American character, and specifically involved not the creation of a native compositional tradition but primarily a reform in the performance and appreciation of music. Our contemporary focus on "original" American composition during that period, a focus that has led to the privileging of music outside the fine-art tradition, is an anachronistic focus. The early American concern was not to create a body of original, distinct musical works that could express the "idea" of America; rather, the concern, a uniquely American concern, was to institute a program that held the promise of forming a future society not only of refined musical taste but, as a consequence, of refined and homogeneous moral character.

NOTES

1. Reprinted as *The Euterpeiad or Musical Intelligencer*, 3 vols., intro. Charles E. Wunderlich (New York: Da Capo Press, 1977). For a discussion of Parker and *The Euterpeiad*, see H. Earle Johnson, "Early New England Periodicals Devoted to Music," *Musical Quarterly* 26 (April 1940): 153–61, and John C. Haskins, "John Rowe Parker and *The Euterpeiad*," *Notes*, 2d ser. 8 (June 1951), 447–56.

2. For a general study of popular music in antebellum America, see H. Wiley Hitchcock, *Music in the United States: A Historical Introduction* (Englewood Cliffs, N. J.: Prentice Hall, 1969), 96–129, and Russell Sanjek, *American Popular Music and Its Business,* 3 vols. (New York and Oxford: Oxford Univ. Press, 1988), vol 2: 25–222.

3. Hitchcock, 51. This privileging of the vernacular tradition is, to be sure, largely a reaction to earlier histories of American music, centrally those of Frederic Ritter, Oscar Sonneck, Louis Elson, John Tasker Howard, and H. Earle Johnson, which privilege the fine art traditions while disregarding indigenous popular music. Gilbert Chase, *contra* this tradition in American musical historiography, opens his history of American music with the warning that the "genteel" tradition is his own personal "bête noire" (*America's Music* [New York: McGraw Hill, 1955], xvii) and so turns most of his attention to the "noncultured" traditions. This revised perspective, focusing mainly on popular music and on "serious" composers such as Charles Ives, who spurned imitation of European models for an often cranky sort of American originality, has come to dominate American musical historiography over the last three decades. The central studies along these lines are those works of Gilbert Chase, H. Wiley Hitchcock, and Russell Sanjek cited above; Ronald L. Davis, *A History of Music in American Life*, 2 vols. (Malabar: Krieger, 1982); and Charles Hamm, *Music in the New World* (New York: Norton, 1983).

4. For early histories of these institutions as well as early concert programs, see Charles C. Perkins and John Sullivan Dwight, *A History of the Handel and Haydn Society of Boston, Massachusetts* (Boston: A. Mudge, 1883, 1893); Louis C. Madera, *Annals of Music in Philadelphia and the History of the Musical Fund Society from its Organization in 1820 to the Year 1858*, ed. Philip H. Groepp (Philadelphia: J. B. Lippincott, 1896); Henry Edward Krehbiel, *The Philharmonic Society of New York: A Memorial; Published on the Occasion of the Fiftieth Anniversary of the Founding of the Philharmonic Society* (New York and London: Novello, Ewer & Co., 1892). A complete list of concert programs for the Philharmonia Society can be found in Krehbiel, pp. 95–163.

5. *Musical Magazine* 1.1, Jan. 5, 1839: 1

6. "A Dissertation on Musical Taste," *The Euterpeiad* III, (June 22, 1822): 54.

7. T. B. Hayward, "Our Criticisms," *Musical Magazine* 2, no. 48 (Oct. 24, 1840): 366.

8. On the early American tunesmiths, see especially Irving Lowens, *Music and Mu-*

sicians in America (New York: Norton, 178–93), and Hamm, 112–28. For musical education in early America generally, Lloyd F. Sunderman, "The Era of Beginnings in American Music Education (1830–1840)," *Journal of Research in Music Education* 4 (1956): 33–45; James H. Stone, "Mid-Nineteenth-Century American Beliefs in the Social Value of Music," *Musical Quarterly* 43 (1957): 38–49.

9. *Musical Magazine* 1.1, Jan. 5, 1839: 1.

10. For Mason and Hastings as musical reformers and educators, see Hamm, 161–72, and Sanjek, 203–8. For Woodbridge, see John J. Silantien, "The Contributions of William Channing Woodbridge to American Music Education," *Contributions to Music Education* 4 (1976): 80–84.

11. "Our Criticisms," *The Musical Magazine* 1. 1, Jan. 5, 1839: 2.

12. For a general study of Johann Pestallozi, see Kate Silber, *Pestalozzi: The Man and His Work* (New York: Schocken, 1960). The central American versions of Pestalozzian musical pedagogy include Joseph Neef, *Sketch of a Plan and Method of Education Founded on the Analysis of the Human Faculties and Natural Reason Suitable for the Offspring of a Free People and for All Rational Beings* (Philadelphia: 1808), and Lowell Mason, *Manual of the Boston Academy of Music for Instruction on the System of Pestalozzi* (Boston, 1834). See also Gerald Lee Gutek, *Joseph Neef: The Americanization of Pestalozzianism* (Mobile: Univ. of Alabama Press, 1978) and Howard Ellis, "The Influence of Pestalozzianism on Instruction in Music," Ph.D. diss, University of Michigan, 1957.

13. William Channing Woodbridge, *A Lecture on Vocal Music as a Branch of Common Education, Delivered in the Representatives' Hall. Boston, August 24 1830. Before the American Institute of Instruction* (Boston: Hilliard, Gray, Little and Wilkins, 1831), 12. The ability of music, in its performance and appreciation, to unite a group of individuals practically, morally, and intellectively was the most immediate practical justification for the establishment of musical education and a common, cultivated concert culture: "It [the love of music] is just the kind of influence which promises to check the vicious tendencies most peculiar to our state of society; . . . it disposes men to blend, while other influences to which we are subject all tend to disunion" (*Boston Musical Gazette*, 1 [1838–39]: 205). The same idea appears in an anonymous article in *The North American Review*: "Another circumstance which renders music of extraordinary and almost inappreciable value in this country, is the necessity of discipline, strict conformity to rules, the subordination of the different parts and voices, and the distinctness of each department. In music, every one, from the highest to the lowest, has his appointed, fixed place . . . . What an inestimable incident is this, in any study to be pursued in this country, where every man is so apt to entertain the idea that he is born with a genius for any thing he may choose to undertake . . . . Every one, in short, places himself on his reserved, natural right of rebellion; and the constitution itself is made to maintain the most self-destructive doctrines. We consider it providential that there is one pursuit of an attractive character, which cannot be thus inverted; in which learners must submit to teachers, the less advanced must yield to those who are more so, and where every one must take his appropriate place, and not seize upon another for which his natural and acquired powers do not fit him . . . . There is only one evil of which we are apprehensive, and that is disunion . . . . Great effects can be produced by combination alone, especially in music" ("Music in America," *North American Review* 111 [Apr. 1841]: 325).

14. *Musical Magazine* I. 12, June 8, 1839: 184.

15. Stone's summary of the moral justification postulated for musical cultivation in early nineteenth-century America is typical of modern accounts: "Most importantly, the Boston School Committee called attention to the moral values of music instruction. It believed that music had mysterious charms which enlivened mind and body. Youthful savagery and uncouthness were subdued by singing" (James H. Stone, "Mid-Nineteenth Century Beliefs in the Social Value of Music," *Musical Quarterly* 43 [1957]: 40). Although American writers on music and musical education were frequently inarticulate as to the specific causes of the salutary moral effects of the cultivation of musical taste, there can be little doubt that the moral effect of music was considered as arising out of a (quantifiable) affective influence on character which had little to do with "mysterious charms." For Descartes's specific influence on musical theory, see Denes Zoltai, *Ethos und Affekt* (Berlin: Akademie-Verlag, 1970); John H. Neubauer, *The Emancipation of Music from Language: Departure from Mimesis in Eighteenth Century Aesthetics* (New Haven and London: Yale Univ. Press, 1986), 42–59. Parker explicitly draws on Cartesian affective psychology: "The manners of any people are best denoted by the prevailing state of the music of their country; and this is certainly true; as the mind will always seek its repose and delight in pursuits the most similar to its general tendency and direction" ("The Use and Abuse of Music," *The Euterpeiad* 3 [Apr. 27, 1822]: 19).

16. *Musical Visitor,* Boston, 1841, 2.1: 8.

17. The anonymous author of "Music in America" cited above justifies musical education with an essentially identical argument. Since "men are governed more by feeling and impulse than by reason and reflection" (322), what better vehicle than music, which through its affect, can be the "means by which a deep and permanent impression is to be made on men's minds and character" (322). An immediate example of the difference between European and American attitudes may be found in the last half of the essay, "Music and the Temperance Reform," which are selections from an British essay by one "Professor Raumer," who spells out the particular virtue music may have in the reformation of alcoholism among the lower classes. Whereas Hayward's lengthy introduction to this letter sets out the relation between affect and ethical development, which introduces a powerful social justification for a specifically reformative musical education project, Raumer merely finds music to be a more wholesome distraction or entertainment for the working class than the beer or gin hall: "You must offer the poor man some substitute for intoxication; you must make other thoughts and other feelings accessible to him . . . . A singing and dancing people are certainly higher in the scale of morality than a sotting people . . . . The hundreds who resort to a museum cannot at the same time be sitting in an ale-house or a gin-shop . . . . I am convinced . . . . that drunkenness would decline, if music, dancing, and all the less sensual and animal recreations were allowed . . . . A man who enjoys singing, dancing, or the drama, cannot possibly be very drunk; nor is brutal grossness of behavior compatible with social recreation" ("Music and the Temperance Reform," 186–87). The relation between ethos and affect was not to be so explicitly confused in European justifications of the arts as it was in American writings. On European justifications of music based on affect theory, see Neubauer, *Emancipation of Music.*

18. Hayward and Hach, "Prospectus," 1.

19. Woodbridge, *A Lecture*, 11. For Woodbridge and his principles of musical education in relation to this lecture, see Lloyd Sunderman, "The Era of Beginnings in American Music Education (1830–1840), *"Journal of Research in Music Education* 4 (1956): 33; John J. Silantien "The Contributions of William Channing Woodbridge to American Music Education," *Contributions to Music Education* 4 (1976): 80–84; Estelle R. Jorgensen, "William Channing Woodbridge's Lecture, 'On Vocal Music as a Branch of Common Education,' Revisited," *Studies in Music* 19 (1985): 1–32.

20. Woodbridge, *A Lecture* 12.

21. See Kevin Barry, *Language, Music and the Sign: A Study in Aesthetics, Poetics and Poetic Practice from Collins to Coleridge* (Cambridge: Cambridge Univ. Press, 1987), 118; John H. Neubauer, *Emancipation of Music,* 184–92; Adolf Nowak, *Hegels Musikästhetik* (Regensburg: Gustav-Bosse, 1971), 163–88; Marlene Schmidt, *Zur Theorie des musikalischen Charakters* (Munich: Musikverlag Emil Katebichler, 1981), 123–30.

22. The concern with interpretation of the musical text is not unique to Romantic theories of music; the interpretive concern in the late eighteenth and early nineteenth centuries, however, begins to specifically address the expressivity of music—"expression" in musical aesthetics of the time primarily signifying the "imitation" or "representation" of feeling, sentiment, or emotion. This project, as all interpretive projects of musical experience, is more or less literary in quality. Romantic musical aesthetics, however, exploited the emptiness of the musical sign and the consequent indeterminacy of musical language. There is never in European aesthetics the notion of a single correct or proper response or interpretation of a musical text. On the precise meaning of "expression" as the representation of emotion, see Neubauer, *Emancipation of Music,* 149–67. On European views of the emptiness or indeterminacy of the musical sign, see Barry *Language, Music, and the Sign,* 10–18.

23. For a discussion of how recordings of music get mobilized 100 years later in American culture, see Holly Kruse "Early Audio Technology and Domestic Space," *Stanford Humanities Review* 3 (Autumn 1993).

24. Thomas Hastings, *A Dissertation on Musical Taste* (Albany: Websters and Skinners, 1822), 5.

25. Ibid., 16.

26. Ibid., 4.

27. Ibid., 5.

28. Ibid., 13–14.

29. Ibid., 198.

30. Ibid., 6–7. Hach and Hayward's journal, the same interpretive imperative is laid on the conductor as well: "He is, or ought to be . . . . an impersonation of the mind of the composer" ("Duties of a Musical Conductor," *Musical Magazine* 1. 7 [Mar. 30, 1839]: 109). In both passages, mimesis operates at the level of textual production: the conductor or performer becomes a second, but specular, composer.

31. *A Dissertation,* 7.

32. Ibid., 18–19.

33. The composer's project is first and foremost an interpretive project: "But though the productions of the musician are of a less durable nature than those of the poet, yet the experience of many generations has proved, that their durability may be

materially promoted by a proper selection and treatment of ideas; and this part of the composer's art, as we have seen, is chiefly derived from extensive analytical examinations of the most approved specimens of ancient and modern composition" (*A Dissertation,* 90).

34. Ibid., 91

35. Ibid., 92.

36. Ibid., 84.

37. Ibid., 84–85.

38. Ibid., 85.

39. This self-centered aspect of "perverted" music is stressed also by "Professor Nixon": "[Music] if perverted in its offices, may subserve the views of unholy ambition" ("On the Influence of Music," *American Annals of Education* 5 [Nov. 1835]: 508).

40. *A Dissertation,* 18.

41. Ibid., 71.

42. Ibid., 19.

43. Ibid., 53.

44. Ibid., 66.

45. Ibid., 132.

46. Ibid., l05.

47. Ibid., 108.

48. Ibid., 22.

49. Ibid., 88.

50. Ibid., 13. Hastings specifically uses "association" to explain how the music of the theater, which attempts to imitate natural events, acquires its meaning: "Hence it happens, that one who but rarely visits the theatre, is usually displeased with much of the musick that he hears on such occasions. The constant frequenters of the theatre have acquired by means of habitual association, such powers of conception as are quite unknown to him" (ibid., 115–16).

51. Ibid., 13.

52. Ibid., 88.

Part 2
Disciplined and Disciplining
Music

OLA STOCKFELT

Adequate Modes of Listening
(Translated by Anahid Kassabian and
Leo G. Svendsen)

Towards evening, I am totally exhausted, but I can finally sink into the seat and relax. The roar of the engines and the hiss from the vents is almost deafening.[1] Under normal circumstances, I detest those sounds, but now they give me the marvelous confirmation that I have made it—I have finally got past all those unexpected and absurd obstacles that forced me to run around and around, all day, in the heat, from office to office and from airport to airport, even though I had my reservation and was ready to depart in the morning. Between this buzz and the noise from fellow passengers, mild individual flute tones find their way to me, tones that further confirm my impression that I have finally reached a place where I can relax. It takes a few minutes before I can even muster the attention to listen to what is actually being played: it is the first movement of Mozart's Symphony no. 40, the "Great G-minor," in an arrangement for flute soloist and some kind of rock group. The flutist seems totally unengaged; as do the other musicians, when it is even possible to distinguish what they are playing. Moreover, the arranger has mutilated the movement quite brutally—large sections are simply absent. As long as I wasn't listening closely, it was perfect music for the situation, but now I start to be both irritated and interested—and not at all at home any more.

What does it mean to treat good music like that?

It is clear that, during its two-hundred-year history, Mozart's Symphony no. 40 has been not *one* work but rather a series of different works with different meanings in different contexts. It is unclear whether the symphony may be said to have existed at all as a "living" work during the fifteen years following its composition insofar as it may not have been performed.

J. J. de Momigny, a music encyclopedist who may serve as a spokesman for Paris audiences at the beginning of the nineteenth century, treats Mozart's Symphony no. 40 as a musical drama approximating a verbal, scenic drama. As such, he regards the symphony as a "classic" work (that is, worthy of imitation), but in certain respects too radical to be understood as a continuous entity if the listener lacks the opportunity to study the score (or script) carefully in advance. He considers the central parts of the first movement incomprehensible on first hearing because of their extended experimentation with ambivalent harmonies and their use of enharmonic "tricks";[2] putative dialogues are presented, moreover, in a rhetorically incorrect fashion, so as to seem almost absurd; and certain parts—quite against the rules of drama— lack actors identifiable as subjects.

As the symphony began to be performed more frequently, the earliest German reviews characterized it as a grandiose and innovative work, well worthy of and demanding performance, but also colossal and difficult, an exhausting challenge for orchestras—especially for those musicians with solo parts (!). To perform the symphony counted as at once daring and praiseworthy; to listen to it was to listen to something new, modern, and avant-garde, as well as affording the instructive spectacle of musicians striving to master a technically complicated masterpiece.

As time went on and the concert repertoire expanded (notably through the agency of Beethoven), Mozart's Symphony no. 40 began to be regarded as a relatively balanced work, a work with "classical" proportions—something to which one could refer and which one could use as a model when arguing against the "excesses" of newer music.[3] By the end of the 1820s, the symphony was definitively established as a normal, familiar part of the orchestral repertoire—a standard work that was no longer particularly exceptional but still enjoyable. In fact, the symphony was beginning to seem old-fashioned and unusually small in scale. Enhanced orchestration, however, rendered it sufficiently powerful to remain part of the standard symphonic repertoire.

Such adaptations of the symphony, fitting it to new listeners and new listening contexts, however, raised protests on the part of those "educated" listeners who considered "classical" music the carrier of eternal values. In opposition to the contemporaneous commercially controlled concert practice dominated by novelty and modernity, such classicizing listeners managed to establish a sort of "refuge for the higher art," encompassing both performances and academic discussion. This refuge reified a classical repertoire, a classicist performance praxis, explicit normative rules for an adequate approach to this classicist-performed classical repertoire, and an explicit language for discussing the music as it was recreated by listeners under these conditions: in short, a musical discourse reified these conditions as basic human principles inseparable from the concept of music. Within the confines of this refuge, the Symphony no. 40 could be given a specific eternal value insofar as it constituted a part of the normative structure of classical music. The work, as it was recreated by the educated listener through established performance praxis, could in this way become its own norm.

At the same time, the symphony continued to live on in other forms outside the "refuge for the higher art." These other forms, however, established no basis either for academic discussion or for any explicit ideological frame. Thus the refuge and its privileged denizen, the "classical cultural heritage," can be seen as a special case of a more general tendency. The performance and reception of the symphony have always changed to a greater or lesser extent as new listening situations have arisen, and the "work" has correspondingly taken on different types of meaning in these different situations— all of which have differed more or less radically from those that existed when the work was composed or when it was performed for the first time.

In the concert hall, the symphony was adapted to the other repertoire and to the audience's expectations of orchestral sound. Inside concert halls, the physical preserves of the "refuge for the higher art," an idealized picture of Mozart and Viennese classicism, in tandem with an ideologically based picture of an ideal relation between individual and music, shaped the symphony's performance. As the concert hall tradition evolved, the symphony also became a medium for interpretation, something on which a conductor could leave his own personal stamp; and listening for differences in interpretation, for marks of the conductor's artistry, became an obvious part of this tradition. The symphony was much rearranged to render it performable in the context of the bourgeois salon, that is, to render it a plausible backdrop for conversation and flirtation. Restaurant orchestras, theater orchestras, organ players, and brass ensembles presumably each dictated changes to the work so that it would correspond to the conventions and requirements of these respective groups and modes of performance—changes that in different ways stemmed from the music's subservience to other simultaneous activities. Towards the 1960s and 1970s, music listening became simultaneous with an ever-broader range of situations; consequently, as the vacillation of attention between music and other activities became the norm, the symphony would be rewritten with rather arbitrary break points to facilitate "soundbite" listening.[4]

One should note that with the exception of adaptations for "sound bite listening," these changes have mainly involved aspects of reorchestration, either of the symphony as a unified work or at most of its four relatively independent movements. In other words, the formal structure of the single movements has been left untouched in those situations in which the music is intended to occupy the center of the listener's attention, whether in the concert hall, in the bourgeois salon, or performed by the radio orchestra. However, in situations in which the music has a secondary function, or in which listening is one of several equally important activities, changes to the formal structure of individual movements have replaced development over time, and attention has tended to focus on single musical moments that become increasingly independent and free-standing.

Renditions of Mozart's Symphony no. 40, or indeed of any work, have hence always been adjusted to the activity of the listener and to the listener's way of listening: partly according to the different musical contexts; partly according to different views of the relation between music, the individual, and society; and partly according to the different activities the listener could be expected to perform at the same time as listening to the music. As contemporary society and the role of music in that society have changed, new ways of listening have developed that have made the experience of the symphony a meaningful part of these new contexts.

To denote these different ways of listening, to denote the different things *for which* a listener can listen in relation to the sound of music, I have chosen to use the term *modes of listening*.[5] Identically-sounding musical works, listened to through different modes of listening, may engender different kinds of music experiences and even experiences of fundamentally different musical works. New modes of listening have been developed for new relations between listener and music and in relation to new repertoires. Moreover, these new modes of listening have demanded changes in established performance praxis and in rearrangements of established works—the composition of new music being only one obvious change. Today, when a vast spectrum of musical styles are an available, nearly unavoidable part of everyday life, and when the same piece of music can exist in a number of widely differentiated listening situations, each listener has a great repertoire of modes of listening that corresponds to the great repertoire of styles of music and listening situations in the everyday soundscape.

Western industrialized nations today form a more or less homogeneous culture dominated musically by European and North American "art music" and Anglo-American popular music. Through the phonograph record, radio, and television, the same music is to a great extent scattered across the entire world.[6] Each hearing person who listens to the radio, watches TV, goes to the movies, goes dancing, eats in restaurants, goes to supermarkets, participates in parties, has built up, has been *forced* (in order to be able to handle her or his perceptions of sound)—to build up an appreciable competence in translating and using the music impressions that stream in from loudspeakers in almost every living space. Such competence results not primarily from any formalized schooling but from different everyday learning processes as we teach ourselves which of the sounds that ebb and surge across the modern cityscape at every instant of the day should be clustered together and understood as music and which should be understood as something else; which different types of music correlate with which activity and which subculture;

which type of intramusical meanings attach to different types of sound in different musical contexts. The mass-media musical mainstream (in the widest sense of the phrase) has hence become something of a nonverbal lingua franca, one common cultural repertoire transcending traditional culture, class, and age boundaries.[7] Alongside this common cultural competence, many listeners also live in one or several more or less profiled subcultures with a more specialized musical language.[8]

At the same time, the same listeners have the competence to use the same type of music, even the same piece of music, in a variety of different ways in different situations. The symphony that in the concert hall or on earphones can give an autonomous intramusical experience, tuning one's mood to the highest tension and shutting out the rest of the world, may in the café give the same listeners a mildly pleasant, relaxed separation from the noise of the street. At the movies (like the use of Mozart's Symphony no. 40's first movement in a James Bond film)[9] or on television (like the main theme from the same movement in the introduction trailer for the 1987 world ice hockey championships in Vienna), parts of the same work may clearly designate the persons and environments shown according to categories of class and cultural status. And on the car radio in rush hour traffic (if the radio can't be shut off) the same music may constitute an annoying hazard to road safety.

In this way, the situation in which one encounters music conditions the music itself. Particularly with regard to music within the communal repertoire, one can even assume that daily listening is often *more conditioned by the situation in which one meets the music than by the music itself, or by the listener's primary cultural identity*, at least within that more or less homogeneous cultural sphere that comprises Western industrialized environments. Which mode of listening the listener adopts in a given situation depends mainly on how the listener chooses to listen—that is, which mode of listening he or she chooses to develop or adopt. And yet this choice is neither totally free nor accidental.

In part, every mode of listening demands a significant degree of competence on the part of the listener (and the competence will not be less by being shared by many), and no listener can have an infinite repertoire of modes of listening. The mode of listening a listener can adopt is in this way limited by the competences in modes of listening that he or she possesses or can develop in a given situation. Momigny, for example, could only with difficulty discern the second theme in the Symphony no. 40's first movement, and then only after having studied the score.[10] *In part*, not every mode of listening is in any immediate way adaptable to every type of sound structure or even to every type of musical work. The kind of rhetoric Momigny listened for when he heard the exchanges between instrument groups in the second theme was not to be found in the music he was hearing.

In part, different modes of listening are in different ways more or less firmly connected to specific listening situations. For example, to dance during a symphony concert (practically impossible because of the fixed seats) is to commit a gaffe, a breach of social convention, even if one is hearing Viennese waltzes or other music originally meant to accompany dancing. It is likewise inappropriate to sink into prolonged intramusical contemplation when one is squeezed into a 7-11-type convenience store.

In part, finally, the listener's choice of strategies is not entirely free. It can be impossible, for example, to choose to listen in an autonomously reflexive mode if too many other things are competing for attention, and impossible to refuse to listen—to dishearken—to very strong and profiled sounds, or to musemes with a special significance for the listener.[11] Different listeners are also conscious to different degrees of their own choice of mode of listening, and are moreover able to adapt a chosen mode of listening in different situations in relation to different types of sound structures.

See figure 6.1 below for a graphic representation of listening. The screening field between the listener's repertoire of modes (vertical lines), listener situation (lines running from upper left to lower right), the music (lines running from upper right to lower left), and listener strategy (horizontal lines) composes in this way for a given listener in a given situation the number of different possible modes of listening (center of the diagram).

In this way, the field of "possible modes of listening" above is of different breadths for different listeners.[12]

Modes of listening may be described, like listening experiences themselves, as transcendental insofar as any mode of listening is always developed by an individual as she/he strives to make her/his picture of the world com-

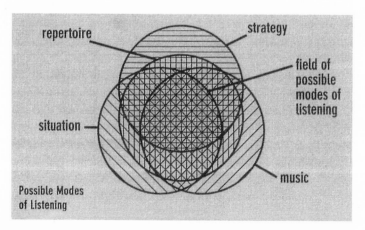

Figure 6.1. A Graphic Representation of Listening.

prehensible. In this fashion, every form of knowledge is, on the other hand, transcendental. Inasmuch as the modes of listening are a more general category than the experience of listening—a mode of listening contains a basic structure for the experience of listening, *for whatever* a listener listens, not the specific result of this experience in relation to a specific piece of music in a specific situation—they are also more generally communicable. This discussion of modes of listening primarily touches not the individual subject but the epistemic subject.[13] Hence it is possible to make constructive generalizations about the type and result of different modes of listening (in music experience) where one analyzes the listening. The possibility of communicating in and about specific modes of listening has also been demonstrated through the theoretical framework that was developed during the late nineteenth century to explain bourgeois concert listening. In the same way, it is possible and constructive to make such generalizations when one shapes music education in order to impart the knowledge and the concern for knowledge that are the prerequisite for specific modes of listening (i.e., when teaching situations are laid out such that the students will develop such knowledge and desire for knowledge).

Different opinions about what one can or ought to listen for in a piece of music, which mode of listening one has to develop, and in which situations of listening one can or ought to meet the piece of music have resulted in different ideals of performance practices, in different kinds of program design, and even in radical rearrangements. Mozart's Symphony no. 40 is a piece of music that has, over nearly two hundred years, been varied in each of these ways in order to be fitted to different specific situations of listening.

Today, one can hear almost any style of music in any surrounding and in any situation. The sound of big opera ensembles can be fitted onto a windsurfing board, and the sound of a nylon-stringed guitar can fill a football stadium; one can listen to march music in the bathtub and salon music in the mountains. This state of affairs is still quite novel. Not that long ago, one was obliged to go to the opera to hear opera, and the only way to hear the guitar was to sit rather close to the performer. Various musical styles were implicitly bound to specific environments and specific relationships between the performer and the listener.

Today the coupling of musical style and listener situation is less a result of enforcing material conditions than of the relatively free choice of the listener. (On the other hand, the choice can never be totally free—it demands a goodly amount of material investment to be able to listen to any kind of music style in any situation, but in the industrialized world these investments ought not to be wholly insurmountable for more than a few adults.)[14]

That all music *styles* today can take place in almost all environments does not mean, however, that all music has an equal relation to each different environment. Opera's style developed first of all in relation to the spaces, the economic means, the listeners, and the listeners' actions, that were typical for the opera environment. Symphonies developed primarily in relation to the concert hall. That both opera and symphonies have been performed in many different environments, and today can be listened to (even if not performed) in almost any environment, does not change the fact that opera and concert halls, as buildings and social environments, have played a central role in the development of opera and symphony: through the development of modes of listening, these environments have created the structure and made understandable the sound structures of operas and symphonies. The opera house and the concert hall as environments are as much integral and fundamental parts of the musical *genres* "opera" and "symphony" as are the purely intramusical means of style.[15]

Each style of music, even if it can make an appearance almost anywhere today, is shaped in close relation to a few environments. In each genre, a few environments, a few situations of listening, make up the constitutive elements in this genre: "The distance between musician and audience, between spectator and spectator, the overall dimension of the events are often fundamental elements in the definition of a genre, and often guide the participants, in the right or wrong way in determining what they should expect about other rules of genre; often 'how you are seated' says more about the music that will be performed than a poster does."[16]

Such an environment can be concretely tangible, like a concert hall, a *palais de danse*, or a church; but it may also be more difficult to localize. Loudspeakers constitute a sort of musical environment, just as one can say that in certain contexts "radio offerings" in their own right constitute a musical environment—not as tangible as a church but not less real.

For recently produced works of music, the style-specific and genre-specific environments have often been identical. Music that is intended for performance in a concert hall has been produced for the concert hall situation. For music mainly targeted toward play on car stereos, one can, for instance, use small speakers that simulate car stereos during the mixing. For works of music that have existed for a longer time, however, the discrepancy can be considerable: this is the case, for example, when liturgical or predominantly dance music is performed in the concert hall for a seated public engaged in aesthetic contemplation. In these instances the changed situation of listening has meant greater or lesser changes in the work of music as sound and especially in the *perceived* work of music.[17]

For each musical genre, a number of listening situations in a given historical situation constitute the genre-specific relation between music and listener. These determine the genre-defining property and the ideal relation between music and listener that were presumed in the formation of the musical style— in the composing, the arranging, the performance, the programming of the music. I have chosen to call these *genre-normative listening situations.*

Genre-normative listening situations are not absolute but are perpetually changing in tandem with the changes in society, in the same way that musical styles change. The private music rooms of late eighteenth-century connoisseurs, for example, engendered a totally different relationship between the listener and the music from those attaining in the opera hall or concert hall, relationships that in their turn differed from those characteristic of the bourgeois salon and restaurant. These different situations hence demanded or made possible different types of musical performance (in spite of the fact that the works being performed might be identical on paper). The situations, and the different performances, also demanded or made possible different modes of listening, and hence resulted in different musical experiences.

Consequently, each genre also has a number of *genre-normative modes of listening*, and even these have changed over time in relationships corresponding to styles of music, to choices of strategies of the listener, to the genre-normative situations of listening, and to a series of social factors. The reflexive, active attitude of musicians to music is a mode of listening that is probably (to some extent) common to almost all forms of "music" (for instance, if one also counts electronic music composers as performing musicians). Other normative modes of listening, like the normative user situations, can almost become defining characteristics for other genres of music.

I have chosen to call each listening in a genre-normative listening situation with its situation-associated genre-normative mode of listening *adequate listening*. Adequate listening hence occurs when one listens to music according to the exigencies of a given social situation and according to the predominant sociocultural conventions of the subculture to which the music belongs.

As a rule, a genre comprises several types of adequate listening. The person who performs music listens with a different type of concentration than do people who are simply listening; but both types of listening can surely be adequate to the genre. Both those who are caught up in the music and dance wildly out on the floor and those who stand close to the stage and concentrate, admiring and studying the virtuosity of the solo guitarist, show adequate attitudes at a blues-rock concert; on the other hand, someone who leans back and with half-closed eyes tries to follow the tonal and thematic tension, relations, and dissolutions is probably not listening adequately.

To listen adequately hence does not mean any particular, better, or "more musical," "more intellectual," or "culturally superior" way of listening. It means that one masters and develops the ability to listen for what is relevant to the genre in the music, for what is adequate to understanding according to the specific genre's comprehensible context. Adequate listening is not a prerequisite of assimilating or enjoying music, of learning how to recognize musical styles, or how to create meaning for oneself from what music expresses; it *is* a prerequisite of using music as a language in a broader sense, as a medium for real communication from composer, musician, or programmer to audience/listener. In live situations, an adequately listening audience may also be the prerequisite for the performers' ability to perform genre-adequate music in genres that build on reciprocal communication between executors and listeners. Adequate listening, with adequate modes of listening in an adequate situation, is a normative part of music genre, in the same way that sounding material is.

Adequate listening is, like all languages, always the result of an informal (although sometimes formalized) contract between a greater or smaller group of people, an agreement about the relation of the musical means of expression to this group's picture of the world. Adequate listening is hence always in the broadest sense ideological: it relates to a set of opinions belonging to a social group about ideal relations between individuals, between individuals and cultural expression, and between the cultural expressions and the construction of society.

In contemporary Western society, idealized bourgeois concert hall listening—which was developed especially in the latter part of the nineteenth century in relation to the listening and repertoires of concert hall situations—is situated in a special position. This is so for two reasons: (1) such listening was given priority in state cultural policy and educational policy efforts and was a part of the cultural legitimacy of the governing elite; and (2) perhaps most importantly, this musical language more than any other has become formalized and made translatable into other formalized languages, i.e. the verbal, which in turn was enriched and accommodated to meet the need for effective means of translation.

Up to a point, a relatively functional explicit language has been created, in verbal and graphic form, to describe the experiencing and experiences of a certain type of music, of a certain type of listening. This language, to some extent and for lack of alternatives, could be used to communicate verbally and graphically even about other forms of listening. It has hence become one of the material prerequisites for developing communication and value systems around music even in environments that show few external similarities with the bourgeois idealized concert hall.[18]

The total formal dominance of this language in parts of the academic tradition and music education during the past one hundred years has reified the value categories on which the bourgeois concert-hall listening ideal of adequacy were based. This reification has played a crucial part in the academic (de-)valorization of musical genres that split radically from classical music: the bias in language means that deviations from the concert hall's ideal of adequacy also make it impossible to reply to the reified, absolute, value criteria that were formulated to express that ideal. According to the presumptions of this language, for example, it is logical and correct to create "types of listening" ordered hierarchically according to their relation to the reified norm.[19] On the other hand, it is unclear what value this type of partitioning can have outside the specific genre-related normative situation of listening. Like other modes of listening, this autonomous "expert listening" is adequately applicable to a limited number of genres, and, for certain genres, musical autonomy can even make an adequate listening impossible (as in the example above of the person listening for the tonal and thematic relations in blues-rock who in this way loses the genre-defining adequate expression in the music).

This autonomous reflexive listening is not the only adequate listening to develop and establish itself: people have listened adequately to different music in a number of different ways, even though not all these modes of listening were carried on in a formalized fashion into the present. There has never been only *one* adequate autonomous listening in existence—disagreement between different theoretical schools can be seen as oppositions between different autonomous adequacy ideals that can, perhaps by splitting hairs, be said to constitute different musical genres within the frame of one and the same musical style.

Analysis of a musical genre, or of a work in a musical genre, must contain and be based on analysis of the listening adequate to that genre, of the music as it is experienced as adequate to the genre in the normative listening situations, with an adequate mode of listening, adequate extramusical connotations, and adequate simultaneous activities—this is a prerequisite for the possibility of analyzing the "right" piece of music. However, for analyses of everyday music listening, this is not always enough. Analysis of music in everyday listening situations must be based on listening adequate to the given situation. Such adequacy is not determined by the music style in and of itself, or by the genre within which the music style was created, or by the genre to which it primarily belongs today, but rather by the location of the music in the specific situation. That location determines, for instance, who can fulfill the role of "transmitter" in "the musical communication chain." When analyzing background music that targets a general audience in a specific situation, one might therefore develop a strategy of making the music understandable as it is meant to be made understandable by the arranger and programmer. An analysis based on a one-sided, concentrated, autonomous listening will be an analysis of the wrong object, even if the music analyzed originally was created for such a mode of listening. This constraint naturally creates special methodological problems, inasmuch as an adequately adapted "background listening" makes continuous reflexive consciousness impossible. An analysis must therefore begin from such shifts between modes of listening, between foreground and background.

A characteristic common to the various "popular music" arrangements of Mozart's Symphony no. 40 is that, in comparison to the original, they are (today) better suited to listening modes directed towards momentary identification, and worse suited to listening modes directed towards the intramusical developments over long periods of time that the sonata form, for instance, presupposes. The arrangements are consequently better suited than the original for the type of shifts that occur when music is used in certain contemporary everyday listening situations, as accompaniment to different occupations—shifts between attention to the music and attention to other simultaneous activities.[20]

Such shifts between different listening modes, between different forms of attentive listening and more or less complete disregard of (or "dishearkening" to) the music, are not solely a contemporary development, although they have perhaps become more common since technical developments have made music more generally available. Such shifts between listening modes can even be regarded as the normal case when the music has been used in assembly halls, in restaurants, and the like, and of course when it has been a part of more integrated complexes, such as opera or film. It is the continuous and one-sided autonomous concentrated listening that must be regarded as a special case—the point at the extreme left in the following figure.

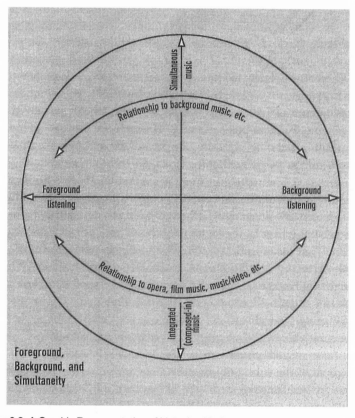

Figure 6.2. A Graphic Representation of Listening Modes.

The axis from left to right concerns musical experience, the listener's action toward the music: toward the left is music as foreground and listening as the major activity, while to the right, music tends toward background and listening toward secondary activity. The axis from top to bottom concerns the piece of music—the composer's, the performer's, the arranger's, or the programmer's intentions concerning the music's relations to intended simultaneous activities: at the bottom music is a totally integrated part of a greater totality that occupies all the listener's senses (as part of a *Gesammt-kunstwerk*), whereas at the top the music is a completely separate activity, simultaneous to others. The two arched arrows represent the usual listener activity, with shifts between different degrees of foreground listening and background listening: the upper for usual background listening, the lower for usual music listening in connection with film, opera, and so on. The point to the extreme left, the total and continuously concentrated, completely autonomous listening, has its counterpart farthest to the right in the complete "dishearkening" of the music. Both these extreme points, which can be exemplified with the Adornian "expert listener's" ideal activity at one end and the acts performed by those who "without will" let themselves be seduced and ruled by background music without even being conscious of its presence at the other, must be considered as just that: extreme points, exceptions. More interesting are the more usual listening activities in which the listener's strategy is to shift between different listening modes and to pay various degrees of attention to the music.

An example of the tension between idealized concert hall listening and one of the more common everyday "idle listening" modes occurred when I heard the strains of Mozart's Symphony no. 40 on an airplane just about to take off from Montreal to Amsterdam in a recording with Berdien Stenberg. The experience signaled a shift from an "idle listening" totally adequate to the situation to an attempt to adopt an autonomous, reflexive, concert-hall-like listening inadequate to the situation. The final question—"What does it mean to treat good music like that"—was obviously an incongruous one. In the given situation of listening, criteria other than those of the concert hall should have applied. There must be a relation between form and dynamic structure in applied music, for instance, such that the music's central features remain perceptible even in a sound environment that drowns all finer nuances, even at a volume low enough for passengers to talk, which itself is a prerequisite of carrying out smoothly the primary activity in the situation, locating seats in an airplane. In other words, it must be possible for almost all travelers both to "dishearken" and to enjoy (or at least to be appropriately soothed by) the music in that somewhat vacuous situation that reigns at intercontinental departures as feverish activity alternates with enforced aimless waiting. Mozart's original version in such a situation could hardly be unambiguously "good" music: any recording preserving the original orchestration in such a sound environment would either register as completely silent during certain passages or as deafeningly strong during others, for the volume of all such recordings is too varied, and they contain too many finely tuned nuances. Sections of the symphony, especially parts of the development section, would demand the concentrated and virtually continuous attention of those who are seated and waiting for departure if they were to understand the work in a manner adequate to the genre, and those hitherto unfamiliar with the symphony would probably need to hear at least a movement in its entirety for their listening to "measure up." On the other hand, Stenberg's recording, almost constant in volume, its clearly mixed melodic voice serving as the carrying and always audible unifying factor, and its avoidance of fundamental harmonic and thematic changes over time, must be considered "good" music—music well suited to the circumstances. The arrangement is thus utterly in accordance with the established principles that also have produced, for example, the "standard concert hall versions": it is an adequate adaptation to the demands of a new user situation on the music.

Different listening situations give different norms of quality, both for the piece of music and for the activity of the listener. As long as I listened with dispersed interest, I was charmed by the sound without analyzing the source more closely. I adopted an adequate mode of listening (out of several possible ones), and the music could therefore play a meaningful role in relation to the world (the music was "pleasant for the ear" without being "too much of a symphony," as Theo van Leeuwen expressed it.)[21]

When I began to listen concentratedly, however, I applied an inadequate mode of listening—not because the music shouldn't or couldn't be adequate to listen to in a concentrated way, but because I measured it according to norms appropriate to other listening situations and other music. I applied an incorrect concentrated mode of listening. Rather than paying attention to the qualities that were in fact present in the music, what I experienced was the lack of a set of expected but unrealized musical qualities: the work acquired meaning as a focus for irritation, but not as a meaningful work of music. As an "idle listener," I possessed the competence that was necessary for an adequate dedication to the music, but as a concentrated listener I was excluded by the exclusiveness of the music, insofar as I was not able to develop (or did not master) a genre-adequate mode of listening.

When considering music that, like Stenberg's recording, is especially suited (possibly with intent) to "sound bite listening" with its rather arbitrary breaking points, to shifting between different activities (of which listening to the music is one), and to shifting between different modes of listening, our analysis of that music should center precisely on its suitability for such shifts between modes of listening and between varying degrees of attention. The shift between different modes of listening is hence both an object of analysis and a means of analysis. In other words, for it to be possible to analyze this music adequately as it appears in everyday listening situations, a fragmented listening must guide us in determining both *which* parameters in the music merit closer consideration in a more concentrated and reflexive study and *how* these parameters should be considered. Hence we must develop our competence reflexively to control the use of, and the shifts between, different modes of listening to different types of sound events. In the same way that we must listen to the urban soundscape as "music" in order to make it more human, thereby developing the competence to draw up active goals for the "composition" of a more human sound environment, we must develop the competence to listen to that music precisely *as* a part of the soundscape in order to explain and change the position of the music in this soundscape. Insofar as we strive to understand today's everyday music and want to develop pedagogical programs with real relevance to those who will live and participate in this musical life, we must develop our own reflexive consciousness and competence as active "idle listeners."

NOTES

1. This article is a translation of the final chapter of Ola Stockfelt's *Musik som lyssnandets konst (Music as the Art of Listening)*. In the work as a whole, he analyzes Mozart's Symphony no. 40 in G minor (K. 550), in a variety of arrangements and contexts over its 200-year history, arguing that the listening that grounds the academic study of music—autonomous, reflexive, concert-hall listening—misses the features of music that are most important for analysis. *Music as the Art of Listening* presents close studies of performance and reception in Paris at the turn of the nineteenth century, in central Europe in four periods from 1798 to 1848, in bourgeois salons and homes, in public places such as restaurants at the turn of the twentieth century, in arrangements for phonograph recordings, and in arrangements intended as background music in public places. Analyzing the shifts and changes in the work in each of these contexts, Stockfelt contends that music is composed, arranged, and performed in relation to specific listening contexts and activities, that different modes of listening create or recreate the sound patterns as different pieces of music, and that the different productions and consumptions are more or less appropriate to, or adequate to, each other.

The opening paragraph of this selection is also the opening paragraph of the entire work, where it is set off, as it is here, as an epigraph.

2. Techniques or procedures that seemed, according to the compositional standards of the period, to imply an obvious disdain for the common listener.

3. It was in this way the discussion of Beethoven's work, rather than that of Mozart's work itself, that indirectly turned Mozart's Symphony no. 40 into a balanced, "classical" work: see the discussion of Beethoven's "Eroica" symphony, *Allgemeine Musikalische Zeitung*, Apr. 1805.

4. In Swedish, *momentant lyssnande* implies both speed and discreteness (definitions of *moment* include "factor," "element," and "instant"). We have chosen "soundbite" here at Stockfelt's suggestion to convey both these senses—trans.

5. Modes of listening are of course not limited to music, though listening that results in some sort of music experience is the primary interest in this context. In a more general discussion of an individual's relation to her or his sound environment, it may be more appropriate to separate more clearly the listening modes that contain a focusing toward the sound's and sound structures' qualitative, information-carrying, nonverbal aesthetic aspects. Musical listening modes would then describe such listening modes in which the listener in some way selects, structures, and experiences a part of the sound environment as music. The speech-choirs on Chicago's first LP, the sirens in Varèse's "Ionization," John Cage's "4'33"," Schaffer's concrete music, and the current rich flowering of music in which sampling synthesis has begun to employ the most varied everyday sounds (especially as rhythmical accompaniment) are all examples of nonmusical sounds that have become musical by being placed in a context where the listener has been able to perceive it from an aestheticizing perspective, a musical listening mode, in some way. The same process accounts for the introduction of the trumpet in European Renaissance music. Neither speech-choirs, sirens, nor trumpets instantaneously lost their original extramusical content by being worked into a musical context—on the contrary, their commonly known (if ultimately transient) extramusical connotations enriched the music's nonverbal communicative meaning-bearing function for those who were able to fit an adequate listening mode for this music (see the third section of this essay). As the society and sound environment changed, the knowledge of different sounds' extramusical connotations also changed—for an average listener it is reasonable to expect that the trumpets, for example, will be understood today as musical instruments to approximately the same extent as saxophones or flutes, whereas quite different sounds tend to be used nowadays to signify war. In this way, the competence for listening to music with trumpets that was adequate just a couple of centuries ago has since been lost. Instead, new intramusical modes have been formalized as "adequate." This means, from a listener-historical perspective, that in practice a new "music" has been created from the sound material in old compositions, even if one performs the music "faithfully to its original" without changing one single tone or one single instrument.

The development of such musical listening modes in relation to the daily sound environment can be seen as a presumption for the type of soundscaping R. M. Schafer has proposed.

6. See Roger Wallis and Krister Malm, *Big Sounds from Small People: The Music Industry in Small Countries* (Göteborg, Sweden: Skrifter från musikvetenskapliga institutionen vid Göteborgs Universitet, no. 7, 1984), and Jeremy Tunstall, *The Media Are American: Anglo-American Media in the World*, Communication and Society series (London: Constable, 1977).

7. Philip Tagg convincingly demonstrates both the common competence of adequately understanding and contextually placing different musical structures through the process of reflexive listening and the fact that listeners for the most part understand the musical semiotic content in such situations in the same way, across cultural areas in other ways considerably separated (Tagg and Clarida, unpublished report on listeners' responses to film and television title themes).

8. See Ulf Hannerz's discussion of "cultural repertoires" in Hannerz, "Research in the Black Ghetto: A Review of the Sixties," *Discovering Afro-America*, ed. Roger D. Abrahams and John F. Szwed (Leiden: International Studies in Sociology and So-

cial Anthropology, E. J. Brill, 1975) and Hannerz, "Delkulturerna och helheten" ("Subcultures and the Totality"), *Kultur och medvetande (Culture and Consciousness)*, ed. Ulf Hannerz, Rita Liljeström, and Orvar Löfgren (Göteborg: Akademilitteratur, 1982).

9. *The Living Daylights*, 1988.

10. Stockfelt discusses Momigny's responses in chap. 3 of *Music as the Art of Listening*—trans.

11. Minimal fragments of musical meaning. See Philip Tagg, *Kojak, 50 Seconds of Television Music—toward the Analysis of Affect in Popular Music* (Göteborg: Skrifter från Musikvetenskapliga institutionen vid Göteborgs Universitet No. 2, 1979)—trans.

12. To broaden this field—to develop the listener's register of modes of listening and to develop the possibility, the freedom, to adapt as many parts as possible of the register in as many situations and in relation to as many parts of the sound environment as possible, in a way that enriches and expands the interaction of the listener with her- or himself and her or his capacity to control the sound aspects of her or his existence—what could be called "musical listener-emancipation"—may be seen as a pedagogical goal.

13. These terms are used here according to Piaget's dictum that "structuralism calls for a differentiation between the individual subject, who does not enter at all, and the epistemic subject, that cognitive nucleus which is common to all subjects at the same level" (Jean Piaget, *Structuralism* [London: Routledge and Kegan Paul, 1973], 139).

14. Assuming, of course, that we are not speaking of live performance here; see below. It should also be noted that the investments involved are probably prohibitive for fewer adults in Sweden than in the U.S., despite the fact that stereos, walkmen, and the like are cheaper here—trans.

15. In the distinction between style and genre I have followed the definition of the term *genre* that Franco Fabbri has proposed: "A musical genre is a set of musical events (real or possible) whose course is governed by a set of socially accepted rules" (Franco Fabbri, "A Theory of Musical Genres: Two Applications," *Popular Music Perspectives*, ed. David Horn and Philip Tagg [Göteborg and Exeter: International Association for the Study of Popular Music, 1981], 52). He gives this definition in relation to and as critique of the praxis: "In most musicological literature which has tackled the problem of genres . . . [in which] . . . the formal and technical roles seem to be the only ones taken into consideration, to the point where genre, style and form become synonymous" (55), a critique which I mainly share, but which began to be out of date after Fabbri's article (cf. Björnberg, *En Liten Sång*). Fabbri's concept of genre is in line with the arguments I have put forward above about the social exclusivity and about the concept of music. For the formally and technically specific elements in isolation, I have used the term *style*.

16. Fabbri, "A Theory of Musical Genres," 57.

17. One could even say that changes in the listening situation, and therefore in the modes of listening, have created totally new works of music—in cases where the sounding structure in the original context wasn't being perceived as music.

18. For many of autonomous music aesthetics' valorized concepts, such as "personally deep impression," "intense," "dramatic," "introduction-climax-ending," etc., agreements with other genres have been found and developed (perhaps first and foremost the ones that build on vocal forms like blues and jazz). These valorized concepts

partly constitute what is understood as "real music" even in other contexts. But it is not obvious that they are the most important parameters in all forms of music usage—in many contexts they are directly unwanted. The same thing goes for autonomous listening as such, which is often held up as an ideal even for styles that developed in genres without musical autonomy.

19. See Theodor Adorno, *Introduction to the Sociology of Music*, trans. E. B. Ashton (New York: Continuum, 1989), 1–20.

20. The same thing can be said to hold true for Theo van Leeuwen's use of the first part of the Symphony no. 40 in background music contexts, when at low volume it accompanies primary simultaneous activities. In an interview with the author, van Leeuwen said he uses (i.e., has obtained the reproduction rights to) a recording with the mysterious "Salzburg Mozart Orchestra! Whatever it may be, but it can be . . . The Dutch . . . ah . . . or the symphony orchestra of Amsterdam, acting under another name or . . . maybe it's an additional recording, that you don't know," a rather placid recording in which the first movement takes 7'47". But in the contexts in which van Leeuwen intends his program to be used, the choice of recording plays a minor role, as long as it isn't too catchy or technically deficient, since the programs are not intended for more than occasional active listening. See also note 20—trans.

21. Van Leeuwen produces background music packages for Philips Background Music Service in the Netherlands, one of the largest producers in the world of the music known colloquially as "elevator music" and are roughly as well known in Europe as is the company whose name has become the other standard colloquial term for the genre in the U.S. *Music as the Art of Listening* contains the extended interview with van Leeuwen quoted in note 20—trans.

ROBERT WALSER

"Out of Notes"
Signification, Interpretation, and the
Problem of Miles Davis

I played "My Funny Valentine" for a long time—and didn't like it—and all of a sudden it meant something.

Miles Davis

A flurry of posthumous tributes to Miles Davis almost managed to conceal the fact that jazz critics and historians have never known how to explain the power and appeal of his playing. Of course, there has been no lack of writing about Davis and no shortage of praise for his accomplishments. For example, *Musician* magazine, which covers jazz but is not primarily devoted to it, launched a cover story with the extraordinary statement "In the entire recording age, no one has meant more to music than Miles Davis."[1] But histories of jazz, biographies of Davis, and jazz journalism often beg the question of *why* he ought to be so highly regarded: there is a curious absence of engagement with Davis's music, and especially with his trumpet playing.

Miles Davis has always been difficult to deal with critically: along with his controversial personal life and his even more controversial decision to "go electric" around 1969, Davis has long been infamous for missing more notes than any other major trumpet player. While nearly everyone acknowledges his historical importance as a band leader and a musical innovator, and while for decades large audiences flocked to his concerts, critics have always been made uncomfortable by his "mistakes," the cracked and missed notes common in his performances. "The problem of Miles Davis" is the problem Davis presents to critics and historians: How are we to account for such glaring defects in the performances of someone who is indisputably one of the most important musicians in the history of jazz?

Often critics simply ignore the mistakes. In his history of jazz, Frank Tirro delicately avoided any mention of the controversies surrounding Davis, whether missed notes, drug use, or electric instruments. Joachim Berendt, in *The Jazz Book*, regretfully mentions Davis's "clams" but quickly passes on, and the widely used jazz appreciation text by Mark Gridley, like that of

Donald D. Megill and Richard S. Demory, similarly whitewashes Davis's career.[2] When Howard Brofsky and Bill Cole independently transcribed and published the trumpet solo of Davis's 1964 recording of "My Funny Valentine," both chose to leave out the cracks, slips, and spleeahs, enabling them to produce nice, clean texts and to avoid many problematic aspects of the performance.[3]

Critics sometimes apologize for Davis's flaws or try to explain them away. Bill Cole acknowledges that Davis had what he calls "mechanical problems," but asserts that Davis "used them well to his advantage," building a style out of his weaknesses, forging "his mistakes into a positive result." Gary Giddins similarly credits Davis with "a thoroughly original style built on the acknowledgment of technical limitations." Giddins comments: "By the time of 'My Funny Valentine,' which contains one of the most notorious fluffs ever released, one got the feeling that his every crackle and splutter was to be embraced as evidence of his spontaneous soul."[4] But Giddins himself does not seem convinced by this argument, and he remains unable either to embrace the fluffs or to excuse them. The best that can be said of Miles Davis in this light is that he was a good musician but a bad trumpet player.

James Lincoln Collier, as usual, is bolder than most other critics: "But if his influence was profound, the ultimate value of his work is another matter. Miles Davis is not, in comparison with other men of major influence in jazz, a great improviser. His lines are often composed of unrelated fragments and generally lack coherence. His sound is interesting, but too often it is weakened by the petulant whine of his half-valving. He has never produced the melodic lines of a Parker or Beiderbecke, or the dramatic structure of Armstrong or Ellington. And although certainly an adequate instrumentalist—we should not overstress his technical inadequacies—he is not a great one. Perhaps more important, he has not really been the innovator he is sometimes credited with being. Most of the fresh concepts he incorporated into his music originated with other men, ironically, in view of his black militancy, many of them white. . . . He has to be seen, then, not as an innovator, but as a popularizer of new ideas."[5]

Collier's complaint is that Davis lacks originality, formal regularity, timbral purity and consistency, and technical facility. But would Davis's playing really be better if his sound were more pure and uniform, or his phrases more regular? By claiming that Davis failed to measure up to presumably objective musical standards, Collier suggests that Davis was not a good trumpet player *or* a good musician, despite the popularity and respect he has earned from fans and musicians. Though he is more blunt in his denunciation of Davis than most other jazz critics, Collier's assessment is not unique. But when critical judgments become so out of synch with the actual reception of the music they address, it may be time to reexamine some basic premises. Perhaps there are other methods and criteria to use in analyzing and evaluating jazz; perhaps there is a way of theorizing Davis's playing that would account for its power to affect deeply many listeners.

Miles Davis may be the most important and challenging figure for jazz criticism at the present moment, because he can't be denied a place in the canon of great jazz musicians, yet the accepted criteria for greatness do not fit him well. (The complexity of Duke Ellington's scoring or the virtuosity of Charlie Parker's improvisation, for example, seem to be much easier to explain and to legitimate than Davis's performances.) The uneasiness many critics display toward Miles Davis's "mistakes," and their failure to explain the power of his playing, suggest that there are important gaps in the paradigms of musical analysis and interpretation that dominate jazz studies. Understanding Davis's missed notes, and accounting for his success as a performer, may require rethinking some of our assumptions about what and how music means.

Some useful ways of doing so are implicit in the theory of signification presented by Henry Louis Gates Jr. in his book *The Signifying Monkey: A Theory of African-American Literary Criticism.* I am not the first to remark how much this book has to offer music scholars: John P. Murphy has drawn upon Gates's work in his discussion of dialogue among jazz improvisers; Gary Tomlinson has used Gates's ideas in his excellent essay on jazz canons and Miles Davis's fusion period; and Samuel Floyd has deployed Gates's theory in his insightful analysis of the dialogue of rhythmic relationships and formal conventions in Jelly Roll Morton's "Black Bottom Stomp."[6] But I will argue that Gates's theory of signifying might yet be applied at a finer level of musical analysis, to illuminate the significance of specific musical details and the rhetoric of performance.

At the core of his theory is Gates's delineation of two different ways of thinking about how meanings are produced. Gates distinguishes between two cultural traditions, white "signifying" and black "Signifyin(g)"; as I find the latter a rather cumbersome alteration of the vernacular term, I will refer to these as *signification* and *signifyin'* respectively (*signification* also has the advantage of preserving the static, foundationalist character of the theories of meaning to which Gates refers, while *signifyin'* retains the vernacular focus on agency). The two modes contrast sharply. Signification is logical, rational, limited: from this perspective, meanings are denotative, fixed, exact, and exclusive. Signifyin', conversely, works through reference, gesture, and dialogue to suggest multiple meanings through association. If signification assumes that meanings can be absolute, permanent, and objectively specified, signifyin' respects contingency, improvisation, relativity—the social production and negotiation of meanings. We might compare the way a dictionary prescribes meanings with the ways in which words constantly change meaning in actual usage by communities of language users. The difference is akin to that between semantics and rhetoric: signification assumes that meaning can be communicated abstractly and individually, apart from the circumstances of exchange; signifyin' presumes performance and dialogic engagement.

As Gates himself insists, signifyin' is not exclusive to African-American culture, though it is in that culture that signifyin' has been most fully articulated theoretically, not only by scholars but also in folklore and song lyrics. In fact, the concept could be compared to literary critic Mikhail Bakhtin's ideas about dialogue in the novel or to a variety of other twentieth-century philosophical interrogations of the nature of language and meaning, from Wittgenstein to the American pragmatists to the French poststructuralists.[7] But Gates, while certainly influenced by these critics and theorists, means to illuminate African-American literature by taking seriously the modes of signifyin' developed within black vernacular traditions.

Gates is not the only African-American literary theorist to draw attention to the importance of signifyin', or to attempt to define it. Houston A. Baker Jr. recently equated signifyin' with deconstruction, and Ralph Ellison had earlier defined signifyin' as "rhetorical understatement" in his book *Shadow and Act*.[8] Both definitions highlight the richness and slipperiness of signifyin' as a cultural tradition and a rhetorical strategy. Like Gates, Baker and Ellison point to performance, negotiation, and dialogue with past and present as features of this mode of artistic activity.

Clearly, Gates's theory of signifyin' is opposed to the perspective of modernism. For the modernists, the art work had to be autonomous from mass culture and everyday life; it was the expression of a purely individual consciousness, without social content; such art was supposed to be self-referential, exploring the medium itself. Modernist aesthetic theory has long dominated academic study of the arts, and consequently it has seemed attractive to many jazz critics and scholars as a route to academic prestige and legitimation. At a recent symposium on jazz theory and criticism, Gunther Schuller pondered the question of how to judge jazz, coming up with a characteristically modernist dual answer. On the one hand, he says, we must judge jazz performances or recordings on their own merits, based on the composer's and musicians' intentions and study of the work. On the other hand, we can rely upon certain standards of performance quality and authenticity, the latter encompassing technical accuracy, appropriateness to the style, and originality. That is, art can be understood as intentional, its meanings owned by the artist; but it can also be held accountable to a set of critical standards that are assumed to transcend particular statements or artifacts.[9]

In a response to Schuller's comments published in *New Perspectives on Jazz*, Olly Wilson points out that musical techniques, styles, and procedures are never autonomous; they are organized at a conceptual level, a level of cultural priorities and modes of thought, which must be addressed by criticism. Amiri Baraka argues in the same volume that the critic must understand *how* the work means: an aesthetic, he pointed out, is expressive of a worldview: "subjective, yet reflective of objective political and economic existence."[10] In other words, reactions to art feel personal, but they nonetheless reflect the ways in which even our most personal feelings are socially constituted.

Some jazz critics, then, resist the modernist attitudes that are so antithetical to signifyin'; such critics are dissatisfied with analytical methods that radically reduce musical activities to formal abstractions that often shed little light on how music is experienced. But overall, academics (and some jazz musicians) seem increasingly drawn to what I will call "classicizing" strategies for legitimating jazz. Now, it seems natural enough that people who are trying to win more respect for the music they love should do so by making comparisons with the most prestigious music around, classical music. But the price of classicism is always loss of specificity, just as it has been the price of the canonic coherence of European concert music (the disparate sounds of many centuries, many peoples, many functions, many meanings all homogenized and made interchangeably "great"). Too often, jazz education and scholarship mimic the elitist moral crusade that created the canon of classical music in the last half of the nineteenth century. Audiences are assumed to be passive, the content of jazz is rarely discussed, its relevance to people's lives never examined. It is simply presumed that increased exposure to jazz is somehow good for people: appreciation takes the place of understanding. Moreover, history is distorted when devotees work to separate jazz from the rest of popular music, a move that is meant to put them on the right side of the mass culture/modernism divide.[11]

Such classicization of jazz has even facilitated a nationalist distortion of jazz in the United States. According to such prominent spokespeople for jazz as Billy Taylor, Wynton Marsalis, and Gunther Schuller, jazz is "America's classical music" or "America's one truly indigenous musical art form." It "developed steadily from a single expression of the consciousness of *black* people into a *national* music that expresses American ideals and attitudes to Americans and to people from other cultures all around the world," and it makes a single kind of political statement: "In a typical jazz performance each individual performer contributes his or her personal musical perspective and thereby graphically demonstrates the democratic process at work." Jazz idealizes "the concept of individual freedom."[12]

But characterizing jazz in this way effaces both its complex cultural history, including the myriad effects of racism and elitism on the music and the people who have made it, and the dialogue that is at the very heart of the music. Taylor praised individualism, but what of collaboration: in collective improvisation, in composition, in the ongoing collective transformation of the discourse of jazz? What of the ways in which musicians, as they play, converse with one another, with their audiences, with their forebears? Taylor celebrates the fact that jazz has received substantial support from the U.S.

State Department and that it has been featured on Voice of America radio broadcasts, without considering why this might be so. The answer is that the sort of reading of jazz articulated by Taylor, which emphasizes individualism rather than collectivism, autonomous statements rather than dialogue and collaboration, helped enable the use of jazz as propaganda for capitalism by distorting the nature of the music, by blurring its variety and its debt to the collective struggles of African-Americans, and by effacing the fact that jazz has long flourished outside of the United States.[13] The most obvious failing of the movement to classicize jazz, however, is that it has never been able to do justice to the music: for example, it offers no means of accounting for why Miles Davis misses notes, or even of understanding what he is really doing the rest of the time.

This is in part because musicological treatments of jazz have also been chiefly devoted to legitimation, the main argument having been that jazz is worthwhile because even its improvised solos demonstrate organic unity and motivic coherence.[14] Virtually the whole tradition of musicological analysis of jazz, from Winthrop Sargeant on, has been caught between the admission that jazz is different from classical music (and probably inferior), and the desire to legitimate jazz according to the criteria commonly used to analyze classical music. Jazz scholars have long neglected opportunities to learn about the different premises and values emphasized in African-American culture from scholars and theorists of that culture. The two writers most often credited as the foremost musical analysts of jazz, André Hodeir and Gunther Schuller, applied the vocabulary of academic musical analysis to jazz, labeling chords and motives without seriously questioning the appropriateness of such wholesale methodological transference. Hodeir's allegiance to the European canon allowed him only a single yardstick against which to measure every musical object, regardless of its history, its discursive premises, or its values. And even though Schuller has written an excellent explanation of the sedimented African priorities in jazz, transformed by African-Americans in their new contexts, he has also accepted from musicology the idea that Western art music operates in an autonomous domain; his writings on jazz are colored by his desire to prove that jazz is equally autonomous and thus equally worthy of respect.[15]

Both Hodeir and Schuller often referred to the importance of "objectivity"—a common priority among those who prefer not to interrogate their premises. Schuller celebrated "real quality and musical talent" without any reflection on how those categories come to be created and understood by various social groups; indeed, he searched for "purely musical qualities," deliberately stripping away the "historical and social trappings" that enable sounds to be meaningful to people.[16] In his famous analysis of Sonny Rollins's "Blue 7," Schuller consistently avoided commenting on rhetoric or affect, and reduced the force of Rollins's improvisation to the articulation of unity and order. Though it is clear that Schuller, along with everyone else, hears much more than that in this recording, his precise labeling of musical details and persuasive legitimation of jazz according to long-standing musicological criteria caused many critics to hail this article as a singular critical triumph.[17] All it really tells us about Rollins, however, is that his improvisations are coherent; it says nothing about why we might value that coherence, why we find it meaningful, or how this solo differs from any of a million other coherent pieces of music.

The price of such classicizing formalism is always the loss of affect and history; most jazz analysts and many critics have been modernists willing to make the trade. But Miles Davis, in such terms, would have to be called postmodern. He refused to be constrained by genre boundaries; his music embraced and explored contradictions; he dismissed questions of authenticity or purity; he was unwilling to separate art, life, and politics. These are the traits that led Stanley Crouch to place the blame for contemporary jazz, which he sees as being in a colossal mess, squarely on Davis: he refers to "the mire Miles Davis pushed jazz into." But as Robert Palmer argues, such polemics signal cultural contestation of great import: "Critics and musicians who are still trying to hold the line against this cultural democratization, mostly from the classical and jazz camps, are classist bigots fighting a losing battle with musical and social realities. . . . Davis had a particular knack for getting under these purists' skins."[18] As we will see, Davis's consistent and deliberate use of risky techniques and constant transgression of genre boundaries are antithetical to classicism and cannot be explained by formalism; from such perspectives, unusual content looks like flawed form. That is why so many critics have responded to Davis's music with puzzlement, hostility, or an uneasy silence.

Gates's theory is useful precisely because his goal was to create the means to deal with cultural difference on its own terms, as an antidote to theoretical assimilation by more prestigious projects. Gates does not shy away from questions of value and analysis, yet his work unmasks the shallowness of attempts to show that African literature is worthy of study because it is fundamentally the same as European literature or that jazz is worthy of study because it is just like classical music. Gates's notion of signifyin' codifies a set of ideas about processes of signification, and in the process offers us a bag of new conceptual tools for musical analysis and challenges us to rethink not only the tactics but also the goals of such work. I want to illustrate the productive potential of these ideas through a detailed analysis of Miles Davis's 1964 recording of "My Funny Valentine." But since audiences hear Davis's recording up against a long history of other performances of the song, I will begin with the issue of intertextuality.

Consider a pop vocalist's treatment of the song, such as Tony Bennett's 1959 recording.[19] Bennett's voice is warm, with constant vibrato throughout.

Figure 7.1. Transcription of Miles Davis solo on "My Funny Valentine," 1964 Recording.

Like many singers, he uses vibrato as a component of the vocal sound rather than as an ornament, so that it projects sincerity and expressivity evenly over the course of the entire song. Bennett follows the original printed version of the song closely, but he often slightly alters the rhythm of the melody to make his delivery of the text seem more natural and intimate; he also changes a note here and there, to suggest even more personal earnestness. A few deft appoggiaturas serve to underline his casual control of the music, and to complete his modest customizing. Bennett's rich tenor presents the singer as an ostensibly benevolent patriarch, for when the song is sung by a man to a woman (the opposite of the original context in the Broadway musical *Babes in Arms*), the text's enumeration of faults ("Is your figure less than Greek? Is your mouth a little weak?") becomes somewhat condescending, even insult-

ing, however well masked by the tender music. The pianist's nod to "Green-sleeves" at the very end completes the atmosphere of poignant sincerity Bennett has worked to create.

"My Funny Valentine" was composed by Rodgers and Hart in 1937. By the time of Bennett's recording, Davis had already recorded the song twice himself, in 1956 and 1958; his live recording was made five years after Bennett's. Now can we say that Davis is signifyin' on—commenting on, in dia-

logue with, deconstructing—Bennett's version? The question is made more complex by the idea that as a performer, Davis is signifyin' on all of the versions of the song he has heard; but for his audience, Davis is signifyin' on all of the versions each listener has heard. What is played is played up against Davis's intertextual experience, and what is heard is heard up against the listeners' experiences. Moreover, Davis is no doubt engaging with the many Bennett-like performances of "My Funny Valentine" he must have heard, but

× = half valved note

~ = swallowed, burbled, or ornamented note

he is also signifyin' on many jazz versions, including his own past performances.[20] This chain of signifyin' spins out indefinitely, though most fundamentally Davis is in dialogue with the basic features of the song itself, as jazz
musicians would understand them, and as listeners would recognize them.
The whole point of a jazz musician like Davis playing a Tin Pan Alley pop
song could be understood as his opportunity to signify on the melodic possibilities, formal conventions (such as the AABA plan of the thirty two-
measure chorus), harmonic potentials, and previously performed versions of
the original song.[21]

Davis signifies from the very beginning of his 1964 performance: after
Herbie Hancock's piano introduction, Davis understates the first two phrases
of the melody as shown in the transcription above.[22] His tone is soft and
without vibrato, and he has clipped the long notes of the song, making
his statement seem idiosyncratic yet restrained. Without a constant vibrato

such as Bennett uses, there is no warm surface to hide behind; Davis's state-ment seems stark and vulnerable. After each phrase, he pauses, and the empty time creates a sense of dramatic engagement as we wait for the con-tinuation we know must occur. On the third phrase (m. 5), Davis deceives us: he begins on the proper note, but instead of ascending to follow the melody, he descends into the lowest register of the trumpet before seeming to gain momentum that shoots him up to almost an octave higher than where he should be, if he were still following the tune. The melody of "My Funny Valentine" was so familiar to his audience that Davis did not need to state it before signifyin' on it: two brief phrases serve to establish the tune. The third phrase not only deceives but contrasts sharply with the first two (mm. 1 and 3): during this eruption Davis plays loudly for the first time, and adds some vibrato while he holds the final high note. Unlike Tony Bennett, Davis uses vibrato selectively so that its presence or absence is significant: here he uses it to intensify the end of this outburst before he retreats back to a soft note in his middle range.

That next note, in the last measure of the first A section (m. 8), is rich in signifyin'. Davis plays an A-flat in the normal way, with the trumpet's first valve depressed.[23] He then slides down to a G without changing valves. This is a technique that, on the trumpet, is difficult, risky, and relatively rare. Acoustically, the trumpet should not be able to play any notes between A-flat and E-flat with only the first valve depressed; Davis must bend the note with his lips without letting it crack down to the next harmonic.[24] The result is a fuzzy sound, not quite in tune. There is no conceivable situation in classical trumpet playing where such a sound would be desirable. Yet in this solo it is the audible sign of Davis's effort and risk, articulating a moment of strain that contributes to the affect of his interpretation. If we explain this measure in terms of quarter tones or, as Howard Brofsky does, transcribe it as simply two notes, an A-flat and a G, we gain a neater description but miss the point of the music. Davis deliberately risks cracking that note because it is the only way to achieve that sense of strain. Here, he manages to hold onto the note; at other moments in the solo such wagers are not won. However, it is crucial to appreciate the extraordinary lengths to which Davis goes to make playing the trumpet even more difficult and risky than it already is, and to understand the musical results of his doing so.

For the trumpet, like most wind instruments, underwent a continual pro-cess of "improvement" throughout the nineteenth century and, to a lesser extent, the twentieth. In particular, instrument makers sought to adapt the trumpet to the needs of the expanding nineteenth-century orchestra by striv-ing for a smooth, even timbre across the whole range of the instrument, one that would be consistent at all dynamic levels. In contrast, the eighteenth-century trumpet parts of J. S. Bach made use of the inconsistencies of the instrument as Bach knew it. On the trumpets of that time, every note had a different timbre and a different degree of stability. Bach carefully exploited these characteristics, using weaker or fuzzier notes in harmonically strained passages, and returning to cadence with the most gloriously solid notes on the instrument. Players of the time also developed a very flexible technique, practicing a great variety of articulations, working to make their lines uneven and musically subtle. All of this particularity was undone in the nineteenth century, as both instruments and pedagogy became standardized for the needs of the symphony orchestra. As a consequence, jazz trumpet players like Miles Davis have had to wrestle with an instrument that was literally designed to frustrate their attempts to produce a wide variety of timbres.[25]

Throughout the solo, Davis uses another risky technique: he half-valves— depresses a valve only part of the way down, which creates a split, unfocused airstream—to create a variety of timbres and effects. In measures 10 and 11, half-valving is combined with dissonant pitches and halting, fragmented rhythms to create a temporary sense of dislocation. Another half-valved slide blurs the beginning of a reference to the original melody in measure 12. After his unnerving silence during the major seventh chord in the next measure— an important point of arrival in the song—Davis uses a grace note and a slight half-valve to make the high point of the phrase seem delicately virtuosic (m. 14). A quick reprise of the risky bend finishes off the phrase, and we must wait almost two measures for another utterance from Davis.

When it comes, the next phrase contrasts sharply with the previous state- ment, for its climb is loud and brash, featuring no fewer than three cracked notes in two measures. I suspect that the last of these was done deliberately, to make the other two seem thematic in retrospect. This is not uncommon among jazz musicians, who are free to signify on the music they have played just seconds before. Improvisers can comment on what they have just played by spontaneously repeating, embellishing, and developing their best ideas. But jazz musicians can also engage with their most infelicitous phrases: though they cannot be unplayed, they can be resituated and reinterpreted by subsequent statements. Thelonious Monk was particularly adept at using mu- sical accidents as material for development and elaboration. But of course jazz musicians vary greatly in their attitudes about such things. Many abhor technical imperfections and strive to avoid uncontrolled noises. Some, like Monk or Davis, play in ways that create such unforeseen sounds, though Monk seemed to find them fascinating while Davis simply accepted them as consequences of the way he played.

I don't mean to suggest that Davis wanted to make mistakes, or that he was not bothered by them. He had absorbed a dislike of technical failings from many sources, including his first trumpet hero, Harry James, who was famous for his stylish phrasing and flawless technique. And when Davis had to choose among various takes after a recording session, he is said to have invariably picked the one with the fewest mistakes.[26] Yet Davis has also been quoted as saying: "When they make records with all the mistakes in, as well as the rest, then they'll really make jazz records. If the mistakes aren't there, too, it ain't none of you." [27] Despite his dislike of failure, Davis constantly and consistently put himself at risk in his trumpet playing, by using a loose, flexible embouchure that helped him to produce a great variety of tone colors and articulations, by striving for dramatic gestures rather than consistent demonstration of mastery, and by experimenting with unconventional techniques. Ideally, he would always play on the edge and never miss; in practice, he played closer to the edge than anyone else and simply accepted the inevitable missteps, never retreating to a safer, more consistent performing style.

After the glaring "clams" of measures 17 and 18, Davis returns with a soft nod to the original melody of "My Funny Valentine" in the following two bars. The next lick again goes beyond the classical boundaries of trumpet technique by using an alternate fingering to produce a different timbre and slightly low pitch. Davis plays a lazy triplet of Ds, the first and last with the normal fingering of open, but the middle one with the third valve. Another curt nod to the melody sets up a tremendous silence, a charged gap of almost three full measures. Gates, in one of his few explicit comments on African-American music, explains how such a pause can be understood as signifyin': "[A] great musician often tries to make musical phrases that are elastic in their formal properties. These elastic phrases stretch the form rather than articulate the form. Because the form is self-evident to the musician, both he and his well-trained audience are playing and listening with expectation. Signifyin(g) disappoints these expectations; caesuras, or breaks, achieve the same function. This form of disappointment creates a dialogue between what the listener expects and what the artist plays. Whereas younger, less mature musicians accentuate the beat, more accomplished musicians do not have to do so. They feel free to imply it." [28] To create a pause of such length, during one of the most tense harmonic moments of the song is, among other things, Davis's confident assertion of his stature as a soloist. Would an audience wait eagerly through such a gap for a lesser musician? Would a lesser musician dare to find out? Davis indulges in that sort of manipulation that is the prerogative of the virtuoso and at the same time illustrates his freedom from having to articulate all of the chords; rather, the chords are there as a field upon which he signifies.

In a deviation from the standard thirty two-bar form, Rodgers and Hart extended the final A section of "My Funny Valentine" with an extra four measures (beyond the usual eight). In the ninth bar of this section (m. 33), we can hear Davis signal, with a single pair of notes, a doubling of the tempo, which is immediately picked up by the other musicians. A high rip, solidly on the downbeat, gets their attention, and the subtle swing of two eighth-notes on the second beat is enough to cue the band to shift tempo. The eighth-notes are signifyin' on the previous rhythmic feel and cannot be contained within it, prompting the change.[29] By starting the new rhythmic feel four measures before the start of a new chorus, Davis cuts against the regularity of the song's formal plan, building momentum at what should be the most predictable point in the song, the turnaround into the next chorus, where the melody relaxes. That he succeeds in sparking increased engagement with the audience is clear from their spontaneous applause here, in the middle of his solo.

Davis begins the second chorus of his solo with a striking contrast, a splattered high note followed by one that is neatly and precisely placed (m. 37). The first note comes across as a scream, particularly since it is on the tense ninth degree (D over C minor); the second note not only resolves harmonically to the tonic but also resolves the gesture of wildness with a demonstration of control. Precise placement of even more dissonant notes in the following measure emphasize Davis's willfulness and strength, as he clashes deliberately with the harmonic context.

The third measure of this chorus (m. 39) is a mess. Clear, distinctly pitched notes are almost wholly absent; what we hear is a raucous, complex ascending gesture. Davis keeps his embouchure very loose and uses breath accents on the higher notes to shape the line. What results is indeterminate in pitch but rhetorically clear. It is a chaotic, almost frantic climb that briefly shoots past the tonic to the flat ninth degree, then spins back to the tonic and down an octave by way of a deft flip into bluesier terrain. Again, Davis is less interested in articulating pitches than in signifyin': the two halves of this phrase are in dialogue, the messy scramble upward answered by the casual, simple return. Their juxtaposition furthers our sense of Davis's playful, adventurous, multifaceted, sometimes strained but ultimately capable character.[30] Davis doesn't present his audiences with a product, polished and inviting admiration; we hear a dramatic process of creation from him as from few others. And as we listen, we can experience these feelings of playfulness, complexity, struggle, and competence as our own.

For the next seven measures, Davis works primarily with rhythm: his phrases are simple and exquisitely swung, and he places substantial pauses in between them so that the rhythm section can be heard swinging in response. Skipping ahead, we hear him doing something similar at the start of the last A section (m. 61), creating a space for dialogue just before he ascends into a series of stratospheric screeches that must have surprised those critics who have insisted that Davis is a weak trumpet player with a limited range. The solo ends (m. 74) with a series of fading quarter notes on the beat, pitched in Davis's midrange, a dissonant tritone away from the tonic; an appoggiatura both blurs and emphasizes each note, making the end of his solo seem enigmatic and inconclusive.

Characterizing Davis's style as "prideful loneliness," Nat Hentoff has argued that Davis's power as a soloist was due to his "relentless probing of the song, of himself and of the resources of his horn. There is also the constant drawing of melodic and emotional lines as taut as possible before the tension is released only to build up again. And there is the unabashed sensuality of tone, together with the acute pleasure of surprising oneself in music." [31] Hentoff's comments are certainly evocative of what I have called signifyin' in Davis's music. And Ben Sidran's book about orality in African-American music similarly directs our attention toward the dialogic aspects of jazz, as do LeRoi Jones's *Blues People* and Christopher Small's *Music of the Common Tongue: Survival and Celebration in Afro-American Music.* [32]

Such arguments, however, seem not to have influenced jazz scholarship much: with the exception of Hentoff, these writers are not often cited in jazz bibliographies. [33] The reason for this, I think, has been the lack of attention within jazz scholarship and criticism to articulating links among the impressions of listeners, the techniques of musicians, and the actual sounds that result. Bill Cole remarked of this solo that Davis "holds his listeners' interest by playing every note as if it were the most important note he would ever play. It is this intensity that is so persuasive in his playing." This argument is itself persuasive, but how do we actually hear an abstract quality like "intensity"? Gary Tomlinson has nicely described "the technical revolution brought to the trumpet by black Americans, a revolution that toppled the prim Arban methods and military precision of Victorian cornet virtuosos and broke wide open the expressive range of the instrument." Tomlinson goes on to say specifically of Miles Davis: "The power of his vision was such that he could make even his famous cracked and fluffed notes a convincing expressive aspect of it." [34] Like Gary Giddins, Tomlinson is trying to valorize aspects of Davis's performances that escape conventional accounts; like Giddins's attempt, though, it appeals to a fairly misty notion of "vision." But most important, none of these comments are very specific musically; jazz criticism has lacked detailed analyses of specific performances that articulate links among reactions, theories, performance choices, and technical details.

My analysis of "My Funny Valentine" is certainly not exhaustive—a more extensive treatment might move beyond Davis's rhetorical choices to examine how the other musicians similarly signify on the conventions of the tune (Hancock's chord substitutions are particularly important). And while I have touched upon a few points of dialogic interaction among the musicians, there is also much more to be said about that. I have focused selectively on certain aspects of one solo in order to make a number of methodological points and to present an example of a kind of analysis that takes us into the notes but acknowledges the centrality of rhetoric, that leads us into the trees but also sees the forest. The value of a theory of signifyin' is that it can help direct our attention to aspects of jazz performance and reception that have not been cogently addressed, and it helps provide a language for doing so. And by grounding his theory in African-American practices but not limiting its applicability to African-American culture, Gates helps us to gain a new perspective on many different cultural practices. Prevalent methods of jazz analysis, borrowed from the toolbox of musicology, may provide excellent means for *legitimating* jazz in the academy. But they are clearly inadequate to the task of helping us to *understand* jazz and to account for its power to affect many people deeply—issues that ought to be central to critical scholarship of jazz. They offer only a kind of mystified, ahistorical, text-based legitimacy within which rhetoric and signifyin' are invisible. Such methods cannot cope with the problem of Miles Davis: the missed notes, the charged gaps, the technical risk-taking, the whole challenge of explaining how this powerful music works and means.

Why must it be explained? Because it will be, somehow, unavoidably. Artistic experiences are never unmediated by theoretical assumptions, whether positivist or formalist, mystifying or signifyin'. And how we think about Davis's solo on "My Funny Valentine" has implications far beyond our response to this particular performance. The work of Miles Davis seems to repudiate conventional notions of aesthetic distance and to insist that music is less a thing than an activity; his music itself provides the most eloquent argument for analysis to open itself up to issues of gesture and performativity. The problem of Miles Davis is that if technical perfection is assumed to be a universal and primary goal, the deliberate efforts of musicians like Davis to take chances are invisible, and their semiotic successes are inaudible. If individuality and originality are fetishized, signifyin' is lost, for it is fundamentally dialogic and depends upon the interaction among musicians, their audiences, and the experiences and texts they exchange.

For example, one of Davis's biographers asserts that the "My Funny Valentine" solo demonstrates "no readily apparent logic," while another waxes enthusiastic about the "dramatic inner logic" of the same solo.[35] Each critic finds it a powerfully moving performance, but both lack an analytical vocabulary that could do justice to their perceptions. Pianist Chick Corea muses: "Miles' solos are really interesting to look at on music paper, because there's nothing to them. On a Trane solo or Charlie Parker solo, you can string the notes out and see all these phrases and harmonic ideas, patterns, all kinds of things. Miles doesn't use patterns. He doesn't string notes out. It's weird. Without the expression, and without the feeling he puts into it, there's nothing there."[36] Corea's comments dramatize the problems of accounting for the rhetorical power of aspects of Davis's performances that escape conventional notation and theorization.

Davis himself once said: "Sometimes you run out of notes. The notes just disappear and you have to play a sound."[37] The title of this essay takes as a motto Davis's insistence that musical creativity need not be limited by abstractions such as notes, and it signals a call for critics and scholars not to allow such concepts to constrain *their* work. Musical analysts need to confront the challenges of signifyin', the real-life dialogic flux of meaning, never groundable in a foundationalist epistemology, but always grounded in a web of social practices, histories, and desires. Modernism and classicism can't take us into notes, where choices and details signify; nor out of notes, onto that risky rhetorical terrain Miles Davis never stopped exploring.

NOTES

Material presented in this article was performed as lecture-demonstrations at the African-American Music Forum, University of Michigan, April 26, 1990; the IASPM conference in New Orleans, May 1, 1990; McGill University, January 31, 1992; the University of California—Riverside, March 11, 1992; and the University of California—Berkeley, January 22, 1993. The article has benefited from the comments and questions of the audiences at those presentations, and from correspondence with Krin Gabbard, George Lipsitz, and Christopher Small. Slightly different versions of this article were published in *Musical Quarterly* 77 (1993): 343–65, and Krin Gabbard, ed. *Jazz among the Discourses* (Durham: Duke Univ. Press, 1995), 165–88. I am grateful for the corrections and challenges issued by the anonymous reviewers for *Musical Quarterly* and Duke University Press and to John Puterbaugh for setting my transcription. The epigraph appears in Nat Hentoff, "An Afternoon with Miles Davis," in Martin T. Williams, ed., *Jazz Panorama* (New York: Da Capo, 1979), 162. This version of the article previously published in *Musical Quarterly* used with permission Oxford University Press—eds.

1. *Musician* (Dec. 1991), 5. Other important tributes appeared in *Down Beat* (Dec. 1991) and *Rolling Stone* (Nov. 14, 1991).

2. See Frank Tirro, *Jazz: A History* (New York: Norton, 1977); Joachim E. Berendt, *The Jazz Book: From Ragtime to Fusion and Beyond* (Westport: Lawrence Hill, 1982); Mark C. Gridley, *Jazz Styles: History and Analysis,* 4th ed. (Englewood Cliffs, N. J.: Prentice-Hall, 1991); and Donald D. Megill and Richard S. Demory *Introduction to Jazz History* (Englewood Cliffs, N. J.: Prentice-Hall, 1989). Tirro does mention fusion, but without any hint that it was controversial, that it was anything other than natural evolution.

3. *My Funny Valentine: Miles Davis in Concert* (Columbia CS 9106). This is a live recording of a performance at Philharmonic Hall in New York City, Feb. 12, 1964. Davis performed with George Coleman, Herbie Hancock, Ron Carter, and Tony Williams. Ian Carr's transcription is much better in this respect: see Ian Carr, *Miles Davis: A Critical Biography* (London: Paladin, 1982), 306. See also Howard Brofsky, "Miles Davis and *My Funny Valentine*: The Evolution of a Solo," *Black Music Research Journal* (1983): 23–45; and Bill Cole, *Miles Davis: A Musical Biography* (New York: William Morrow, 1985). While most critics refer to "missed notes" or "cracked notes," trumpet players themselves tend to prefer more colorful, onomatopoetic terms, such as "spleeah," "clam," or "frack."

4. Gary Giddens, *Rhythm-a-ning: Jazz Tradition and Innovation in the '80s* (New York, Oxford Univ. Press, 1985): 79, 84.

5. James Lincoln Collier, *The Making of Jazz* (New York, Dell: 1978), 435. For Giddens's comments, see Gary Giddens, *Rhythm-a-ning,* 79, 84.

6. Henry Louis Gates Jr., *The Signifying Monkey: A Theory of African-American*

Literary Criticism (New York: Oxford Univ. Press, 1988). Floyd's fine essay, "Ring Shout! Literary Studies, Historical Studies, and Black Music Inquiry," *Black Music Research Journal* 11 (Fall 1991): 265–87, actually appeared long after its publication date, when my article had largely been completed; his reading of Gates and his analytical focus differ somewhat from mine, but our goals are quite similar. See also John P. Murphy, "Jazz Improvisation: The Joy of Influence," *Black Perspective in Music* 18: 1–2, 7–19; Gary Tomlinson, "Cultural Dialogics and Jazz: A White Historian Signifies," in Katherine Bergeron and Philip V. Bohlman, eds., *Disciplining Music: Musicology and Its Canons* (Chicago: Univ. of Chicago Press, 1992), 64–94; and Krin Gabbard, "Signifyin(g) the Phallus: *Mo' Better Blues* and Representations of the Jazz Trumpet," *Cinema Journal* 32 (Fall 1992): 43–62.

7. See M. M. Bakhtin, *The Dialogic Imagination* (Austin: Univ. of Texas Press, 1981). It might seem that semiotics would be highly relevant to musical signifyin'. But scholars working in the area of musical semiotics have typically assumed that the production of musical meaning is a matter of semantics, following older models developed by structuralist linguistics, or they remain tied to a foundationalist epistemology that is unable to cope with the social and contested production of meanings. See, for example, Jean-Jacques Nattiez, *Music and Discourse: Toward a Semiologic of Music* (Princeton: Princeton Univ. Press, 1990).

8. Houston A. Baker Jr., "Handling 'Crisis': Great Books, Rap Music, and the End of Western Homogeneity," *Callaloo* (Spring 1990): 183; and Ralph Ellison, *Shadow and Act* (New York: Random House, 1964), 249.

9. Gunther Schuller, "The Influence of Jazz on the History and Development of Concert Music," in David N. Baker, ed., *New Perspectives on Jazz* (Washington, D. C.: Smithsonian Institution Press 1990), 9–24.

10. Olly Wilson, "The Influence of Jazz on the History and Development of Concert Music [response]," and Amiri Baraka, "Jazz Criticism and Its Effect on the Art Form," in Baker, *New Perspectives*.

11. See Lawrence W. Levine, *Highbrow/Lowbrow: The Emergence of Cultural Hierarchy in America* (Cambridge: Harvard Univ. Press, 1988); and Andreas Huyssen, *After the Great Divide: Modernism, Mass Culture, Postmodernism* (Bloomington: Indiana Univ. Press, 1986). Note that the *New Grove Dictionary of Jazz*, ed. Barry Kernfeld (New York: Grove's Dictionaries of Music, 1988) contains no articles under any of these headings: "Analysis," "History," "Historiography," "Criticism," "Audiences," "Fans," "Concerts," "African Music," or "Afro-American Music."

12. William "Billy" Taylor, "Jazz: America's Classical Music," *Black Perspective in Music* 14 (Winter 1986): 21–25; and "Jazz in the Contemporary Marketplace: Professional and Third-Sector Strategies for the Balance of the Century," in Baker *New Perspectives*. See also Grover Sales, *Jazz: America's Classical Music* (Englewood Cliffs, N. J.: Prentice-Hall, 1984).

13. As Martin Williams (*The Jazz Tradition*, new and rev. ed. [Oxford: Oxford Univ. Press, 1983]) points out, "Jazz not only exalts the individual finding his [*sic*] own way, it also places him in a fundamental, dynamic, and necessary co-operation with his fellows" (256). Compare the individualist, monologic understanding of jazz in Ted Gioia's *The Imperfect Art: Reflections on Jazz and Modern Culture* (New York: Oxford Univ. Press, 1988). See also the critical review of Gioia's book by David Horn in *Popular Music* 10, no. 1 (1991): 103–7.

14. See, for example, Frank Tirro, "Constructive Elements in Jazz Improvisation,"

Journal of the American Musicological Society 27 (Summer 1974): 285–305; Lewis Porter, "John Coltrane's *A Love Supreme*: Jazz Improvisation as Composition," *Journal of the American Musicological Society* 38 (Fall 1985): 593–621; and Gunther Schuller, "Sonny Rollins and the Challenge of Thematic Improvisation," in *Musings* (New York: Oxford Univ. Press, 1986) (orig. pub. in *The Jazz Review*, Nov. 1958).

15. See Gunther Schuller, *Early Jazz: Its Roots and Musical Development* (New York: Oxford Univ. Press, 1968), chap. 1, "The Origins"; and André Hodeir, *Jazz: Its Evolution and Essence*, updated ed. (New York: Grove Press, 1979; orig. pub. 1956), 92 et passim. For an overview of discussions of African retentions in African-American music, see Portia K. Maultsby, "Africanisms in African-American Music," in Joseph E. Holloway, ed., *Africanisms in American Culture* (Bloomington: Univ. of Indiana Press, 1990).

16. Gunther Schuller, *The Swing Era: The Development of Jazz, 1930–1945* (New York: Oxford Univ. Press, 1989), 63, 199, et passim. Thus when Schuller boasts of listening to over 30,000 recordings while writing this book, one might ask, "But what was he listening *for?*"

17. Even John Gennari ("Jazz Criticism: Its Development and Ideologies," *Black Literature Forum* 25 [Fall 1991]: 449–523), who criticizes Schuller for stripping away the cultural meanings of jazz, nonetheless credits him with having produced comprehensive and precise analyses of the music.

18. Stanley Crouch, "Jazz Criticism and Its Effect on the Art Form [response]," in Baker, *New Perspectives*; Robert Palmer, "The Man Who Changed Music," *Rolling Stone* (Nov. 14, 1991): 39–42, 47.

19. First issued on Columbia CS-8242, this recording also appears in the Smithsonian Collection *American Popular Song* (Smithsonian Institution and CBS, RD-031). Most of the comments that follow could apply just as well to Frank Sinatra's recording on *Songs for Young Lovers* (Capitol, 1954).

20. See Brofsky, "Miles Davis and *My Funny Valentine*" for a comparison of three different performances by Davis of "My Funny Valentine."

21. We might say that the early bebop musicians were signifyin' on Tin Pan Alley popular songs when they stripped away the melody, doubled the tempo, and explored the harmonic possibilites they found in such tunes as "I Got Rhythm" and "Cherokee." But bebop practice would have been to give "My Funny Valentine" a new melody and not acknowledge that the tune had any connection with popular song. Davis, when he used Tin Pan Alley songs, always said so, making the signifyin' less private and esoteric, more explicit and popular. See W. T. Lhamon Jr., *Deliberate Speed: The Origins of a Cultural Style in the American 1950s* (Washington, D. C.: Smithsonian Institution Press, 1990), 172–73.

22. My transcription is provided as a guide to the analysis that follows. The analysis, though, is based on the sounds of the performance, not the sight of the transcription. It should be clear that I have no illusions about the capacity of musical notation to represent musical performances completely or accurately. I have tried, however, to furnish a transcription that acknowledges its own limitations, one that records the existence of aspects of the performance that are not notatable or that are usually overlooked by analysis. Even so, an enormous amount of important musical information is left out, especially nuances of pitch and timbre. Note the key to special symbols that appears at the end of the transcription.

23. Pitches are given in the text at concert pitch, so as to match the transcription. A trumpet player would think of this note as a B-flat.

24. Acoustical properties permit a valveless brass instrument, such as a bugle, to play only the notes (or harmonics) of an overtone series, such as A-flat, E-flat, A-flat, C, E-flat, G-flat, A-flat, B-flat, etc. The trumpet's valves allow it to switch quickly among various series.

25. Davis is certainly not the only trumpet player to wrestle with the instrument in this way. For example, Charles Schlueter, principal trumpet of the Boston Symphony Orchestra, has throughout his career struggled to produce a great range of timbres. Schlueter's experiments with equipment and his risky playing techniques and interpretations have made him perhaps the most controversial trumpet player in American orchestral circles. Like Davis, he has often missed more notes than many think he should, but his risks have also paid off in unsurpassedly rich and beautiful performances. On the controversies surrounding Schlueter, see Carl A. Vigeland, *In Concert: Onstage and Offstage with the Boston Symphony Orchestra* (Amherst: University Press, 1991). On the history of the trumpet, see Edward Tarr, *The Trumpet* (Portland, Ore.: Amadeus Press, 1988), and Robert Walser, "Musical Imagery and Performance Practice in J. S. Bach's Arias with Trumpet," *International Trumpet Guild Journal* 13 (Sept. 1988): 62–77.

26. Berendt, *The Jazz Book*, cites unnamed "recording directors" who agree on this point. On Davis's admiration for Harry James, see Miles Davis, with Quincy Troupe, *Miles: The Autobiography* (New York: Simon & Schuster, 1989), 32.

27. Ralph J. Gleason, *Celebrating the Duke* (Boston: Little, Brown, 1975), 134.

28. Gates, *The Signifying Monkey*, 123.

29. It is quite possible that this tempo change was planned, or that it was at least an option that had been taken in previous performances. But it is made to feel spontaneous, to seem musically cued by Davis.

30. Krin Gabbard (1992: 60) cites this solo as a perfect example of how Davis alternated strongly phallic gestures with moments of postphallic vulnerability.

31. Nat Hentoff, liner notes to Miles Davis, *My Funny Valentine*, Columbia (1964). "Prideful loneliness" is from Hentoff, *Jazz Is* (New York: Random House, 1976), 141.

32. Ben Sidran, *Black Talk* (New York: Da Capo, 1983 [orig. pub. 1971]); LeRoi Jones, *Blues People* (New York: William Morrow, 1963); Christopher Small, *Music of the Common Tongue: Survival and Celebration in Afro-American Music* (New York: Riverrun Press, 1987). See also Amiri Baraka, "Miles Davis: One of the Great Mother Fuckers," in Amiri and Amina Baraka, *The Music: Reflections on Jazz and Blues* (New York: William Morrow, 1987), 209–301.

33. For example, Martin Williams's "Suggestions for Further Reading" for the *Smithsonian Collection of Classic Jazz*, rev. ed. (CBS Special Products, 1987) ignores Sidran and Jones, as does Max Harrison's entry on "Jazz" in the *New Grove Dictionary of Music and Musicians* (New York: Grove's Dictionaries of Music, 1980), 9:561–79.

34. Tomlinson "Cultural Dialogics and Jazz," 90–91.

35. See Eric Nisenson, *Round about Midnight: A Portrait of Miles Davis* (New York: Dial Press, 1982), 187. See also Ian Carr, *Miles Davis: A Biography* (New York: Morrow, 1982), 175.

36. Ibid., 187. Another important biography of Davis (besides Cole) is Jack Chambers's *Milestones: The Music and Times of Miles Davis* (New York: Quill, Wiliam

Morrow, 1985), a tremendous compilation of facts and quotes, but a book that offers little analysis of the music and its meanings. Barry Kernfeld's dissertation *Adderly, Coltrane, and Davis at the Twilight of Bebop: The Search for Melodic Coherence (1958–59)* (Cornell University, 1981) uses traditional musicological tools to generate detailed descriptions of Davis's music. For Corea's comments, see Howard Mandel, "Sketches of Miles," *Downbeat* (Dec. 1991): 16–20.

37. Kephra Burns, liner notes for Miles Davis, "Aura" (CBS, 1989 [recorded 1984]).

PETER WINKLER

Writing Ghost Notes: The Poetics and Politics of Transcription

> The real issue is whether there can be a true representation of anything
> or whether any and all representations, because they *are* representations,
> are embedded first in the language and then in the culture, institutions,
> and political ambiance of the representer. If the latter alternative is the
> correct one (as I believe it is), then we must be prepared to accept that
> a representation is *eo ipso* implicated, intertwined, embedded, inter-
> woven with a great many other things besides the truth, which is itself
> a representation.
>
> **Edward Said**

In this essay I wish to reconsider some habits of thought and modes of inquiry that I have been pursuing for many years. If what follows seems excessively autobiographical or self-absorbed, I must beg the reader's indulgence. My hope is that I can present the issues I am addressing more clearly by framing them in terms of my own experience, rather than by referring to them in a disembodied, abstract way.

My involvement with the study of popular music began rather late in my musical training, while I was studying composition in graduate school in the late 1960s. When I first heard Aretha Franklin's earliest Atlantic recordings in 1967, I was both thrilled and shaken. I had already become intrigued with the music of the Beatles, but it was not difficult to understand and appreciate the Beatles in terms of the Western European art tradition that had shaped my education and musical perceptions. I could point to elements in the structure of their songs—subtleties of form, details of voice-leading, metrical shifts, text-setting—that would demonstrate to my own satisfaction that what the Beatles were doing was a kind of "art song." But Aretha Franklin's records affected me even more strongly: I felt her music was profound and deeply moving, yet I knew of no techniques of music theory or analysis that could account for her effect on me. I kept asking, "What is really going on in this music?"

I began reading everything I could find about popular music, and then

169

working outward to other traditions—older popular song, jazz, country, gospel music. Gradually I was able to build up a picture of the social, historical, and economic context in which this music existed. But rarely did the literature address the music *itself*. This, alas, is still largely true today, even though the literature has multiplied enormously. Our understanding of the context in which popular music exists has become increasingly sophisticated, but, with a few notable exceptions, most popular music scholarship still treats the music itself as a kind of "black box"—undiscussed, unknown, perhaps unknowable.[1] The question, now as then, is What is really going on in this music?

It seemed reasonable to me that to answer the question, I would first have to answer another question: Exactly what notes are being played and sung? The first step, then, would be to make transcriptions—that is, to listen to records and write down what I heard in the form of a musical score. With a definitive score I could go on to produce an analysis, generalizing about the patterns and structures I had discovered. But the process of making transcriptions turned out to be far less straightforward than I had anticipated. It took hours to get a single phrase down; transcribing an entire record took days. Every time I listened to the music, I found more problems with what I had written down. Despite these difficulties, I found the process of making transcriptions absorbing and enlightening. More than twenty years and hundreds of transcriptions later I still feel that, for all the problems and frustrations they involve, transcriptions are worth doing. I rely heavily on them in my own research, and I always require them of students in the popular music courses I teach.[2]

But today many academics are seriously examining the presuppositions behind the work we do and our motivations for doing it. Many of our old notions—about the nature of our understanding of music, society and culture, about the "autonomy" or "universality" of music, about the possibility of scientific objectivity in our work—have been challenged. We find it increasingly difficult to pretend that music can be comprehended in and for itself, without regard to its social and cultural context, that scholarship can be ideologically neutral, or that the work we do is innocent of political ramifications.

Hence I feel that it is time to examine the presuppositions behind my transcriptions. What exactly do I do when I make a transcription? What happens when I represent recorded sound in graphic form? What is the relation of my transcription to the actual recorded sound? What does transcription help me to learn or discover? Are there things that the act of transcription obscures or minimizes? What are my motivations for making a transcription? Do the uses to which a transcription is put have deeper social and political implications?

I am by no means the first to ask such questions. Although transcription is fairly uncommon in studies of popular music (because studies that focus on the music itself are still rare), it has been standard procedure in the field of ethnomusicology since that discipline began to develop in the last century. And transcription is frequently used in the study of jazz, as an aid both to analysis and pedagogy. For years there has been a thoughtful ongoing dialogue in the literature of ethnomusicology regarding the difficult problems that the act of transcription raises; this discussion will draw on that dialogue.[3]

My contribution to that dialogue here can be described as phenomenological in the sense that it investigates the perceptual and cognitive acts that underlie the act of transcription. I will discuss a transcription of a portion of Aretha Franklin's recording of the song "I Never Loved a Man (The Way I Love You)," one of the songs that originally inspired me to take up the serious study of popular music.[4] The object of my inquiry here is not the song, nor its stunning performance by Aretha and the band, but rather the process of transcription itself and the questions that arise about the meaning, use, and value of such an activity.

NOTATION, ORALITY, AND LITERACY

I begin with a basic question: What does it mean to write music down? As a musician trained in the Western tradition, it is easy for me to accept our notational system as natural and inevitable. In our language the word *music* has two very different senses that are often confused or conflated: *music* can mean actual musical sounds (as in "listen to the music"), and it can mean the representation of those sounds through notation (as in "I can't play the piece without the music"). Many Western musicians think of a piece of music not in terms of musical sounds but in terms of a musical *score*: not as an aural phenomenon but as a visual representation. As Bruno Nettl put it, "We think of a piece of music as existing in its truest form on a piece of paper."[5] This essentially "visualist" orientation can be seen as an outgrowth of the high value Western culture places on visual evidence in general and writing in particular.[6] Such an orientation easily leads to ethnocentrism. In the curricula of many of our music schools, "musicianship" is synonymous with "musical literacy": the clear implication is that if you can't read music, you are not really a musician. And music that does not rely on a notated score for its transmission tends to be seen as an abnormality, a musical Other, something that is not really, or not fully, music.

Walter Ong, in his study of orality and literacy, says, "Without writing, the literate mind would not and could not think as it does, not only when engaged in writing but normally even when it is composing its thoughts in oral form."[7] It is clear that musical notation has a profound effect on the ways in which musicians make and think about music. What is the nature of that effect?

As sound, music exists in a temporal stream—indeed, it can only exist *because* of that temporal stream, and hence can only be perceived within that stream. As Ong puts it: "All sensation takes place in time, but sound has a special relationship to time unlike that of the other fields that register in human sensation. Sound exists only when it is going out of existence. It is not simply perishable but essentially evanescent, and it is sensed as evanescence. When I pronounce the word 'permanence,' by the time I get to the '-nence,' the 'perma-' is gone, and has to be gone." [8]

Notation enables us to transcend the evanescence of music. Its effect is to neutralize time—to *kill* time. When we write music down, we represent musical sound by means of a sequence of visual symbols that we apprehend independently of the temporal stream. Thus we can focus on a particular musical event for as long as we want, scan instantaneously back and forth in time, or make side-by-side comparisons of temporally distant moments. Through notation we can escape the inexorable flow of time and comprehend the totality of a piece of music in an instant. We become as gods, viewing music from outside time, free of the constraints of past, present, or future. But this godlike vantage point tends to distract our attention from the existential immediacy of the musical event. Any particular musical performance is seen as just one possible realization of a timeless, atemporal model.

So far I have been speaking of musical notation in general. Throughout the world there are many notations, each adapted to the requirements of a particular tradition. The system of notation I use, which was developed for the tradition of European art music, separates the musical continuum according to a number of discretely notated parameters. Two of these parameters—pitch and rhythm—are represented within precisely defined grids: scale and meter. Other parameters—tempo, volume, instrumentation, expression, variation of timbre, and such ametrical rhythmic elements as ornaments—are represented with less precision by a variety of arbitrarily assigned symbols and verbal indications. When we use this system to write music down, we tend to pay the most attention to those elements that are most precisely determined, pitch and rhythm. And our perception of these elements is unavoidably conditioned by the grids our notational system offers: the division of the octave into twelve perceptually equal steps and the organization of musical time into even subdivisions or multiples of equally spaced musical pulses.

Written notation, of course, is just one possible mode of musical transmission. Many musical cultures rely primarily on oral transmission: one learns music from other musicians by receiving oral instructions, listening to them play, and imitating their actions. Recording technology has made possible what Walter Ong calls "secondary orality"—learning music not directly from other musicians but from recorded performances. This is a primary mode of transmission for jazz and popular musicians. For a musician working in an oral tradition, fixing a piece in notation may be not only unnecessary, it may be an actual *impoverishment*. Once the details are immutably frozen, it is no longer possible for the musicians to respond to particular performance situations: to interact with the audience, for example, or to capitalize on the individual moods, skills, and proclivities of the performers. Under such circumstances, notation can seem like a form of tyranny.

Having drawn this theoretical distinction between orality and literacy, I must hasten to add that it breaks down in practice. No musical culture, not even European art music, is solely dependent on notation; in the final analysis musicians learn any tradition primarily by listening and performing, not by reading. Bruno Nettl remarks: "The Western system of notation . . . is still essentially a mnemonic device."[9] And Pandora Hopkins adds: "There is no such thing as a non-oral tradition in music."[10] Indeed, many traditions today are hybrids of all three forms of transmission.

Consider "I Never Loved a Man." Does this song exist in a literate or an oral tradition? How was the recording created? I have not been able to find specific information about how Aretha Franklin learned the song, but popular singers typically learn material either by reading a "lead sheet" consisting of the lyrics, a skeletal version of the melodic line in musical staff notation, and schematic indications of the harmonies by means of chord symbols, or by listening to a "demo" recording of the song, or by a combination of the two. We do have information about how the recording session was conducted, from Jerry Wexler, who produced the session: "[Aretha] played [the song] to the rhythm section, Charlie Chalmers went into Rick's office to write out the horn parts, and when he came back out with the arrangement, we played the whole band together. There are no overdubs on that record. . . . Oh yeah, we did overdub her voice double tracking on the long open break—that was Chips Moman's idea."[11] The music of this recording, then, was created in a collaborative effort involving a number of musicians, technicians, and advisors, in a complex process involving all three of Walter Ong's basic types of modes of transmission: oral (Aretha teaching the song to the band, presumably by playing and singing it several times); "secondary oral" (the recorded demo); and written (the lead sheet and horn arrangements). Here, as in most instances of musical transmission, the relationship between orality and literacy is a continuum, not a binary opposition.

Let me return to my first question: What is really going on in this music? Our investigation of orality and literacy suggests that the attempt to answer this question by making a transcription may be doomed from the start. As an atemporal, graphic representation of a temporal phenomenon, a transcription cannot represent our hearing of the music as it unfolds in time. And as a rendering using the Western notational system, it necessarily emphasizes some dimensions of the musical continuum and marginalizes others. Many of the elements that were orally transmitted during the making of this recording—especially the all-important rhythmic feel, or "groove"—were not transmitted through notation, and capturing them in notation will be difficult, if not impossible. But could a transcription at least answer the more limited question: Exactly what notes are being played and sung? To answer that question, let me turn to the actual process of transcription.

AURAL TRANSCRIPTION: FINDING THE NOTES

Transcriptions can be of varying degrees of detail and complexity, according to the uses for which they are intended. Charles Seeger proposed the distinction between "prescriptive and descriptive uses of music writing—between a blueprint of how a specific piece of music shall be made to sound and a report of how a specific performance of any music actually did sound." [12] For members of a band that wanted to learn to play "I Never Loved A Man," the diagram below could serve as an adequate prescriptive transcription. It indicates the meter, identifies the sections of the piece, indicates which instruments play in which sections, marks off the number of measures in each section, and gives the basic chord progressions.

Of course this diagram could not stand alone; the players would also need to listen to the record and know how to perform in the style; figure 8.1 is a supplement, a memory aid, to a process that remains primarily oral. But to answer the question: Exactly what notes are being played and sung? I need a descriptive transcription. This is what I attempt in figure 8.2, and this is where the troubles begin.

The indispensable tool for a transcriber is a well-trained ear, that is, skill at taking music dictation. This skill is taught as part of musicianship courses; it involves being able to remember and reproduce stretches of music and write them down. Few musicians possess ears or memories sharp enough to transcribe more than a short span of music on a single hearing. In the early years of ethnomusicology, before the advent of recordings, transcription was an inexact craft. The arrival of recorded sound was a great boon to transcribers. Indeed, most ethnomusicologists feel that the discipline would have been impossible without it. With a recording, one can (and must) hear a brief passage over and over again, until one feels one has "got it right." In addition to repetition, transcribers have developed many strategies for manipulating the recorded sound in order to hear the details more clearly. One of the oldest of these strategies is to slow the playback speed; since the details unfold at a slower pace, one has a better chance of catching them. Another technique is to filter the sound—to boost or attenuate certain areas of the frequency spectrum in order to better hear a particular element and screen out the interference of other elements. A more recent and sophisticated piece of technology is what I shall refer to as a "time stretcher." This is a device that can alter the tempo of a recording while retaining the original pitch. It does

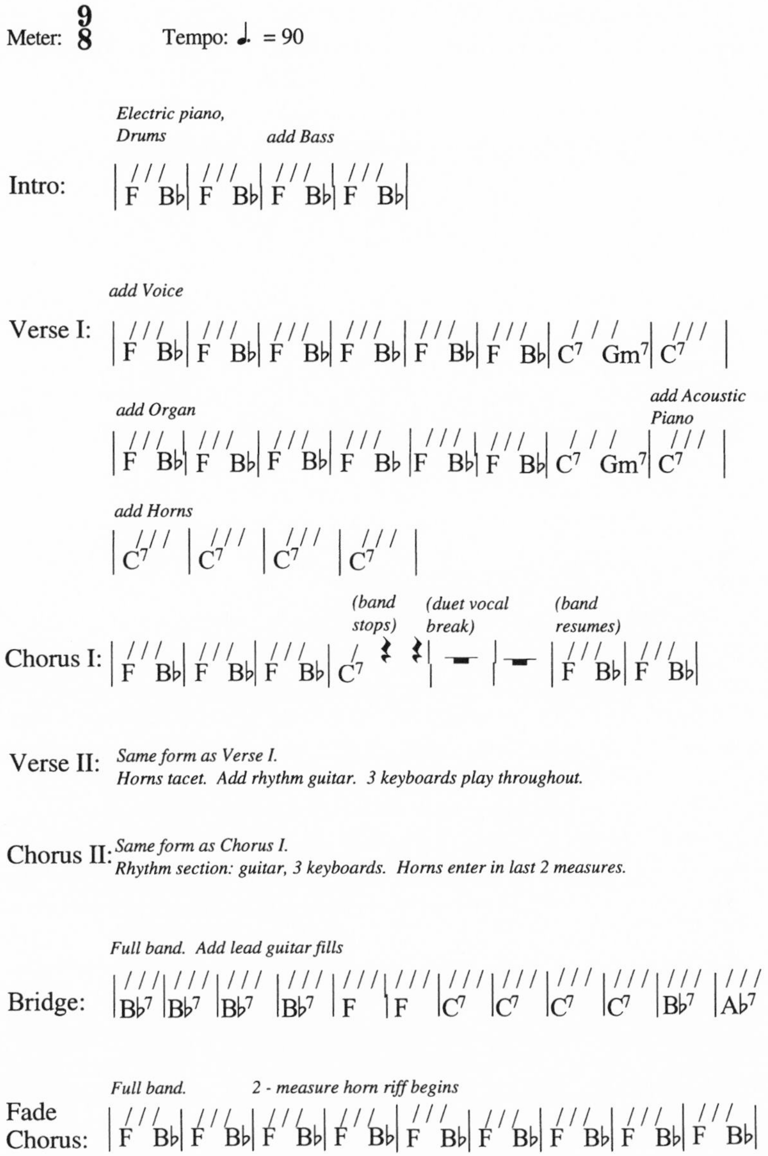

Meter: $\frac{9}{8}$ Tempo: ♩. = 90

Electric piano,
Drums   add Bass

Intro: | F B♭| F B♭| F B♭| F B♭|

add Voice

Verse I: | F B♭| F B♭| F B♭| F B♭| F B♭| F B♭| C⁷ Gm⁷| C⁷ |

add Organ   add Acoustic
                                                   Piano

| F B♭| F B♭| F B♭| F B♭| F B♭| F B♭| C⁷ Gm⁷| C⁷ |

add Horns

| C⁷ | C⁷ | C⁷ | C⁷ |

                     (band   (duet vocal   (band
                     stops)   break)   resumes)

Chorus I: | F B♭| F B♭| F B♭| C⁷ | — | — | F B♭| F B♭|

Verse II: *Same form as Verse I.*
Horns tacet. Add rhythm guitar. 3 keyboards play throughout.

Chorus II: *Same form as Chorus I.*
Rhythm section: guitar, 3 keyboards. Horns enter in last 2 measures.

Full band. Add lead guitar fills

Bridge: | B♭⁷| B♭⁷| B♭⁷| B♭⁷| F | F | C⁷ | C⁷ | C⁷ | C⁷ | B♭⁷| A♭⁷|

Full band.   2 - measure horn riff begins

Fade
Chorus: | F B♭| F B♭| F B♭| F B♭| F B♭| F B♭| F B♭| F B♭| F B♭|

Figure 8.1. "I Never Loved a Man": Prescriptive Transcription.

that by sampling extremely brief segments of the musical signal and interpo-
lating additional copies of that sample into a newly created, lengthened
signal.[13]

Armed with these tools, I begin my transcription. The primary focus in
the recording is Aretha Franklin's voice and her magnificently subtle and var-

Figure 8.2. "I Never Loved a Man": Descriptive Transcription, Score of First Verse and Chorus. "I Never Loved a Man" (Ronny Shannon) (c) 1968 Pronto Music (BMI) and Fourteenth Hour Music (BMI). All rights administered by Warner-Tamerlane Publishing Corp (BMI). All rights reserved. Used by Permission. Warner Bros. Publications U. S. Inc., Miami, FL 33014.

ied ornamentation and phrasing. It is clear that transcribing her singing is going to be extraordinarily difficult, so I decide to begin with the instrumental parts, which ought to be easier to write down. But the first sound in the recording already plunges me into difficulties. It is not hard to identify the first chord on the electric piano as F major. But how is the chord voiced? Is the top note a middle C or the F above? At first I think it is a C, but as the riff pattern repeats I am less and less sure. Do I hear an F above the C? If my ear follows the descending pattern in the second part of the measure— E-flat/D—it wants to complete the pattern with a C. On the second triplet of the third beat, however, there is a decorative F, easy to hear because the piano plays no other note with it. But is that F struck again on the following downbeat? The full F chord on the downbeat makes it difficult to tell.

The ambiguity with which I am struggling points to a fundamental inde-

terminacy a transcriber encounters when dealing with more than a single pitch sounding at the same time. To understand this indeterminacy we need to take a brief detour into the realm of musical acoustics. Any musical tone is a combination of a number of frequencies: in addition to the fundamental frequency (the perceived pitch) there is a series of higher frequencies, or partials. When several tones are heard in combination, the complex interaction of their partials can create the illusion of additional tones (through the reinforcement of particular partials or the appearance of "sum" and "difference" tones). This distortion can come about at several different stages of the transmission process, including resonances in the acoustic space of the recording studio, in the electronic medium, in the acoustics of the listening environment, and in the processing of the acoustic event by our ears and brains. The high F I hear could simply be a particularly strong reinforcement of the partials of an F in a lower octave.

I resort to several tricks to try to hear the chord more clearly: at half-speed,

I can hear the chord for a longer period of time, but it is even more difficult to distinguish which note is on top. Since the pitch is proportionately
lowered, the timbre of the sounds is drastically altered, the sound is mud-
died, and the interference effects are, if anything, amplified. I try the time
stretcher, but again, the effect is to amplify the existing distortions rather
than to expunge them. In the end, I decide to rely on musical intuition and
write F as the topmost note.

Once past this initial barrier, the electric piano part is not hard to write
down, since it is based on a repeated pattern (a riff) that is apparently not

varied. But as more instruments are added to the ensemble, new ambiguities arise. Masking becomes a problem: when a softer sound is played in combination with a louder sound, especially one that is lower in pitch, there is a threshold beyond which the softer sound is not just difficult to hear but completely inaudible: the ear cannot respond to it. This begins to happen to the low notes in the electric piano as soon as the bass enters, and once the horns enter, I lose much of the electric piano part, and fill in the blanks by guesswork.

The bass part, since it is a monophonic line, initially seems to be easier to transcribe than the electric piano. A filter helps to make the part more prominent by cutting out the higher frequencies, and my transcription goes smoothly until I encounter the eighth-note runs beginning in measure 6. Here I find myself at another threshold of perception: though it is easy to tell the general direction of the runs, and the notes with which they begin and end, I have difficulty filling in the intermediate notes. When notes go by so rapidly in such a low register, my ear has difficulty distinguishing between whole-steps and half-steps, or major thirds and minor thirds.

Despite these uncertainties, transcribing the bass part is a delight, because it focuses my attention on Tommy Cogbill's elegant playing: I listen as he subtly varies the basic riff pattern in response to what is going on around him, punctuating the pauses in Aretha's vocal lines and articulating the larger boundaries of the form. I am especially intrigued to discover that after measure 12, Cogbill has expanded his 1-measure riff pattern to 2 measures, by varying what happens at the end of each measure, thus helping the music to breathe in longer spans. These details are things a casual listening may not reveal, but they are integral to the effect of the song.

After eight measures of the verse, Aretha begins playing acoustic piano. According to Wexler, the song was recorded without overdubs, so Aretha must have been singing and playing at the same time. Her piano part is flexible, nonrepetitive, and complements her singing: it fills and punctuates the pauses between her vocal lines. One can hear in the flow of her piano part the seeds of the more circumscribed, riff-styled parts played by the other instruments; it is easy to see how the band parts evolved from Aretha's piano playing during the rehearsal process. Needless to say, her part, with all its complexities, is far more difficult to capture on paper than the others. Aretha is playing in gospel style, often using full chords in both hands; the difficulties in resolving harmonies into individual pitches are compounded here. In addition, the horns are playing at full volume, and the electric piano continues, often masking the details of the piano part.

A moment particularly troubling to my ears is beat three of measure 22. I keep thinking I hear some sort of glissando, a descending cascade of notes from a high B-flat. It is not a sound I can satisfactorily duplicate on the piano. I'm not always sure I hear it; the "phantom glissando" disappears when I modify the playback in some ways (for example, slowing the speed) but reappears under some other modifications (using the time stretcher). It might be some sort of complex resonance or other acoustical quirk, but why then does it sound like a cascade of notes rather than a single sound? After agonizing over this moment for hours, I conclude that the "phantom glissando" must be an illusion: not something that Aretha actually played but something that my ears persist in constructing out of ambiguous audio signals.

I could go on to chronicle the problems I have in discerning what notes are played by the organ, the horns, and some of the details of the drumming, but the essential point should be clear. In the parts I have examined so far, the chief obstacle to transcription has been perceptual difficulties, a fundamental uncertainty over which notes were being played. The precise, gridlike representation of pitch in figure 8.2 does not really represent my perception, or the perception of any possible listener. I look at the clear little dots I have written on the staff, with their implication of a clear, binary simplicity—either this pitch is sounding at this point in time or it is not—and I know that it is a lie. As I listen, I can make out some notes clearly, but much of what I perceive is a Gestalt in which the component parts are not easily separable or identifiable. I can identify a chord, but not necessarily its exact voicing or scoring. I can hear that a line is descending, but I cannot make out the individual stages of the descent.

In jazz parlance, "ghost notes" are "notes more implied than actually played."[14] The elusive notes I pursue while trying to make this transcription are "ghosts" of a different sort—not implied by the performer but inferred, guessed at, assumed by the listener/transcriber. Were they actually played, or am I just imagining them? I begin to suspect that the task I have set myself is not just difficult, but impossible: there is an uncertainty principle at work here. Too many of the details I am trying to represent are, in the final analysis, beyond the threshold of perception and hence irretrievable; no amount of careful listening or electronic tinkering will enable me to determine them with absolute certainty. A more honest notation might be in shades of grey—from black for the notes I am sure I can hear to almost invisible for the ones of which I am least sure.

AUTOMATIC TRANSCRIPTION: MEASURING THE GROOVE

Faced with the difficulties and the limitations of perception that have frustrated my attempts so far, I begin to think about turning from aural transcription to automatic transcription—that is, making use of some sort of machine that mechanically converts recorded sound into a graphical representation. Ethnomusicologists began experimenting with such devices in the 1920s, in hopes of finding a more objective means of representing the music they were studying. But despite enormous advances in digital sound technology in the past few decades, the capabilities of existing transcription devices are still quite limited. The melograph, which was first developed at UCLA in the late 1940s, generates a graphical representation of the changes in pitch and loudness of a melodic line. But a melograph is of no use to me in my study of this recording, because it can only track a single line. The recording of "I Never Loved a Man" compresses a great deal of musical information into a single audio signal (or a pair of signals in the stereo version). When we listen to the recording, our ears easily resolve this signal into the sounds of a number of distinct instruments and voices. Yet our understanding of the neurological and physiological mechanisms by which the ear accomplishes this feat is incomplete. And there is as yet no computer algorithm that can successfully emulate the perceptual activity that makes this resolution possible. It will be a long time before we can ask a machine to produce a full score from a recorded signal.

Given the current state of our technology, then, an automatic transcription cannot answer the question, Exactly what notes are being played and sung? because it cannot aspire to such completeness; it can only reflect particular aspects of the musical sound. But it might provide the answer to some more limited questions.[15] At the very least, an automatic transcription might free me from the inherent subjectivity of transcribing by ear, and show me a picture of the sounds that are "really out there." To see what kinds of insights an automatic device might make possible, I decide to experiment with computer sampling software that generates a visual display of the envelope (that is, the variation in loudness, the attack and decay) of a recorded sound.[16] This is of no help in studying pitch, but it might help me to understand something about the rhythmic nature of the music. Of course, I am asking a very different kind of question now: What can I use this device to discover? My inquiry is being driven by the technology, not the other way around. When the texture of the music is complex the sampled display is of little use, since there is no way to distinguish the individual parts. But at the very beginning of "I Never Loved a Man" only a few instruments are playing, and when I use a filter to eliminate the lower frequencies of the signal, I can focus the display on the envelopes of Aretha's voice and the higher drum sounds: the hi-hat cymbal and the snare drum. Figure 8.3 is a graph of a portion of that display: the last beat of measure 4 through the first two beats of measure 6—Aretha's first vocal line.

I begin by looking at the drum sounds. Since the attack—the onset—of these sounds is quite sharp and fairly regular, it is easy to pinpoint the point in time at which they begin. My software is able to measure the distance between any two attacks in terms of microseconds, and I decide to measure all the attacks in the drum pattern for the nine measures beginning in measure 4. Perhaps these measurements can yield some insight into the nature of the rhythmic articulation—the "groove"—created by Roger Hawkins's drumming. This is a crucial element in the song, but one that Western notation does not represent, since it is a matter of minuscule deviations from a metronomically exact meter. As Charles Keil has observed, "It is the little discrepancies within a jazz drummer's beat, between bass and drums, between rhythm section and soloists, that create 'swing' and invite us to participate."[17]

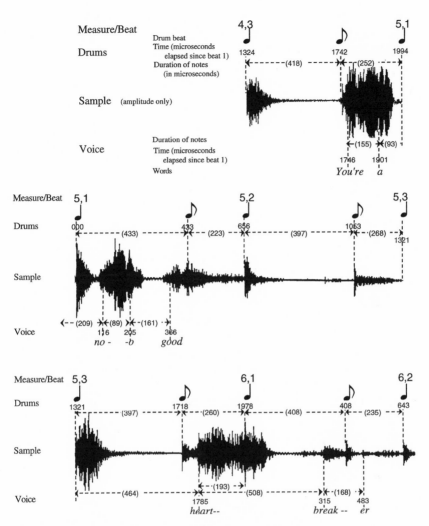

Figure 8.3. Sample and Measurements of First Line of Vocal Part.

The results of my measurements appear in figure 8.4.

By themselves, these measurements mean little. To interpret the data, I need to resort to some rudimentary number-crunching. I calculate the average duration of a beat (a dotted quarter-note) to be 660 microseconds. Although Roger Hawkins's beat sounds rock-steady, my measurements reveal slight deviations from mechanical exactness. The discrepancies range within ±48 microseconds, or roughly 17 percent of the value of a beat, a difference

$\frac{9}{8}$ ♩   ♪   ♩   ♪   ♩   ♪

Measure	Beat 1			Beat 2			Beat 3			
	Quarter	Total	Triplet	Quarter	Total	Triplet	Quarter	Total	Triplet	Measure Total
4	428	666	238	420	670	250	418	670	252	2006
5	433	656	223	397	665	268	397	657	260	1978
6	408	643	235	401	624	223	434	673	239	1940
7	399	654	255	378	614	236	424	658	234	1926
8	419	657	238	418	639	221	423	685	262	1981
9	418	685	267	412	650	238	482	691	209	2026
10	435	671	236	418	656	238	471	691	220	2018
11	486	679	193	415	636	221	453	702	249	2017
12	413	656	243	418	656	238	418	612	194	1924
Average	**427**	**663**	**236**	**409**	**646**	**237**	**436**	**671**	**235**	**1980**

Average Quarter	424	In NUTs:*	64
Average Eighth	236	In NUTs:	36
Average Dotted Quarter Beat	660	In NUTs:	100

Average Deviation from exact metrical time:

-13		16	-31		17	-4		15
	3			-14			11	

In NUTs*:

-2		2	-5		3	-1		2
	0			-2			2	

Subdivision of the beat, comparative Ratios (in NUTs*; Beat = 100)

Observed Ratio:	64 : 36
(Compound Meter) Quarter + Eighth :	66.7 : 33.3
5 32nds + 3 32nds :	62.5 : 37.5
Golden Section :	61.8 : 38.2

*NUTs = Nominal Units of Time (see Jairazbhoy,1983)

Figure 8.4. Analysis of Drum "Groove."

that is, I would guess, virtually imperceptible. To get at the "groove," though, I have to ask whether there is a consistent pattern to Hawkins's discrepancies.

The meter of this song—I notate it as 9/8, though it could also be notated as 3/4 with triplet subdivisions—is unique. I have heard it in Afro-American gospel music, but as far as I know this particular "groove" has never been used in any other Top 40 popular record, before or since. Hawkins does not subdivide the beat into exact triplets, but instead systematically shortens the quarter notes and lengthens the eighth-notes. The chart at the bottom of figure 8.4 compares the ratio created by Hawkins's subdivisions (64:36) to a few other ratios: it is somewhere between 2/3 + 1/3 and 5/8 + 3/8 of a beat; a trifle closer to the second of these. (This ratio is also close to the Golden Section—a proportion some theorists delight in discovering throughout nature and the arts—but it is closer to the other two ratios.)

The "groove" of a song depends not only on subtle shadings of the subdivisions of the beat but also on shadings of different beats within the measure. A "backbeat"—the accentuation of metrically unstressed beats—is often a central element in a groove. In a triple meter such as this, both beats 2 and 3 are unstressed, and Hawkins places a sharp snare drum accent on beat 3. (Later on, this backbeat is supplanted by an even stronger emphasis on beat 2: listen to the horn accents in mm. 25–27, and Chips Moman's guitar part in the second verse.) My measurements reveal that this backbeat is emphasized in most of the measures by a slight shortening of beat 2 and lengthening of beat 3: that is, the accented third beat comes slightly early. This anticipation doesn't sound like Hawkins is rushing the beat, however, possibly because the final eighth-note subdivision of beat 2 is given its full value; instead, the time is "robbed" from the initial quarter-note subdivision of beat 2 (see my calculations of "average deviation from exact metrical time" at the bottom of figure 8.4).[18]

This little experiment in automatic transcription gives me some insight into the nature of the groove: Roger Hawkins slightly equalizes the shuffle subdivisions of the beat, and he emphasizes the accented third beat with a slight anticipation (I find the second observation particularly interesting, because it runs counter to my intuitions: I would have guessed that the accented third beat came *late*, not early). But I must emphasize that this mini-study is far too limited to warrant drawing any final conclusions. An adequate account of the groove of this piece would have to embrace the full range of Charles Keil's "participatory discrepancies." I would have to find ways of detecting and measuring all the slight distortions and asynchronicities within and between all the instrumental and vocal parts that bring the beat to life. Clearly, if appropriate technology could be developed, automatic transcription would be of great use in such a task. But even by ear, with the aid of the time stretcher, I can hear some of the discrepancies: for example, Hawkins's eighth-notes often seem to anticipate the eighth-notes in Tommy Cogbill's bass.

I turned to automatic transcription in the hope that it could clarify my musical perception. By now it should be clear that this was a false hope. In a thoughtful essay on the limitations of automatic transcription, Nazir Jairazbhoy demonstrates the enormous discrepancies between music as it is represented in an automatic transcription and music as it is perceived by a human listener. He concludes: "An automatic transcription should not be thought of as a replacement for aural transcription. They perform different but equally justifiable functions. The primary value of automatic transcriptions would be to throw light on what we do *not* 'hear,' what we change in the process of 'hearing,' or what we take for granted. They can also provide an insight into some of the extremely subtle elements of music which we cannot readily distinguish aurally, but which might nevertheless influence our perception of the music on a subconscious plane." [19]

REPRESENTING THE VOICE

I can no longer postpone my transcription of the most important and challenging part of this recording: Aretha Franklin's voice. The instrumental parts, despite all the difficulties I have experienced in determining their details, are quite unambiguous in several important respects. All the instruments are tuned to the 12-note tempered scale, so whatever I can hear of their parts can be represented with confidence in terms of that pitch system. And for all the slight inflections and variations of timing that bring the rhythm to life, the basic rhythmic patterns the instruments play are clearly tied to the underlying 9/8 meter. But Aretha Franklin's singing is another matter altogether. Her flexible molding of pitch, rhythm, and timbre bursts through the arbitrary confines of our notational system. It will be very difficult to represent what she is singing in terms of the tempered scale or unambiguous subdivisions of the beat.

I decide to begin by trying to use the sample shown in figure 8.3 to determine the exact rhythm of Aretha's first vocal phrase. Locating the beginning of her notes is much more difficult than locating the drum attacks, since vocal attacks are far more smooth and gradual. Once I have arrived at a (somewhat arbitrary) method for locating the beginning of each of her notes, I measure the distance between them, and try to find an appropriate notation for the rhythmic relationships. As an aid to finding the best notation I construct a rhythmic grid (figure 8.5), dividing the beat (660 microseconds) into all the possible subdivisions between 2 and 9, plus 12 and 16.

Of all the tasks I have attempted in the course of this transcription, this turns out to be the most annoying and frustrating. I repeat my measurements on several different days, and each time the results are wildly divergent: my methodology has an extremely wide margin of error. Furthermore, trying to shoehorn the durations I measure into a coherent rhythmic scheme is an exercise in futility: my rhythmic grid makes distinctions that are far finer than my margin of error, or the 7% variability I noted in Hawkins's drum part.

Subdivisions of a quarter-note beat = 660 microseconds

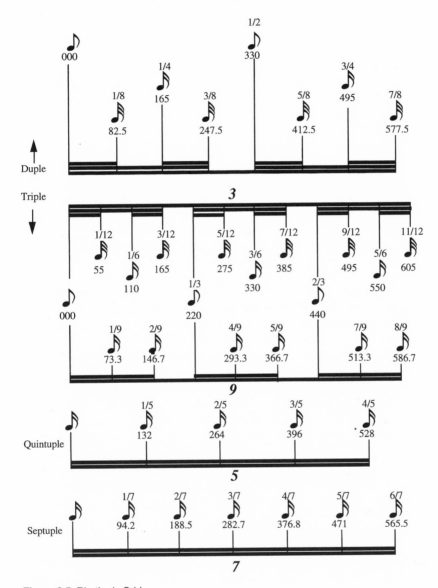

Figure 8.5. Rhythmic Grid.

The results of this exercise are shown in figure 8.6, which, with figure 8.5, I include here only for cautionary reasons: they may look very scientific, but they are pseudo-science, based on dubious methods of data collection, and far too many steps removed from the actual phenomena they purport to analyze.

To me, the most annoying thing about this experiment is how far my pursuit of objectivity has taken me from my experience of the actual sounding music. I sit silently in front of the purring computer for hours, taking measurements and crunching numbers. The only sounds I hear are the grotesque and obnoxious noises produced by "scrubbing" back and forth across small segments of the sample to try to determine the beginning of each syllable.

With relief I return to aural transcription. For all the starts and stops and obsessive repetitions of tiny scraps of sound, I feel in touch with the music again. And here, the time stretcher is a welcome aid. By slowing the speed while retaining the original pitch, it enables me to hear the intricate details of Aretha's singing in clear relief. Although the stretcher's resampling introduces a buzz into the timbre, to my ears the sound is by no means grotesque; it has its own hypnotic beauty. Every subtle shading, ornament, and articulation is drawn out and dwelled upon, and as I listen repeatedly and attempt to capture what I hear on paper my respect for Aretha Franklin's art continues to grow.

What do I hear? Let me attempt to find words to characterize one brief passage—measures 9 and 10—at the words "And I don't know why." Aretha begins with a dramatic leap of a tenth, from a very quiet low F on the word *and* up to an intense rising ornament on the word *I*: a slightly flat A moving immediately up to B-flat. She reverses this figure on the next syllable, *don't*, singing a downward thrusting B-flat / A-flat appoggiatura. The next two words, *know why*, are separated by a subtle passage across the vocal break—a slight catch in her voice, a hint of falsetto, almost a sob (the pitch of the falsetto note isn't exactly clear, but I have written it as a slightly sharp C). The word *why* continues with a four-note descending melisma: B / B-flat / A-flat / F; the final F trails off into aspirated breath, as do the endings of many of the other phrases. This is powerful text-setting: the way the melody twists around a central B-flat seems to mirror the lyrics' painful ambivalence ("I don't know why I let you do these things to me").

Attempting to capture her singing in musical notation is only a little less awkward than attempting to characterize it in prose. The basic premises of our notational system may be inappropriate to such a task. As Robert Gjerdingen has written: "Poets know that notes warble. They know that notes glide and soar, quaver and shake, bend and curve sinuously in ways that communicate subtle feelings to receptive listeners. . . . our traditional conceptions of a tone hamper our ability to analyze the fluid shapes and motions that mean so much in fine singing."[20] Gjerdingen suggests that a highly ornamented

Figure 8.6. Attempts at Rhythmic Notation of the first Vocal Line.

vocal style such as Aretha's cannot adequately be represented as a succession of notes understood as "atoms of pitch—single, static points in musical time and space."[21] Points have no insides, but the essence of Aretha's singing lies in what happens "inside" the notes: pitches are not fixed; they glide up and down, they shift in color and timbre, they are shaped into ornamental arabesques. Gjerdingen has developed an elegant variant of the melograph to represent these details, but, as we have already seen, a melograph cannot be used here. So I decide to try to adapt Western musical notation to my purposes.

In the effort to portray such effects in Western notation, transcribers have devised an array of special symbols; the ones I have employed in my transcription are listed in figure 8.7.

| Slightly (c. 1/4 - tone) flat | Slightly (c. 1/4 - tone) sharp | Vibrato upward from pitch | Vibrato downward from pitch | Appogiatura (Upper note is on the beat) |

Glides (note bends):

| Pitch-glide beginning as note is attacked | Pitch sustained, then gliding upward | Glide between two pitches; second pitch sustained | Glide at end of phrase; final note heard but not sustained | Glide at end of phrase; final note not clearly heard |

Other vocal sounds:

| "(hhh)" Aspiration at end of phrase | "d" or "t" Terminal consonant, end of phrase | Passage across vocal break (see m. 9) | "you - (ah)" vowel shift |

Rhythmic stress:

| Primary stress (downbeat) of a phrase |

Figure 8.7. Symbols for Transcription of Vocal Part.

With these symbols I attempt to show some of the features of Aretha's style: the range of her inflection of pitch (the area between the third and fifth of the scale is particularly rich in inflections—in addition to the various glides and glissandi within this region, I think I can separate ten distinct stable pitches); her use of precisely controlled vibrato, her shifts in vowel sounds, her use of aspiration at the ends of phrases and her careful placement of terminal consonants, and special sounds such as the catch in her voice mentioned above. Although I have tried to be as precise and consistent as possible, these representations are—once again—ultimately based on subjective judgments. The distinctions I have attempted to make between various kinds of pitch-glides or note-bends might be drawn very differently by another transcriber. The distinction between a fixed note and a glide or bend is not always unambiguous, especially when the note is short. And my judgments about the exact pitch of a note, particularly when I attempt to distinguish microtonal inflections, are often arbitrary and conditioned by the context in which I hear the note.

My representation of the rhythm of Aretha's singing is similarly subjective. It is always difficult to decide how fussy to be about rhythm. Many notes fall slightly before or after a particular beat or subdivision; should I attempt to pinpoint these inflections exactly? I attempt a compromise between excessive complexity and oversimplification in my notation. But my choices about how to realize this compromise are conditioned as much by the limitations of the notational system as by the realities of the rhythms I hear.

Despite the compromises, my rhythmic notation is extremely complex. This complexity stems in part from the inadequacies of the notational system, and in part from the genuine complexity of Aretha's rhythmic phrasing. I am quite sure, for example, that I hear her moving back and forth between triple and duple subdivisions of the beat. The duple subdivisions are polyrhythmic to the basic triple subdivisions of the 9/8 meter (depending on the context, I notate them either as dotted values or as quadruplets); furthermore, she does not always begin them on the beat. The clearest example is in measure 23, on the words "stuck like glue": these notes are evenly spaced a duple eighth note apart, but the group begins on the third (triple) subdivision of beat 2. The tension this kind of polyrhythmic interplay creates against the beat is part of what makes Aretha's singing so expressive and vital.

The rhythmic tension between Aretha's singing and the underlying meter is particularly striking when we look at the placement of her phrases. I have used an acute accent (´) to indicate where I think Aretha places the primary stresses of each phrase. Rarely does she place two stresses in the same metrical position, and nearly all of her stresses are off the beat. In the first twelve bars her only on-beat stresses are in measure 9 ("I" on beat 2), and in measure 12 ("me" on the downbeat): both of these on-beat stresses are important structural boundaries (the first stress of the second half of the verse, and the final stress of the verse), and could be thought of as momentary resolutions of the tension between her rhythm and the meter. Could it also be significant that both are first-person pronouns? In the midst of her anger and confusion about her abusive lover, when she refers to herself she grounds herself in the beat. As the song moves into the chorus, Aretha places more and more of her stresses on the beat, until, beginning in measure 28—the climax of the chorus and the beginning of her three-measure vocal break—each stress is placed squarely on the downbeat of the measure. The concluding "hook" of the chorus thus resolves the rhythmic tension she had set up earlier, just as the words turn from ambivalence to affirmation.

There are other important dimensions to Aretha's singing, such as dynamics and timbre, that I haven't even tried to represent in this transcription. Aretha's shaping of dynamics is as intricate and flexible as her shaping of every other aspect of her singing. I could pepper the score with *crescendi* and *decrescendi, piani* and *forti*; but these are crude indicators, and again, I would have to make difficult decisions about how much detail to show, for every note has a unique dynamic shaping. It would be even harder to show anything about her use of vocal timbre. I have indicated places where she shifts her vowel sounds, but beyond that I would have to invent a whole new set of symbols to indicate how she varies the brightness and darkness of her voice. And so far I have only mentioned the lyrics of the song, and Aretha's declamation of them, in passing.

I must remember that in separating out these discrete "dimensions" or "aspects" of Aretha's singing—pitch, rhythm, dynamics, timbre, text-setting—I am being highly influenced by the notational system. These distinctions have little to do with the actual act of performance, or with how I experience her voice. It would be ludicrous to imagine her first deciding what notes to sing, then where to place them rhythmically, then what dynamics to apply. As she sings, I hear, not an assemblage of discrete ingredients, but a single entity, the result of a unified impulse. When I listen to her singing, I can feel that impulse, but it is not anything I can describe with any precision. On paper I have no way of representing that impulse; the best I can do is to hope that it might somehow be inferred through the traces it leaves in the various dimensions my notational system is able to represent.

''WHY TRANSCRIBE?''

Having completed my transcription, I must ask: Why have I done this? What are my motivations for spending all this time fussing over an old record? Why is it so important to try to find out what is "really going on" in this music, especially when the process has proved so difficult and the results so indeterminate? What is the value of such a transcription? What uses can it be put to? There are several possible answers to these questions, but each answer raises further questions.

One: To Show What's "Really There"

Musical notation is an undeniably useful tool when writing about music. It can give a reader who has no access to a recording of the music a sketchy notion of what it might sound like. In particular, notation can function as an efficient way of isolating and referring to specific passages or individual elements in the musical stream. (Such functions may become obsolete in the next generation of media technology: for the reader/listener with access to the proper gadgets, written text and recorded sound may be dynamically linked.) This modest function of notation—as a kind of index or blueprint— cannot be faulted. But it must be remembered that a transcription is a blueprint drawn *after* the building is built. And one must resist the temptation of mistaking the blueprint for the building.

The narrative of my struggles to notate this recording should be enough to demonstrate that even the most scrupulously detailed transcription is full of guesses, suppositions, and arbitrary decisions. My old question, What notes are being played and sung? can never be answered definitively. It is a mistake to think of a transcriber as a scientist, objectively recording aural phenomena. The transcriber's role cannot really be passive or detached. When transcribing, I do not listen to the notes one by one in the attempt to assign a frequency and rhythmic value to each. I really hear larger shapes, Gestalten, which I attempt, with varying degrees of success, to break down into constituent elements. Predicting and guessing are essential parts of the process. Do I hear a D or an E-flat? Is this rhythm based on duple or triple subdivisions? I try to hear it either way in turn; I sing it both ways, or play it on the piano, or beat out the rhythm as I listen. The disturbing thing is that I can often hear it *both* ways (though not simultaneously). My mindset, my mental image, has a great deal to do with what I hear.

Throughout this essay I have written of notation as the unreal approximation of real music. But what is the nature of this reality? Is it the set of physical wave forms encoded in the recorded media, reproduced through amplifiers and speakers? Or is it what we as listeners hear? Every listener hears slightly different things, and every time I hear this recording I hear something different. Perception is not merely the intake of sense data; it involves actively interpreting the data and matching them against imagined models. Nazir Jairazbhoy writes: "When listening to a familiar tradition, our 'hearing' is influenced by very specific memories, as well as musical syntax, both of which induce feelings of anticipation, frustration, suspense, and reso-lution. These feelings result from an interaction between what we expect to hear and what we actually do hear . . . . There is, and perhaps always will be, a large gap between what an automatic transcriber would 'hear' and what an experienced listener of a particular musical idiom might 'hear.'"[22]

There is an important corollary to this observation. At the outset of this project, I suggested a simple procedure for the study of this music: first make a transcription, then analyze it. We can now see the fundamental flaw in this procedure: the transcription must itself rest on analytic presupposi-tions. Though my aural transcription (figure 8.2) seemed to stand on its own, it was in fact conditioned by my knowledge of the style, my years of listening to this recording, my instincts as a composer and performer. I was looking for specific things in the music, and I found them. As the transcription pro-cess went on and I focused on more specific questions, I tacitly abandoned the idea of separating transcription from analysis.

What this all suggests is that a transcription is not so much a scientific measurement of data as it is, as Pandora Hopkins has suggested, a kind of work of art in itself: "The notion . . . of notation as a different and distinct art form [from music]—a way of manipulating visual designs to communicate one's individual impressions—one's opinion—of music to other people (or even to oneself), seems to us not only valid but utterly fascinating."[23] The criteria I have invoked in making decisions about how and what to transcribe have been as much aesthetic as scientific. My activities as a transcriber are less like a physical scientist taking readings from instruments than they are like a translator rendering a poem from one language into another.

Two: To Support Arguments about Its Historical and Social Significance

Why fuss over this particular record? I have made no secret of my admiration for it. But so far I have spoken of it as though it were an "autonomous" work of art. It may appear that I am fetishizing this song, that the point of lavishing such attention on it is to demonstrate its value in and for itself, to canonize it as a work of "Great Art" that "transcends the social, the political and the everyday."[24] In so doing I am guilty of reproducing the very habits of thought I am attempting to criticize. As a corrective, let me return to the story behind this recording, to give a brief account of what I see as its social and historical significance.

"I Never Loved a Man" was the song that initiated Aretha Franklin's rise to stardom and hence represents a pivotal moment in the diffusion of Afro-American styles to a mass audience. Though she was not the first black artist to achieve success singing popular music in a Gospel-based style, Aretha

Franklin was the first woman to do so, and her popularity with the mainstream pop audience eclipsed that of precursors such as Clyde McPhatter, Sam Cooke, or even Ray Charles. The genre she established still occupies a central position in popular music: contemporary examples include the work of such pop/soul divas as Whitney Houston and Mariah Carey, and the obligatory "soulful" ballads that accompany the end-credits of so many contemporary Hollywood films.

The record is also significant because of the racial and gender politics that surrounded its making. For all the power and assurance of the recording, it couldn't have been an easy session for Aretha. A great deal was riding on this, her first session for Atlantic. She was singing and playing with an all-white band, recording at Fame Studios, near Muscle Shoals, Alabama, a small studio in a small southern town. Aretha and her husband were the only African-Americans present in the studio, and as far as I can tell, Aretha was the only woman present. Jerry Wexler, Atlantic's producer, had asked studio owner Rick Hall to hire a horn section with some black musicians in it: "I didn't want to present Aretha and her husband, Ted White, with the spectacle of a wall-to-wall white band . . . But Rick didn't bother to get 'em, so the whole thing was white."[25] We don't have to guess whether there was racial tension at the session, we *know* there was: late in the evening a fight erupted between Ted White and one of the horn players, who had used a racial epithet. The remaining Fame sessions were canceled, and from then on Wexler recorded Aretha in New York, flying in his southern musicians and making sure that the band was integrated.

But despite the tension, I think it is fairly clear that the most powerful figure at the session was not the producer, the composer, or the arranger, but Aretha Franklin herself. This was atypical of recording sessions at the time, and was even atypical of Aretha's own recordings in later years. It was she who chose the song, taught it to the other musicians, and shaped the style of the performance through her singing and piano playing. As Roger Hawkins put it, "Aretha's emotion made everything work . . . . I played to her voice."[26] Though she is not credited as a composer, her florid gospel-styled vocal line must have amounted to a fundamental recomposition of Ronny Shannon's original melody, just as her later versions of such songs as "Eleanor Rigby" or "Bridge over Troubled Water" recomposed those melodies. And I am sure that she improvised the additional lyrics that are just barely audible in the fade-out, lyrics that strikingly reverse the passive victim's role portrayed in the body of the song:

> I ain't never had a man that hurt me so bad
> But this is what I'm gonna do about it
> I tell you I'm gonna hold on

Early in this essay I complained that popular music scholarship too often treats the music itself as a kind of unknowable "black box." Can the knowledge we have gained of this music through transcription and analysis shed any light on the racial and gender politics surrounding the production of the recording? I believe that many of the musical details I discovered in the course of making this transcription confirm Aretha's dominant position in this recording and her influence on how the other musicians played. Can we go farther than that? How exactly did her style affect the playing of the white musicians? Did their style have an effect on her? Did this musical collaboration succeed in resolving the racial and gender tensions implicit in the situation, or did those tensions leave residual traces in the music? Can we "read the text" of this recording for evidence of the unresolved contradictions in the society that produced it?

There isn't room to explore such questions here, but if we were to compare this transcription with transcriptions of other records—of later sessions where Aretha's own input had diminished, of her work with black bands such as King Curtis' Kingpins, of the Muscle Shoals band's work with other performers—we might begin to find some answers. Nevertheless, it is a tricky business to connect specific musical observations to broad social issues. It is all too easy to generalize from meager evidence, to mistake subjective reactions and prejudices for hard data, or to assume that framing one's observations in the language of the latest French intellectual fashion will automatically confirm their validity. Yet if we fail to attempt to make such connections, we can rightfully be accused of being irrelevant.

Three: To Establish the Legitimacy of the Music

I have not yet answered the charge that, in the act of transcribing and analyzing this song, I am making claims for its transcendent value, or "canonizing" it. Could my transcription be interpreted as an attempt to establish its legitimacy?

This is an overtly political use for notated transcriptions: to endow a musical tradition with respectability by presenting it in the same trappings as one presents Western concert music. In announcing plans for the Jazz Masterworks Editions, a series of published transcriptions of classic jazz performances by Duke Ellington and other jazz masters, Gunther Schuller stated: "In our society, jazz will never be recognized as a fully respectable, serious art until we have available a representative and substantial jazz literature to be studied, to be performed, to exist in music libraries and stores, and thus to be revered just as much as we revere classical music." [27] Schuller's aim is to establish a jazz canon that can be archived and enshrined in university libraries alongside complete editions of European composers and the national "monument" collections like *Denkmäler Deutscher Tonkunst*. This is a shrewd political strategy and deserves to be taken seriously. I feel that not only jazz but many other kinds of music marginalized by the academy (many of which Schuller would oppose admitting into the canon)—including the music of Aretha Franklin—deserve serious respect and attention, and their study should be a part of any musician's education. In that sense, I am arguing for the "canonization" of this song.

But Schuller's statement makes me uncomfortable, because it seems to imply judging the music by inappropriate standards. It appears to battle Eurocentrism but ultimately capitulates to it: if only notated music is truly "respectable and serious," then this music must be notated. My notations of Aretha Franklin's singing may look as complex as many "serious" contemporary scores. But that should not be the measure of the value of her art; as we have seen, the complexity of the notation is as much a critique of the notational system as it is a reflection of the true complexity of her singing. A transcription is a very poor substitute for actually hearing her voice. If we are to take this music seriously, we must take it seriously on its own terms. A transcription can be an aid to this, but we must avoid the temptation of thinking of the notation as a substitute for the music itself.

The danger of a notated score of "I Never Loved a Man," then, is the tendency for such a representation to place it in the alien context of the European art music tradition. If we are to expand the canon to include music such as this, it is important that we expand our frame of reference as well. We should understand that recorded sound, not a transcribed score, is the primary medium in which this song exists. And we must regard this song not as an autonomous, timeless production of a transcendent artistic "genius" but as the product of social and historical milieu in which it was created and through which its meanings are constructed.

Four: To Reproduce the Music in Live Performance

For most of this essay, I have been concerned with descriptive transcription. But we shouldn't ignore the practical uses of prescriptive transcriptions. This has been the most frequent motivation for transcription in jazz. The use of written transcriptions of improvised solos for pedagogical purposes dates back to the publication of books of "hot trumpet breaks" in the 1920s.[28] More recently, similar pedagogical transcriptions—both in Western notation and in guitar tabulature—have been published for rock musicians. Such practical transcriptions, of course, do not have to capture matters of style; performers are always encouraged to use the transcriptions in tandem with recordings, and even if they are not able to do so, they are expected to understand how to "swing" and how to achieve idiomatic phrasing and articulation through aural means. Learning notated solos can be an efficient way to develop a repertory of improvisational "licks."

A more problematic employment of transcriptions is in the recent "Jazz Repertory" movement, in which classic recordings are recreated in live performance. In announcing the "Jazz Masterworks Editions," Gunther Schuller said, "While it's true that we have great jazz performances on records, records are not a living legacy . . . any music that is not kept alive in live performance will die, sooner or later."[29]

I have made and used many such transcriptions myself, transcribing piano rags by Eubie Blake and James P. Johnson for myself and solos by such players as Benny Goodman, Sidney Bechet, and Stéphane Grapelli for other musicians. But I am uneasy about this practice. Is using a transcription to facilitate the note-for-note reproduction of a solo improvised many years ago truly a way of "keeping the music alive?" It involves a fundamental alteration of the way in which the music was produced. What had been an improvisation, a crystallization of a particular time and place and combination of musicians, is treated as a composition, a score to be reproduced as Western art music is reproduced. In order to bring the music to life, I must attempt to infuse it with my own musical spirit, just as I do when I am playing Chopin or Mozart. As Charles Keil puts it, a notated score is only "a petrified skeleton on which to hang the flesh and blood of actual music-making."[30] But I am playing music that was never meant to be transmitted and reproduced through notation, and that calls the entire enterprise into question. When I play, say, a Jelly Roll Morton piece from one of James Dapogny's excellent transcriptions, am I bringing the music to life, or am I embalming it? Should I be compared to Vladimir Horowitz performing Chopin—or to Robin Williams imitating Louis Armstrong?

Five: To Appropriate the Music as Currency for Academic Exchange

The ultimate site for the politics of transcription is the academy. As an academic, operating within the paradigms of the academic community, I need to consider what unspoken motivations might lie beneath my own urge to transcribe. I must own that there is a sense in which making a transcription is like claiming possession of the music: transcription can function for me as a kind of vicarious composition or performance. As Bruno Nettl notes, "Having made a transcription gives . . . [ethnomusicologists] a certain sense of direct ownership and control over the music that they have laboriously reduced to notation."[31]

The urge toward possession, toward rational control, is of course a strong motivation for scholarship. Susan McClary and Robert Walser have pointed out some of the painful contradictions this urge can involve: "It is . . . the intellectually committed among us who become academics—those who are uncomfortable with inexplicable sensual responses and who wish to be able to control those responses rationally. Yet musicologists also are individuals who find themselves drawn to music so irresistibly that they dedicate their careers to trying to figure out what makes it tick. This combination of intense attraction and fear of the irrational or of the sensual creates a strange set of priorities: to seize the objects that are most profoundly disturbing and to try to explain away—through extensive verbalization and theorizing—that which caused the disturbance."[32]

In addition to these mixed personal motives for transcribing, I must acknowledge the role of academic politics. By bringing popular music into the province of scholarly discourse, I and scholars like me are establishing a new beachhead for academic colonization, claiming new territory for the production of items of exchange in the academic economy: conference papers, journal articles, doctoral theses, and books such as this one. By contributing this essay to a book devoted to critical reevaluations of musicological paradigms, I am participating in a debate that, whatever its other motivations and outcomes, is part of the further proliferation (if not outright inflation) of such academic currency. This currency has a measurable economic value: it is the basis on which we are evaluated when we are considered for academic positions, for promotion or for tenure.

There is no easy escape from such dilemmas: these are the rules of the game, the conditions under which academic production is made possible. When the study of popular music—or of any phenomenon of mass culture— is reduced to this economic bottom line, it can seem trivial, if not ludicrous. It is not surprising that the popular press and the recent crop of conservative critics of academia treat such pursuits with scorn or derision. We need to retain a sense of humor about what we do—as Philip Tagg remarks, "It *can* be hilarious at times"[33]—but we should not lose sight of the importance of what we are attempting to do: to understand our musical environment and the effects music has on our lives.

TRANSCRIPTION RECONSIDERED

If a truly objective transcription is impossible, if the act of transcription is inevitably suffused with the subjectivity of the transcriber, if the connections one can draw between a transcription and the music's social and political context are tenuous, if a transcription can be misappropriated as a means of faking an improvisation, establishing "legitimacy," or furthering one's academic career, then why bother?

Despite the negative tone of the last remarks, I still believe that transcription is an indispensable tool for studying music. But we must rethink its uses. Rather than seeing it as a way of distancing oneself from the music, transcription should be seen as a deep and intimate involvement in musical processes. The goal should not be an objective representation but just the opposite: transcription must be recognized as an intensely *subjective* act. And this should be recognized not as a fundamental weakness, but as a fundamental strength.

Bruno Nettl emphasized the importance of transcription as a learning device: "Transcription by ear amounts to careful listening which is organized so that various aspects of a musical style can be perceived in some kind of order. Listening to a piece without the aid of transcribing it is, in a sense, like hearing a lecture without taking notes—something which has its values but which results in a more general, superficial impression than does the intensive listening with the help of paper and pencil." [34]

I would state Nettl's remarks even more strongly: the *primary* usefulness of transcription is the process, not the product. For me, the act of transcription is a form of meditation. When I transcribe, I am interacting with the music. I focus my attention on every event, straining to hear what the musicians were doing, matching what I hear against what I can reproduce, what I can manage to represent on paper, sharpening my awareness of those nuances and details that elude transcription. At every turn I learn something new as I match my expectations and my experience with the sounds I actually hear. I am not always able to verbalize or notate what I learn in this process, but I feel that the music is shaping me, changing me, as I go along. I am being transformed by the music; I am living inside it. Far from feeling that transcription allows me to posses the music, I feel that the music possesses *me*.

If we think of the work of the transcriber as an art form in itself, analogous to the art of the translator, then the strictures Rudolf Pannwitz set for translation should apply: the translator should "allow . . . his language to be powerfully affected by the foreign tongue . . . . He must expand and deepen his language by means of the foreign language." [35] The experience of transcribing a song like "I Never Loved a Man" should lead to a deformation, an expansion and deepening, of our notational system and of our habits of musical thought.

The chief value of a transcription, then, is to the transcriber. If I were to take this notion to its logical conclusion, I would argue that transcriptions should be tossed into the wastebasket as soon as they are completed. But I must own that a completed transcription has some value to others, so long as the readers have access to the original recording. Following the recording with the transcription might enable the reader to muster up a faint shadow of the understanding and involvement that the transcriber originally gained from the process. Without that recording, the capacity of a transcription to do good is enormously diminished, and its capacity to do harm is enormously enlarged.

To present a notated score as an objective representation of a complex piece of music such as "I Never Loved a Man" is an act of arrogance. But to attempt to transcribe it, as any ethnomusicologist knows, is a lesson in humility. It is this spirit of humility that we must never lose while pursuing our scholarly enterprises. And it is this spirit of humility that we can pass on to our readers and our students. We must tell them: "Listen. Listen again. There is more to this music than you think."

NOTES

For their help, comments, and suggestions about earlier drafts of this paper, I am grateful to Jane Sugarman, Robert Gjerdigen, Joseph Auner, Daniel Weymouth, Rob Walser, David Brackett, Krin Gabbard, and David Schwarz.

1. The seminal work in the analysis of popular music is by Philip Tagg. See his *Kojak: 50 Seconds of Television Music* (Göteborg: Skrifter från Musikvetenskapliga Institutionen, 1977) and "Analyzing Popular Music; Theory, Method, and Practice," *Popular Music 2* (1982): 37–68. More recent analytical work can be found in Richard Middleton, *Studying Popular Music* (Milton Keynes: Open Univ. Press, 1990); Susan McClary, *Feminine Endings* (Minneapolis: Univ. of Minnesota Press, 1991); Sheila Whitely, *The Space between the Notes* (New York: Routledge, 1992); Robert Walser, *Running with the Devil* (Hanover, N. H.: Univ. of New England Press, 1993); David Brackett, *Interpreting Popular Music* (Cambridge: Cambridge Univ. Press, 1995); and in the pages of such periodicals as *Popular Music* and *Journal of Popular Music Studies.*

The reasons why most popular music scholars avoid examination of the music itself would take another full essay to explore. An excellent summary of the dilemmas involved may be found in Susan McClary and Robert Walser, "Start Making Sense! Musicology Wrestles with Rock," in Simon Frith and Andrew Goodwin, eds., *On Record: Rock, Pop, and the Written Word* (New York: Pantheon, 1990).

2. See Peter Winkler, "Randy Newman's Americana," *Popular Music* 7, no. 1 (1988): 1–26, and "Toward a Theory of Popular Harmony," *In Theory Only* (1978): 1–26.

3. The most thoughtful survey of the dialogue is in Bruno Nettl, *The Study of Ethnomusicology: Twenty-nine Issues and Concepts* (Urbana and Chicago: Univ. of Illinois Press, 1983). See especially chap. 6, "I Can't Say a Thing Until I've Seen the Score."

4. The recording, made in Muscle Shoals, Alabama, in January 1967, was originally released on Atlantic 2386, and has been reissued frequently. My study is based upon Atlantic CD 81668–2, Aretha Franklin: 30 Greatest Hits (1986).

5. Nettl, *The Study of Ethnomusicology*, 65.

6. See Walter J. Ong, *Orality and Literacy: The Technologizing of the Word* (1982; reprint London: Routledge, 1988).

7. Ibid., 78.

8. Ibid., 31–32.

9. Bruno Nettl, *Theory and Method in Ethnomusicology* ([New York:] Free Press, of Glencoe, 1964).

10. Pandora Hopkins, "The Purposes of Transcription," *Ethnomusicology* 10, no. 3 (1966): 310–17.

11. Charlie Gillett, *Making Tracks: The Story of Atlantic Records* (London: Souvenir Press, 1974), 209.

12. Charles Seeger, "Prescriptive and Descriptive Music Writing," *Studies in Musicology, 1935–1975* (Berkeley: Univ. of California Press, 1977), 168.

13. The device I used was an Eventide Ultra-Harmonizer, which had been fitted with a "studio sampler" chip.

14. Gunther Schuller, *The Swing Era* (New York: Oxford Univ. Press, 1989), 864.

15. Only a few attempts to apply automatic transcription to the realm of popular music have been made so far. David Brackett, for instance, has used frequency spectrograms to analyze the timbral qualities of recordings by Hank Williams, James Brown, and Elvis Costello. See David Brackett, *Interpeting Popular Music* (Cambridge Univ. Press, 1995).

16. The software I used was Sound Designer 2.

17. Charles Keil, "Participatory Discrepancies and the Power of Music," *Cultural Anthropology* 2, no. 3 (1987): 277; reprinted in Keil and Feld, *Music Grooves* (Chicago: Univ. of Chicago Press, 1994).

18. For ease of comparison, I have represented the ratios and deviations from mathematical accuracy in figure 8.4 by means of Nazir A. Jairazbhoy's system of Nominal Units of Time (NUTs), which represents durations in terms of 1/100 of a beat. See Jairazbhoy, "Nominal Units of Time: A Counterpart for Ellis' System of Cents," *Selected Reports in Ethnomusicology* 4 (1983): 113–24.

19. Nazir A. Jairazbhoy, "The 'Objective' and Subjective View in Music Transcriptions," *Ethnomusicology* 21, no. 2 (1977): 270.

20. Robert Gjerdingen, "Shape and Motion in the Microstructure of Song," *Music Perception* 6, no. 1 (1988): 35–36.

21. Gjerdingen, "Shape and Motion," 36.

22. Jairazbhoy, "The 'Objective' and Subjective View," 268.

23. Hopkins, "The Purposes of Transcription," 313.

24. Janet Wolff, "The Ideology of Autonomous Art," in Richard Leppert and Susan McClary, eds., *Music and Society: The Politics of Composition, Performance, and Reception* (Cambridge: Cambridge Univ. Press, 1987), 1.

25. Mark Bego, *Aretha Franklin, the Queen of Soul* (New York: St. Martin's Press, 1989), 84. The information in the remainder of this paragraph is from the same source.

26. Ibid., 94.

27. Gunther Schuller, prospectus for Jazz Masterworks Editions, quoted in *RPM* 13 (1989): 16.

28. For a concise survey and discussion of jazz transcription, see Mark Tucker, "Transcription," in *The New Grove Dictionary of Jazz* (London: MacMillan, 1988), 545–47.

29. Schuller, prospectus, 16.

30. Keil, "Participatory Discrepancies," 279.

31. Nettl, *The Study of Ethnomusicology*, 78.

32. McClary and Walser, "Start Making Sense!" 286.

33. Tagg, "Analyzing Popular Music," 39.

34. Nettl, *Theory and Method in Ethnomusicology*, 127–28.

35. Quoted in Walter Benjamin, "The Task of the Translator," in *Illuminations* (New York: Schocken, 1969).

JENNIFER RYCENGA

Sisterhood: A Loving Lesbian Ear Listens to Progressive Heterosexual Women's Rock Music

I have always had a passion for richly complex popular music and a deep desire to hear women musicians engaged in such music. For decades, it seemed, such opportunities were rare; the complex musics appeared to be the boys' preserve, and the women musicians were far too often props for male sexist fantasies than their own self-creations.[1] But, as Gillian Gaar so brilliantly chronicles in *She's a Rebel*, women have "worked hard to overcome the dismissive 'novelty' tag they have so often been saddled with" and are now in a position where "the opportunities for determining the direction of rock & roll's future are virtually unlimited."[2] This raises new questions for women, as the simple fact of our representation in the music world is replaced by the quixotic nature of multiple representations and their resulting musical, political, and sexual meanings. As a lesbian listener, musician, composer, and scholar, I am intrigued by my strongly positive *lesbian* response to the music of three leading women composer/performers: Kate Bush, PJ Harvey, and Tori Amos. This essay addresses how their music can be heard lesbian-i-cally, without appropriating them as pseudolesbians or critiquing their ambivalent allegiance to heterosexuality (which all three of them criticize with a mercilessness that would be labeled instantly as man-hating if sung by an out lesbian), and without suggesting that a lesbian-ic hearing is limited only to lesbians.

THEORETICAL MUSINGS

In her essay "Uses of the Erotic: The Erotic as Power," Audre Lorde pithily suggests a female and/or lesbian ontology of experience, located in "the erotic." Her definition of this much-maligned word avoids foreclosure by adopting a cumulative process of expansion. In the first three pages of the work, she describes the erotic as "a resource within," "the power of our unexpressed or unrecognized feelings," a "power" and "energy for change," which under oppression is corrupt, distorted, suppressed, not considered. The erotic is source, resource, power, teacher, immediate experience. And, paradoxically, it is "*firmly* rooted in the *unexpressed* or *unrecognized*" (emphasis mine): in other words, the erotic is definitively located in the undefined.[3]

Such deliberate ambiguities breathe in feminist philosophies that stress the material.[4] By valuing the particularities of personal experience and our interactions with the physical world, Lorde's "erotic" provides an open-ended mode of apprehension, born from her Black lesbian experience but eminently capable of analogous development by others. Her approach values both specificities from her experience and a general function of the erotic as an agent of growth and transformation. In postulating a "lesbian ear" I am working in the spirit of Lorde's erotic: suggesting that the intensities of our interactions with other bodies parallel the intensities of our interactions with sound, with thought, and with our work.[5] Just as Lorde can see the world in a packet of yellow coloring for margarine,[6] or Julian of Norwich can mystically apprehend the universe in a hazelnut,[7] likewise, the lesbian ear can auditorily perceive a singular yet shared world via the materiality of sound, musical motion, and temporality.[8] Thus, my analysis suggests that any individual's experiences of sound, music, and materiality are both idiosyncratically unique and simultaneously locatable within certain interpretive grids, at least some of which are determined by the material conditions of our physicality.

This postulated loving lesbian ear is an effort to overlap formal, political, literary, relational, interpersonal, subjective, and physical modalities of listening. It is "loving" because, while I do not eschew criticism, I prefer to focus on the positive, without investment in strategies of exclusion.[9] My smorgasbord methods incorporate formal analysis, critical theory, musicianship, theories of power, philosophy, and more.

I have chosen to analogize sexuality and the act of listening in order to stress the physicality and temporality of both activities. To use the word *lesbian* as if it were a simple term is not possible, because all universalizing definitions that have been proposed—sexual activity of women with women, affectional preference, political opposition to heterosexism, stylistic "butch-femme" performance—are inadequate. In fact, the only people who seem to be able to agree on who the lesbians are would be those who demonize us, such as the authors of antiqueer ballot initiatives.[10] But musicians should know better than to freeze concepts of identity, since we deal in a genre located in the ex-static: time and movement. This is why it behooves us to avoid an uncritical adoption of postmodern methods of linguistic deconstruction.

Fastening on the unmaking and making of verbal meaning may be just as inimical to music analysis as a detached analytic viewpoint. To speak of lesbian identity as a fixed given or biological essentialism will not work philosophically, but swinging to the opposite pole of lesbian identity as a construction is a negligible achievement that short-changes both the political struggles of queers and our creative originality. It is no accident that postmodernism has consigned to the dustbin of its theories all narratives of revolution and utopia as well as those of imperialism and other tyrannies: it seems more concerned with demonstrating the dependent origin of all activities, styles, and other elements of bricollage, than envisioning what lies beyond the reassembly of the given.

Instead, I would suggest an approach that stresses difference and agency, understanding that differing epistemologies and resulting different worldviews emerge and are crafted from different physicalities, different subject positions, and different experiences. At the same time, these epistemologies are by no means mutually exclusive: I conceive of them as intertwined and refer to them as "bunched epistemologies."[11] Thus, all sexualities (heterosexuality, bisexuality, gay male sexuality, etc.) can include intimacy of all kinds. Every sexuality has the potential to evoke a Lordesque sense of the erotic, in the midst of or in addition to genital activities. What I am suggesting is that the difference between sexualities can neither be generalized away nor essentialized into irreconcilable and unknowable otherness.[12]

Likewise, as implied in the title, I am concerned not only with lesbian sexuality per se but also with the solidarity possible between women of different sexualities. Identity politics was never intended to render solidarity impossible, though it has had that effect in some quarters. Rather, difference can be what provokes mutual interest and attention, not isolation and leveling.[13] In this sense, the relationality between women that is a constituent component of lesbian life and theory is here extrapolated to include a nonappropriative but still physical relation between the lesbian ear and music by heterosexual women. The compelling fact is that as a lesbian I can have a somatically based intense relation with these heterosexual women that involves neither party denying or surrendering our own sexual identities. This involves people meeting with the autonomy of difference intact and the possibility of profound communication open.

Freezing sexuality with denotative labels will achieve only theoretical and political stagnation.[14] Understanding sexuality as a connotative web of significance and valuation proposes something quite different and dynamic, something that is much more like music than like language. And, as any lover, mystic, or musician knows, ineffability is not a lack or loss of words but a state that describes those moments when life and language do not overlap on a simple grid. This, I feel, can be well illustrated in music itself, where no amount of analytic explanation or genre definition can effectively defuse or render obsolete the temporal flow of the music itself. Likewise, the experience of sexuality—as a physical, temporal, relational, spiritual experience—can be described linguistically, but never exhaustively. Analogously, sexuality can be partially described musically, and music partially described sexually.

Judith Butler has forefronted the notion of "gender performatives" in her *Gender Trouble*.[15] In a revealing paragraph she quotes Nietzsche's claim in *On the Genealogy of Morals* that "there is no 'being' behind doing, effecting, becoming; the 'doer' is merely a fiction added to the deed—the deed is everything." In an application Nietzsche himself would not have anticipated or condoned, we might state as a corollary that there is no gender identity behind the expressions of gender; that identity is performatively constituted by the very "expressions" that are said to be its results.[16] This could very well be applied to music: there is no nominal music behind musical expressions, music is performatively constructed.

But such statements are themselves too sweeping in their nominalism: I think that there is some reality *within* performative flux, which is *not static*. The implicit unity that enables us to employ a concept like "music" signals the existence of categories, but categories that grow, change, expand, build, and dissolve. Musicians, scholars of music, and listeners all have experiences of music's present-ing time: the ways in which music focuses on the ontologically significant dynamic qualities of time.[17] Theories about what this means are legion, from Bergson to Kramer. But the key philosophical starting point is that time and music are inseparable, intertwined at the fact of existence—ontologically—and in the experience of what and how we know—epistemologically. While the contingency created by temporality makes Butler's "performative" possible, to refer to all temporality/time in the terms that Butler uses to define the performative would be an unnecessary limitation: performative suggests a dramatic and contingent construction of meanings.[18] And further: "Acts, gestures, and desire produce the effect of an internal core or substance, but produce this on the surface of the body, through the play of signifying absences that suggest, but never reveal, the organizing principles of identity as cause. Such acts, gestures, enactments, generally construed, are performative in the sense that the identity that they otherwise purport to express are fabrications manufactured and sustained through corporeal signs and other discursive means."[19]

Music and time are not well served by the postmodern stress on language and visual representation or unexamined assumptions that still, perhaps unconsciously, resist an ontological ascription of significance to the flux of temporality.[20] To do this is to repeat the error of various simple-minded Platonisms, in which the noneternal quality of history supposedly sullies the ontological Reality of events in time. To banish ontology is an overreaction; I am willing to risk starting with the (forever unstable and open) existence of the body, of touch, of sound, of time.

Furthermore, the notion of gender or sexuality as performance cannot be taken over uncritically into the world of music, where we know that performance necessarily includes allied concepts such as reading, rehearsal, and run-through.[21] Yes, music is performative, but that may be simply because all *present*-ations take place *in time*. The performative, as a philosophic category, may be empty for forms such as music. Music is performance *plus* time and the physical materiality of sound. These integrated aspects generate and sustain interdependent relations—the performance gives rise to the sound, but time gives the occasion to the performance, and the sound manifests time. The broader category is that of activity: music is an activity, a making of time in time, and therefore its qualities are best described *adverbially*.[22] We know this in and through our bodies.

Reflecting on the lesbian ear, I returned to the work of a feminist theorist who is also a musician: composer/film maker/writer Trinh T. Minh-ha. She makes the key point that "we do not have bodies, we are our bodies, and we are ourselves while being the world. . . . We write—think and feel—(with) our entire bodies rather than only (with) our minds or hearts. . . . it takes time to tolerate greater aliveness."[23]

I am a lesbian; I do lesbianism all day. I am my body, my lesbian body, which is "biophilic,"[24] and "excruciatingly alive."[25] My daily actions, whether eating Bran Chex, filling the car's gas tank, correcting student papers, or cleaning up my office, consist of do-ing lesbianism. Similarly, everything I hear I hear as a lesbian. My way of listening to music is adverbially part of the on-going act of creatively interpreting lesbian-i-cally. It is not a question of an identity called "lesbian" or of the politics of representation. Rather, the lesbian ear is part of a politics and philosophy *with* the body, a politics and philosophy *with* embodied experience. "With" here means alongside, simultaneous, unseparated, in tandem each with the other: the inseparability of body, experience, time, and the (elusive) subject/self. The qualities of the be-ing, do-ing, creating of ourSelves and the universe—the adverbial sense of be-ing lesbian—that is the subject of a self-defined yet still inclusive lesbian ear. This leads me to postulate "the be-ing lesbian" and/or "the do-ing lesbian"—that to be a lesbian is neither a permanent cloak nor a changing set of stage costumes. It is an ontological, ethical, and epistemological process that is a predisposition, a history, and an ongoing conscious set of decisions. In this, "the be-ing/do-ing lesbian" resembles the practicing/performing musician—both are awash in a practice, a habit, a joy, a drudge, a performance, and an orientation toward the world, ways of apprehending reality, and of do-ing these apprehensions in their totality of intense and quotidian moments. Such a subjectivity is neither an isolated atomized individualism nor an erasable difference. It simultaneously participates in the many and the single.

Like a religion or an art form, a lesbian is an interpretation of the world, an interpretation based on tendencies, ways of seeing, ways of highlighting and editing the world with an eye to significance. For example, Buddhism examines the world and proceeds to construct its interpretive categories around suffering, desire, ignorance, knowledge, and nirvana. These categories are hardly unique to Buddhism, but their prominence and the specifics of their interactions, do form a distinct nexus that can be recognized and named Buddhist. Similarly, lesbian interpretations start with positive valuations of women, the body, and tactility (touch). Lesbian interpretation finds little sustenance in systems that reject or debase women and the body; thus lesbian theory tends to be highly critical and politically opposed to dualism and other inquisitorial systems of religious/political male dominance.

How, then, does music fit into possible lesbianic readings? Music easily achieves a place of potential prominence here because it has both a palpable and abstract materiality that makes it accessible to the lesbian ear, which then makes it susceptible to an interpretation by the be-ings and do-ings lesbian.[26] Hence, I offer this lesbian reading not in the hopes that one of these musicians turns out to be lesbian or bisexual, nor to claim that their heterosexuality is an insurmountable barrier to a lesbian hearing of their music, but to speak as a lesbian philosophia-er[27] *with* their music to reveal how tactility/materiality is present in the music at a place where be-ing Lesbian can make meaningful contact with them in an interconnected universe.

My use of the word *lesbian* is therefore simultaneously more universal and more idiosyncratically personal than general usage. It does not exclude those whose experience (sexually and musically) is distinctively different, but it also is born from my specificity. The "lesbian ear" is active, physical, interpretive, female, immersed in sound. It is "hearing the body," closely allied to "writing the body," which Trinh T. Minh-ha explains is "that abstract-concrete, personal-political realm of excess not fully contained by writing's unifying structural forces. Its physicality (vocality, tactility, touch, resonance), or edging and margin, exceeds the rationalized 'clarity' of communicative structures and cannot be fully explained by any analysis."[28]

Difference and multiplicity are vital to the current representation of knowledge and study in and outside of the academy. Hearing each other's stories, understanding the borderlands[29] between interpretive frames, and incorporating the tensions and paradoxes of an unresolvably chaotic universe are certainly challenges to all people, from all subjectivities. By presenting a lesbian analysis of songs that have no overt lesbian content, and no lesbian political agenda, I am stating that all of women's culture, all of world music, all of history, is part of lesbian culture as well: this is the world in which we (lesbians and nonlesbians) live.[30] Thus, a lesbian experience of this music presents a way of hearing music that operates within parameters of valuation (as outlined above) and which presents (through the medium of music) a location for sharing that experience (with lesbians and nonlesbians). I am not suggesting that this hearing can *only* be achieved by lesbians or that the listening experience of others is invalid. What I am saying is that the physical experience of lesbianic living can lead to ways of hearing and interacting with music and that musical thinking can lead to certain ways of living erotically (in Audre Lorde's sense) as a lesbian. It is precisely the fact that there is overlap between different experiences that makes possible the creative sharing of differences: "Each of us understands each other through analogies to our own experience or not at all."[31]

This is a work in process. I don't mean that it is incomplete but that it is about listening to the process of music-making, and metaphorically and non-metaphorically relating that to lesbian interactions with the material world. And I say "in process" instead of "about process" because the form and intent of the paper is to listen together, to be in the musical moment together (even at the distanciated remove of print).

This is also a continuation of the work I did in "Lesbian Compositional Process," where I discussed the philosophical and practical ways in which lesbian experience can influence compositional decisions.[32] Herein, I ask the listener to listen (along) with one woman's lesbian ear: to hear with, perhaps, a different set of perceptions and experiences. In this regard, it is essential for the reader to also *be* a listener, meaning that I hope the reader knows and/or listens to the pieces discussed along with reading the article.

Kate Bush, PJ Harvey, and Tori Amos have attracted the attention of feminists for the content of their lyrics as well as their high-profile successes as headliners in the male-dominated world of popular music. But, as is often the case, what is noticed is their visual image—their personæ—and their language: the lyrics, the interviews, the easily verifiable outside "data" which function in the conceptual worlds established and dominated by language. The possibilities of musical meanings, locations, decisions, effects, politics, are overlooked in the rush for the easily translated and discussed.

However, all three of these women have declared their desire to have their full musical, instrumental, and compositional skills recognized. Kate Bush, Tori Amos, and PJ Harvey have each taken the prerogative to self-title their musical ensembles and to place themselves in the role of lead instrumentalist as well as vocalist in their ensembles. They claim their own names as the name of their musical efforts and actively center their multiple musical capabilities. The sheer amount of compositional decision-making that occurs in the work of these artists is immense; their pride in these skills is likewise obvious and effectively conveys itself in each woman's forthright, self-possessed stage presence.

The analyses that follow are based on oral listening. My decision to present these analyses without relying on transcriptions is not a renunciation of that form of musical discourse but rather an affirmation of considerations of timbre, orchestration, and texture that are not effectively relayed in musical notation, coupled with a desire to valorize close listening in a context that praises the lesbian ear. I am going to both listen *past* the words *and* listen *with* the words. Bush, Harvey, and Amos unite music and lyrics, so we cannot separate them utterly, even for analysis. In fact, the interplay of vocal lines, contrapuntal instrumental lines, and large-scale formal decisions about vocal and instrumental sections is a revelatory part of their work.

Starting from one's own taste is a seldom recognized but frequently operative principle in arts scholarship, and I acknowledge that my own involvement with these pieces is a loving one. Like a lover, I may well continuously delineate their (essentially innumerable) good qualities and ignore their (to me insignificant) shortcomings. I also intend to illustrate why these are, in my mind, *valuable* pieces, music that repays attention. Implicit in this is not so much a value judgment but an ethical principle of attention. I am willing to analogize sexuality and music because both are revelatory when all the participants—the musicians, performers, listeners, and the lovers—attend, and discover further meaning in each other, immersed in the temporal.

Musically these compositions partake of a tactility that can easily be a part of a be-ing lesbian interpretation, and this tactility may well lead to solidarity in the music that goes beyond identity into shared realities: that is, the attention paid by Harvey, Bush, and Amos to sonic detail is an attention commensurate with be-ing lesbian, which, if these women are heterosexual, represents a place of analogy/metaphor/contact, a way of be-ing and interacting with material that can be shared by listeners whose sexualities vary. But these points of contact are not meant to reduce difference; my hope is that shared intensity of attention will produce richly varying reports which are complementary, not oppositional.

THE MUSIC

Kate Bush

Active as a solo artist since the late 1970s, Kate Bush is the best established of the musicians under discussion. She has become progressively more detailed and conceptual in her production of albums. With her 1985 release, *Hounds of Love*, Bush dedicated an entire side of the album to a "dream sequence" piece. But it is the enigmatic "Running up That Hill" that I consider here. The orchestration in this work breaks down into three classes of instruments: (1) voices; (2) instruments that sound programmed (and humanly untouched); (3) instruments that sound as though they are being played in real time. "Running up That Hill" works, in large measure, because of the tensions created by having these three types of human sound production present in unusual proportions. There is a prominent drum machine throughout, as well as a synthesized organ sounding the C/E-flat drone and articulating chord changes. Only late in the piece are there some drum turnarounds and float guitar lines that seem to be played manually.

The drone is one of the most immediate and significant aspects of the piece. Pulsing and humming on the minor third C/E-flat, the drone renders the piece sonically immobile; it does not "run" anywhere. It is precisely this that the singer makes reference to, saying "if only I could," and then making it clear that what she cannot do is to "be running up." The piece remains in place, held by the drone and by the severely muted envelopes of the mechanized instruments. The place where it breaks off and tries to break free is in the bridge. The drums break their pattern, the singing voice persistently tries to convince the unnamed, ungendered other to do voluntarily what neither she nor God can accomplish. The doubts and ambivalences of the first two verses are here abandoned in favor of an unabashed attempt to get the better part, to "exchange the experience," and "to steal *this moment* from you *now*."[33] The drum turnaround on "Let's exchange the experience" then unleashes rhythmic and timbral possibilities and nuances for the rest of the piece, including the tantalizingly brief float guitar solos, and finally issues in the hybrid phase-shifted voices near the end.

Kate Bush chooses to highlight the basic elements of the song, as well as differing sounds, when she sings of "you," "me," and "oh." The "oh" is that which is too impossible to speak, a place where speech is lost or abandoned.[34] There is a stress on these simplest of words, revealing and reveling in their differing vowel sounds. But when it comes time to ask a key question "Tell me we both matter, don't we?" the text-setting rhythm is very fast, and Bush decrescendos on the line, almost mumbling it. So, the individuals—the you and me—are clear, while the relationship—its purposes, its interactions, its negotiations—is rendered highly ambivalent. Also, the narrative of the song is constantly self-revising. The second verse, in talking of the extent to which the lovers hurt each other, gives the lie to the easy assertion with which the piece opens: "It doesn't hurt me." Then, the bridge, in its willingness to steal from the lover, negates the rhetorical question in "We both matter, don't we?" In contrast, the music is additive: we never lose the sonic landscape with which the piece begins, but the (albeit tightly circumscribed) entrance of the 'live' drums and guitars, and the increasing complexity and dramatic extremes of the voices, suggest that the landscape may contain much more than we originally (re)cognized, in the same way that a desert reveals itself as a complex ecosystem when one gives it time/attention.

The women's voices that accompany Bush are present almost throughout the piece. The mix attempts to match their background quality to that of the

C/E-flat drone, so that the voices may sometimes appear to grow out of or fade into that texture. The women's voices do not function as an angelic chorus; rather they heterophonically follow Bush in her own self-imposed limitations. Finally, the gorgeous sweeps of the melodic lines themselves are a kind of movement, and yet they too end up going in circles. Bush highlights this by avoiding the tonic middle C as a cadential pitch until the final measures of the piece. In both the bridge and the devolving, shrinking coda, the voice tries but is unable to free itself from the constraints of the piece and falls back down into the sea of sound Bush has created. Thus, even her lead vocals drop to a lower timbral range, and, instead of the swooping intervals of the earlier melodies, the final phrases (on the words "If I only could be running up that hill") take place within a fourth from C-F, except for one reach to a flattened fifth, which slides melodramatically to the fourth. Bush's voice falls into the textural gravity of the cadential ending, where it loses its distinctiveness. When the final cadence is reached, the resolution stops the cycle by fading into the pitch and tonality of the C minor drone.

Kate Bush is a composer who is interested in sonic texture at every step of the musical process. She built her own studio before recording the *Hounds of Love* album because, she said, "you can't experiment forever (in paid studio time), and I work very, very slowly."[35] Bush is aware that she is composing in direct contact with sounds: "I think that the combination of very acoustic real sounds and very hard electronic sounds is fabulous. . . . I like to create contrasts and extremes for the atmosphere that you're building around a particular song. . . . It's always the song that tells you what to do. . . . The song is controlling you. It's telling you what to do really."[36]

The integrity of the song, the concern with relational interaction in the compositional process (between composer and sounds and song), and the attention bestowed on these considerations are all crucial points of contact with a loving lesbian ear. While a lesbian reading of this song could proceed from the lyrics (the relationship under discussion is not gender-specific), I find it more interesting to observe the convergence of lesbian materiality/physicality and musical materiality/tangibility invoked by Bush's compositional decisions. This song is susceptible to a lesbian reading because it does not erase women or the body and because it invokes the Lordely erotic in its delectable delightful play of sound.

Even more immediately, the timbres used, and their persistence through the course of the song, offer, simply by virtue of their distinctiveness, a self-contained sonic world. While "envelopes" in the technical acoustic sense, create this effect, the particular sounds themselves *are* enveloping: in their physical effects on listeners, in their striking difference from most other contemporary production sounds, and in their overlapping continuous, drone,

and circular presences. My own lesbian ear hears and touches here a deliberately sensual aural world, in which time both stands still and accumu-
lates. This lesbian ear hears explorations of time, of touch, of relation, of
embodiment that analogize to lesbian sexual, sensual experience in ways that
can be mutually revelatory.[37]

PJ Harvey

"Oh My Lover," the opening song from PJ Harvey's first commercial album,
Dry, presents a rich contrast to "Running up that Hill." "Oh My Lover"
opens with a thickly textured chord in voice, guitar, and bass, but then, for
the entire first verse, consists of a sparse duet between Harvey's voice and
a very physical, humanly played bass line. The rawness and immediacy of
Harvey's sound—vocally, instrumentally, ensemble-wise, and in the recorded
mix—is crucial to her embodiment of musical tactility. Throughout this album the textures and sounds of each instrument are given space to sound, to
be alive: one hears fingers move, variations in timbre on a sustained pitch or
chord, a wide variety of visceral attacks and envelopes, guttural vocals, and
noisy guitar effects. The vocal style in this particular song is highly dramatic—
self-effacing, angry, conceding, begging, desperate—without ever being sar-
castic or simpering, without removing her dramatic persona from the immediacy of the scene: she never distances herself, even when she is obviously
adopting a role. The constantly returning phrases "It's all right" and "there's
no time" create bitter ironies inside and outside of the music. Obviously, nothing is "all right" in this narrative. But the demand that women *pretend* that
everything is always "all right" permeates the critique implicit in the piece.[38]

   As in "Running Up That Hill," Harvey leaves the gender of the lover un-
specified (although we know that the lover is with another woman, which
eliminates both the "He left me for a he" anxiety of the heterosexual woman
or the biphobia of lesbians). Also, as with Bush, the narrative of the song
changes focus with each verse and line.[39] In contrast, though, Harvey employs
audible orchestrational decisions to mark these changes, rather than Bush's
obsessive timbral continuity. The first verse, without drums, is an intimate
counterpoint, a conversation; the second verse, in its liltingly moribund way,
shows the narrator willing to selflessly take on the lover's cares, forgetting
her self. The third, instrumental verse is an extended austere moment in musical time. This is a *durée* of thought, a space of and for reflection. Its narrative impact is most clear in the explosion that issues from it in the fourth
verse, where the narrator comprehends the loss of attention and care from
her lover, the painful loss of intimate contact.

   What makes this self-reflexive musically is that it takes place in a context
that explicitly evokes time—music's constituent theme/medium/existence—

as a topic. There is the narrator's wrenching realization that, for her lover, for her, "There's no time." Yet the openness of time, the nonurgency of the third instrumental verse, illustrates that in the music there *is* time, but it is lost in *this* particular human relationship, gone with the slackening of intensity between these lovers. As the instruments grow noisier, denser, more complex in their sounds and interactions from the fourth verse to the conclusion of the coda, we have three worlds presented simultaneously: (1) the despairing loss in the words and vocal timbres; (2) the actual chaos and pain of difficult relationships in the instrumental trio; and (3) the creation of a world of touch and time, where things *are* all right and there *is* time, in the thick wealth of sound and rhythm. It is not surprising when the tensions between these worlds issue forth into a confusion of backwards tape noises, seemingly emanating from the final chord.

In his effusive review of *Dry*, Timothy White focuses on "Oh My Lover": "The conflicts inherent in the songs' cerebral issues and carnal urges are boldly sketched by Polly's reverberate guitar, Stephen Vaughan's libidinous bass, and the temperamental percussion of Robert Ellis. The album's conceptual axis, however, is 'Oh My Lover,' in which a jilted lover wrestles with arousal and rejection. The track can be perceived as heart rendingly tender or richly ironic, yet its deeply erotic spell prevails. This disquieting ambiguity is precisely the point of Harvey's songwriting, which is why she customarily declines to discuss it."[40]

Excusing the adjectival excesses of popular rock criticism, one can still take from the review a sense of the tactile, material quality of the music. Even if White intended the word *erotic* in its strictly sexual sense, a lesbian reading would include the Lordesque erotic: a vital, physical intensity (which White implies in the epithet "libidinous bass"), not limited to, but often drawn from, sexuality. Also, the reference to her silence about her lyrics is important: I suspect that she knows that her music and lyrics are inextricably entwined, and that to isolate and/or remove the lyrics to the site of an exclusively linguistic political discussion would be to deny the music (or reduce it to the role of a highlighter pen!).

PJ Harvey has quickly become a favorite among rock critics and writers.[41] As Jim Arundel states, *Dry* revels in ambiguity, it "tantalises . . . intrigues and thrills but doesn't tell the full story; that lets her keep control."[42] Part of this ambiguity has centered on gender issues.[43] In her public self-presentations, PJ Harvey adopts a gender-ambivalent form of her name, repeatedly makes provocative comments about gender in interviews, uses her sexuality as part of her artistry, *and* defines it herself, studiously and self-consciously fitting no one's agenda. She sports a postmodern edge filled with gender ambiguity and repositionings of sexist discourse.[44] For instance, there is the deeply unsettling "Man-Size." This song, purportedly sung from a male perspective, is heard twice on the *Rid of Me* album, once with string quartet and once with rock trio. The lyrics are alternatively hostile, self-destructive, macho, and violent: "I'm coming up man-sized, skinned alive . . . I'll measure time / I'll measure height / I'll calculate my birthright . . . . Silence my lady, get girl out of my head, douse her with gasoline, set it live and set it free." Similarly the song "50Ft. Queenie" (*Rid of Me*) mocks the male emphasis on penis size: "Hey now I'm king of the world, you oughta hear my song / you come and measure me, I'm fifty inches long!"

At the same time, she can also appeal to the cultural feminists when her lyrics concern such topics as women primping themselves to please men. Examples include "Me-Jane" (*Dry*), where an angry Jane confronts Tarzan's treatment of her; or "Legs"(*Rid of Me*), which describes the self-defense killing of a spousal abuser ("did it hurt when you bled . . . I bet you never thought that I would try"); or her debut single[45] "Dress" (*Dry*), in which she comically relates the trials and tribulations of trying to find if "there is someway I can dress to please him" even while she is "tipping over like a heavy-loaded fruit tree" in some piece of absurd clothing.

Yet despite these obvious ties to feminist concerns, PJ Harvey consistently denies any explicit feminist aspects in her music, a move that cost her the support of some feminists in England.[46] In their interview of Harvey and their resultant angry article about her denial of feminism, Sally Margaret Joy and Everett True seem determined to cut the theoretical ground out from under the musician:

> When you say feminism doesn't enter your vocabulary, why doesn't it? What do you envisage it meaning?
>
> "I don't think about it," she replies. "I don't spend time thinking about feminism as an issue."
>
> But maybe the people who have needed feminism are the people who've suffered because of sexism, and have found it difficult to get on. To become a successful woman and then say openly you don't consider feminism a valid perspective for yourself implies you think feminism's useless. Maybe what you're saying is that you haven't struggled and hence you haven't needed feminism.
> She denies this.
>
> "I've struggled quite a lot. It's really hard work."
> And you've never encountered sexism?
>
> "Of course I have."
>
> But you've always dealt with it on your own, right?
> She nods.
>
> Some would say that's putting yourself above feminism.

"For me, that's backtracking," she says. Basically, Polly doesn't want to be restricted by people's expectations. The constraints that any term—even one as encompassing as "feminism"—places on someone, she sees as counter-productive.

"It's negative. It's going the other way," she continues. "You can talk about things too much and nothing will de done. I'd prefer to just go ahead and do things and not think about them; you get more done that way."[47]

I quote this extended interview both to illustrate the tone of betrayal and feminist consciousness of the writers and to show how Harvey keeps returning to the work. Her words very closely echo those of another creative white woman artist who appeals to lesbian sensibilities, Georgia O'Keeffe: "O'Keeffe repeatedly said that if the young (women) artists worked more and complained less, there would be more of their paintings and sculptures to hang in museums and galleries. . . . 'Women never helped me,' she once declared in old age. 'The men helped me.' Perhaps she forgot that few women art critics and museum curators were in a position to help her as much as Stieglitz. Not remembering and not feeling obligated to other women, O'Keeffe came to resent those who tried to appeal to her through feminism—and when feminist Gloria Steinem arrived in Abiquiu with a bouquet of red roses, O'Keeffe refused to see her."[48] Like O'Keeffe, Harvey has a tough sense of self-definition that appeals to lesbian sensibilities. Even if she is herself denying the solidarity of an overt political sisterhood, Harvey's self-determination has the kind of gritty independence that has characterized the lesbian break from socialized femininity.[49]

My central concern here is that the strength of her music—and her own insistence on its centrality ("I'm in a band because I want to play music")[50]—are overlooked. The specific musical moments and textures are lost in the flurry of words in and about the songs, and thus the skillful interweaving of music and text is likewise lost. In her more aphoristic and less lyrically obvious songs, the interpretive potentials are multiplied. In turning to "Water," the listener finds few words and only the outline of lyric continuity. The interpretation cannot exist independently of the music in time.

"Water," also from *Dry*, is a complex combination of myth, meter, minimalist text, materiality of sound, and formal repetition and expansion. The lyrics play with the sound of the word *water*, and with the small syntactical units created by "water, walking, I'm walking, I'm walking on."[51] This sequence can work either as a repeating cycle, in which case the singer is "walking on water," or as a linear lead to the verses, in which case the singer is "walking on for years and years and years." The lyrics certainly suggest the song is concerned with overcoming a mind/body dualism, specifically one imposed by (Christian) religion. To overcome this, the female singer "leaves (her) clothes on the beach" and walks *into* (not *on*) the sea. Her solidarity is with a woman—"Mary Mary"—a reference to the mother of Jesus but also a name that is literally the source of mari-time vocabulary: there is a family of goddesses with names like *mari* who are related to the sea.[52] As if to confirm this, Harvey has added the reference to Icarus: "Think of him all waxy wings melted down into the sea." This reference is to a death by water, the death of Icarus, which, unlike that of Jesus (who is referred to in this song as "the very man"), promises no redemption, only mortal finality. The fate of the singer, on her walk into the water, is left ambivalent—the last line of the final verse is "Mary Mary hold on tightly *over* water *under* the sea" (emphasis mine).[53]

The passage of time—whether it be in "years and years and years" or in "nine or eleven years" or in the constant walking—these passages of time are marked in time, felt in the music. Most significantly this happens in the palpable passage of time in the instrumental redevelopment of the introduction. Here, the 5/4 meter is repeated, with its regularity and vivid presence marked by the harmonic guitar pitch that enters in the fifth measure of the section. Further, the regularity of this meter often has a slight hesitation leading to the downbeat, the steady motion of the meter thus being consciously renewed and marked with each measure. This tendency is highlighted during the instrumental interlude, an interlude that seemingly introduces no "new" musical material. Outside of these moments, the 5/4 meter has two striking interruptions to its continuity. Three extra beats are added right after the singer declares that she is "walking down into the sea," and again just after "Mary Mary hold on tightly, under water over the sea." These two moments report self-directed activity that defy and deny the miraculous quality of "walking on water." Instead, in both places, Harvey holds on to physical reality, immerses herself in the water, and in the embrace with Mary. Even within orthodox Roman Catholic theology, Mary represents the flesh—albeit a valorized image of flesh in obedience to the deity.[54] Harvey's rescuing of Mary, even if it is to drown her in the waters that cannot be walked on, is a significant reclaiming of this often impossible and contradictory female mythological character. Harvey accomplishes this critically within the context of a specific Christian reading of the relation between deity and nature, in which the deity is seen as having established nature. Given this creator deity, he (Jesus/God the Father) can either live within creation itself and play by its rules (incarnation) or he can defy the natural world as secondary to his own power (miracles, such as walking on water), taking either stance at his own preference. Harvey's own voice and the character of "Mary Mary" are suggesting a simultaneous alternative to "what the very man said" in their connection to the physical immersion in water. The singer and the figure of "Mary Mary" have a shared female solidarity (even as they are both shaped in relation to "the very man") that is also a theological solidarity in favor of the physicality of life.[55]

In the music, Harvey's obsession with the sound and length of the word *water* is likewise itself an immersion. As the coda repeats the chorus, with extended vocal elaborations, Harvey ends the piece with voice alone—ending this album entitled *Dry* (a reference to feeling "left dry" by one or another [male] lover) with the word *water* and bringing us full circle orchestrationally from the opening bass/vocal duet of "Oh My Lover."

In a musical analysis of "Water," what emerges is that PJ Harvey is compositionally creating multiple representations of religious images and spiritualities. The fact that music itself has temporality, and that the presence of that time is made palpable in the song, is one such representation of a spirituality. The layers of myth include the Christian scriptures, the Greek Icarus, and the christian-appropriated figure of water and sky, Mari/Mary. Perhaps the reason that PJ Harvey does not choose to embrace the word *feminist* is that that "very word" has ceased to carry multiple ambiguities of the sort Harvey senses are necessary to her art. It is not that feminism is a frozen political subjectivity as that it has, so often, become a totalizing subjectivity.[56] The need for feminism as a verb, as an activity, itself needs music, and it needs the active subjectivity and materiality of lesbian touch.[57]

Tori Amos

Reviewing a Tori Amos[58] concert, critic Simon Reynolds explicitly compares her to both Bush and PJ Harvey.[59] He then compliments the "angry young women" of rock, who "have something to say about their lives/life . . . who really want to connect and confound."[60] In Amos's case, because so many of her songs are concerned with the travails of growing up female, her solidarity with women and with feminist concerns is obvious.[61] Some examples from her lyrics can demonstrate that: "She's been everybody else's girl, maybe one day she'll be her own" ("Girl"); "I want to smash the faces of those beautiful boys, those Christian boys, so you can make me cum it doesn't make you Jesus" ("These Precious Things").

Given this last example, Tori Amos would appear to have a better understanding of the real-life nonconsensual S/M dynamics of Christianity than a host of professional theologians. She also has an explicitly consensual (if resigned and unenthusiastic) S/M song—"Leather"—on her debut album, *Little Earthquakes*. But it is the events in the musical textures and details of "Crucify," the song that opens the album, that create a materiality worthy of close lesbian attention.

Amos begins the piece with her voice and the piano—her own complete musical presence—and *neither of these elements ever bows out of the piece*. The utter continuity of the vocal line—which lends an air of necessity to the frequent use of breath sounds in the piece—is astounding. The lyric content—concerning the self-inflicted pain that results from living under cultural, religious, social, male-imposed expectations—and the physical facts of her voice's utter continuity and her breath not sounding as if it is hers to define (or even to comfortably regulate), combine to create resonances beyond their literal representation.

There is a small metric detail worthy of note: the piece is entirely in 4/4, except on the chorus line "Nothing I do is good enough for you," where there are two added beats to comprise a 6/4 bar. It is as if that bitterness cannot be contained, yet this metrical transgression proves again that what she has done is not objectively good, as it throws the meter off its track. Further, there is the horrifying draining sound, not unlike a straw at the bottom of an empty glass, that accompanies the chorus and adds a disturbing level of air and noise.

The bridge section is pivotal: the cry of "Please please" is accompanied by other female voices that surround Amos's lines heterophonically. The words are fewer, simpler, elemental, repeated on top of themselves. They point to their end, when Amos's voice is alone, saying "I cry": there is no savior.

Overall, Amos effectively conveys the physical and emotional realities of teenage female life: sex, guilt, intellectual confusion, anger, and resentment. What makes "Crucify" an especially important example of her art is how this is conveyed in the physical anxieties of the music itself: the vocal restlessness and the keyboard textures that dance around the vocal lines. Clearly this density of sound is related to her live-performance style, but it is rarely as unrelenting as in this song.[62] Another notable example is the slower rhythmic densities that occur on the chorus line "My heart is sick of being, my heart is sick of being in," where her act of spitting the consonants both obscures the words and literally replaces the percussion. Further, this suggests a philosophical ambivalence: is she sick of life/being itself, or of being in chains, or of being unable to think beyond those chains, or all of these?

Like PJ Harvey's, Amos's songs and lyrics show considerable religious reflection and study. Her father was a Methodist minister,[63] and her grandfather conveyed to Tori the wisdom of her great grandmother, who was a full-blooded Cherokee, on matters concerning "nature and spirituality."[64] While this may lead the cynical to describe her as a "vaguely New Age hippy-chick"[65] or as "Joni Mitchell with a pagan streak,"[66] the connection of her personal and immediate style to a self-determined philosophy seems clear to me. Male critics seem embarrassed by the level of bodily and emotional involvement in her live performances and compositions: words and phrases like "confessional,"[67] "maudlin,"[68] "ecstatic anguish,"[69] "emotions are declared in a state of undress," "heightened sense of self-exposure," "explosive articulations of suppressed desire and repressed agony,"[70] "a little too explicit"[71] reappear in almost every review of her work. Her response to these expressions of uneasiness is that of a woman who appraises her own musicianship as spiritually, physically immediate. To the female interviewer who suggested that she was "grinding her pelvis into the piano bench," she unabashedly explained: "The energy's got to go somewhere; it gets caught in the hips," says Amos. "You feel the spirit of the piano running through you. As women, we've been taught to deny our sexuality, and I think that's one of our biggest crimes. This is bringing together the physical, emotional, mental, and spiritual. I feel like I act as a channel for these forces."[72]

Even more tellingly, she maintains that, as a musician, she is in a dialogue with music, and with her physical instruments (piano and voice) themselves: "I wrap my arms around the piano and embrace it. I see the piano as a living being . . . . I feel like the piano has not been explored to its full potential. I'm not talking about synthesizers either. I mean *really* working with the acoustic instrument. I started to approach it as something that has its own consciousness. It thinks. We collaborate together. It's not like master and servant. At times—and we're all guilty of this—you start whipping your instrument. Domination. Not that I don't like domination. But when it comes to the piano, it's not going to work unless there's give and take . . . . it's that intuitive place of respecting the instrument and respecting the song. Music, it has an opinion."[73]

When a performer relates to music this way, and then chooses "sexual politics" as her subject matter,[74] it will make some uncomfortable. But I maintain that it is commensurate with a lesbian aesthetic of attention; that, indeed, it suggests a parallel to a lesbian ear. Musical do-ing for Amos is relational, with music and in solidarity with other women, with youth, with queers. Musical do-ing is overtly, unabashedly, sensuously physical in Amos's live performances and recordings.

CONCLUSIONS

What, in any of these pieces, does the loving lesbian ear hear? Attention to women, to claiming one's own voice,[75] to interacting with musical structure and sound as living beings: all of these things imply to me the physicality and woman-loving world in which lesbians function, in which the be-ing and do-ing lesbian interprets. I said before that lesbianic interpretations of the world deploy positively valued entities, such as women, body, and tactility, simultaneously rejecting or ignoring (or attempting to ignore) what is inimical to lesbian existence, such as the structural erasure of women, and authoritarianism.[76] On the level of linguistic content, each of these pieces is concerned with critiquing religious systems (principally Christianity) that call for separation from body, and substitute a form of immanent sacrality. Further-more, they do this in the context of singing about women.

The theology in "Running up That Hill," "Crucify," and "Water" is far more cogent and suggestive than much professional critical theology. But what is of more interest to me is that the music in its mode of contact with the world evidences an involved philosophy that *is contact* with material, with flesh, with sound, with time. This is a philosophia *with* music that does not need to be expressed abstractly, since it is about (concrete) materiality. The attention that these women performer/composers lavish on the instrumental sounds for which they are responsible indicates a relationship with sound that, whether expressed technically or immediately, points to an involvement that is erotic in the Lordesque sense. The relationship to music that a com-poser or an ensemble can create is as crucial a part of an erotic, physical, embodied continuum as the literal contact of genitals. The loving lesbian ear hears women into being, trying to ensound the entirety of women without limits, resulting in

> A hearing engaged in by the whole body that evokes speech—a new speech—a new creation. The woman *had* been heard to her own speech. *Deep in the experience itself is the source of the new imaging.*[77]

Hearing creatively and lesbianically is walking into the sea of immersion in Sound/Life, in the *now* that exists in music's temporality.

NOTES

1. There are, of course, significant exceptions to this: namely, Aretha Franklin, Martha Reeves, Diana Ross and the Supremes, Janis Joplin, Judy Collins, and Joan Baez, to name a few. But I am drawing a comparison between the time when such women were rarities to our present day, when there are so many women performers and composers of popular music that even a brief representative list from different styles would go on for pages.

2. Gillian Gaar, *She's a Rebel: The History of Women in Rock and Roll* (Seattle: Seal Press, 1992), 441–42.

3. Audre Lorde, "Uses of the Erotic: The Erotic as Power," in *Sister Outsider: Essays and Speeches* (Freedom, Calif.: Crossing Press, 1984), 53–55.

4. For another examination of ambiguity, see Gloria Anzaldúa, *Borderlands/La frontera: The New Mestiza* (San Francisco: Spinsters/Aunt Lute, 1987), 79–80.

5. Lorde quite explicitly condemns the warped situation of exploited labor as a direct cause of the absence of the erotic in our work; see Lorde, *Sister Outsider*, 55.

6. Ibid., 57.

7. Julian of Norwich, *Revelations of Divine Love*, trans. Clifton Wolters (New York: Penguin, 1967), 68, 80.

8. No matter how hackneyed and overquoted they may seem, Blake's words in "Auguries of Innocence" are especially apt for the topic of materiality and temporality in music:

> "To see a World in a Grain of Sand
> And a Heaven in a Wild Flower
> Hold Infinity in the palm of your hand
> And Eternity in an hour."

The sense here that time itself ("an hour") , in conjunction with our physical bodies ("the palm of your hand"), produces a qualitatively different experience of time ("Eternity") is, to my mind, an insight remarkable to find in language but commonplace in music.

9. For more on "a positive focus" in feminist work, see Emily Erwin Culpepper, "Philosophia: Feminist Methodology for Constructing a Female Train of Thought," *Journal of Feminist Studies in Religion* 3:2:7–16, 8–9.

10. On lesbian identity, see Vera Whisman, "Identity Crises: Who Is a Lesbian, Anyway?" in *Sisters, Sexperts, Queers: Beyond the Lesbian Nation*, ed. Arlene Stein (New York: Plume, 1993), 47–60. In this context, it is worth quoting Toni Morrison that "definitions belong to the definer, not the defined" and that it was the Nazis who decided if one was Jewish or not (regardless of one's religious practice) and the racist authorities who decided if one had any "color" in one's blood lineage in the racist genetics of U.S. politics. Interestingly, our current enemies link all sexual and intellectual deviants into a "homo"-genous group.

11. See my unpublished paper, "Bunched Epistemologies: Mysticism and the Ineffability of the Queer Body," delivered at the Society for the Study of Ancient Philosophy, Binghamton, N. Y., October 1994.

12. To clarify, I am saying, for instance, that the fullness of heterosexual experience can lead to the exclusivist distortions of heterosexism—"The belief in the inherent superiority of one pattern of loving and thereby its right to dominance" [Lorde, *Sister Outsider*, 45]—or to the cosmological vision of the unity of energy and matter expressed in the Hindu reflections on Siva-Shakti, among many other possibilities. To maintain that the experience of *specifically* heterosexual activity does not enter into the shaping of such worldviews is to separate the mind and the body in ways that are unconscionable.

13. See Eve Kosofsky Sedgwick's "axiomatic" discussion of difference for more explorations of this theme, in *Epistemology of the Closet* (Berkeley: Univ. of California Press, 1990), 22–27.

14. Though I disagree with substantial portions of this article, I think Judith Butler makes this point quite nicely in "Imitation and Gender Insubordination," in *Inside/ Out: Lesbian Theories, Gay Theories*, ed. Diane Fuss (New York: Routledge, 1991).

15. Butler, "Imitation and Gender Insubordination," 134–49.

16. Butler, *Gender Trouble: Feminism and the Subversion of Identity* (New York: Routledge, 1990), 25.

17. I have referred to this elsewhere as doing "philosophy with music" rather than "philosophy of music": see Jennifer Rycenga, "Lesbian Compositional Process: One

Lover-Composer's Perspective," in *Queering the Pitch: The New Gay and Lesbian Musicology*, ed. Philip Brett, Elizabeth Wood, and Gary C. Thomas (New York: Routledge, 1994), 280.

18. Judith Butler, *Gender Trouble*, 139, emphasis hers.

19. Ibid., 136, emphasis hers.

20. One interesting account of time and postmodernism is Elizabeth Deeds Ermath, *Sequel to History: Postmodernism and the Crisis of Representational Time* (Princeton: Princeton Univ. Press, 1992), esp. 45 ff.

21. This point was elegantly made by Charles Kronengold in his paper "Piecing It Out: Performance of Sound and Thought," delivered at the conference "Music, Gender, and Performance," Berkeley, Calif. October 1993.

22. Another interesting critique of the postmodern emphasis in queer theory, from a gay male perspective, can be found in Randy P. Connor, *Blossom of Bone: Reclaiming the Connections between Homoeroticism and the Sacred* (San Francisco: Harper Collins, 1993), 7–9.

23. Trinh T. Minh-ha, *Woman, Native, Other: Writing Postcoloniality and Feminism* (Bloomington: Indiana Univ. Press, 1989), 36; parenthetical entries and emphasis hers.

24. Mary Daly, *Gyn/Ecology: The Metaethics of Radical Feminism* (Boston: Beacon Press, 1978), 10.

25. Anzaldúa, *Borderlands*, 38.

26. See also the discussions of music and lesbian be-ing in Rycenga, "Lesbian Compositional Process," esp. 278–82.

27. The word *philosophia* meaning "a love of wisdom, especially a love of the wisdom of women," has been developed by Culpepper, "Philosophia," 6.

28. Trinh, *Woman, Native, Other*, 44.

29. See Anzaldúa, *Borderlands*.

30. Adrienne Munich states this bluntly when she says: "That Cervantes was a male writer is a fact of women's history" ("Notorious Signs, Feminist Criticism and Literary Tradition," in *Making a Difference: Feminist Literary criticism*. ed. Gayle Green and Coppélia Kahn [London: Routledge, 1985], 250, emphasis hers). Likewise, the fact that, say, Kate Bush is a heterosexual woman does not imply that lesbian interpretation should turn away from her music, nor that lesbians should appropriate her, nor that lesbians are privileged (or marginalized) interpreters of her work.

31. David Tracy, *The Analogical Imagination: Christian Theology and the Culture of Pluralism* (New York: Crossroad, 1987), 451.

32. Rycenga, "Lesbian Compositional Process."

33. Side two of *Hounds of Love* has a stress on the multiple musical/linguistic meanings of the term *moment;* listen especially to "Jig of Life." I have addressed the question of moments in music in my dissertation "The Composer as a Religious Person in the Context of Pluralism," 52–55.

34. This is not ineffability in the sense which I discussed earlier.

35. Ted Mico, "Fairy Tales," *Melody Maker* 60 (Aug. 24, 1985): 19. Building her own studio was a step in her self-definition and shows the seriousness with which she undertakes and makes compositional decisions. As reported by Peter Gabriel's former manager, Gale Colson, "Kate told me after *The Dreaming* they sat her down at EMI and said they wanted her to have a producer, that she couldn't produce herself. And

she was so angry that she went home and built a studio and made *Hounds of Love*"
(Gaar, *She's a Rebel*, 269–70; see also 266).

36. John Dilberto, "Kate Bush: From Piano to Fairlight with Britain's Exotic Chan-
teuse," *Keyboard* 11: 64.

37. Readers and listeners familiar with Bush's work will recognize similar elements
in the title song that opens her 1989 release "The Sensual World." Based on her reading of James Joyce's *Ulysses*, her extension of his work seems both deliberately feminist and definitively somatic. She says of this piece: "Gradually it started to unfold into
this idea of Molly Bloom *stepping away from her author, into the sensual world*"
(Rogers, 16, emphasis mine). Likewise, the song "Eat the Music" from *The Red Shoes*
demands a lesbian reading—in fact, it explicitly uses imagery, such as pomegranates
and "fruits" in general, which are in the common parlance of queerdom), to speak of
full involvement in music.

38. As David Schwarz pointed out, Harvey is also inverting the masculine self-pity
that the blues so often indulges (personal correspondance).

39. Bush acknowledges the strong narrative element in her music, saying: "To me,
that's what songwriting is about: human relationships and telling stories" (Sheila Rogers, "The Sensual Woman" *Rolling Stone* [Feb. 8, 1990]: 16).

40. Timothy White, "P J Harvey: A Lover's Musical Meaning," *Billboard* 104:33:
3 (1992): 3.

41. For the drooling praise of male critics, see White, "A Lover's Musical Meaning"; Jim Arundel, "Thrist and Foremost," *Melody Maker* 68 (Mar. 28, 1992): 38;
Craig Marks, "20 Best Albums of the Year," *Spin* 8, no. 9 (1992): 69; and Gene Santoro, "Review of *Dry*," *The Nation* 255:21: 780. For a dissenting opinion, see Steve
Simels, "Review of *Dry*," *Stereo Review* 57:10:90 (1992). (For some twenty years I
have *always* disagreed with Simels.)

42. Arundel, "Thirst and Foremost," 38.

43. One (male) critic writes "Her lyrics are *too* embarrassing: any male who contends otherwise is simply being insensitive" (Everett True, "Too Clever by Harvey?"
Melody Maker 68 (Jan. 25, 1992): 22, emphasis—and pipeline to God?—his). It is
worth noting that the male reviewers don't even mention issues of lesbianism: the logic
seems to be that her songs are about heterosexual relations and that no matter how
viciously critical she may be toward men and male arrogance, this is unrelated to
choosing (or valuing) women. If my analysis of "Water" has any merit, this failure
to conceptualize a lesbian reading may be due to a fetishization of genital contact as
the only definition of lesbianism, since Harvey connects with women's anger at many
levels that call forth implications of female solidarity, if not lesbian sex. Critics even
ignore the much more overt sexually lesbian thematics of the song "Yuri G" ("I drew
her down to me . . . . Yeah, I wish I was Yuri G, it's just the things that she does
to me").

44. Harvey's acknowledged influences include Roland Barthes, Captain Beefheart
(White, "A Lover's Musical Meaning," 3), William Burroughs (Santoro "Review of
Dry," 780), Marianne Faithful, Elvis Presley, and Howlin' Wolf (Jim Arundel, "PJ
Harvey: Sex and Bile and Rock and Roll," *Melody Maker* 68 [Feb. 8, 1992]: 37)—
surely a fragmented collection of postmodern curiosities! For a psychologically reduc-
tive view, see Simon Reynolds and Joy Press, *The Sex Revolts: Gender, Rebellion and
Rock'n' Roll* (Cambridge: Harvard Univ. Press, 1995), 242–43, 337–40.

45. Arundel, "Sex and Bile and Rock and Roll," 36.

46. See Santoro "Review of *Dry*," 780, and Sally Margaret Joy and Everett True, "PJ Harvey: Bare Essentials," *Melody Maker* 68 (Apr. 11, 1992): 34–35. Some of this was fueled by PJ Harvey's decision to pose nude for the British music magazine NME; see Joy and True for response to this, as well as Arundel, 1992. I am not going to dwell on this visual aspect of the feminist controversy around Harvey; however, my argument would proceed in similar directions, that focusing on the verbal and visual discourse to the exclusion of the musical discourse is an unnecessary reduction. But ignoring the visual (and marketing) aspects of such controversies also leaves vital questions unaddressed. Permission to reprint this portion of the interview granted by *Melody Maker*—eds.

47. Joy and True, "Bare Essentials," 35.

48. Laurie Lisle, *Portrait of an Artist: A Biography of Georgia O'Keefe*, rev. ed. (New York: Washington Square Press, 1986), 426–27.

49. One should also note that Alfred Stieglitz took volumes of naked photographs of O'Keeffe before she achieved her own renown. Like PJ Harvey's decision to pose for NME, this does not erase the problematic nature of the male gaze on the nudity of women artists; rather, it complicates questions of female artistry, agency, and objectification.

50. Joy and True, "Bare Essentials," 35.

51. I believe that this focus on the sonic, emotional, and syntactical possibilities of a single word is a deliberate compositional technique in Harvey's work: compare, for example, the song "Ecstasy" on *Rid of Me*, in which Harvey extends the vowel sounds of the title word, one syllable at a time.

52. Barbara G. Walker, *The Woman's Encyclopedia of Myths and Secrets* (San Francisco: Harper and Row, 1983), 584–85. My thanks to Mari Gasiorowicz for sparking my interest.

53. Insofar as the well-educated Harvey's songs have invoked such varied cultural artifacts as the Celtic Sheela-na-gig, the Hebrew Bible ("Samson and Delilah"), and Bob Dylan ("Highway 61 Revisited"), I don't think that her use of allusion is either accidental or unstudied. Similarly, Kate Bush thanks Joseph Campbell in the liner notes of *The Red Shoes*.

54. In her brilliant analysis and history of the Virgin, Marina Warner states that "in the very celebration of the perfect human woman, both humanity and women were subtly denigrated": *Alone of All Her Sex: The Myth and the Cult of the Virgin Mary* (New York: Vintage, 1983), xxi.

55. Nana Peazant, the wonderful matriarch in Julie Dash's film "Daughters of the Dust" similarly says: "I'm not going to be watching from no heaven while there's soil still here for me for planting" (Julie Dash, *Daughters of the Dust: The Making of an African-American Woman's Film* [New York: New Press, 1992], 159).

56. I am speaking here of two dimensions: the media misrepresentations of feminism, and (far more serious) the criticism raised by many marginalized women (e.g., women of color, lesbians of all races, working-class women) that feminism, in its sweeping assumption that sexism was at the root of all oppressions, has erased valuable dimensions of experience.

57. Mary Daly suggests that "feminism is a verb; it is female be-ing . . . . It was/is inevitable that women who conceive of feminism as a thing, a state, would come at

some point to believe themselves to have moved 'beyond feminism.' But . . . one does not move 'beyond' it. One moves with it" (*Pure Lust: Elemental Feminist Phiolosophy* [Boston: Beacon Press, 1984], 194). This is, of course, a critique of Harvey's disavowal of feminism; on the other hand, there may be no need to cling to the specific word *feminism.*

58. Just as I was finishing this essay, Amos released her second album, *Under the Pink* (Atlantic 82567–2, 1994). Her choice of orchestrations and piano textures is more akin to art music than is *Little Earthquakes*. One might productively note Amos's connection to gay male culture. She got her first performance experience playing in a gay club in Washington, D. C. (Alec Fogue, "Music: Vogue Arts," *Vogue* 182: 64), and in the liner notes to *Under the Pink* she includes a prominent thanks to "the Faeries." She certainly credits gay men with helping her own sexual awareness—and technique: "I had forty-year-old congressmen coming on to me, which was interesting, and all the gay waiters teaching me how to give head with a cucumber. So if I get teeth marks on it, I didn't get chocolate milk that night" (Caren Myers, "Famous Amos," *Details Magazine* [March 1994]: 193).

59. Commenting on PJ Harvey, Tori Amos said, "That was just so current, the concept of dry. Feeling dry. I loved that. I don't wanna be dry. I'm a mango" (Caren Myers, "Famous Amos," 194).

60. Simon Reynolds, "Tori Amos: The Borderline, New York," *Melody Maker* (May 2, 1992), 26.

61. Amos has stated that her new album looks at female betrayal of women, inspired in part by Alice Walker's *Possessing the Secret of Joy*. She also clarifies her feminism: "Amos said she is still an avowed feminist, but one, she added, who believes in men's rights and children's rights and even the rights of rats" (Stephen Holden, "Songwriter Explores Women's Injustices toward Women," *Fresno Bee* [Feb. 6, 1994]: H20).

62. A significant difference between Amos's live and recorded performances involves her extensive use of rubato in her live shows. The entire metrical organization of her pieces is transformed by her live practices.

63. Elysa Gardner, "Tori Amos Keeps Her Head," *Musician* 171: 46–49 (1993): 46–49; and Alec Foege, "Music: Vogue Arts," *Vogue* 182: 64. The songs "God" and "Icicle" on *Under the Pink*, are creating a storm of religious controversy: "Icicle" brings Christian hymn-singing into simultaneous presentation with Tori's masturbation.

64. Gardner, "Tori Amos Keeps Her Head," 49.

65. Paul Lester, "Tori Amos: Froebel's Institute, Roehampton" (concert review) *Melody Maker* 68 (Jan. 11, 1992): 22.

66. Glenn Kenny, "Record Review: Crucify," *Stereo Review* 57: 8: 76 (1992): 76.

67. Lester, 22; Jon Wilde, "Vote Tori!" *Melody Maker* 68 (Jan. 4, 1992): 29; David Fricke, "Tori Amos: BMG Studios, New York" (concert review) *Melody Maker* 68 (Mar. 14, 1992): 25.

68. Lester, 22.

69. Simon Reynolds, "Tori Amos: The Borderline, New York" (concert review), *Melody Maker* 68 (May 2, 1992): 26.

70. Fricke, 25.

71. Reynolds, 26.

72. Melinda Newman, "Tori Amos: Atlantic's Golden Girl," *Billboard* 105 : 8: 86.

73. Greg Rule, "Tori! Tori! Tori!" *Keyboard* 18, no. 9 (1992): 49, 50, emphasis Amos's. Compare this to the quote by Bush cited earlier: "The song is controlling you. It's telling you what to do really" (Dilberto, "Kate Bush: From Piano to Fairlight," 64).

74. Allen Brown, "Tori Amos: Café Royale, Edinburgh" (concert review), *Melody Maker* 68 (July 4, 1992): 12.

75. The title character of Christa Wolf's *Cassandra* summarizes this feminist theme: "To speak with my voice—the ultimate" (Christa Wolf, *Cassandra: A Novel and Four Essays*, trans. Jan van Heurck [New York: Farrar Straus Giroux, 1984], 4).

76. According to lesbian linguist and thinker Julia Penelope: "If there's one thing most Lesbians have in common, it's the ability to say 'no' to coercion. Tell one of us *not* to do something, and she'll turn right around and do it. That's the essence of the Lesbian" (Julia Penelope, *Call Me Lesbian: Lesbian Lives, Lesbian Theory* [Freedom, Calif.: The Crossing Press, 1992], 5, emphasis hers). The term *essence* here should be understood ironically. Philip Brett makes a similar point about gay men's coming-out processes concerning consensus, alliance, and respect for difference rather than respect for authority ("Britten's Queens," talk at the Berkeley conference "Music, Sexuality, and Performance," October 1993).

77. Nelle Morton, *The Journey Is Home* (Boston: Beacon Press, 1985), 128, 127, emphasis hers.

JENNY KALLICK

Janáček's Jenůfa *and the Tyranny of the Domestic*

INTRODUCTION

Relationships binding drama and music have been crucial throughout the history of opera. Librettists and composers, negotiating these relationships, have turned again and again to stories centering on the domestic. Duty, ritual, property, and marriage pervade the genre in a variety of dramaturgical modalities, portraying daily life across the strata of economic and social class. Domestic stories reveal the competing interests of public and private, community and individual, men and women within overarching societal traditions. Oppositions such as these are often nested in the foreground of plot development. In opera, tension can exist beneath the narrative surface in a clash between explicit or implicit *textual* ideologies and explicit or implicit *musical* ideologies. Through the routine of common practice, some musical styles have acquired gender associations, just as some musical formal designs have become the site for politicized dramatic enactments. Consequently, in compositions that combine text and music, the words may seem to tell one story, the music, another. It is precisely through such polyphonic voices that an operatic "realism" can represent the ambiguity of daily life.

This essay on Leoš Janáček's *Jenůfa*, an opera predicated on the imperatives of Moravian rural life, examines a domestic tale centered on an uncommon subject—infanticide. This investigation will demonstrate how Janáček's work renders the terror, guilt, and claustrophobic paranoia experienced by those who have challenged village morality. I shall also look closely at the composer's use of traditional operatic conventions as they strengthen or weaken "realism." Where expressive passages in *Jenůfa* blur the perception of realism, they open up an idealized domestic world of romantic love.

Remarkably, despite idealized representation of gender roles, Janáček projects a deep empathy for women trapped in a tyrannical domestic order.

Along with *La Bohème* and *Cavalleria Rusticana*, *Jenůfa* (1894–1903)[1] is considered part of the *verismo* operatic tradition.[2] Its libretto was crafted by Janáček, drawing directly on the realist-style play *Její pastorkyňa* (*Her Stepdaughter*, 1890) by Gabriela Sekerová Preissová (1862–1946). According to the author, it incorporates "two real-life incidents, though much idealized!" More specifically: "In the first a lad wounded a girl, his brother's sweetheart, while slicing cabbage. He wounded her in the face deliberately because he loved her himself. In the second a woman helped her stepdaughter get rid of the fruits of her love (the girl threw the baby into the sewer), but I didn't want to have two murderesses. Jenůfa falls through love, but she has enough goodwill and strength to live a better life."[3] Preissová, a precocious and well-educated Bohemian-born writer, refined her progressive ideas in the lively cultural milieu of cosmopolitan Prague. After her marriage, she went to live in Hodonín, a German-speaking town in the center of Moravian Slovakia, and there became intrigued with portraying rapidly disappearing Moravian village traditions. She first learned the Moravian dialect, then studied daily life in the surrounding Czech villages, and finally, produced *Její pastorkyňa,* an uncompromising portrait of the harsh reality of daily life.[4]

Janáček (1854–1928) developed a similar fascination with ethnography and, in particular, with the endangered Moravian folk song traditions. He participated in numerous field trips aimed at collecting every possible fragment of surviving folk melody. No doubt his intense patriotism fueled his ethnographic interests as he scouted for folk materials that he could later use in his own compositions. The joining of folk materials with high art, he believed, would help promote social and national progress in the Czech lands.[5] In preparing the libretto for *Jenůfa*, the composer sought to preserve Preissová's authentic depiction of Moravian life. Substantial deletion and limited textual repetition were a practical necessity. About a third of Preissová's text was removed, including two entire scenes; various individual lines or phrases were repeated to delineate poetic units; and minor adjustments were made to satisfy grammatical considerations. The only new text was that of a folk-style song in Act I, which Janáček introduced to dramatize a scene of community singing and dancing included in Preissová's own stage description.

As suggested by M. M. Bakhtin, material carried across discourses, such as from drama to opera, is changed both in its cultural meanings and representational impact.[6] Janáček, in working out a shortened version of the play, also created a new poetic and dramatic order that paved the way for very specific musical and dramaturgical structurings. In particular, some of the libretto's prose units and their musical settings inscribe meanings distinct from those of Preissová's. In her version, for example, Jenůfa and her lover

Števa argue about their unborn child and their fear of society's judgment. In the libretto, the composer takes this argument, crafts a traditional operatic love duet, and thereby connects the quarreling lovers to a meta-world filled with amorous operatic couples. Preissová's realistic dialogue suddenly glows with a romantic hue: traditional musico-dramaturgical signifiers transform the couple's quotidian dilemmas.

I shall begin by considering Preissová's work in the context of late nineteenth-century domestic narrative archetypes, and *Jenůfa* in the context of a group of relevant operas. Next, I shall examine the play-to-opera transformation. Finally, I shall analyze Janáček's musico-dramatic structures and the emergence of his voice counterpoised against that of Preissová.

MARRIAGE PLOTS AND THE "REGULATION FINISH"

What manner of woman was Gabriela Preissová? In her correspondence with Janáček she appears urbane, sophisticated, and deeply suspicious of the politics that control artistic reception.[7] Before the dismal failure of *Její pastorkyňa* at the Prague National Theatre in 1890, her work was widely admired for its frank depiction of rural life. Numerous commissions encouraged her to produce new works in the same vein. But with *Její pastorkyňa*, she pleased neither the more progressive forces at Prague's German-language theater, who favored the most radical sorts of new realism, nor the more conservative thinkers at the Czech-language theatre, who preferred milder varieties.[8]

In the broader literary landscape, Preissová's progressive inclinations were not uncommon. Domestic narrative archetypes were changing; Thomas Hardy, in an article from 1890, predicts the gradual disappearance of literature endorsing the ideology of domesticity.[9] He suggests that the novel will become "honest" again when the marriage plot with its "regulation finish," namely, "they married and were happy ever after," disappears.[10] The traditional cultural endorsement of marriage and the means by which "patterns of passions and patterns of property are always brought into harmonious alignment" will be replaced by "catastrophes based on sexual relation as it is."[11] Whether we turn for evidence to Hardy's own works, such as *Jude the Obscure* or *Tess of the Durbervilles*; to George Eliot's *Adam Bede* or *Daniel Deronda*; or to continental works such as Flaubert's *Madame Bovary*, Ibsen's *A Doll's House* and *Hedda Gabbler*, or Tolstoy's *Anna Karenina*, literature at this time takes on what Jane Tompkins refers to as the new "cultural work" of fiction. This cultural work provided its readers with a redefined "social order," and "a blueprint for survival under a specific set of political, economic, social, or religious conditions."[12]

Also influencing narrative models, alongside Hardy's "marriage question," was the "woman question" and the threatening specter of two emerging female stereotypes, the "odd woman" and the "new woman." The first of these stereotypes, devised as a way of organizing the emotional chaos created by changing social roles, took center stage in George Gissing's eponymous novel of 1891, bringing to bear resonances of the "lesbian, the angular spinster, and the hysterical feminist." [13] The "new woman," on the other hand, was that anarchic figure, who, according to Elaine Showalter, "threatened to turn the world upside down." Unlike the odd woman, who, Showalter reminds us, is "celibate, sexually repressed, and easily pitied or patronized as the flotsam and jetsam of the matrimonial tide, the sexually independent new woman criticized society's insistence on marriage as woman's only option for a fulfilling life." [14]

In addition to narratives addressing the marriage and the woman question were a limited number of depictions of what I term the tyranny of the domestic. Often set in a small village, these are tales in which the absolute imperatives of domestic order take on life-threatening proportions. [15] Even in the early twentieth century, sexual activity before or outside of marriage brought irreparable shame to the woman and ostracism for any child who might result. With abortion widely banned and virtually unavailable outside the more liberal cities, infanticide was considered a practicable solution both in the countryside and in the city. John Lukacs, in his profile of Budapest around 1900, remarks that direct statistics on abortion are unavailable since it was illegal and carried a stiff penalty. What has been documented, he continues, is the practice, not just among the poor, of "farming out babies to wet nurses." But Lukacs points out that the Hungarian name for these wet nurses translates as "angel maker," suggesting that few of these babies were meant to survive. [16]

The progression from "the marriage plot with its regulation finish" to "catastrophes based on sexual relation as it is" is also reflected in changing libretto archetypes, some incorporating women's stories, and some even told from a woman's perspective. Three crucial operas—Bedřich Smetana's *The Bartered Bride* (1866), Peter Ilyich Tchaikovsky's *Eugene Onegin* (1879; in Brno, 1888), and Pietro Mascagni's *Cavalleria Rusticana* (1890; in Brno, 1892)—were all heard by Janáček soon after their premiers. He described them admiringly in newspaper reviews for Brno's *Hudební listy* and found that each work, despite varying domestic scenarios, aimed for opera's highest purpose: "to pursue the truth." [17]

Smetana's *The Bartered Bride,* a light-hearted representation of the domestic, eventually became the most popular Czech opera of all time and an icon for any aspiring Czech-language opera composer. [18] Its story invokes a folkloristic setting of idyllic village life and provides a humorous overlay to Hardy's "marriage plot." Musically, choruses of villagers affirm in strophic accord the happy state of matrimony, while bride and bridegroom exchange in symmetrical and mutually affirming duets the unanimity of their passionate commitment. Dramaturgical predictability thus reaffirms marriage contracts and domestic order. *The Bartered Bride* grants enormous prestige to the folk traditions that order daily life. Likewise, Preissová's narrative, *Její pastorkyňa,* embraces the ingrained conservatism of Czech nationalism with its notion that only the isolation of the countryside nurtures an authentic national spirit. Nevertheless, the author challenges the vision of the idealized village and makes clear that traditions rigidly imposed can fester and become dangerous. Janáček, deeply committed to an authentic portrayal of village life, represented the village in *Jenůfa* as both more boisterous and even more deadly than the simple, rustic village in *The Bartered Bride.*

Tchaikovsky's *Eugene Onegin,* based on Pushkin's epic poem, polarizes romantic love and a prudent choice of marriage partner. For the central female character, Tatyana, her unrequited love for Onegin is followed by a socially and economically important marriage; years later, she strongly defends her commitment when Onegin reappears and wants another chance. What is most remarkable about this opera, presenting perhaps a singular example before Janáček, is Tchaikovsky's success in portraying the complexities involved in resolving the conflicts between romantic love and sensible marriage from a woman's vantage point. In the letter-writing scene, we receive Tatyana's thoughts without the interpolation of a male narrative voice. Later, when she confronts Onegin, we again are given Tatyana's reactions without the telltale signs of a male interlocutor. The instinct to inscribe a woman's perspective and permit a woman's self-narration would soon emerge as a hallmark of Janáček's operatic style.[19]

In a final example from the operatic context surrounding the production of *Jenůfa*, Mascagni's *Cavalleria Rusticana* portrays domestic life as a brutal panorama of jealousy, revenge, and domestic chaos. Janáček wrote of the Brno premier of *Cavalleria Rusticana* in 1892: "Indeed there are several passages in his opera that surprise by their modernity of harmony and formal perfection. . . . From a dramatic point of view, the scene between Santa [Santuzza] and Turiddu is masterfully constructed. A pernicious passion grows out of the icy calm of their first meeting. You think that an explosion will take place any moment, yet by Lola's scene, the blazing fire is only fed; and Santa's repeated tearful pleas stop Turiddu several times, finally culminating in the unpitched cry: '*A te la mala Pasqua, spergiuro!*' "[20] His remarks make clear that he was attracted both to the opera's dramatic realism and to its strongly delineated structures. In *Cavalleria Rusticana*, the conflict between respect for marriage as a sacrament of the church and sexual desire cannot be easily resolved. Eventually, *Cavalleria Rusticana* endorses domestic order at any cost, requiring punishment for those who block the way to domestic stability. Dramaturgically, Mascagni's use of traditional structures signals the opera's conservative bent and anticipates the final restoration of domestic order. In *Jenůfa,* Janáček will similarly employ conventional operatic forms to order both musical structure and domestic space.

Critic Carl Dahlhaus writes with puzzlement of Janáček's attraction to *Cavalleria Rusticana*, a work that Dahlhaus considered intrinsically melodramatic. He proposes that the values of dramatic realism are threatened by Mascagni's melodramatic approach, especially by the composer's use of the love duet and other conventional formal models.[21] By contrast, Dahlhaus applauds Janáček for avoiding the melodramatic in his own works. But there can be no doubt that Janáček also relied on traditional dramaturgical structures. Acting as his own librettist, the composer prepared a text that supports strongly articulated operatic scenes. On balance, the composer's meticulous transformation—from Preissová's textual realism to a libretto marked by overarching structures of powerful operatic dramaturgy—does, as Dahlhaus notes, successfully avoid the melodramatic. To discover how the composer retains a tone of realism within a dramaturgically traditional framework, we turn to a brief comparision of play and libretto.

FROM PLAY TO LIBRETTO

Její pastorkyňa tells the story of three young adults, Jenůfa, Števa, and Laca, bound together in a tragic love triangle. Števa's and Jenůfa's fathers, now deceased, were brothers. Laca's mother, a wealthy widow, was the second wife of Števa's father. Her inheritance has all gone to Števa. He owns most of the mill, making him the most desirable bachelor with the means to avoid the army. Laca had to serve in the army and must work for a living in Števa's mill. After the death of her mother, Jenůfa's father, Tomas, married the Kostelnička, who serves as church sextoness. Tomas was a dishonest and abusive husband. At his death, the Kostelnička was left destitute. She takes on small tasks and permits Jenůfa to work at the mill. Grandmother Buryja, mother of two sons—the father of Jenůfa and the father of Števa—also has no property and depends on the mill for her pension. Other characters include villagers, soldiers, companions of Števa, the mayor and his wife, their daughter Karolka, the mill foreman, a young boy Jano, and a servant girl.

Preissová distributes the action among three acts: the first—eight scenes—in which Jenůfa's pregnancy is revealed; the second—nine scenes—in which Jenůfa's newborn is drowned by her stepmother, the Kostelnička; the third—twelve scenes—in which Jenůfa marries Laca, and the Kostelnička confesses her crime.[22] Janáček retains the three-act structure, omitting Preissová's Act I, sc. 3, much of Act I, sc. 5, and Act II, sc. 3—all scenes dominated by the Kostelnička. This reduction in the Kostelnička's part is paralleled by significant cuts for Grandma Buryja, Laca, and Števa. Although the Kostelnička,

Števa and Laca maintain dramatic significance, Jenůfa's presence becomes dominant.

The composer's revisions rely primarily on 1) cutting of text in order to shape regular, symmetrical textual units that support architectonic musical structures, and 2) repeating text to emphasize the boundaries between formalized musical units. In addition, cutting and repeating helps match distinctive textual units with prominent speech-derived rhythmic motives and passages of expanded lyricism.

Two musical ensembles are developed outside the dramaturgy of the play: in Act I, Števa and his companions celebrate at the mill in high spirits, and in Act III, the villagers react to the Kostelnička's confession. Both rely on text repetition to produce tableaux of Moravian daily life. By contrast, conversations in the play are routinely tightened, making them less dialogic, and consequently less natural. For instance, in Act I, sc. 1, Grandma Buryja's interactions with Jenůfa are cut to a minimum, giving Jenůfa's anxiety greater emphasis; Laca's words of anger and jealousy are greatly reduced, shifting the presentation of his emotional tone to the orchestra.

Two duet structures in Act I and three monologues in Act II demonstrate Janáček's various libretto strategies. Looking more closely, for example, at the Jenůfa/Števa duet mentioned above (Act I, sc. 7 in the play, Act I, sc. 6 in the opera), the composer's substantial textual deletions in combination with textual repetitions produce four, equal-sized blocks of text marked off by repetitive textual delimiters. As a result, the words no longer flow comfortably as a dramatic scene; rather, they present a well-crafted set piece ready for operatic realization.

In the three monologues, Janáček capitalized on Preissová's stream-of-consciousness depiction of characters on the brink of madness. For the setting of the Kostelnička's anticipation of her confrontion with Števa (Act II, sc. 2), the composer allows her to begin calmly with Preissová's text intact. As she becomes angry and agitated, the final words of her original utterances from Preissová are repeated: "I have been praying, *praying;*" and "It is all quite useless, *quite useless.*" The orchestra hears her obsessiveness, repeating a single rhythm incessantly.

For the setting of the Kostelnička's gathering resolve to drown the infant (Act II, sc. 5 in the opera; Act II, sc. 6 in the play), the composer both cuts back and repeats Preissová's original words right from the start of the scene, locking in an obsessive tone. "In a moment, *in a moment,*" the Kostelnička chants plaintively to open the scene. If she can reconcile herself to God, she will be able to act, and thus "God understands how things stand, *God understands how things stand.*" This full sentence, once repeated, is heard for expressive purposes up a half step, thrusting her into a state of paranoid delusion: "They [the villagers] would all turn on me and Jenůfa, *they would all turn on me and Jenůfa,*" and, pointing at herself, she shouts "Look at her, look at her, *look at her.*" The orchestra, hearing the Kostelnička's madness, also looses its grip, its music now fragmented, even chaotic.

For the setting of Jenůfa's monologue as she awakens from her drug-induced sleep (Act II, sc. 6 in the opera; Act II, sc. 7 in the play), Janáček repeats numerous crucial phrases: "Mama keeps reproaching me, pricking my heart with thorns, *pricking my heart with thorns*"; "Števa still does not come, *Števa still does not come*"; "He [my baby] is terribly cold; don't leave him there, *don't leave him.*" Suddenly, Jenůfa resorts to prayer; the composer regularizes the musical phrases of lyrical rapture, mimicking a familiar pietal mode of reverential pleading. On the one hand, the music empathizes with Jenůfa's agony, giving her comfort. On the other hand, the music allows the listener to sense an ironic discrepancy between this imposed regularity and the chaos that underlies the domestic structure: she sings in the too bright B *major*, as opposed to B-flat—her characteristic, lyrical key.

In Janáček's struggle to balance realism with musical expressivity, he discovered that repeated text supports the latter, and not the former. Text repetition joined to musical motivic material punctuates both dramatic themes and musical structures; text repetition linked to lyrical expansion must be used sparingly, and only in support of authentic emotional catharsis. Tempering passionate lyricism throughout the score, Janáček employs powerful modernist gestures—dissonance, rhythmic irregularity, and abrupt shifts. For a full exploration of the composer's balancing of realism and expressivity, we turn to the score.

THE MUSIC AND DRAMA OF *JENŮFA*

Act I takes place by the mill, the village's center of power. Jenůfa, pregnant by Števa, awaits news of his draft status. Having just found out that that he will not be drafted, Števa returns in a celebratory mood with his companions. A scene of wild singing and dancing, based on the folk-style song inserted by the composer, generates one of the opera's relatively few extended ensembles. This ensemble introduces a folkloristic musical mode that will function throughout the opera as an important signifier for unbending traditional values. The Kostelnička interrupts the festivities, and a pair of dramatic confrontations follows. In the first, Jenůfa pleads with Števa that they marry immediately to avoid scandal. In the second, Laca teases Jenůfa and, when she spurns his advances, he slashes Jenůfa's cheek in full awareness that Števa will probably abandon Jenůfa once she has been disfigured.

The opening scene establishes Jenůfa's ambivalent relationships to her extended family, the village hierarchy, and the church, making clear that her private concerns cannot easily be reconciled with the values of these public institutions. Jenůfa's distraction from her pressing domestic responsibility, namely, aiding Grandma Buryja with the potato peeling, draws us toward her private anxiety. Janáček emphasizes the central dramatic theme of Jenůfa's guilt-ridden anxiety by using a series of short textual repetitions. With a musically intensified repetition of the second half of her initial line, "Števa has not come back, *Števa has not come back*," the composer depicts her escalating worry (rh I.5 + 4); see note 23 for an explanation of the numbering system used in this article.[23]

The introduction of Jenůfa's lyrical mode concludes this first scene; this musical style soon emerges as her most characteristic expression. In Act I, this lyricism expresses Jenůfa's sense of the tension between public and private; in Acts II and III, her lyrical mode will epitomize her association with an idealized maternal. Jenůfa's educational aspirations, hinting at her affinity with the "modern woman," are brought out by a brief vignette, centering around the young shepherd Jano. Jano bursts on the scene announcing his delight that he has successfully learned to read (rh I.24). Grandma Buryja reminds us of Jenůfa's common sense and strength of mind (rh I.28 + 2); Jenůfa sighs, responding that her "common sense has long ago flowed away like the water in the mill stream" (rh I.29).[24]

The musical setting for Jenůfa's sighs casts an otherworldly shimmer of E Major, inflected by A-sharp; upper strings and woodwinds play *ppp* with arpeggiating harp (rh I.29).[25] With the intrusion of a more active texture of motivic material, the initial lyricism is obscured by a sense of the public world and its bustle (rh I.30 beat two). A motivic contour associated with Jenůfa, first sounded by the oboe over Jenůfa's prayers to the virgin Mary, is most prominent (rh I.6 + 20). With a pattern of rising and falling stepwise motion, followed by a turn figure, the motivic contour mirrors the enclosed domestic circle in which Jenůfa must operate as shown in figure 10.1.

Scene 4 introduces the opera's first hint of formalized dramaturgy in the form of a strophic song. At the beginning of the scene, Števa and his comrades seize full control, eventually culminating in a regular song struc-

Figure 10.1. *Jenůfa,* Act I, sc. 1 (rh I.30): Jenůfa's Motivic Contour. Janáček *Jenůfa.* Copyright 1917 by Universal Edition. Copyright renewed. Copyright 1969. All rights reserved. Used by Permission of European American Music Distributors Corporation, sole U.S. and Canadian agent for Universal Edition.

ture. The shift from intimacy to boisterousness announces the opening of a public space (rh I.48). After the celebratory outburst, Jenůfa opens scene 5 by gently scolding Števa for his drunkenness (rh I.54). He quickly acknowledges his drunkenness, dragging her B-flat Major down to A-flat in a kind of tonal stagger (rh I.54 + 9–14). With real nastiness, he challenges Jenůfa and calls for the singing of a highly charged erotic song with accompanying tarantella-like dance (rh I.57 + 10). Števa's song suggests the widespread

Figure 10.2. *Jenůfa,* Act I, sc. 5 (rh I.61): Wild Dance. Janáček *Jenůfa.* Copyright 1917 by Universal Edition. Copyright renewed. Copyright 1969. All rights reserved. Used by Permission of European American Music Distributors Corporation, sole U.S. and Canadian agent for Universal Edition.

European tradition of "rough music," the kind of "rude cacophony . . . which usually directed mockery or hostility against individuals who offended against certain community norms." See figure 10.2.

Characteristic properties of these musics include "raucous, ear-shattering noise, unpitying laughter, and the mimicking of obscenities."[26] The element of eroticism in Števa's song points to a powerful underlying gender structure. Števa claims that he has chosen this particular song because it is Jenůfa's favorite, although suspicion is in order. The gendering is classic: the girl in the song is shown to experience her sweetheart in eroticized terms just as Števa, focusing on Jenůfa in sexual terms, imagines her to be the sexual aggressor. In fact, Jenůfa is offended by the depiction of herself as sexualized; she concentrates on what she perceives to be their spiritual or emotional closeness, leading her to assume that marriage is inevitable.

At first hearing, the song represents a simple folk style marked by regular, strong rhythmic accentuation. But to let us hear this music as Jenůfa hears it, the composer interferes with its inherent simplicity by imposing modernist techniques. The tension between apparent simplicity and modernism produces a frenzied, threatening tone that captures Jenůfa's horrified response to the whole scene. The folk idiom, as pointed out by E. P. Thompson, "at its very origin carried [a] sense of patronising distance."[27] In general, folkloric representations tend to idealize, and as Michelle Perot describes, "rural private life, its image frozen in folklore, more often than not eludes our grasp."[28] The musical equivalent of this "image frozen in folklore" controls the nationalistic representations of Smetana and other earlier Czech composers, where folk elements radiate the community's idealized common purpose.

By contrast, Janáček tends to distance himself and the listener from folk customs introducing elements of social criticism and realism. For example, the opera opens with the dark and ominous sounds of the incessant turning of the village mill wheel. This haunting sonority emanates from the rhythmic layers of a xylophone eighth-note ostinato, a quarter-note lower-strings pizzicato on the pedal C-flat, a dotted half-note melody in the violins, and counterpoint in violas doubled by clarinets. Together, they convey the mill's ceaseless energy, the lifeblood of the village, as well as the source of an inescapable destiny as shown in figure 10.3.

Dahlhaus has observed that the doubled-edged tone of Števa's erotic song illustrates Janáček's remarkable ability to bring modernist and nationalist musical styles together: "Janáček . . . has incorporated the conflicting elements of this scene into his music: the (for Jenůfa) heartrending levity of the chorus, seemingly a folk-song quotation; the ambiguous uninhibited dance; and the orgiastic conclusion, resembling a force of nature. He does this by progres-

Figure 10.3. *Jenůfa,* Act I, sc. 1 (rh I m. 1): the Turning of the Mill Wheel. Janáček *Jenůfa.*

sion from a major tonality in the chorus to a folklike modality and finally to a bitonality hovering at the brink of twentieth-century modern music." [29] The stylistic mixture described by Dahlhaus conveys the clash between the village's conservative nationalistic tendencies and the advance of modern life. One should bear in mind that Janáček counted on an elaborate Moravian style of costume to sharpen this irony. The use of a rather generic mode of rural dress in most recent productions diminishes the irony that the composer had so carefully mapped on to the folkloristic. We need only recall Max Brod's report that Janáček broke into tears at the Vienna premier when the Kostelnička made her first entrance dressed in a "soiled everyday dress" rather than "in her Sunday best . . . carrying a beautiful lace shawl over her arm as is the custom." [30]

The chromatically-inflected rising triplets at the end of figure 10.2 depict the Kostelnička raising her hand and bringing the orgy to a halt. She announces a one-year waiting period before the marriage of Števa and Jenůfa (rh I.64). [31] A fugue for the entire village counters with the popular wisdom that "love must always endeavour to triumph over misfortune" (rh I.84 + 1). [32] Števa's song jolted us into uncomfortable territory. In the real village, he could not have made public his sexualized feelings for Jenůfa. Thus the opera had to recover from his disclosure. The fugue freezes the action, placing the village into a state of suspended animation. Through the neutralizing effect of contrapuntal singing, the villagers re-enter the decorum of public space, cleansed of the revelation of sexual transgression.

Act I concludes with a pair of duets—the first duet involving Jenůfa and

Števa, the second, Jenůfa and Laca. In the first duet, the text falls into four musical units that alternate active and lyrical expressions:

> Unit I: Allegro, Jenůfa confronts Števa (rh I.87 + 5)
> Unit II: Andante, Jenůfa reflects her despair (rh I.92)
> Unit III: Allegro, Števa and Jenůfa argue (rh I. 95)
> Unit IV: Moderato, Števa sings of his desire (rh I.101)

The mill motive, functioning as a refrain, prepares the duet (rh I.87). A brief recitative follows in which Jenůfa forgives Števa for his drunkenness (rh I.87 + 1). The recitative leads directly to Unit I (rh I.87 + 5). Three stanzas, each using text repetition to mark the close, unfold the dramatic development: stanza one builds upon a distinctive motive of two descending seconds separated by a perfect fourth as Jenůfa explains to Števa, "You know my situation" (rh I.87 + 13); stanza two has a more expansive feeling and ends in a dramatic presto juxtaposed with an adagio in which Jenůfa explains on her highest pitch, "You know my pain" (rh I.90 + 6); stanza three, after a fermata, begins with voice alone in a contrasting low tessatura to the text "God help us so we can marry" (rh I.90 + 8). The orchestra alone rounds out the unit.

Unit II shifts to a lyrical function, with three tightly-compacted parts. Each incorporates an obsessive rocking motive reflected in the following ways: 1) Jenůfa's worries about her mother's reproaches (rh I.92), 2) Jenůfa's mounting despair (rh I.93), and 3) Jenůfa's suicidal thoughts (rh I.94). Finally, her outpouring is cut short when Števa scolds Jenůfa, warning her to stop "pulling such a face" (rh I.94 + 7).

After a brief recitative (rh I.94 + 7), Unit III returns to an active mode, characterized by a duple meter with patterns of rhythmic accentuation and stepwise melodic contour that recall the folkloristic element from the erotic folk song of Števa and his companions. Števa brags "the girls like me!" until Jenůfa seizes hold of Števa's folkloristic material and scolds him (rh I.97). The tempo increases as does her anger and, finally, reaching presto, she sings, "You can't look at others; don't be like that!" (rh I.99).

Similarly, a brief recitative precedes Unit IV in which Števa's lyricism offers reassurance and pledges his loyalty (rh I.100 + 4). At the outset of the unit, he sings rhapsodically to Jenůfa's cheeks, "like rosy apples" (rh I.101). Unit IV continues with the opera's most lyrical music as Števa serenades in D-flat Major, "O Jenůfa, O Jenůfa" (rh I.102). Grandma Buryja returns and suggests that the evening has gone on too long. Jenůfa, singing in ensemble and still despairing, reiterates that she will have to kill herself if she doesn't marry Števa (rh I.102). The reappearance of the mill theme, recomposed, provides a transition to the second duet between Jenůfa and Laca (rh I.103 + 3).

Turning briefly to the second duet, it, too, alternates active and lyrical materials. The mill motive agains opens the scene (rh I.104). In contrast to the first duet, various triple meters define the individual sections. Text repetition is a primary agent for structural demarcation. The first allegro presents energetic, petty bickering between Jenůfa and Laca (rh I.104 + 10). The triple meter establishes a hard, aggressive waltz which cadences with a presto in duple meter and a measure of silence (rh I.111 + 6). Jenůfa seizes control of the lyrical, second section with her ironic, unaccompanied pronouncement that she is proud to wear a flower given to Števa by another girl (rh I.111 + 7). The triple meter that follows for section three becomes sexy, suggesting a Viennese waltz. Jenůfa ends her sexual teasing with what are obviously empty gestures (rh I.112), emphasized by a decisive ritardando and maestoso that lead to an instrumental transition to the next section (rh I.113). The transition builds on the motive from the maestoso, then to a brief recitative, where Laca mocks Jenůfa's willingness to wear the flower, and, finally, to a six-measure presto that brings back the folkloristic rhythms from the previous duet (rh I.114). The presto is violent with its ferocious tempo, accents, leaping melodic line, and charging accelerando. Finally, in an andante, over an A-flat pedal, Laca grabs the lyric role to chilling effect (rh I.115). He repeats three times that Števa sees nothing in Jenůfa but her cheeks—rosy, like apples. Just as the lyricism suddenly ends, the mill motive reappears, and Laca, glancing at his knife, realizes that he can separate Jenůfa from Števa for good (rh I.118). Laca cuts her cheek, and the scene climaxes with an extended ensemble that closes the act (rh I.120 + 2).

The duets are similar, not only to each other, but also to the dramaturgical structure described by Harold Powers as "the prototypical situation in Italian Romantic melodrama, the dramatic confrontation [referred to as] the Grand Duet."[33] Philip Gossett describes its essential dramatic rhythm as consisting of an alternation between lyrical (or static) and confrontational (or kinetic) sections.[34] We can also expect the first lyrical section to be slow, and the second—faster.[35] The second lyrical section, called the cabaletta, is sung in ensemble, as a "vent for the emotion which was strictly controlled in the andante."[36] What does Janáček achieve by choosing this particular operatic structure for the first duet? One result is to enhance our sense of Jenůfa and Števa as a romantic couple. The Grand Duet model also idealizes their relationship. We find ourselves attracted to Števa as his rhapsodic outpouring connects him to other ardent lovers in opera history. Only Jenůfa remains skeptical of his sincerity and refuses to sing the traditional lyrical cabaletta; instead, she threatens to kill herself if they do not marry as shown in figure 10.4.

In the play, Števa's reassurances to Jenůfa are given less weight in the context of an extended dialogue. In the opera, this dialogue has been radically

Jenůfa

Smrt bych si mu - se - la u - ro - bit!

(If you left me, I'd have to kill myself!)

Figure 10.4. *Jenůfa,* Act I, sc. 6 (rh I.102): Jenůfa's Threat. Janáček *Jenůfa.* Copyright 1917 by Universal Edition. Copyright renewed. Copyright 1969. All rights reserved. Used by Permission of European American Music Distributors Corporation, sole U.S. and Canadian agent for Universal Edition.

cut back so that the cabaletta, even without Jenůfa's participation, immediately recasts the moment. The Grand Duet was designed to express mutally-held passion; its distinctive dramaturgical framework insists that passion and romantic love overrule the imperatives of money and position. As Števa sings, his words, taken on their own, are not dishonest. Rather, they reveal that he desires Jenůfa, not as a whole person, but as a sexualized being. His admiration for her rosy cheeks becomes the emblem of this desire, and Jenůfa's body becomes the site of the drama. In the scene that follows, the narrative will literally be written upon her body by Laca's knife.[37]

By the end of Act I, Janáček has established the terms of the opera's conflict. The music of the mill and the folkloristic modality are mapped on to power, sexuality, betrayal, and violence. Through this mapping, the tyranny of the domestic gains a visceral dimension that increases the sense of dramatic realism. Two Grand Duet structures organize the central dramatic confrontations, valorizing romantic love and reinforcing gender archetypes. Preissová's play, by contrast, conveys a tougher, unromanticized confrontation between Jenůfa and Števa and an unavoidable outburst between Jenůfa and Laca. The playwright inscribes the reactions of the two couples within the intense demands of a village life. In addition, Preissová is more generous in her characterization of the Kostelnička, giving her a chance to be understood as acting out of rational conviction. In the opera, she is hardly noticed before she pronounces that the marriage of Jenůfa and Števa must wait at least a year. When the villagers declare that she is a "hard woman," the audience can only concur, having not been given the opportunity to hear an explanation. This hardness, which Janáček emphasizes, will emerge as irrationality during the next act.

Act II takes place in winter inside the Kostelnička's tightly shuttered house six months after Jenůfa has given birth to her son.[38] The Kostelnička is planning to force Števa to assume responsibility for Jenůfa and their child. Jenůfa expresses a desire to sleep and her stepmother drugs her. When Števa rejects his responsibilty, the Kostelnička offers Laca a much desired opportunity to marry his beloved Jenůfa, telling him in panic that the child is dead. Feeling trapped by her assertion to Laca, she drowns the child in the frozen river. When Jenůfa awakens, her stepmother claims that the child has died while Jenůfa was seriously ill.

An orchestral introduction, firmly grounded in C-sharp melodic minor and a compound meter, conveys the mood of nightmarish panic that engulfs the household. A sixteenth-note triplet explosion in the timpani spawns perpetual-motion string triplets, suggesting the rushing waters of the mill. With woodwinds and horns, Janáček echoes the state of siege felt by the Kostelnička as the sounds of everyday life penetrate the walls of her safe haven. The outside world with its ever-churning mill and village customs, once compliant in the face of her moral authority, is now the enemy. A series of dramatic C-sharp Minor tutti chords climaxes with a four-against-three figure (rh II.1). The figure's two leaps of a perfect fourth, followed by a falling second, introduce a tragic-sounding D-natural, giving Phrygian inflection to the Kostelnička's anxiety as shown in figure 10.5.

Without pause, the curtain rises on the first scene (rh II.1 + 11). Unlike Preissová's play, in which Jenůfa and her stepmother engage in lengthy discussion of their shared problems, Janáček greatly reduces their dialogue, separating Jenůfa and her stepmother by a wall of feeling. Each is assigned distinctive musical gestures and modes of expression that come to define their opposing positions in the domestic hierarchy. The Kostelnička speaks first, asking Jenůfa why she has been praying all the time (rh II.4). Jenůfa replies that she has a tormented soul (rh II.4 + 8), but her sweetly delivered reply draws our attention away from her torment and toward her glow of maternal bliss. As they continue their musical interaction, the Kostelnička becomes increasingly anxious and insists upon bringing back the tragic-sounding Phrygian D-natural and the jagged four-against-three-figure that comes to embody the Kostelnička's sharp-edged personality (rh II.4 + 11–18).

Jenůfa, drawing comfort from her sleeping infant, begins to establish her characteristic key of B-flat Major. She tries to calm her baby, herself, and

Figure 10.5. *Jenůfa,* Act II, prologue (rh II.1): Kostelnička's Obsession Motive. Janáček *Jenůfa.*

(Good night, mama!)

Figure 10.6. *Jenůfa,* Act II, sc. 1, (rh II.15): "Good night, mama, good night." Janáček *Jenůfa.*

her stepmother who continues to fret about the past. Eventually, the Kostelnička's four-against-three motive is transformed by Jenůfa's presence into a gentler profile with simplified rhythmic motion held inside the span of a triadic harmony (rh II.9). Jenůfa's lyricism opens into an expansive passage of F-sharp Major tranquillity, made transcendent by its spaciousness, stability, and flowing harp accompaniment (rh II.15). This same combination of musical elements will signal domestic reconciliation in the opera's final scene. On a local level, this F-sharp arrival resolves a long preparation, thereby conveying a strong sense of inevitability. The text is brief, the words those of a simple daughter with a pure heart as Jenůfa repeats, "good night, mama, good night," as shown in figure 10.6.[39]

We are unprepared for Jenůfa's outpouring of affection, for when we last saw her she was engaged in conflict with Števa and Laca. This beatific moment announces Jenůfa's transformation: she has become the essential maternal figure, taking on the personae of the Madonna, to whom she has addressed her prayers from the opera's opening moments. Jenůfa's lyricizing encodes her essential feminine nature, as if a lullaby or prayer is never far from her lips. Even when she learns of her child's death and suffers excruciating pain, she responds with a painful lyricism, affirming her belief that young Števa, now an angel, must be with God. This first scene has established dramatic and musical oppositions that propel the dramatic action throughout the remainder of the opera. Dramatically as well as musically, the two women have been polarized: Jenůfa is now fully feminized—passive, pure, the maternal icon; the Kostelnička is defeminized—aggressive, guilty, the "odd woman." It is now around Jenůfa that domestic order will be reconstructed.

The impending infanticide constitutes the opera's central dramatic event.

The Kostelnička's contemplation of this act is expressed in two monologues that excruciatingly prepare for Jenůfa's singular monologue (see discussion above). In drama, monologue epitomizes the secret self; like a diary entry read aloud, it aligns itself with women in private spaces.[40] In opera dramaturgy, an aria presents an individual's emotional state in highly formalized terms; a monologue works directly and spontaneously to intensify personal expression. We may even feel a tinge of voyeurism in listening to these very private expressions delivered in the hidden space within the Kostelnička's parlor.

As mentioned earlier, each musical monologue presents Preissová's text virtually verbatim, although text repetition is required to support the substantial musical repetition that characterizes all three monologues. In many cases, the repetition mirrors what Lawrence Kramer has described as the "feeling carried by Romantic repetition usually involv[ing] distress, disturbance, or turbulence," a feeling associated with "abnormality, particularly of obsessiveness."[41] For the Kostelnička, the repetitions signal her paranoia—imaginary angry villagers hovering at the cottage. For Jenůfa, musical repetition signals an oscillation between pulling back from, and giving into, a psychotic break.

The Kostelnička's first monologue opens with one more representation of the churning of the mill (rh II.18). Initially the mill churns smoothly until an increasing rhythmic intensity generates an angular motive in the violas—a dotted sixteenth and three thirty-seconds—that conveys the Kostelnička's obsessive thinking (rh II.20). During the constant repetition of this obsession motive, the Kostelnička dwells on her disgust at the baby's physical resemblance to his father, confessing that she fasted and prayed that the child not be born. The orchestra, building in volume through sweeping Mixolydian-inflected glissandi, climaxes on a tutti F-sharp ninth chord (rh II.22 + 2). The Kostelnička's desperation overflows into an unaccompanied recitative concentrated at the bottom of her vocal range: "It is all quite useless, *quite useless*" (rh II.22 + 2). The orchestra seizes the obsession motive adding a prominent tritone to signal that the dreaded external world is getting closer. Števa's arrival will confirm this fear. See figure 10.7.

Two tightly structured duets follow, paralleling those of Act I.[42] For the Act II Kostelnička/Števa duet, Janáček, as in Act I, carves out blocks of text to serve as structural units. Within this multi-sectional duet, he incorporates strong musical contrasts linked to discrete textual units. In the first section, the nervousness that Števa feels as he arrives in answer to the Kostelnička's summons translates into an innovative texture consisting of a smooth, rhythmically calm bass clarinet bass line doubled by B-flat clarinet against ghostly thirty-second note figures in the upper strings, embodying the tritone that

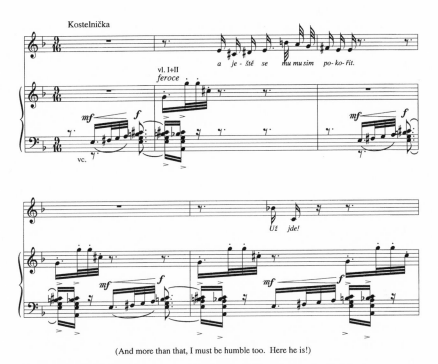

(And more than that, I must be humble too. Here he is!)

Figure 10.7. *Jenůfa,* Act II, sc. 2 (rh II.23): Obsession Motive with Tritone. Janáček *Jenůfa.*

had joined the obsession motive in the previous scene (rh II.24). When Števa learns that the baby has been born, a quarter-note ostinato on the tritone A-flat / D, seemingly escaped from the obsession motive, begins in the horns, raising the tension substantially as shown in figure 10.8.

The Kostelnička mimics Števa's fear in the contour of her tritone-driven melodic line and clearly feels that she is in control (rh II.27 + 2). She permits Števa to rationalize his absence as the orchestral texture shown below continues in obsessive ostinato throughout his insistent, repeated lines. A second section, marked by a French horn and viola ostinato built on Jenůfa's characteristic melodic contour, underscores their bitter arguing (rh II.31) until the arrival of the third section, marked Allegro, when the Kostelnička pleads her case (rh II.33). The music is touching, yet we continue to harbor a sympathy for the young romantic hero to whom Janáček had granted lyrical persuasion in Act I. The Kostelnička falls to her knees before Števa who is moved to tears (rh II.37 + 3).

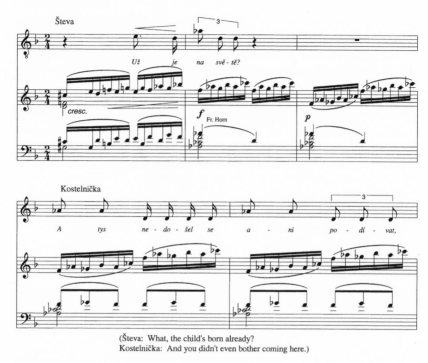

(Števa: What, the child's born already?
Kostelnička: And you didn't even bother coming here.)

Figure 10.8. *Jenůfa,* Act II, sc. 3 (rh II.26 + 6): A-flat/D Tritone in French Horn. Janáček

The fourth and final section, marked presto, belongs to Števa (rh II.41). Recovering his composure, he uses the folkloristic idiom to take control. His counter-attack culminates in the announcement that he is engaged to Karolka, the mayor's daughter. In essence, Števa has seized power in the tradition-bound Grand Duet structure. As the duet closes with Števa's departure, Jenůfa cries out from a nightmare in a disturbing moment of unconscious premonition. The Kostelnička and Jenůfa join in a simultaneous wail as Jenůfa dreams that a rock has fallen on her. Jenůfa's somnolent premonition is even more horrifying given her unshakable religious convictions. With the return of the mill music, we are reminded of the omnipresent force of nature and its control over the village destiny as shown in figure 10.9.

Laca enters, initiating the second tightly-structured duet (II.51 + 5). The Kostelnička sees him as a last hope for Jenůfa, whose chances for marriage are dismal. The dialogic quality of their encounter reflects the eagerness of both the Kostelnička and of Laca to come to an agreement. In a striking passage of mutuality, his marriage to Jenůfa is secured (rh II.53).

The Kostelnička's second monologue divides into three sections, demarcated by increasing tempi: 1) largo (rh II.64); 2) con moto (rh II.68); 3) poco più (rh II.69). Each single section rushes forward with greater intensity, feeling more out of control than the one before. All are filled with disjunct, obsessive, and dramatic gestures, strong harmonic turns, and heavy chromaticism. The third section, in particular, displays the Kostelnička's final

(Števa: So it's finished, really finished!
Kostelnička: Steva!
Jenůfa: Mama, see a stone will crush me!)

Figure 10.9. *Jenůfa,* Act II, sc. 3 (rh II.47 + 4): Jenůfa's Somnolent Premonition. Janáček

degeneration into hallucination, as cascading chromatic scales announce her delusional self-accusation in which she points her finger in the air, shouting, "Look at her, look at her, *look at her!*" The Kostelnička grabs the baby and departs. With music that seems to come directly from the Kostelnička's own terror-stricken psyche, Janáček creates one of the most gripping scenes in the operatic repertoire.

In contrast to the Kostelnička's paranoia, Jenůfa feels no threat from the outside. Initiating the scene 5 monologue, a solo violin beckons Jenůfa from her sleep with an expansive lyricism that is partner to her own (rh II.72). She looks about anxiously for her stepmother, but is calmed by her companion violin and opens the shutters, admiring the beautiful night and its stars (rh II.76). Jenůfa's gradually mounting anxiety arises first from worry of her stepmother's disapproval, and then from the presentiment that her baby is in trouble and crying for her (rh II.80 + 4). Her monologue develops through waves of emotion while she struggles to remain calm. Finally, sensing that horrid events are occurring at a distance, she briefly loses touch with the immediate reality of her surroundings. Still, unlike her stepmother, she is not deluded: her perception of the world outside her hiding place is absolutely accurate. Quickly, she regains her senses, asking, "Where am I?" (rh II.84 + 6). Although the orchestra has filled the musical space with the ominous sounds of the mill stream and its cold waters, Jenůfa turns to God and prays as shown in figure 10.10.

In Act II, Janáček creates a musical representation of the tyranny of the gender-specific domestic. Števa demonstrates that he is free to come and go from the household, and when pressed, calls upon folkloric music for protection. Laca, too, has choices, moving free between public and private spaces. The tyranny of the domestic is a problem that women alone must face. We encounter Jenůfa and the Kostelnička imprisoned in the primary domestic space—the home. Jenůfa's essential feminized nature determines her expressive mode. The resultant lyricism takes emotional precedence as all vestiges of her individuality and any desire for a life apart from the domestic are erased. The gentleness granted to Jenůfa, originally by Preissová, is amplified through her musical representation: she is completely collapsed into the role of the essential domestic female. From her stepmother emanates the music of paranoia: she moves toward a dark madness that makes her seem cruel and inhuman. Jenůfa and the Kostelnička are thus positioned as an opposed gender pair. Jenůfa emerges as a passive Nietzschean "cultured maiden"; the Kostelnička becomes an aggressive outcast or "odd woman" with no legitimate place in the domestic order. Whereas Preissová defined the feminized space, allowing us to hear the private thoughts of women, Janáček's music brings out the claustrophobia and paranoia that such space can produce.

Act III takes place two months later inside the Kostelnička's house where

(Hail to Thee, Holy Queen,
Hail, Mother of mercy.)

Figure 10.10. *Jenůfa,* Act II, sc. 6 (rh II.88): Jenůfa's Prayer. Janáček *Jenůfa.* Copyright 1917 by Universal Edition. Copyright renewed. Copyright 1969. All rights reserved. Used by Permission of European American Music Distributors Corporation, sole U.S. and Canadian agent for Universal Edition.

Jenůfa and Laca prepare for their wedding. The act opens with a series of short scenes: the tone is one of forced gaiety accompanied by darkly orchestrated music. The mayor, his wife, Števa, and the latter's fiancée Karolka join Jenůfa's immediate family in anticipation of the wedding. In rapid succession, a traditional wedding dance offered by the young village women, and blessings given by Grandma and the Kostelnička culminate in the discovery of little Števa's frozen body. The Kostelnička's confession brings forth the villagers' desire for vengeance which can only be assuaged when Jenůfa insists that she be forgiven.

Janáček prepares the moment of the corpse's recognition and the confession of the Kostelnička by compressing the beginning of the act. In Act I, Jenůfa had felt at odds with community institutions; in Act III, she waits eagerly to take her place in the domestic order. Through it all, the Kostelnička is visibly on edge. Explosive gestures, encapsulating the Kostelnička's fear of impending retribution, interrupt attempts at celebration. With the shutters now fully open, every outside sound seems to her to be threatening. Jenůfa is tender and encourages her to think about the future when things will be better. The major's wife draws attention to Jenůfa's unadorned mode of dress, a detail that anticipates the discovery of young Števa, who is easily identified by his clothing, into which Jenůfa has sewn her ribbons. A brief scene of privacy between Jenůfa and Laca reveals the complicated feelings between them (rh III.19). This scene constitutes a real love duet tinged with lament. Laca vows to devote his life to Jenůfa as penance for having injured her. His vow releases the tension between them as shown in figure 10.11.

The drama moves swiftly through Karolka's inane chattiness, smoothed over by Jenůfa, who is gracious in her hospitality. This hospitality reminds

(Ah, but I have sinned so deeply against you,
My whole life I'll spend tring to make it up to you.)

Figure 10.11. *Jenůfa,* Act III, sc. 3 (rh III.22): Laca's Vow. Janáček *Jenůfa.* Copyright 1917 by Universal Edition. Copyright renewed. Copyright 1969. All rights reserved. Used by Permission of European American Music Distributors Corporation, sole U.S. and Canadian agent for Universal Edition.

us that Jenůfa in her status of bride-to-be has the authority granted to women over their assigned domestic space. Although the home of the Kostelnička is filled with the symbols of marriage and household, she herself, once a moral pillar of the community, has forfeited her legitimacy in the domestic realm. A ceremony of song and blessings moves the action toward the discovery of the corpse and the Kostelnička's subsequent confession (rh III.37). In Act I, Jenůfa's cheek was the site for narrative inscription. In the final moments of Act III, an analogous inscription shifts to young Števa's body.

The relatively concise unfolding of the first part of Act III contrasts with the second part's expansiveness, conducted fully in a public space. Even the last duet between Jenůfa and Laca, although it is sung in private, speaks to the community's requirements for domestic order (rh III.75). Janáček's music fills out: phrases develop more slowly, more organically, and musical sections seem less constrained. As a result, there is time for extended musical statements, first by the Kostelnička in her confession, then by Jenůfa in her response, and finally by Jenůfa and Laca in the closing duet. Moreover, the music is held rapt by the lyricism of reconciliation and forgiveness inherent in the feminized expression of Jenůfa. With the reconciliation between private and public, *Jenůfa's* "happy ending" is attained.

CONCLUSION

At the start of this essay, I suggested that issues surrounding private life and the domestic are important for Janáček's musico-dramatic realization of Preissová's drama. The composer's choices reinscribe Preissová's text and alter the representation of the domestic. Such is the case with two strategic dramaturgical moves in Act I. First, an expanded ensemble relies on strophic song structure to establish the folkloristic music of the village hierarchy and its authority. Music of this sort is crucial in *The Bartered Bride* and *Eugene Onegin* as well, but only in *Jenůfa* does the folkloristic warn of the danger inherent in public custom and folk tradition. Second, the double duets in Act I employ the Grand Duet model to invoke idealized, romantic love. In *Jenůfa,* this dramaturgical model causes the harsh reality of village life to soften and to expand into lyrical expression.

In Act II, Janáček expresses the confinement experienced by Jenůfa and the Kostelnička in their tightly shuttered home. Perhaps only the Countess's Act II cavatina in *The Marriage of Figaro* or the letter-writing scene from *Eugene Onegin* captures so well a woman alone. These are extraordinarily empathetic portraits of women held captive in domestic spaces.

In Act III, Janáček intermingles sounds of celebration with representations of the Kostelnička's frightening specter of the outside world. Once young Števa's corpse is found and the confession intoned, the composer offers healing consolation. The balm of Jenůfa's lyricism creates a palpable sensation of relief as described by Janáček scholar, Jaroslav Vogel: "The music and action . . . touch the limits of endurance. . . . Janáček heals all wounds with a liberating, uplifting catharsis."[43]

Among other things, this essay has pondered what happens when a story is re-told. It is worth noting that Preissová's frank, realistic representation of infanticide hastened the end of her active career. Years after the opera's successful premier, she undertook revisions of her play, seeking to have it resemble *Jenůfa* more closely in a novel with a softer ending.[44] But her efforts never succeeded. It was in Janáček's operatic arena that this overwhelming story could best be rendered. It is a work to be deeply cherished.

NOTES

1. For *Jenůfa*, the period of composition is established in John Tyrrell, *Turn of the Century Masters* from *The New Grove Series* (New York and London: Norton, 1985), 8; for *Její pastorkyňa*, the date cited is that of the premier as given by Karel Brusak, "Drama into Libretto," in *Jenůfa/Katya Kabanova* from *English National Opera Guide Series* (New York and London: John Calder, 1985), 13.

2. Realism in literature and *verismo* opera are distinct from each other in important ways. As Carl Dahlhaus suggests, opera is not particularly well suited to the projection of social criticism, an important feature of realism in literature. In particular, opera's obligatory lyrical moments, the show-stopping arias, for instance, interrupt unromanticized representations of daily life (*Nineteenth-Century Music*, [Berkeley and Los Angeles: Univ. of California Press, 1988], 353).

3. John Tyrrell, *Janáček's Operas* (Princeton: Princeton Univ. Press, 1992), 41.

4. Ibid., 22.

5. Many of his compositions over the years can be linked to a specific political cause or social principle to which the composer felt a deep commitment. His first effort to combine folk material and opera involved the adding of melodies to *Počátek románu* (*The Beginning of a Romance*), a Preissová novella. The composer later dismissed this effort, more incidental music than opera, as "an empty farce" (see Patrick Lambert, "Leoš Janáček and T. G. Masaryk," in *T. G. Masaryk*, vol. 3, ed. Harry Hanak [Houndmills: Macmillan, 1990], 207.)

6. M. M. Bakhtin, "Discourse in the Novel," in *The Dialogic Imagination*, ed. Michael Holquist (Austin: Univ. of Texas Press, 1981), 419–21.

7. John Tyrrell, *Janáček's Operas* (Princeton: Princeton Univ. Press, 1992), 21–39.

8. Karel Brusak, "Drama into Libretto," in *Jenůfa / Katya Kabanova* from *English National Opera Guide Series* (New York and London: John Calder, 1985), 13.

9. Thomas Hardy, "Candour in English Fiction," quoted in Ann Ardis, *New Woman, New Novels* (New Brunswick: Rutgers Univ. Press, 1990), 33.

10. Ibid., 34, 73.

11. Ibid.

12. Jane Tompkins, *Sensational Designs* (New York: Oxford Univ. Press, 1985), xi, xviii, quoted in Ardis, 29.

13. Elaine Showalter, *Sexual Anarchy* (New York: Penguin, 1990), 23.

14. Ibid., 38.

15. In a bitter portrait of village life (*The Power of Darkness* [1888]), Tolstoy depicts a ruthless battle between men and women, rich and poor, powerful and powerless. The story's climactic scene presents the agony of the newborn's father, who, up to this terrible moment, has been presented as more callow than evil. He returns from the cellar where he has crushed his infant son to death at the insistence of his intended mother-in-law. The baby's cries haunt him as he asks rhetorically: "What have they made me do? What have they made me do?" A joyless wedding scene follows, forcing a proper close for the "marriage plot." Tolstoy's story fulfills Hardy's prediction: the marriage plot is portrayed cynically, replaced by a view of domestic life that rejects the romantic dream of living happily-ever-after (*The Portable Tolstoy*, ed. John Bayley [New York: Penguin, 1978], 804).

16. John Lukacs, *Budapest 1900* (New York: Weidenfeld & Nicolson, 1990), 82.

17. See n. 5: Lambert, 206.

18. John Tyrrell, *Czech Opera* (Cambridge: Cambridge Univ. Press, 1988), 69.

19. Janáček's considerable admiration for Tchaikovsky is laid out in full in an essay on *Eugene Onegin* (1891) (Zemanová, 160–63).

20. Ibid., 174–75.

21. Dahlhaus, 358.

22. The following modern edition was used in comparing play and opera: Gabriela Preissová, *Její pastorkyňa: Drama z Venkovského Života Moravského o 3 Jendánich* (Praze: J. Otto, 1923).

23. Act numbers in upper-case Roman numerals and rehearsal numbers in Arabic numerals are preceded by "rh" (for "rehearsal"). A plus sign (+) followed by an Arabic numeral may be used to indicate a location so many measures following the rehearsal number. Note that rehearsal numbers are identical in the Universal (1969) piano-vocal and full orchestral scores. Sometimes rehearsal numbers are printed directly over bar lines; in such cases, the numbers refer to measures to the right of the bar lines.

24. Translation by Otakar Kraus and Edward Downes from the full score, ed. by J. M. Dürr (Vienna: Universal Edition, 1969).

25. In Janáček's music, major and minor modes occur only rarely without modal inflection. I shall use "major" and "minor" occasionally as shorthand indications of tonal centers, where the specification of more precise modal characteristics is not required.

26. E. P. Thompson, "Rough Music," in *Customs in Common* (New York: New York Press, 1993), 467, 469.

27. E. P. Thompson, "Custom and Culture," in *Customs in Common* (New York: New York Press, 1993), 2.

28. Michelle Perot, *A History of Private Lives*, vol. 4 (Cambridge: Harvard Univ. Press, 1990), 4.

29. Dahlhaus, 358–59.

30. Charles Susskind, *Janáček and Brod* (New Haven and London: Yale Univ. Press, 1985), 51.

31. In the play and in an earlier version of the opera, the Kostelnička is allowed to explain her reasons for this harsh pronouncement, namely, that Števa's drunkenness portends a difficult path for the couple, not unlike the misery she endured with Števa's brutal, irresponsible father. Without this material, the Kostelnička's actions appear rather arbitrary and bitter. The omitted portion of the opera is included in the piano/vocal score, Universal Edition, (rh I.66) – (rh I.73 + 3), and more recently has come to be reinserted by some conductors (for example, by Sir Charles Mackerras on his recording for London 414 483–2).

32. This extended ensemble has been criticized for detracting from the realism of both the text and music. Although this objection has some validity, the fugue serves an important ideological purpose as will be explained below.

33. Harold S. Powers, "'La solita forma' and the Uses of Convention," *Acta musicologica* 59 (1987), 70.

34. Philip Gossett, "Verdi, Ghislanzoni, and *Aida*: The Uses of Convention," *Critical Inquiry* 1 (1974): 304–6.

35. Philip Gossett, "The 'Candeur Virginale' of *Tancredi*," *Musical Times* 112 (1971), 327.

36. Julian Budden, *The Operas of Verdi*, vol. 1 (New York: Schirmer, 1973), 16.

37. The idea that a body part can be transformed into a linguistic sign is developed by Peter Brooks in *Body Work* (Cambridge: Harvard Univ. Press, 1993).

38. Jenůfa has named her child Števa after his father. As shown above, a complex geneology among the main characters in the opera fosters rifts and conflicting financial interests. For example, Jenůfa's and Števa's fathers are sons of the previously wealthy Grandma Burya; the Kostelnička is Jenůfa's stepmother; (note: the Czech title of the opera is *Její pastorkyňa—Her Stepdaughter*); Laca and Števa have the same mother and are therefore half-brothers. When the opera begins, Števa has already inherited the family fortune including the mill; Grandma is a pensioner; the Kostelnička is without independent means; Jenůfa must work at the mill; Laca has had to serve in the army, lacking the funds to buy an exemption, and now also works at the mill. Consequently, Laca resents Števa who has taken up with Jenůfa while he was away at the army; the Kostelnička detests Števa due to his physical resemblance to her former husband. To make matters worse, and to provide a crucial motivating factor for the Kostelnička's actions, Jenůfa's son Števa bears an uncanny resemblance to his father.

39. The two key signatures shown in the figure—G–flat in the harp and F–sharp in the vocal part—correspond to Janáček's original manuscript notation. Throughout his music, key signatures often signify personal, expressive topoi, particularly the keys of D–flat, C–sharp, F–sharp, and G–flat.

40. Diaries came to the fore during the nineteenth century together with an increasing interest in the notion of privacy and the higher value placed on the emotional life of an individual.

41. Lawrence Kramer, *Music and Poetry* (Berkeley and Los Angeles: Univ. of California Press, 1984), 27.

42. A scene between the Kostelnička and a widowed friend has been omitted so as

not to interrupt the dramatic drive toward the infanticide; again, any development of the Kostelnička's broader personality is sacrificed, reinforcing the impression of her as the "odd woman."

43. Jaroslav Vogel, *Leoš Janáček* (New York: Norton, 1981), 141.

44. Gabriela Preissová, *Její pastorkyňa* (Praha: Československý, 1978).

ANAHID KASSABIAN

At the Twilight's Last Scoring

(P) ostcolonial theory and the geopolitics of the past ten years have con-
spired to make nationalism a high-profile question in the study of culture. But while articles and books on colonialist educational, linguistic, and
cartographic practices boom, little is said about such practices in film and
music.[1] In this essay, three action-adventure films — *The Hunt for Red October*, *Lethal Weapon 2*, and *Indiana Jones and the Temple of Doom* — provide
a textual gateway through which to consider nationalism in contemporary
Hollywood scores and scoring procedures. From them, I theorize an assimilating identification that borrows from both psychoanalysis and cultural studies to account for some of film music's specificities.

THE HUNT FOR LETHAL RED WEAPONS IN THE
TEMPLE OF OCTOBER DOOM II

Different versions of U.S., or "American," nationalism underpin *Lethal
Weapon 2*, *The Hunt for Red October*, and *Indiana Jones and the Temple of
Doom*. Each organizes what it means to be American, as they call it, in terms
of race and gender, but not identically. *The Hunt for Red October* was released in 1990 to great excitement among spy-thriller fans. Tom Clancy's
book made what a popular video guide book calls a real "edge-of-your-seat
winner" about a Lithuanian submarine captain who defects with the new
silent high-tech Soviet sub and its crew.[2] The audio track seems perfect for a
spy film: it is overwhelmingly sneaky, in two senses. First, it *sounds* like a spy

film in that much of the music is short repeated (or ostinato) chromatic figures; see figure 11.1.

Second, the music constantly edges in under the omnipresent ambient noise of the subs, beginning as a barely audible hum that lasts for long seconds before the musical cue, which seems to come from nowhere. This technique, called "sneaking," is central to classical Hollywood practice: it protects the score from being noticed. Because it uses extremely heavy ambient noise, because it blurs the distinction between sound and music, and because much of its music is very short repetitive figures, the overall sound of *Red October* is very thick, organized by an emphasis on sound over music.

The only melodic music in the film is the anthem of the Soviet Union, which appears again and again. It is sung through the opening titles, in an odd kind of pseudo-Soviet-Army-Chorus style that includes female voices and symphonic orchestration. When Ramius (Sean Connery), who importantly is Lithuanian rather than Russian, informs his crew that their mission is to sneak into U.S. waters, they burst into song. In fact, it is precisely this moment of song that gives them away to the U.S. sub: the virtuoso black sonar man, Jonesy, hears the singing. The anthem is heard again in the Soviet admiral's office, on the radio, as he receives the news that Ramius is defecting; and it is heard several times more during the film. In this way, music and Soviet nationalism become inseparable.

Moreover, the film's dialogue keeps returning to music in strange ways. When Jonesy is introduced teaching a young white seaman sonar technique, he tricks the seaman, and then tells him, "So, like Beethoven on the computer, you have labored to produce . . . a biologic" (i.e., a whale). The camera pans 360 degrees around the small sonar room across a Beethoven poster. A short while later, when an officer wants to tease Jonesy, he tells the story of how Jonesy projected music out into the water to listen to it and had the whole fleet listening to Paganini. Jonesy repeatedly corrects him, saying that the music was Pavarotti, not Paganini: the former is a tenor, the latter a composer. The film distinguishes Jonesy as a genius with sonar technology, but—as his tastes in music indicate—he is neither "one of the guys" nor a leader among them: the intersections of race, class, and sexuality become particularly complicated in a black techie classical music lover.[3]

Moreover, rock 'n' roll has a particular status in the film's world. When Ramius tells the crew that they are headed for American waters, he says, "We will pass through the American patrols, pass through their sonar nets, and lay off their largest city and listen to their rock 'n' roll while we conduct missile drills." When the captain of the *Dallas* wants to express how careless the *Red October* is being, he says, "They're moving close to 30 knots; at that speed, they could run over my daughter's stereo and not hear it." Certainly

Figure 11.1. *The Hunt for Red October:* the Submarine Ostinato.
The Hunt for Red October by Basil Poledouris. Copyright (c) 1990 by Ensign Music Corporation. International Copyright Secured. All rights reserved. Used with permission.

Figure 11.2. *The Hunt for Red October:* Ramius Kills the Political Commissar.
The Hunt for Red October by Basil Poledouris. Copyright (c) 1990 by Ensign Music Corporation. International Copyright Secured. All rights reserved. Used with permission.

the idea that rock 'n' roll is noise is not new, but here it is particularly American.

So rock 'n' roll is U.S. noise. Russians sing. And both narratively and musically, the film is very clear about which characters are real Americans. The first musical cue belongs to Ramius, during the sequence in which he kills the political commissar of the mission in order to be able to defect with the new sub. The music invites identification at this moment of his radical separation from the U.S.S.R.; see figure 11.2

While the music is almost identical to the ostinato for the submarines in figure 11.1, the difference is that here the music expresses Ramius's subjective state.

The next cue is organized around Jack Ryan (Alec Baldwin), who has been set up as the hero by a variety of filmic devices from the outset.[4] At a crucial moment in the film, during a meeting of the Joint Chiefs of Staff as they try to decide what to do about the renegade sub *Red October*, the music enters on a cut to Ryan thinking, and exits on the President's National Security Advisor saying, "You wish to add something to our discussion, Dr. Ryan?" See figure 11.3

This is the moment at which Ryan's identification with Ramius takes over both Ryan and the film. Based on his own intelligence report on Ramius, Ryan imagines, and convinces the National Security Advisor, that Ramius has gathered a mutinous crew to defect with the Soviet Union's most high-tech sub. The music draws them together in opposition to the quite different musicality that the film creates for Russianness.[5]

To be blunt, then: Americans are white and men. Jonesy comes close to earning American status, but he fails on several counts. First, his music listening practices differentiate him from the crew as weird, perhaps even gay. As Philip Brett argues, musicality has an intimate ideological and discursive connection with male homosexuality.[6] Not only do musicality and homosexuality both circulate as deviances, they are to some extent conflatable. While gay men pre-Stonewall used phrases such as "Does he play in the orchestra?" as markers of gay identity, musicality signifies feminization, "queerness," homosexuality in everyday boy locker-room parlance.[7] According to Brett's argument, Jonesy's musicality implies at least the possibility of homosexuality, not because gay men are more frequently "musical," but rather because "musical" slips easily into "queer." Second, the film's score never supports his bid for symbolic citizenship: in roughly thirty musical cues throughout the film, not one accompanies Jonesy directly. The score's message is: pumped-up patriotic anthem-singing is old-fashioned, and real American nationalism opens its very white arms to any Ramius smart enough and man enough to deserve it.

Lethal Weapon 2 tells a slightly different story about race, nationalism, and masculinity. The South African consulate in Los Angeles is a front for all sorts of illegal activities, and the plot details how Riggs (Mel Gibson) and Murtaugh (Danny Glover) unmask and nail the bad guys. The Eric Clapton cool-jazz-rock saxophone-guitar score suggests a musical discourse that crosses racial lines. Unlike classical scores organized around one or more leitmotives, but oddly like *The Hunt for Red October*, this score uses small,

Figure 11.3. *The Hunt for Red October:* Ryan Meets the National Security Advisor. *The Hunt for Red October* by Basil Poledouris. Copyright (c) 1990 by Ensign Music Corporation. International Copyright Secured. All rights reserved. Used with permission.

Figure 11.4. *Lethal Weapon 2:* Riggs' Fusion Style Music—Lead Guitar with Chords. *Lethal Weapon 2:* (incidental music) music by Michael Kamen. (C) Warner-Tamerlane Publishing Corp (BMI). All rights Reserved. Used by Permission. Warner Bros. Publications U. S. Inc., Miami, FL 33014

varying figures of four or more notes to signify danger, and suspense, and the seemingly racially unmarked musical style "fusion"—a combination of jazz and rock—for Riggs and Murtaugh; see figure 11.4.

But over the course of the film—actually over the course of the three *Lethal Weapon* films—it becomes clear that the Eric Clapton and David Sandborn licks really belong to Riggs, not to Murtaugh: they enter with Riggs, they follow him around, the express what his character is experiencing, and so on. Even in the opening sequence, the music really belongs to Riggs. During this long chase sequence, the music enters only on the cut to Riggs crawling out through the shattered windshield of Murtaugh's wife's wrecked car. As in *Red October*, the musical cues have the earmarks (and consequences) of literary point-of-view, and it is Riggs's.

Moreover, fusion signifies race in an at best confused field. Fusion is generally understood to have begun in New York in 1969 with Miles Davis's *In a Silent Way* and *Bitches Brew* (on which virtually every fusion star played). Since then it has been "whitened" in a variety of ways. First, many of its major players were white: Josef Zawinul, John McLaughlin, and Al DiMeola among others.[8] Second, it is defined in part by its considerable roots in rock 'n' roll, which by that time was almost monolithically white in both production and consumption. Finally, it is discursively produced in jazz history as inauthentic and mercenary. As Len Lyons says: "Fusion has been both lucrative and controversial in its short lifetime. According to the music's many critics, its popularity and profits far exceed its aesthetic values, durability, or contribution to jazz's developments. . . . the lure of fame and fortune has lured some promising serious musicians into wasting their talents in pursuing financial goals."[9] In jazz tradition, these musical judgments are very often associated with white jazz musicians. So in many ways fusion signifies as a white jazz genre. On the other hand, it signifies as a *jazz* genre, not as a rock genre. Fusion holds a small place as a supposedly failed experiment in jazz history; but it is altogether absent from most rock histories. To the extent that it sounds "jazzy," then, and to the extent that "jazz" still signifies as "black" music, fusion may well signify blackness or, closely enough, hipness to an audience unfamiliar with jazz history and discourse.

Verbally, *Lethal Weapon 2* is oddly preoccupied with nationalism. Nationality defines the "bad guys" here: once the film introduces the South African consul, it isn't very surprising that he is running drugs, laundering money, and smuggling krugerrands. And since he and his fellow countrymen have diplomatic immunity, the only way to "get them" is to blow them sky-high, which makes it possible for the film to be a Lethal Weapon sequel.

But beyond this, there are two very telling moments at which the film defines for us who gets to be American. When Riggs needs a cover to sneak into the consul's office, Leo and Murtaugh create a diversion by having Murtaugh apply for a visa to emigrate to South Africa. The official, of course, tries to dissuade Murtaugh, who gives a rousing speech about going to South Africa to help his brothers in their struggle for freedom. In other words, if one is black, one's allegiances cross national boundaries. Simultaneously, Riggs gets caught breaking into the consul's office and identifies himself as an American, saying: "I'll make a deal with you, Arjun, or Aryan, or whatever the fuck your name is. You get the fuck out of my country, and I won't blow your head off." The music up to this point in the scene consists of marimba octaves; when Riggs attacks, he is accompanied by Clapton's fusion guitar. For Riggs to identify along racial lines, he would have to side with the bad guys. But he can't: he's the hero. And anyway, why should he? He's American.

In all the ways that the music defines Riggs as (1) a hero, (2) the hero of the movie, and (3) the hero of his country, it excludes Murtaugh from these categories. He can't be American as the film defines it because he is black. Beyond that, he can't (as Danny Glover has noted in interviews) be romantic, which often defines heroes. And neither the music nor the narrative is his. And he has commitments beyond the film's realm of justice: he has a family. In the opening chase scene, Murtaugh worries about destroying his wife's station wagon, but his concern is dismissed by Riggs and ridiculed at the station house. That sequence ensures that we know from the start who the real man is, and he isn't the one with the family: at least since *Rebel without a Cause*, Hollywood has shown perceivers what to think about men who worry about what their wives will say.[10] So, as in *The Hunt for Red October*, to the extent that men of color are included in the film, they are excluded from symbolic citizenship.

The connection to *Rebel without a Cause* raises some interesting questions about the role of masculine sexuality in *Lethal Weapon 2*. Just as Jonesy marks the threat of homosexuality in *The Hunt for Red October*, Leo marks that same threat in *Lethal Weapon 2*. And like Jonesy, Leo is marked as gay not directly but indirectly, through stereotypes of gay masculinity (stereotypes that interestingly assimilate certain ethnic stereotypes to gender categories). The film shows his distance from Hollywood heterosexual white masculinity in his obsession with cleanliness and order, in his constantly fluttering hands, in his continuous talking, and in his affected speech. But the film goes even further in defining the terms of its symbolic citizenship. To the deal he proposes to the consul (quoted above), Riggs adds: "If you stay around, I'm going to fuck your ass." The worst punishment Riggs can threaten, it seems, is that he will penetrate the consul anally. The equivalence—the exchangeability—established is between illicitly crossing national boundaries and crossing illicit sexual ones.

Unlike *Red October*, then, *Lethal Weapon 2* is not generous with its symbolic citizenship. Narratively, the film belongs to Riggs, the only cast member to occupy the "American" position, despite Mel Gibson's protean Australian accent. Musically, too, the film is his, although not in terms as straightforward as those of *Red October*. During the long sequence that shows cops being killed, Riggs is in his beach trailer making love with the consular secretary. The small danger figures accompany the various deaths, while Riggs and the girl get source music—an oldies radio station.[11] At first hearing, it may seem that the danger figures signify the South African villains, as a kind of stylistic leitmotiv similar to Riggs's fusion.

But I want to suggest that this oversimplifies the way the music signifies. The use of source music for Riggs's sex scene parallels the use of source music in other scenes in the movie(s): the Looney Tunes theme, the Three Stooges, and early sixties rock 'n' roll all seem to express his subjectivity by accompanying major subjective moments such as his contemplation of suicide or sex with a new lover. The danger figures for the death of cops, who noticeably and multiculturally include blacks and women, are scored for strings and marimbas, the latter an instrument with a very distinctive sound. Various marimba patterns crop up throughout the film in association with the South African consul and his gang; see figure 11.5.

But Riggs's fusion sound also has marimbas, usually with saxophone and electric guitar. That orchestration gives the film an overall sound: without it, the difference between the strings and the guitar/saxophone combo could be jarring. Moreover, the use of marimbas for both Riggs and the South Africans creates an eerie sense of a threat from within, perhaps related to the diplomatic immunity of the consular staff.

The presence of the marimbas suggests that the deaths of the cops have some direct relationship not only to the consul but also to Riggs: that the

Figure 11.5. *Lethal Weapon 2:* The South Africans' Marimbas.
Lethal Weapon 2 (incidental music) music by Michael Kamen. (C) Warner-Tamerlane Publishing Corp (BMI). All rights Reserved. Used by Permission. Warner Bros. Publications U. S. Inc., Miami, FL 33014

deaths are his issue and his responsibility to avenge. This distribution of musics—fusion for Riggs, strings and marimba figures for danger, and source
music for Riggs's "weak" moments—achieves an overwhelming array of
ideological work. It places Riggs firmly within the discourses of both hegemonic masculinity and Hollywood herodom, such that he seems sensitive and
loving, but his "self"—marked by his "own" music—is located entirely in
action rather than in emotion. It also places him within the discourse of
American patriotism insofar as his self is defined in terms of his commitment
to justice and nation.

Indiana Jones and the Temple of Doom is the only one of these three films
not *overtly* about some form of Americanism. It moves about Asia as if the
continent were the size of New Jersey, crashing an airplane in China, skiing
down the Himalayas in a life raft, and landing in an Indian jungle, a sequence
held together (to the extent that it *is* held together) by continuous music. The
film is about "barbarians" in India who practice human sacrifice. A predictable score would have included a lot of what Jerry Goldsmith has called Hollywood ethnic-oriental music: fourths and gongs in China, snake-charmer
harmonic minors in India. After all, it seems reasonable to expect the John
Williams classical style to resort to Hollywood's musical semiotics of ethnicity. But it doesn't.

There is very little ethnic scoring at all in the film, and most of what is
there is source music. For instance, during the snakes-and-monkey-brains
banquet in Pangkot Palace, the dancing girls dance to music. And during the
Thuggi cult rituals of sacrifice, there is chanting focused on words without
discernible melody. But the dramatic scoring almost never has an ethnic
sound, and when it does, it only lasts a few phrases. The film is mainly a kind
of Ben-Hur epic sound-alike, which suggests that there is a style of music that
we might call "spectacle" or "epic" in its own right; see figure 11.6.[12]

However this music is named, it has room for neither subjectivity nor geography: it only bothers to represent the film's broad comic-book-style action. The two-dimensional ethnic villains never have a chance, a point on
which narrative and score are in wholehearted agreement. And Willy, whose
rendition of "Anything Goes" in a Chinese dialect opens the film, never gets
another musical moment to herself. Harrison Ford, even more blatantly than
Mel Gibson, earns the right to herodom and citizenship by virtue of gender
and color.

In fact, the film has a very clear oedipal trajectory. As Sobchack and
Clough have argued, the 1980s produced a spate of films in which children
become their parents' parents: from *Close Encounters of the Third Kind* to
the first *Back to the Future*, children do what their parents cannot, go where
their parents cannot, and repair what their parents might have broken.[13] In
Indiana Jones and the Temple of Doom, the fantasy of reversal is twisted: Indy,
the father, saves his (real or assumed) son, Short Round, along with hundreds

Figure 11.6. *Indiana Jones and the Temple of Doom:* Epic Style.

of enslaved Indian village children. But Short Round also saves Indy. Willy, who is about to be sacrificed to Kali-ma, begs and pleads with a drugged Indy, crying for her life. But only Short Round can bring him out of his drug-induced trance by yelling, "Indy, I love you, you're my best friend, Indy"; and this only after escaping from the mass of child laborers in an action sequence that only Indiana Jones himself could match. Musically, the extended sequence mainly uses source chanting, which at times becomes source scoring as the crowds begin to chant or sing in four-part harmony with the sudden addition of women's voices. But at two moments, when Short Round is escaping from his shackles and when he approaches Indy, the full-blown symphonic dramatic scoring pulls no punches. French horns and trumpets carry the epic melody, supported by strings and timpani, that accompanies Short Round's escape. The timpani become the drums beating a rhythm for the chanters, who return to their original genders. But when Short Round lands in front of Indy—as he cries "Wake up, Dr. Jones, wake up!"—the horns return, only to thin out, reducing in numbers. Then they give way to high, keening violins that begin a brief tremolo (a classical danger and suspense device), while a solo trumpet reenters in time for Short Round's curative cry.

By juxtaposing chanting and symphonic scoring, the score clearly divides "us" from "them." The chanting pagan hordes will allow their evil leader to tear out someone's heart as part of a ritual sacrifice, but good Americans reserve their hearts for classical Hollywood symphonic techniques and for young boys crying out "I love you."[14]

IDENTIFICATION AS ASSIMILATION

Musically, these films reside resolutely within the classical Hollywood tradition. Some recent Hollywood films have proliferated possibilities of identification, often in part by giving two characters comparable (though never equal) technical and narrative attention. I am suggesting that *Lethal Weapon 2*, *The Hunt for Red October*, and *Indiana Jones and the Temple of Doom* appear to do the same in their casts, but the potential threats posed by the competing (ethnically marked) characters—Murtaugh, Leo, Jonesy, and Short Round—are more than neutralized. They are managed in all the ways film theory has articulated: through narrative, editing, and camera techniques. But I have been arguing throughout this article that music, too, is entirely imbricated in the relationship of characters to filmic positions of power.[15]

Elsewhere I have argued that the use of popular songs in scores invites perceivers to bring their own "music histories" into play with the film.[16] Music editing procedures for popular songs also generally follow different approaches from those for classical scores, taking less care to parallel visual continuity editing. For example, to turn for a moment to *Thelma and Louise*, the sequence early in the film in which they drive off for a weekend in the mountains is scored to "House of Hope." The song is mixed (i.e., the volume is adjusted) according to classical procedures for dramatic scoring, but the editing does not follow that tradition. Broadly speaking, classical cues are relatively short, whereas "House of Hope" lasts for about three minutes, from when Louise and Thelma pull out of the driveway until just before they pull into the parking lot of the bar. It is anything but "inaudible";[17] it is not "sneaked"; it exits in a simple fade, (i.e., the volume drops progressively to inaudibility). In this sequence it would be hard work not to notice "House of Hope." What emerges in part through the mixing and more strongly in the editing is a moment of music that commands a relatively high degree of attention and that is likely to be perceived as either a quotation or at least as an allusion to a genre.

This particular textual profile, a profile created by the postproduction technical decisions of editing and mixing, makes possible a broad field of identifications. In extreme contrast, the scoring of the short underwater sequences of the subs in *The Hunt for Red October* leaves relatively little room for perceiver maneuvering. This scoring signifies strongly within classical Hollywood tradition: for example, the ostinato in figure 11.1, quoted above, clearly marks something in the realm of suspense or danger, predominantly because of its tight voice-leading emphasizing minor seconds. But as a performed piece of music its meaning becomes even more clear. The orchestration is classical Hollywood symphonic, dominated by strings; the phrasing is legato; there is little echo; all recording and mixing features suggest (phantasmatically) acoustic performance. This tiny ostinato figure is pure-bred classical Hollywood.

By this I do not mean to suggest that the procedures of classical Hollywood scoring and the late Romantic symphonic idiom most closely associated with them constitute a monolithic system of meaning. Even contemporary cultural theories with as widely different epistemological commitments as deconstruction and ethnographic cultural studies agree that no semiotic system can completely control or guarantee the production of a particular meaning. Rather, the question of the difference between popular song and composed film scores centers around different relationships to intertextuality and textual competence.

The music in *The Hunt for Red October* refers to Hollywood film music, with the exception of the Soviet anthem, which is used, much like Goldsmith's fourths and gongs, to signify nationality and geography without an unwieldy concern for ethnomusicological accuracy (i.e. the military thematics of the film and the invocation of the Soviet Army could have precluded the possibility of women's voices as the choruses themselves did). Surely the ubiquity of classical Hollywood films' musical procedures in film and television ensures that broad audiences are competent in them. (One would have to work hard, in other words, *not* to acquire competence in them. For example, in the years after the release of *Jaws*, its theme developed a life of its own, becoming *the* sound of ironized film danger whether or not one had seen/heard the film itself). Film scores composed in the classical Hollywood tradition, then, rely on a signification system designed for precisely the same uses to which the scores themselves will put it, so that their perceivers need competence in that system alone.

The score of *Thelma and Louise*, however, requires of its listeners multiple competences: in Hollywood film music, in country and western, in blues, and in rock 'n' roll. Some of these musics are subcultural practices that require particular competences acquired within one or more particular communities. Moreover, competences acquired in the same music in different communities may lead to very different kinds of identifications. For instance, the associations of country and western listeners who grew up in Fort Worth, Texas, might make perceiving *Desert Hearts* a disorienting experience, while the associations of country and western listeners who began listening to it in gay bars in New York City might make the score seem to them perfectly "natural" or oddly feminine.

The *Lethal Weapon* films problematize this distinction in important ways. The music in *Lethal Weapon 2* is not really fusion, in the sense that it would not really stand up as fusion to independent listening. One of fusion's defining features is a virtuoso instrumental technique that would be inappropriate (because distracting) in a classical Hollywood score like this one. On the other hand, the music is unmistakably marked "fusion" in its instrumental, melodic, and textual procedures. This score invites identifications as a classical Hollywood score because the music signifies "urban," "hip," "interracial," without opening particularly onto specific individual or community relations.

If classical Hollywood late-Romantic symphonic scores limit available paths of identification, then it would appear at first that they close the gaps both between audience member and perceiver and between perceiver and spectator position. But no such theoretical collapse is possible. "Spectator position" is the visual film-psychoanalytic version of Hall's "preferred reading": it is the structure of identification that the film strives to make most available and desirable. *Perceivers* is the word I have chosen to designate the theoretical placeholder for audience members: it cannot be reduced either to textuality or to an extratextual "real."[18] While perceivers, as theoretical constructs, can never be the same as "real" audience members, they mark an important distinction from previous theoretical positions both because they are decidedly multiple and because they have ears.

And perceivers come with social histories: they bring gender, race, class, sexuality, and many other axes of identity to the foreground. Unlike the spectator of 1970s and 1980s psychoanalytic film theory, perceivers engage films, complete with visual, verbal, sound, and musical tracks, in a flow of conscious and unconscious operations. And their unconsciouses are not those of traditional psychoanalysis, organized around phallic-centered sexual difference; instead, the unconsciouses of perceivers are organized by the particular differences that strain the match between their subjectivities and the subject positions offered by dominant modes of textuality and narrativity.[19] Perceivers—the theoretical entities produced in the writing of a hearing film-critical practice—engage the films they perceive in identification processes that reproduce, on a microcosmic level, the processes of assimilation that structure their everyday experiences.

Music has a particular relationship to processes of assimilation. As many have argued, music can act as a lubricant to identification processes, smoothing the transition into (often barely plausible) fictional worlds by washing perceivers in a "bath or gel of affect."[20] But this model only begins to describe the more specific relations between perceivers and music, and it does not describe the relations between perceivers and popular songs. More to the point, music facilitates the assimilation of perceivers into available subject positions in the film. In the case of films like *Thelma and Louise* that do not limit those positions to the rigid classical one, the music proliferates possibilities by opening perception onto perceivers' own (socially conditioned) histories. In the case of more classical films, such as *Indiana Jones and the Temple of Doom*, the score limits possibilities by narrowing access to perceivers' histories and focusing instead on their competence in assimilation. If assimilation were yet another model of identification, then nothing would have been gained in terms of maintaining a theoretical distance between spectators and perceivers (and audiences). But assimilation is not *an*other model; it is, rather, a name for a category of subjective processes that share with each other some features but not others. It accounts for structural similarities in the relations of, for example, female, black, working-class, queer, and disabled perceivers, without discounting the important differences among us.

To return to *Lethal Weapon 2*, then, it becomes clear that the identification processes available to gay and black male perceivers will differ significantly, both because black and gay identities operate differently from each other and because the categories of race and sexuality operate differently within the film. Murtaugh provides an eminently accessible path of assimilation: through an initial identification with him, a black male perceiver can be eased into a white male subject position, in part because of Murtaugh's proximity to Riggs and in part because the score directs such a passage. In the opening sequence discussed above, identification with either Riggs or Murtaugh is a wide-open field, but once the score enters as Riggs climbs out the window, the available positions narrow.[21] Assimilation can operate in this way, by metonymy or synecdoche. But the processes available to gay male perceivers are quite different. By making Leo both a clown and stereotypically gay, the film makes three paths most likely: refusal to engage the film on the grounds that it is insulting; a camp identification with Leo; or identification with the homophobic position, organized by Riggs's and Murtaugh's annoyance, that finds him funny. Assimilation can also operate in this way, by making disavowal attractive.

Both sets of possibilities depend, however, on the score's resolute production of a privileged subject position. Where the score is less narrowly committed to one position, more fluid processes of assimilation become possible. Even in *Dirty Dancing*, a film combining popular music with a relatively classical score, the organization of the score around Baby's and Johnny's dancing makes assimilation into a working-class white ethnic male position almost as available as assimilation into a middle-class white Jewish female one. Just as *Thelma and Louise* gives increasing attention to Thelma's character, *Dirty Dancing* speaks from Johnny's perspective with increasing strength over the course of the film: as his subjective experiences accumulate screen time, the possibility of seeing the world of Kellerman's Catskills resort from a working-class subject position becomes increasingly available. But that play of availability would be impossible if Johnny were scored as Murtaugh is.

The final sequence of *Dirty Dancing*, however, makes clear another trajectory of assimilating identifications: they are never completely successful, and therefore remain always up for grabs. There is no reason for a white middle-class perceiver to find the exuberance of the final sequence particularly uncomfortable. Johnny—he of the beautiful and capable body—singles out Baby for her outstanding ability to practice good middle-class values: sticking to principle, honesty, trustworthiness, and so on. And the recording he brings has, of course, a hypnotic effect on everyone in the room, such that the guests at Kellerman's forget their middle-class inhibitions not only by beginning to dance but even by dancing with some of the entertainment staff. The film makes it clear that the music makes them do it, and a happy, middle-class-fantasy, U.N. greeting card ending is had by all.

Or is it? For perceivers of any class who believe in the American Dream, the ending of *Dirty Dancing* seems uncomplicated and right. But for those who have difficulty imagining a happily-ever-after for Baby and Johnny, the film's ending is more complicated. The problem lies in the nature of any moment of narrative closure: what McClary argues for closure in tonal procedures—the cadence—is also true of closure in film narrative: "A significant factor that contributes to the violence of tonal procedures is that the actual reward—the cadence—can never be commensurate with the anticipation generated or the effort expended in achieving it. The cadence is, in fact, the most banal, most conventionalized cliché available within any musical style."[22] In this sense, not even the score can finally seal the arbitrariness of closure, because its own closure is equally arbitrary. The film is most at risk of losing perceivers engaged in these assimilating identification processes at this moment, because the banality of closure makes them more likely to call a halt to the process altogether and step outside again. But the cadence will in some way disappoint even perceivers who are comfortably interpellated in the film: and it is in this sense that assimilation is never successful or complete, but always a continuous process.

The microcosmic process of assimilating identification that I have described here depends on and participates in the macroscopic-level production of U.S. nationality by many layers of accumulated processes of assimilation. As many film historians have argued, film played an important part in the process of immigrants' assimilation into U.S. society in the earlier decades of this century. I have argued, much more broadly, that assimilation is a necessary ongoing function for the constitution of the United States as a nation; that it operates in movie theaters (as in many other cultural venues); and that film scores regularly perform its work.

The debate over whether or not music can contain immanent meaning continues in both art music and popular music studies, ignoring the immense fabric of ideological work performed by musical discourses that, like film music, have been ignored in the constitution of both fields. But the debate itself pushes aside the clear evidence that could help explain the workings of musical meanings and the ways that they circulate in 1997. If, as most film music scholars argue, classical Hollywood film scores are based on German (and Russian) late-Romantic symphonic practice, listeners must hear that high art music very differently as a consequence of film music listening. The conditions of listening to popular songs must undergo a similar dramatic change with their inclusion on soundtrack albums along with other music not bearing any earlier relation to them. Ola Stockfelt's article in this volume contends that the procedures of musical analysis are based on a bourgeois concert-hall listening practice; unless both art and popular music scholarship begin to address everyday listening practices, that are neither focused nor singular, the question of meaning in music, along with the question of subjectivity in music, will have been silenced.

Moreover, film music has important contributions to make to ongoing discussions about the various and complex relationships between culture and society. Those discussions have burgeoned in exciting ways, drawing clear connections between the possibility of social justice and the circulation of representations and discourses under the names of cultural theory, cultural studies, critical theory, and so on. Film music complicates the already thick and textured descriptions and theories in this field in new and different ways and promises to make important contributions to the ways that many other kinds of cultural objects and texts are understood. Without hearing music everywhere it sounds, however, theories of culture and the interrelations of social and cultural processes will themselves be mute.

NOTES

1. For an important exception, see Antonia Lant's *Blackout* (Princeton: Princeton Univ. Press, 1991) on English films around World War II.

2. Mick Martin and Marsha Porter, *Video Movie Guide 1992* (New York: Ballantine, 1991), 897.

3. In this sense, Jonesy's characterization becomes a moment to notice how frequently issues of race surface in films through music. Jonesy's "biologic," moreover, itself opens up a complex of class and gender issues: as the "biologic" echoes Horace's "Mountains will heave in childbirth, and a ridiculous mouse will be born" (*Ars Poetica* 139) from the efforts of the puerile practitioner of a craft, it is in this case to Jonesy, in the place of the admired but conquered Greeks, that the Muse has given a modernized "gift of graceful eloquence" (*Ars Poetica* 323). Despite the power of American technology to produce virtual whales rather than mere metaphorical mice, the very knowlege that marks Jonesy (and that other marginal Hollywood figure, the scriptwriter)

with the cachet of education and artistry traps him into mapping himself (as whatever sort of Hellenist) onto yet another complex of servitude, intellectualism, and dangerously fluid sexuality. My thanks to Robert Dulgarian for pointing out this reference.

4. For example, the entire opening sequence of the film is devoted to Ryan at home with his wife and child, Ryan afraid of flying and on a transatlantic flight, and point-of-view shooting of his arrival by limousine at the Pentagon.

5. In fact, music is one important way that the Russian and American militaries are differentiated in this film. Along with the mise-en-scène—which makes the Russian admiral's office look like a film noir set—the musical nationalism of the Soviets suggests a lack of sophistication, a "primitive" or at least out-of-date organization surpassed by American technology, individualism—and masculinity.

6. See Philip Brett, "Musicality, Essentialism, and the Closet," in Brett, Elizabeth Wood, and Gary Thomas, eds., *Queering the Pitch: The New Gay and Lesbian Musicology* (New York and London: Routledge, 1993). I would amend Brett's argument in two ways: I think that it is specific to *male* homosexuality, and I don't believe it applies beyond art musicality.

7. Brett also notes that homosexuality as part of composers' life histories has been stringently policed until quite recently. He discusses some of the similarities between the "problem" of femininity and the "problem" of sexuality, but not the relays between them or the specificities of lesbian sexuality and its role in music studies.

8. It is interesting to note that many fusion stars who come to mind are white but ethnically marked in some way, unlike, for instance, most of their rock superstar counterparts. It is surprising that the filmmakers chose Clapton, one of rock's premier blues guitarists, to write in an idiom in which he has neither history nor reputation.

9. Len Lyons, *The 101 Best Jazz Albums: A History of Jazz on Records* (New York: William Morrow, 1980), 333.

10. In terms of the debates about "family values" in the 1992 presidential campaign, I find it fascinating but not surprising that *Murphy Brown* was a target of criticism while the *Lethal Weapon* films were not.

11. Source music is music whose source is visible or implied within the film.

12. Note especially the arpeggiated strings, the minor sixth between the F-sharp and D in the winds and brass in mm. 5–7 consisting almost entirely of first inversion chords, and the lack of harmonic motion. The continuous D-major chords in various inversions and arpeggiations are infrequently disrupted by similarly manipulated E-flat major chords. There is relatively little construction of desire here, no real drive to resolution; instead, the music produces a sensation of timelessness.

13. See Vivian Sobchak, "Child/Alien/Father: Patriarchal Crisis and Generic Exchange," *Camera Obscura* 15 (1986): 7–44; and Patricia Ticineto Clough, *The Ends of Ethnography: From Realism to Social Criticism* (Newbury Park, Calif.: Sage, 1992).

14. In this sense, most one-time dramatic scoring used to identify geographical location participates in similar colonialist discourses. While the music of mood and emotion are reserved for white Western heroes, ethnic Others are contained in their places by music that identifies them according to their non-Westernness. Put simply, music positions white Western bourgeois characters as subjects while denying that same subjectivity to non-Western characters.

15. One extension of this argument would question readings of films that make feminine or female spectatorship positions possible. No such argument can be made

compellingly, to my mind, without careful and extensive analysis of the score as well as of what usually passes for the "film" (i.e. the visual track).

16. Anahid Kassabian, "A Woman Scored," *Studies in Symbolic Interaction* 15, no. 1 (1994).

17. That is, composed so as not to be noticeable: see Claudia Gorbman, *Unheard Melodies: Narrative Film Music* (Bloomington and Indianapolis: Indiana Univ. Press, 1987), 76–79.

18. These distinctions mark intense and important debates between psychoanalysis and cultural studies that I discuss elsewhere. The gap between "spectator position" and "perceiver" is larger than that between "perceiver" and "audience member" because ethnographic audience "reports" are also theorizations of the space of the audience member.

19. There are a growing number of attempts to rewrite psychoanalysis along these lines. See, for example, Kaja Silverman, *The Acoustic Mirror: The Female Voice in Psychoanalysis and Cinema* (Bloomington: Indiana Univ. Press, 1988) and *Male Subjectivity at the Margins* (New York: Routledge, 1992); Judith Butler, *Gender Trouble: Feminism and the Subversion of Subjectivity* (New York: Routledge, 1990) and *Bodies That Matter* (New York: Routledge, 1993); and Gayatri Chakravorty Spivak, "Echo," *New Literary History* 24 (1993): 17–43.

20. Gorbman (1987), 5.

21. Of course, black male perceivers might resist any identification on the grounds, for example, that Murtaugh's character is detrimental to the image of black men. Such resistance is even more available to gay perceivers: see below.

22. Susan McClary, *Feminine Endings: Music, Gender, and Sexuality* (Minneapolis: Univ. of Minnesota Press, 1991), 127.

DAVID SCHWARZ

Listening Subjects: Semiotics, Psychoanalysis, and the Music of John Adams and Steve Reich

THEORETICAL POSITIONS

This essay outlines a theory of listening subjectivity for music.[1] In general, I am interested in naming and exploring a middle ground between pieces of music as texts and psychic structures upon which their perception depends. Based on recent psychoanalytic criticism, I discuss listening subjectivity as a site for such a middle ground. More specifically, musical listening subjects are produced when moments in performed music allow access to psychological events that are presymbolic—that is, from that phase in our development *before* our mastery of language.[2] Not that *all* music is supposed to be *always* presymbolic; but certain kinds of music articulate their conventionality in such a way that the listener can have access to vestiges of presymbolic conditions within conventional forms and procedures. The psychic structures that I apply to the music of John Adams and Steve Reich are the "sonorous envelope" and the "acoustic mirror" from recent French psychoanalytic theory and Kaja Silverman's recent book *The Acoustic Mirror*.[3]

PSYCHOANALYSIS AND SUBJECTIVITY

Despite the fact that we can't get out of language, access to the presymbolic can occur through the sounds *within* language that we first heard before we knew what they meant. For us to listen to music as an attempt within the symbolic order to hear echoes of this lost sound-not-yet-with-meaning is to construct a fantasy of musical subjectivity. Though we listen from social, institutional positions, such a fantasy of subjectivity expressed in sound can uncover thresholds between imaginary and symbolic structures (to be discussed below). And subjectivity is in part made possible by the crossing of symbolic thresholds in social space.

Benveniste points out that in addition to linguistic categories of signifiers and signifieds, there are positions of enunciation that have unique binary structures. These positions are the pronouns "you" and "I" which constantly shift back and forth in discourse. Benveniste asserts that subjectivity and language are closely related, that we become subjects in and through language—the quintessential signifier of the symbolic order.[4]

For Lacan, the infant experiences imaginary structures after birth and before language acquisition. Imaginary structures begin with lack of differentiation between the (not-yet-perceived-as-such) self and the world, and move through acoustic and visual differentiation. The symbolic order initiates the infant into language and social structures. The imaginary order is governed by the voice and image of the *mother*; the symbolic order—the name of the *father*. This narrative, left-to-right explanation is, however, a symbolic reconstruction. The binary categories of inclusion and exclusion of the imaginary order are paradoxically *distanced* and *fixed* by language in the symbolic order.[5]

I understand the role of language in subjectivity as the last among many stages in the splitting-off of the self from phenomenal experience. As we move away from immediate sensation and towards language, our subjectivity gradually comes into being, from birth, to the aural mirror stage (to be described below), to the visual mirror stage, the oedipal crisis and triangulation of desire, to language and social structures.[6] Benveniste asserts that with access to language, we are able to say "I" and "you" and thus create ourselves as subjects, though shifting, temporary, and discourse-bound. I would like to suggest that music can remind us of phases in our development when we crossed from imaginary to symbolic experience and that the musical representation of such threshold-crossing produces listening subjects. In music's echo of presymbolic experience we hear into the spaces between symbolic convention and presymbolic sound: this is the listener's space.

In short, by *musical listening subject*, I mean that which is neither exclusively text, nor listener, nor culture, but a product of all three. Thus at times I say "listening subjects are produced" when agency is indirect and difficult to locate; at times I say "we construct ourselves as listening subjects" when an act of listening is crucial as psychological model or as immanent musical experience. Subjectivity in music, as elsewhere, is *intermittent* and is audible only for a moment as thresholds are crossed and enunciated.[7]

THE ACOUSTIC MIRROR AND MUSIC

Recent psychoanalytic writings have developed a theory that sound and the voice play a crucial role in early development. Didier Anzieu, Guy Rosolato,

Denis Vasse, and Michel Chion all discuss the perception of the mother's voice as a primal experience in which the child feels itself enclosed in an oceanic sense of union.[8] This body of French psychoanalytic theory is synthesized in Kaja Silverman's book *The Acoustic Mirror*: "It has become something of a commonplace to characterize the maternal voice as a blanket of sound, extending on all sides of the newborn infant" (72).

Guy Rosolato suggests a connection that this essay will exploit when he writes: "The maternal voice helps to constitute for the infant the pleasurable milieu which surrounds, sustains, and cherishes him. . . . One could argue that it is the first model of auditory pleasure and that music finds its roots and its nostalgia in [this] original atmosphere, which might be called a sonorous womb, a murmuring house."[9]

Neither Silverman nor I would suggest that music *is* by definition a sonorous envelope. Silverman avoids such an essentialist approach to music by pointing out that the sonorous envelope is a *fantasy*. That is, all presymbolic experiences are retrospective reconstructions from within the symbolic order and have a certain function there—in social, cultural space. A recognition at this level is therefore necessarily a *misrecognition*, or what Lacan would call a *méconnaissance*. For Silverman, this relevant function is the engendering of subjects in classic cinema. The point in this study of Adams and Reich is to show *that* and *how* music can reflect the psychological events of the sonorous envelope and acoustic mirroring as moments in which we construct ourselves as listening subjects.

THE MUSIC OF JOHN ADAMS

The relationship between the sound of the maternal voice and the infant within the sonorous envelope is paradoxical. On the one hand, envelopment suggests undifferentiated, oceanic, expansive oneness; on the other hand, it suggests being contained, enclosed, and marked off. Thus, the sonorous envelope can be either a positive or negative fantasy.[10] The fantasies of sonorous enclosure in Adams are neutral; in Reich, they are more negatively charged. See figure 12.1. This music is marked by lack. There is no dialectical relationship between keys that propel, sustain, slow down, speed up the music; there is no regular phrase structure, there is no binary opposition between foregrounded melody and accompaniment; there are no predictable, large-scale structural markers. "Dialectical relationships," "regular phrase structure," "binary opposition," "structural markers": these conventional phrases mark our listening posture within the symbolic order, and their omission, their effacement in the music at the outset of *Nixon in China*, provides an aural glimpse of the presymbolic. Not that the A minor scale is outside of culture: major and minor scales are culturally inscribed conventions that Western

Figure 12.1. John Adams, *Nixon in China*: mm. 1–35.

culture took centuries to develop. The saturation of the texture at the beginning of the opera with this scale, however, creates the illusion of pure basic material stripped of its structural significance.

The passage creates an illusion of the sonorous envelope through very repetitive and metrically regular fragments, on the one hand, and irregular entrances of sustained pitches, on the other. A predictable pattern of ascending A-natural minor scales fills each measure with eighth notes; and pitch classes A-natural and F-natural enter at irregular intervals in the bass, with E-naturals entering irregularly high above the texture. The augmentation of the A natural minor scale notated on the middle staff mediates between the regular scale fragments in eighth notes and the irregular entrances mentioned above.

In psychoanalytic theory, the sonorous envelope precedes the mirror

stage, which is marked by binary oppositions set in motion by the child seeing itself reflected in the mother's face/mirror. Each splitting off of the self from the world brings the child closer to language, to socialization, and further away from the wholeness that the sonorous envelope represents. The first event that propels this series of splits opens the envelope and reveals messages inside—differentiation, language, and social conventions. The child's emergence from a sense of being bathed in the mother's voice is the acoustic

mirror. Anzieu asserts that "we would like to demonstrate the existence earlier still [than the mirror stage] of a sonorous mirror, or an acoustic-phonetic
skin, and its function in the psychic apparatus of the acquisition of the capacity for signifying, and symbolizing."[11]

As the acoustic mirror stage begins, the sense of being bathed in the
sounds of the mother's voice is modified as the child imitates the sounds it
hears and has the illusion of *producing* those sounds. According to Silverman:
"Since the child's economy is organized around incorporation, and since
what is incorporated is the auditory field articulated by the maternal voice,
the child could be said to hear itself initially through that voice—to first
'recognize' itself in the vocal 'mirror' supplied by the mother."[12]

Anzieu maps out the acoustic mirror as several stages that occur between
the child's initial sense of being bathed in the sounds of the mother's voice
(the sonorous envelope) and clear imitation of her sounds (the acoustic mirror). For Anzieu, the basis of the acoustic mirror is vocal communication
between the child and its mother. At birth, children can produce four different cries (described by Anzieu in terms of temporal duration, frequency, and
acoustic signature): hunger, anger, physical pain, and frustration. After the
second week, the mother's voice stops a cry more effectively than any other
sound. After the third week, the child develops the ability to emit a "false
cry" to get attention. At five weeks, the child distinguishes the voice of the
mother from other voices, while still not being able to distinguish visually
among faces. Between three and six months, the child clearly plays with the
sounds it emits, gradually moving closer to imitating the mother's voice.[13]

The acoustic mirror is thus an *aural* precursor of the *visual* mirror stage:
the child both recognizes itself in, and hears itself separated by, the sound of
the mother's voice. Thus we can extend the point mentioned above in connection with Denis Vasse. The child is born, and the cutting of the umbilical
cord severs the child from union with the body of the mother. The child
yearns for identification with the mother and focuses on her voice, her smell,
her image. The voice of the mother thus connects the child again to her, but
this connection is predicated on a primal loss of physical connection. This
suggests that our early acoustic experience involves a gender-specific ambivalence to sound, to the mother's voice, and, by extension, to music. As a result
of such an ambivalence, new music that evokes sonorous enclosure can produce a wide range of affective responses, as will be shown below.[14]

There are moments in Adams's music at which the stability of the text
shifts at the emergence of half-formed quotes—not so much of specific
pieces, but more an appropriation of a preexisting style.[15] One can see from
figure 12.2 how conventional musical materials emerge during the initial
326 measures of the opera.

At m. 297, the music sounds like the opening of *Das Rheingold*; see figures 12.3 and 12.4. While Wagner prolongs an E-flat major chord diatoni-
cally, Adams projects C major across his two-dimensional tonal surface. Both

Figure 12.2. John Adams, *Nixon in China*: an Overview of the Musical Materials of mm. 1–326.

Figure 12.3. John Adams, *Nixon in China*: mm. 294–310.
Nixon in China by John Adams (c) Hendon Music, Inc. All rights reserved. Used by permission.

Adams and Wagner superimpose an ascending arpeggiation of a major triad in dotted rhythm over a static arpeggiation of the same chord in the bass. Both set the stage as well for vocal entries in their respective operas.[16]

In *Nixon in China*, the oceanic, undifferentiated texture of the opening gets charged with musical conventions that gradually prefigure the "quote" from Wagner: the *pitch-class* A-natural is a nonfunctional axis of the cycle of major

Figure 12.4. Richard Wagner, *Das Rheingold*: mm. 51–60.

thirds in the bass from mm. 1 to 159; E-flat and A major *chords* are juxtaposed
from mm. 236 to 292. The oscillation between the keys of C major and E minor
from mm. 297 to 325 is a tip-of-the-hat to contemporary minimal music.

The moment of our recognition of this "quote" opens the space between
John Adams the composer and us as listeners, and here we hear within an
acoustic mirror. We have the illusion that our listening has created an element
of musical structure as we hear the difference between being wrapped in the
sonorous envelope of the initial measures of the piece and being split from it

as the music becomes marked by convention. It is also as if we hear the music's origin at this Wagner quote: as if *The Ring* were bleeding into the score.

What really marks this moment of rupture as an acoustic mirror is the indirect way in which Adams quotes through texture and orchestration as much as harmony. If his music had involved real, clearly articulated quotations, then the binary opposition between text as monumental work and the listener would have remained intact. The quote would have functioned as a clear cross-reference between one work and another. But by having his stylistic pseudoquotes emerge from the music, Adams's music reenacts a sonorous event in the structure of our subjectivity—showing social convention coming directly out of the sonorous envelope.

In Adams's *Fearful Symmetries* (1988) there are intermittent quotes within a pastiche of styles, procedures, and textures. Figure 12.5 shows a parallel progression in Adams that echoes a passage from Berlioz's *Symphonie fantastique*: see figure 12.6. In Adams, the first inversion major chords ascend in semitones within a G to G octave as shown in the figure. In Berlioz, the chords ascend in semitones within a C to C octave, with first-inversion chords beginning in m. 472. Adams echoes Berlioz's texture as well. After the first five chords in Berlioz and the first four chords in Adams, the harmonic rhythm quickens, as shown in the figures by the large arrows. Both passages use syncopation: the progression in Berlioz ascends *on* the beat with accented *second* beats from mm. 477 to 484. In Adams, the progression sounds disjointed, with the syncopated bass "supporting" chords on the beat.

Harmony works differently in the passages. Berlioz's progression sets up a large dominant prolongation of C that resolves in m. 493—not shown in the figure. Adams's appropriation of Berlioz leads to a tone cluster in which B-flat, A-flat, and G-flat are superimposed on the B-F tritone in the bass. The Berlioz resolves to C; the Adams is emptied of tension with an oscillation between E-flat and A in the bass (not included in the figure).

The above-mentioned "quote" from Berlioz is a musical representation of acoustic mirroring. This highly *symbolic* musical reference represents a *presymbolic* acoustic mirror in two ways. First, there is a distinction between a left-to-right psychoanalytic theory of general, Western subjectivity tracking the subject from birth to language acquisition on the one hand, and works of art, literature, film, or music that *represent* or reenact such events on the other. All aspects of Western art music are highly symbolic, and there is a gap between the experience of the presymbolic and music's highly conventional structure. Yet sound is common to both our psychoanalytic model and music, and it is precisely through such highly conventional signs that music can point back to the pre-symbolic, effacing itself, if only for a moment in certain ways, in certain pieces.

Secondly, in "Revolution in Poetic Language," Kristeva's notion of the thetic phase suggests how the presymbolic and the symbolic bleed into one

Figure 12.5. John Adams, *Fearful Symmetries*: mm. 223–229.
Fearful Symmetries by John Adams (c) Hendon Music, Inc. All rights reserved. Used by permission.

Figure 12.6. Hector Berlioz, *Symphonie fantastique*: mm. 463–484.

another. She calls the prelinguistic, maternal phase the *semiotic*, the linguistic, paternal phase, the *symbolic*. That which articulates a move from the semiotic to the symbolic she calls the *thetic*: "We view the thetic phase—the positing of the *imago*, castration, and the positing of semiotic motility as the place of the Other, as the precondition for signification, i.e., the precondition for the positing of language. The thetic phase marks a threshold between two heterogeneous realms: the semiotic and the symbolic." This passage claims that the relationship between the semiotic and the symbolic is one of a mutually exclusive binary opposition. And yet Kristeva also says that there must be a dynamic within the semiotic that enables the thetic to take place: "The thetic originates in the 'mirror stage' and is completed, through the phallic stage, by the re-activation of the Oedipus complex." In short, the thetic can shift back into the semiotic, and Kristeva makes clear a necessary link between the mirror stage and language: "The mirror stage produces the 'spatial intuition' which is found at the heart of the functioning of signification."[17] Rosolato also argues that the child's hearing and responding to the mother's voice is a key phase that sets the stage for more complex and later developments: "It [the mother's voice] carries, in effect, the first *introjections* [emphasis Rosolato's] preparatory to identification."[18]

It might seem unlikely that the thetic could shift back from the symbolic to the semiotic. In *Revolution in Poetic Language*, however, Kristeva clearly suggests that it can: "The thetic permits the constitution of the symbolic with its vertical stratification (referent, signified, signifier) and all the subsequent modalities of logico-semantic articulation. The thetic originates in the 'mirror stage' and is completed, through the phallic stage, by the re-activation of the Oedipus complex in puberty; no signifying practice can be without it." Also: "We might then wonder whether the semiotic's dismantling of the symbolic in poetry necessarily implies that the thetic phase is shifted towards the stases of the semiotic *chora* [emphasis Kristeva's]." And finally: "In all its various vacillations, the thetic is displaced towards the stages previous to its positing or within the very stases of the semiotic—in a particular element of the digital code or in a particular continuous portion of the analog [*sic*] code."[19] This is a crucial point for the logic of psychoanalysis in general, and this essay in particular. The fact that the thetic in Kristeva can shift back to an element within the semiotic means that there is a connection between the imaginary and symbolic orders in Lacanian psychoanalysis. There must be something that links the mirror stage to the oedipal crisis and the triangulation of desire. Kristeva suggests that although the thetic clearly and explicitly inscribes subjects into the symbolic order, it reaches back into the semiotic, and even the *chora* as a structure that moves us out of the binary categories of the Imaginary order into the refigured binaries and networks of the symbolic order. I argue throughout this paper that representations of sound resonate with traces of threshold-crossing in developing subjectivity. Kristeva's shifting thetic makes such threshold-crossing comprehensible.

What makes the Berlioz "quote" a representation of the acoustic mirror is not a matter of whether the music is more or less conventional, since every notation in the score is a mark of the symbolic order; rather, the acoustic mirror is a specific effect of musical representations of such conventions on a listener. Anzieu and Rosolato have shown that in its various phases, the acoustic mirror involves a split from the sense of union with the mother's voice, resulting in a sense that the child produces her sounds, leading to an attempt to imitate such sounds. The source of sound production thus shifts from mother to child, and the child moves from a listener to a producer of sounds. And the acoustic mirror tracks the stages that occur as reception of sound (the child "listening" within the sonorous envelope) yields to production of sound (the child imitating the mother's voice). A similar effect is produced in *Fearful Symmetries* with the Berlioz quote at once bleeding into the sounds of Adams's music and emerging out of our memories of having heard the *Symphonie fantastique.*

In *Grand Pianola Music*, the third movement is an example of a texture of sonorous enclosure opening into a conventional passage of acoustic mirroring that is a veiled reference to the pianistic passagework of the classical piano concerto. For sixty measures, Adams projects an E-flat major/minor seventh chord across the surface of the music. The texture superimposes eighth notes in two pianos with held notes in the brass and winds that alternate entrances, rests, and accents at irregular metric intervals. The nonfunctional nature of the chord is emphasized with the seventh moving up stepwise to E-flat in the first trombone part. This stepwise motion sounds jazzy with the trombone's glissando from D-flat to E-flat.

Dynamics produce an illusion of forward motion: the music gets gradually louder until m. 60. At m. 61, the music "resolves" in a flourish of arpeggiated A-flat major chords reminiscent of classical, pianistic passagework. The conventionality of the A-flat major flourish emerges from, and is made possible by, a condition of the oceanic, static texture of E-flat major; the eighth notes in the piano are first merged with, and then *split from*, the held notes in the winds and brass. From the *Symphonie fantastique* in *Fearful Symmetries*, from the style of the classical piano concerto in *Grand Pianola Music* are derived bits of filler, marked with the merest traces of compositional presence. Adams's appropriation/(re-)composition of such marginal passages opens his music and shifts the name of the composer from Wagner, Berlioz, and "Beethoven," to Adams, to us.

THE MUSIC OF STEVE REICH

Different Trains (1988) by Steve Reich establishes the illusion of the sonorous envelope through a texture that suggests both an internal, oceanic immersion in repetitive fragments of sound *and* an obsessive, external, and iconic representation of trains. While the texture of Adams's music involves moments of sounding like previous styles from the canon, Reich explores the relationship between sound and language. First, intervallic structures in the accompaniment determine the intervallic structure of the language of the taped speech that is a part of the composition.[20] In the first movement, a minor third in the strings is taken over by the voice for the phrase "from Chicago" (0:35—0:40). This technique captures in miniature the way we first hear language as pure sound, then as words, phrases, and sentences with meaning.

Once speech has been introduced into the piece, it is effaced in two ways. First speech sounds like pure syntax through repetition.[21] In this music, repetition as meaning-stripper creates the illusion of hearing the pure sound of the maternal voice before we were speakers of her language.[22] In the first movement, the phrase "one of the fastest trains" is repeated 21 times (1:23—2:37). The meaning-stripping function of repetition is enhanced in this passage through an intermittent additional repetition of the tag phrase "fastest trains." And as an instrument's minor third had prefigured the phrase "from Chicago," so, too, the viola imitates the intervallic structure of the voice throughout the passage.

Second, the voice is often distorted. The piece opens with clearly articulated speech and *moves to* distorted speech. This is a representation of a regression in sound back through the acoustic mirror phase. In the second part entitled "During the War" the phrases "lots of cattle wagons there" (4:49—5:17) and "they were loaded with people" (5:18—5:40) are barely comprehensible. In "La Voix," Rosolato discusses noise and the cry as features of the child's pre-verbal voice: "It [noise] exists as a unique illustration of the voice before the Word in which man strips himself of words"(292).[23]

I hear two temporal structures in *Different Trains*. On the one hand, the piece is a monument to the survivors of the Holocaust: it tells a story of their trauma in the "before," "during," and "after," left-to-right structure that the movement titles suggest. On the other hand, the piece represents a regressive fantasy back to the presymbolic through the meaning-stripping function of repetition, and distortion of the voices. Another feature of the music reinforces this regressive element. In the first movement, motives in the accompaniment precede the melodies in the voices; in the second movement, the motives in the accompaniment and voice sound *simultaneously* to suggest language reaching back to its origins of pure sound.

Why is Holocaust trauma represented as a regressive fantasy? A fantasy of regression suggests taking a contemporary post-Holocaust subjective position back to the past as a way of identifying with those who died in the Holocaust. Also, regressive fantasies can work as a self-protecting response to anxiety. In anxiety, the subject produces a symbolic representation (symptom) that will protect him/her from a trauma whose source or object is clearly anticipated.[24] Thus regressive fantasies project the subject through active construction of symbolic acts back to a position from which it would have been strengthened against trauma. The regressive element of *Different Trains* is thus a representation of a desire not so much to escape back into the mother's womb as to regress back symbolically to a fantasy position from which it would have been possible to protect oneself from traumatic shock and from which direct identification with those who died would have been possible.

"IT'S GONNA RAIN" AND "COME OUT"

Reich's early pieces "It's Gonna Rain" (1965) and "Come Out" (1966) use repetition obsessively to strip meaning just as it is about to take shape.[25] "It's Gonna Rain" is in two parts. Part 1 begins with a thirteen-second taped passage from a street preacher's sermon. After a one-second pause, two tracks of the phrase "it's gonna rain" begin to diverge. As the tracks move out of phase, the language sounds as if it were being ripped apart, with consonants torn from vowels through the violence of phase motion.

From 0:14 to 2:00, words and syllables also fade in and out. This gives sound a spatial quality, as if sounds were moving close (fading in) and receding (fading out). Fading dislodges the stillness of the listener. It is as if we had to brace ourselves against approaching sounds, and "let up" as sounds move away, or we seem to push sounds away at some moments and call them up at others.

In his essay "The Uncanny" from 1919, Freud refers to literary representations of the odd, the horrifying, the fanciful as images of a state of mind in which what was once familiar becomes unfamiliar: this is the essential dynamic of the uncanny. Freud discusses the uncanny *not* in terms of a binary opposition between the comfortable, familiar world "inside" (the mind, the home, society, etc.) and a threatening, external, evil force. Rather the uncanny seems to emerge *out of what had been familiar.* Freud discovers this dynamic within the etymology of the word *heimlich* (familiar, in German). Freud realized that the word first meant "familiar" "trusted" and slowly acquired additional connotations of "secret" and "hidden."

Reich's fading imperatives are uncanny since we first hear "go" as a syllable of the word "gonna"; then we realize that it acquires a new meaning when severed from the other syllable. I find the fading in and out of the syllable "go" particularly haunting, as if a sound within a taped voice found a hidden voice of its own and turned a fragmented syllable into an fully meaningful imperative verb: "go!" A highly charged moment of listening subjectivity is created as the music seems to point directly to the mute listener. More important than the verb form "go" is the understood subject: "you."

With the imperative "go," Reich produces what I would like to call an *acoustic gaze*. Silverman says that "unlike the gaze, the look foregrounds the desiring subjectivity of the figure from whom it issues".[26] The look is concrete: it has a source, a direction, a goal. The gaze is more diffuse, more symbolic: the gaze often suggests both a person who is looking *and* a sense that that person is being looked *at*, often by an inanimate object that represents the look of another. In *Looking Awry*, Žižek provides a clear example of the gaze in *Psycho*. As Lilah walks toward the house in which Norman's mother lives, the camera is focused on the *house* as if *it* were looking at *her*: "Let us return to the scene from *Psycho* in which Lilah approaches the house where 'Norman's mother' presumably lives. In what does its 'uncanny' dimension consist? Could we not best describe the effect of this scene by paraphrasing the words of Lacan: In a way *it is already the house that gazes at Lilah* [emphasis Žižek's]. Lilah sees the house, but nonetheless she cannot see it at the point from which it gazes back as her."[27] Reich's acoustic gaze works to undermine the relationship between us as listeners and the *music* as that to which we are listening. As the house gazes back at Lilah in *Psycho*, so, too, the imperative "go" acoustically "gazes" at us in "It's Gonna Rain."

From 2:01 to 7:44, several tracks go out of, and move back into, phase in one gesture. Here the phase process is audibly prefigured in the "unison" phrase with which the music begins: "It's gonna rain" (2:01). The phrase "it's gonna" sounds doubled at the octave, while "rain" sounds like one voice. This shift in register has an uncanny effect on the listener—as if the voice were closing in on us. In *La Voix au cinéma*, Michel Chion discusses how in film, the viewer/listener tends to identify with voices that are recorded with no echo, or reverberation so that they sound close and intimate. Voices that echo, that reverberate within a space beyond the listener, tend to sound more removed and less aimed at the listener.[28]

Part 1 of "It's Gonna Rain" ends abruptly with a line of taped, spoken speech that extends the text by one phrase: "It's gonna rain after a while." The piece is contained within the musical equivalent of a frame: the one-second pause of silence between 0:13 and 0:14 that sets off the thirteen seconds of taped speech from the rest of the piece, and the return to taped speech at the end with the phrase "it's gonna rain after a while." The frame articulates the piece as a symbolic fantasy.[29]

Part 2 begins with an extended passage of taped speech—0:00—0:40. The rest of the section fragments and superimposes words and phrases from this excerpt focusing on: "open the door," "God," "sure enough," and "Hallelujah." I hear this section not as a fantasy of negative regression (as in part 1), but as a nightmarish fantasy of the external, symbolic world as its voices flood in and overwhelm the ear.

"It's Gonna Rain" is about the horror that can reside underneath the symbolic order. Through the heavily mediated and conventional techniques of tape recording, splicing, and phase motion, Reich produces a nightmare of sonorous entrapment by having language split into its vowels and consonants. The vowels sound like inhuman cries; the consonants, like noises heard from within the body.[30]

In "Come Out," Reich is overtly political. The liner notes describe a black youth who was beaten by police in the Harlem riots of 1964. In order to get medical attention, the youth had to squeeze his wounds to show blood. Accordingly, the piece begins with a taped voice saying "I had to like open the bruise up and let some of the bruise blood come out to show them" (0:00— 0:05). After a two second silence (0:05—0:07), the passage is repeated (0: 07—0:12); after another two second silence (0:12—0:14), the passage is repeated again (0:14—0:19). For the rest of the piece, the listener moves into the spoken voice, through the repetition and phase manipulation of shorter and shorter phrases and words from the text with which the piece began: "come out to show them," "to show them," "come out." As in "It's Gonna Rain," the repetition of "come out" sounds like a direct address to the listener, an imperative.

A quite different effect of acoustic mirroring is represented in Reich's phase music. *Violin Phase* and *Piano Phase* (both from 1967) involve a performer who plays first in unison, then moves out of phase with, a taped recording. As the violinist moves out of phase with the tape in *Violin Phase*, a space opens in which the listener hears first an acoustic tugging, followed by echo-effect, followed by clear out-of-phase voices. Psychoanalytically, this series of moments (roughly 0:00—1:50) renders how the fantasy of sonorous enclosure can only be heard in retrospect. That is, only after hearing voices split away from one another can we imagine their having once sounded together.

After the above-mentioned splits and before the end, the fantasy of sonorous envelope consists both in the listener's hearing intertwined and indistinguishable "voices" *and* the fact that we know that one is stationary (as if deaf), the other mobile and listening. Listening subjectivity is produced as the listener joins the configuration: he/she is stationary, like the taped voice, but while the tape is deaf (it can only speak), the listener is mute (we can only listen).

I referred earlier to the necessary link between the myths of Narcissus and Echo as a parallel to the acoustic and visual mirror stages. What happens to Echo in Ovid's *Metamorphoses* reflects Reich's phase music. In Ovid, Echo first has the power to slow the goddess Juno's search for Jove by her loquacity; Juno in the end punishes Echo by limiting what she says to verbatim repetition of what she hears. Echo is placed into and trapped within an acoustic mirror to match the visual mirror of Narcissus. The role of gender and voice in the developing subject is also reflected in this archetypal story: Echo is female, Narcissus male.[31]

The unison between soloist and tape at the beginning of each of these pieces presents the listener with a fantasy of sonorous oneness: as the soloist and tape diverge, we hear a clear acoustic mirror as one voice literally echoes another. This initial unison-followed-by-divergence is heard as if from the listener's position from within the imaginary order with its binary categories of listener, on the one hand, and immediate perception of sound, on the other. As the pieces end, however, we hear not a symbolic inscription of the imaginary into social space; rather, the fantasy simply reverses itself.[32]

CONCLUSIONS

I hope to have suggested how the fantasy of the sonorous envelope and its rupture in acoustic mirroring can illuminate the formation of the listening subject in music and how these structures work differently in the musical styles of John Adams and Steve Reich. In general terms, the construction of the subject follows a course of divisions between the self and the world of phenomenal experience through the phases of birth, the sonorous envelope, the acoustic mirror stage, the visual mirror stage, the oedipal crisis, and the entry into the symbolic order. Each division both distances the subject from phenomenal experience *and* empowers the subject to master such distance through access to language. As we move from one of these realms to another we never lose what has gone before, and in our symbolic world of socialized structures traces of the imaginary order and preimaginary (dis)order remain.

On the broadest level, I propose a common ground between the sonorous structure of the subject in its early stages of development and music. More specifically, the new minimal style of recent postmodern music invites an intimate exploration of psychic and musical structures. What remains to be explored is more explicitly external ideology: links between psychic and musical structures, on the one hand, and culture, on the other. One might ask, for example, whether *Nixon in China* can, in its monumental power and beauty of orchestration, be a critical vehicle, or whether the music is complicit with the glorification of the global politics of America.

This is a crucial issue for postmodern art in general, for it often seems complicit in structures of dominance in the process of gaining distance from them. *Nixon in China* participates in this structure of resistance and complicity.[33] In his other, less overtly political pieces, however, John Adams's musical representation of the sonorous envelope and acoustic mirror is charged with an untroubled, positive affect. The music of Steve Reich, on the other hand, explores and represents more directly the horror within the human voice and early phases of developing subjectivity.[34]

NOTES

1. An earlier draft of this essay was delivered as a paper at the 1991 Society for Music Theory meeting in Cincinnati. I am grateful for the comments of Patrick McCreless, John Rahn, and Robert Hatten following the presentation. I would also like to thank Dennis Foster for constructive criticism on the psychoanalytic paradigm of the argument.

2. I use "imaginary" and "symbolic" as Lacanian terms. For an overview of Lacan's theories, see chap. 4 of Kaja Silverman's *The Subject of Semiotics* (New York: Oxford Univ. Press, 1983) and Fredric Jameson's "The Imaginary and Symbolic in Lacan," in *Ideologies of Theory*, vol. 1 (Minneapolis: Univ. of Minnesota Press, 1988).

3. I seek adjacency with such works as Lawrence Kramer's *Music as Cultural Practice 1800–1900* (Berkeley and Los Angeles: Univ. of California Press, 1990) in which Kramer reads musical and literary texts as expressions of psychic and ideological structures. Recent studies on subjectivity and music include Anahid Kassabian's work on film music in classic cinema and Kofi Agawu's *Playing with Signs* (Princeton: Princeton Univ. Press, 1991)—an adaptation of semiotic theory to eighteenth-century music. My interest in critical theory and voice bears the indirect influence of Abbate's *Unsung Voices: Opera and Musical Narrative in the Nineteenth Century* (Princeton: Princeton Univ. Press, 1991).

4. See "Subjectivity in Language" in Benveniste's *Problems in General Linguistics*, trans. Mary Elizabeth Meek (Coral Gables, Fla.: Univ. of Miami Press, 1971) and Silverman *The Subject of Semiotics*, 43–44.

5. The (visual) mirror stage and its significance in development are central to Lacan: see "The Mirror Stage," in *Ecrits* (Paris: Seuil, 1966; *Ecrits: A Selection*, trans. Alan Sheridan, [New York: Norton, 1977]). Considerations of sound are marginal to his work. More recent French psychoanalytic writings have developed and extended Lacan's theories to include a prominent role for sound and the voice in human development. For a discussion of the role of the mother's voice in the acoustic mirror, see Didier Anzieu's "L'Enveloppe sonore du soi" (*Nouvelle revue de psychanalyse* 13 [1976]) and Guy Rosolato, "La voix" (*Essais sur le symbolique* [Paris: Gallimard, 1969]) and "Entre corps et langage" (*Revue française de psychanalyse* 37, no. 1, [1976]).

The position of the visual analogy in Lacan and film theory is discussed in Charles F. Altman's article "Psychoanalysis and Cinema: The Imaginary Discourse" (*Quarterly Review of Film Studies* 2, no. 3, [August 1977]). Altman argues that Lacanian psychoanalysis privileges visual experience at the expense of aural experience. He points out that the paradigmatic version of the mirror stage in literature is the myth of Narcissus. What happens to Narcissus is intimately connected, he argues, with Echo: "Even the Greeks . . . knew that the story of Narcissus is incomplete without that of Echo: the audio mirror completes the video mirror"(270). As will be discussed briefly below, it is actually the other way around in Ovid. Echo undergoes a series of reductions in the power of her voice before she falls in love with, and is thwarted by, Narcissus.

6. What I mean by "phenomenal experience" is what we think of anecdotally as "reality": the reality to which Freud refers in his writings when he is not talking about representations of reality, but rather everything that is outside the self. Lacan's notion of the Real is very different, according to Žižek: "In the Lacanian notion of the real, the hard kernel that resists symbolization coincides with its opposite, the so-called 'inner' or 'psychic' reality" (Slavoj Žižek, "Grimaces of the Real," *October* 58 [Fall 1991]: 60). Lacan's Real is perhaps so counterintuitive because it is everything that has not-yet/never-will–be marked by the imprint of our imaginary and symbolic experience.

7. In *The Acoustic Mirror: The Female Voice in Psychoanalysis and Cinema* (Bloomington: Indiana Univ. Press, 1988), Kaja Silverman also discusses subjectivity as transitory. She discusses "projection" and "introjection" as two simultaneous aspects of the viewer's gaze: sending-out (projection), and pulling-back information from the text in the opposite direction (introjection) (23). In introjection, "representations are taken into the self, and provide the basis for a *momentary subjectivity* [emphasis mine]—a spectator's previous structuration" (23).

8. See Anzieu, "L'Enveloppe sonore du soi," 161–62; Rosolato "Entre corps et langage," 81; "La Voix," 292; Denis Vasse, "L'Ombilic et la voix," *Le champ freudien* (Paris: Seuil, 1974), 1–23; Michel Chion, *La Voix au cinéma* (Paris: Cahiers du cinéma, 1982), 25–26 and 47–50.

9. This is Silverman's translation of "Si la voix maternelle contribue a constituer pour l'enfant le milieu agréable qui l'entoure, le sustente et le choie, elle peut, inversement, en cas de refus massif ne devenir que pénétration agressive et térébrante contre laquelle il n'a guère de protection a déployer. On peut avancer qu'elle est le premier modèle d'un plaisir auditif et que la musique trouve ses racines et sa nostalgie dans une atmosphère originelle—a nommer comme matrice sonore, maison bruissante" (81). Silverman omits that part of the French that opens the possibility for the sonorous envelope to be experienced negatively—as a structure of terror and entrapment. Michel Chion's theory of the voice in cinema is based on this negative aspect of the mother's voice. Esther Bick's work shows clearly how a child's identification with the smell, the voice, the image of the mother can lead to pathological development in the case of severe neglect: see "The Experience of the Skin in Early Object-Relations," *The International Journal of Psych-analysis* 49, nos. 2–3 (1968). My thanks to Prof. Philip Solomon of the Foreign Language Department at Southern Methodist University for assistance in the French-English translations in this paper. For the French, see Guy Rosolato "Entre corps et langage," 81.

10. The potential for the sonorous envelope to produce a negative fantasy in Rosolato and Chion is reinforced by the work of Denis Vasse, who argues that as the child is severed from the umbilical cord, he or she experiences the first in a long series of splits from phenomenal experience. Vasse argues that the role of the primal identification with the voice of the mother is to attempt to create a bond across that severed connection. Thus, for Vasse there is always a paradoxical sense of union with, and distance from, the voice of the mother (Vasse 17–18, Chion 57–58).

11. "Nous voudrions mettre en évidence l'existence, plus précoce encore, d'un miroir sonore, ou d'une peau auditivo-phonique, et sa fonction dans l'acquisition par

l'appareil psychique de la capacité de signifier, puis de symboliser" (162). Esther Bick takes the metaphor of sound as skin quite literally in her work: "The need for a containing object would seem, in the infantile unintegrated state, to produce a frantic search for an object—a light, a voice, a smell, or other sensual object. . . . Material will show how this containing object is experienced concretely as a skin" (484).

12. Silverman, *The Acoustic Mirror,* 80.

13. Anzieu points out that there is disagreement on one aspect of the acoustic mirror: whether the child first makes as many different sounds as possible, followed by a narrowing down to match those of the mother, or whether the child seeks to imitate the sounds of the mother from the outset of the acoustic mirror and imitation takes time to perfect (168).

14. This Lacanian view of early development might recall Otto Rank. In *The Trauma of Birth* (New York: R. Brunner, 1952), Rank takes Freud's notion of primal repression as his starting point to argue that an immense range of neurotic, psychotic, psychosomatic, nervous, and even physical ailments are manifestations of birth trauma. Rank even argues that epileptic seizures represent an attempt to recapture the motions of a newborn child. Rank is interested in the role of repetition in mastery of trauma, and in a wide variety of spatial anxieties and desires that he links to birth and prebirth states (respectively). Rank also focuses on how the dynamic of transference repeats and masters the covered memories of primal birth trauma. For Rank, there are no gaps in the life of the psyche that cannot be filled, no residues, nothing left out of the process of symbolization. His view of the psyche is one that begins in trauma, and, crucially, he believes that subjects have access to and can master primal birth trauma. Denis Vasse seems to cover similar ground, albeit according to a very different plan: like Rank, Vasse discusses birth trauma as a crucial event in human subjectivity; but unlike Rank, he proposes no global theory subsuming all behavior and illness into an expression of desire for prebirth union with the mother, or of dread at the memory of birth. Vasse is Lacanian in his sense that all representations both reveal and conceal meaning in structures that resist a transparent, immediate access to truth or origins.

15. I use terms such as *quotes, pseudoquotes, half-quotes, references,* to suggest what I consider to be a unique aspect of Adams's music, much of which depends on evoking a style from the standard repertoire, or even moments from specific pieces. It is a particularly postmodern kind of quoting in which the available materials of past works and styles themselves become the basic materials of composition. Another piece of postmodern music in which radical quoting *is* the musical material of the piece is George Rochberg's *Caprice Variations for Solo Violin.* A similar example in postmodern literature is the dense, saturation quoting of the German playwright Heiner Müller.

16. My thanks to Patrick McCreless for pointing out that the Wagner quote at the outset of *Nixon in China* is more resonant still. McCreless suggests that Wagner was interested in beginning *The Ring* with a musical evocation of the root-syllable of nature. Thus these pieces share a concern with sound as origin of consciousness: for Wagner, the root-syllable is the source of meaning in the human body. See Richard Wagner, *Opera as Drama,* trans. Edwin Evans (New York: Scribner, 1913), pt. 3 chap. 2—"The Sounding Vowel of Speech and its Rise to Musical Tone."

17. Kristeva, "Revolution in Poetic Language," *Revolution in Poetic Language,* trans. Margaret Waller (New York: Columbia Univ. Press, 1984) 100–113.

18. "Elle [la voix maternelle] porte, en effet, les premières *introjections* prépara-toires aux identifications" (Rosolato "Entre corps et langage," 80).

19. Kristeva, "Revolution in Poetic Language," 112–17.

20. Citations from Reich's music will be in minutes and seconds read from a compact disc player.

21. By pure syntax I mean a nonlinguistic sonorous structure. My sense of this structure as a pure syntax may seem counterintuitive: syntax is a feature of grammar, of highly symbolic signs that must be inscribed within the symbolic order. My use of the phrase "pure syntax" is meant to echo Kristeva's semiotic phase. See Julia Kristeva, *Desire in Language: A Semiotic Approach to Literature and Art*, ed. Leon S. Roudiez, trans. Thomas Gora, Alice Jardine, and Leon S. Roudiez (New York: Columbia Univ. Press, 1980); *Powers of Horror: An Essay on Abjection*, trans. Leon S. Roudiez (New York: Columbia Univ. Press, 1982) and *Revolution in Poetic Language*, trans. Margaret Waller (New York: Columbia Univ. Press, 1984).

22. Although repetition must work differently in music, art, and literature, it can do many different things. (1) While one image can be absorbed or imprinted on the mind (imagine a painting of one Ballantine beer can) a repetition of the same image says to the viewer: "You are looking at looking." This is the effect of Jasper John's *Painted Bronze Cans*. Hearing hearing is the effect of listening to the second, altered version of John Cage's "A Room." The first version is for piano; the second, for altered piano with objects placed on and around the piano strings to alter the instrument's sounds. (2) Repetition can also emphasize an idea as in "HURRY UP PLEASE IT'S TIME" from *The Waste Land*. (3) Repetition can create a cross-reference as in the use of the song "The End" by the Doors at the beginning and end of the film *Apocalypse Now*. Berg's large-scale cross-reference between the music associated with Dr. Schön and Jack the Ripper in *Lulu* between the first and third acts is one example from music. (4) Repetition can also strip away meaning to create a fantasy of the presymbolic, as in much of Steve Reich's music. (5) Repetition can render a sense of stasis as in the repetition of lines, groups of lines, acts, in Samuel Beckett's *Waiting for Godot*. (6) Repetition can emphasize that a representation is an attempt to reconstruct or imagine a traumatic event, at once signaling a desire on the artist's part to identify with a person, experience, and an acknowledgment on the part of the artist that symbolic reconstructions never bridge the gap entirely between experience and its representation. One aspect of Steve Reich's *Different Trains* involves such repetition as desire for/acknowledgement of the limitations of an identification with the survivors of the Holocaust. See, as well, the repetition of the phrase "before black water entered her lungs and she died" from Joyce Carol Oates's *Black Water*. Also, see the saturation repetition of images that reconstruct the fatal shooting of a Dallas policeman in Morris's film *The Thin Blue Line*. Repetition and chance are crucial structural elements in *Before the Rain*.

23. "Il [l'éclat] existe comme une singulière illustration de cette Voix d'avant la Parole, où l'homme se dépouille des mots." It should be pointed out that the French word *éclat* covers a semantic field far beyond any single word in English: its meanings include: noise, cry, burst of sound. *Parole* with a capital "p" suggests both the spoken word, and the word of God. In the passage at hand Rosolato subtly compares *Parole* and the prelinguistic voice of the child (*Voix* with a capital "v"). The word *mots* (written words) refers to the language of the symbolic order.

24. Thus the difference between *anxiety*, in which the traumatic source is "known" and in which symbolic representation attempts to protect the self, and *fear*, in which the self is flooded by a trauma against which it had no symbolic defenses. See Jean Laplanche and J. B. Pontalis, *The Language of Psycho-analysis*, trans. Donald Nicholson-Smith (New York: Norton, 1973), "Anxiety Hysteria" (37–38), "Anxiety Neurosis (38–39), and "Fright" (174–75).

25. My thanks to Dave Headlam for pointing these pieces out to me and for suggesting the possibilities for applying psychoanalytic concepts to their structures and techniques.

26. For a clear argument about the difference between a "look" and a "gaze," see Silverman's introduction to *Male Subjectivity on the Margins* (London: Routledge, 1982), and 142–43 .

27. Slavoj Žižek, *Looking Awry* (Cambridge: MIT Press, 1991): 118.

28. In the third chapter of *La Voix au cinéma*, Chion explicates his theories of how voices affect the listener; he also uses *Psycho* as an example. First, Chion refers to a voice that we hear in film without seeing its source as *la voix acousmatique*. Chion discusses two different kinds of acousmatic voices in *Psycho*. As we see Norman in the jail cell having been "cannibalized" (Chion's term) by the voice of the mother, her voice is flat, insistent, "close" to the screen, forcing the viewer to identify with Norman's psychosis. As we see (much earlier in the film) Marion driving in her car having stolen money from a client of her company, we hear *her* hear the voices of the men in ·her office earlier in the day. In this example, the voices reverberate in a space clearly beyond the listener; this is the space of Marion's conscience (47–50 and 116–23). Reich's shift in texture from "it's gonna" to "rain" is a purely musical version of what Chion describes in film music.

29. Framing is also essential in film for creating distance between the viewer and the main action. In *Blue Velvet*, the descent into and emergence out of the ear encloses Jeffrey's fantasy. The girl's (Juliette Lewis's) voice-overs at the beginning and end of *Cape Fear* also point to the large-scale significance of the film as a symbolic working-out of the young girl's ambivalence toward her father as she emerges from latency.

30. Two recent psycho-thrillers also touch upon the horror that lies beneath the symbolic order. In both films, the horror is produced when the relationship between imaginary and symbolic phases of development is flawed. Consider the logorrhea of the Speaker in Peter Greenaway's *The Cook, the Thief, His Wife, and Her Lover*, and the obsessive bodily functions to which the profusion of language can barely gain access. In *The Silence of the Lambs*, Hannibal Lechter's major malfunction is clearly related to an infantile desire to bite, to eat, to consume the mother. Though a master of language (a brilliant psychoanalyst and genius criminal), something did not happen in his anal-sadistic phase to free him from equating the desire to consume with the need to know.

31. See "The Story of Echo and Narcissus" in *Metamorphoses*, ll. 338–99.

32. By "symbolic inscription" I refer here to the theory common in film criticism that associates the shot with the imaginary order, and the reverse-shot with the symbolic order (see "Suture" in Kaja Silverman's *The Subject of Semiotics*). As an illustration of this idea's consequences, Dennis Foster has pointed out to me that in *Body Heat*, the character played by John Hurt often is filmed with shots followed by reverse-shots thus inscribing the representation of his character into symbolic, social space.

On the other hand, the character played by Kathleen Turner is often only *shot*—making her a unique object of the camera's desire.

In the classical style, two aspects of musical form suggest a musical equivalent of the reverse-shot: the repetition of a sonata movement's exposition, and the recapitulation.

33. In her book *A Poetics of Postmodernism* (London: Routledge, 1988), Linda Hutcheon inscribes postmodernism within a paradox that crystalizes this sense of resistance and complicity in postmodernism: "Postmodernism teaches that all cultural practices have an ideological subtext which determines the conditions of the very possibility of their production of meaning. And, in art, it does so by leaving overt the contradictions between its self-reflexivity and its historical grounding. In theory . . . the contradictions are not always . . . overt, but are often implied—as in the Barthesian antiauthorizing authority or the Lyotardian master-narrativizing of our suspicion of master narratives. These paradoxes are, I believe, what has led to the political ambidexterity of postmodernism in general, for it has been celebrated and decried by both ends of the political spectrum. If you ignore half of the contradiction, however, it becomes quite easy to see the postmodern as either neoconservatively nostalgic / reactionary or radically disruptive / revolutionary. I would argue that we must beware of this suppression of the full complexity of postmodernist paradoxes (xii-xiii)."

34. See Kristeva's notion of the abject in *The Powers of Horror* and of the chora in *Revolution in Poetic Language* for related theories dealing with the symbolic and pre symbolic in our subjectivity.

Patrick McCreless
Professor of Music, the University of Texas at Austin

Susan McClary
Professor of Musicology, the University of California at Los Angeles

John Covach
Associate Professor of Music, the University of North Carolina, Chapel Hill

Sara Cohen
Lecturer at the Institute of Popular Music, the University of Liverpool

Richard Hooker
Member of the Faculty, Learning Systems Developer, Washington State University, Pullman

Ola Stockfelt
Lecturer in Musicology and Acting Head, Film Studies Department, the University of Gøteborg

Robert Walser
Associate Professor of Musicology, the University of California at Los Angeles

Peter Winkler
Associate Professor of Music, the State University of New York at Stony Brook

Jennifer Rycenga
Assistant Professor of Comparative Religious Studies, San Jose State University

Jenny Kallick
Professor of Music, Amherst College

Anahid Kassabian
Assistant Professor of Communication and Media Studies,
Fordham University

Lawrence Siegel
Composer and teacher, Westmoreland, N.H., and Minneapolis

David Schwarz
Assistant Professor of Music, Amherst College